MASADA

AND

THE WORLD OF THE NEW TESTAMENT

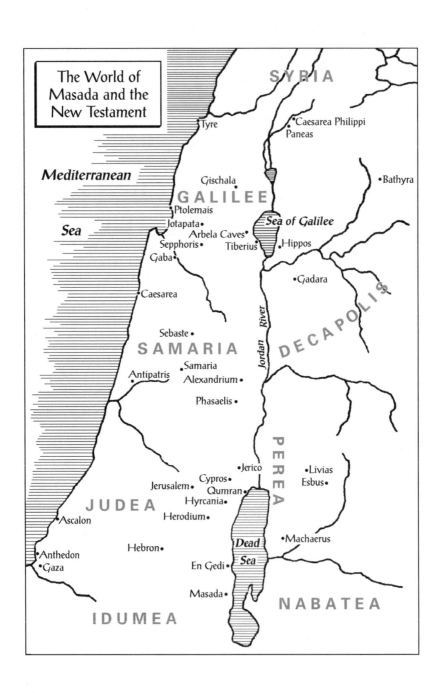

The World of
Masada and the
New Testament

SYRIA

Mediterranean

•Tyre

•Caesarea Philippi
Paneas

•Bathyra

Gischala•

GALILEE

Sea

Ptolemais•
Jotapata•
Arbela Caves•
Sepphoris•   Tiberius
Gaba•

Sea of Galilee

•Hippos

•Caesarea

•Gadara

Sebaste •

SAMARIA

•Samaria
Alexandrium •

•Antipatris

Phasaelis •

DECAPOLIS

Jordan River

PEREA

•Jerico

•Livias
Esbus•

Cypros•
Jerusalem•   Qumran•
Hyrcania•

JUDEA

Herodium•

•Ascalon

•Machaerus

Hebron•

Dead
Sea

•Anthedon
•Gaza

En Gedi•

Masada•

NABATEA

IDUMEA

MASADA

AND

THE WORLD OF THE NEW TESTAMENT

Edited by

John F. Hall
John W. Welch

BYU Studies
Brigham Young University
Provo, Utah

BYU Studies Monographs

The Truth, The Way, The Life:
An Elementary Treatise on Theology

The Journals of William E. McLellin, 1831–1836

Hearts Turned to the Fathers:
A History of the Genealogical Society of Utah, 1894–1994

"We Rejoice in Christ": A Bibliography of
LDS Writings on Jesus Christ and the New Testament

Mormon Americana:
A Guide to Sources and Collections in the United States

Second Crop

Behind the Iron Curtain:
Recollections of Latter-day Saints in East Germany, 1945–1989

Life in Utah: Centennial Selections from BYU Studies

Educating Zion

Library of Congress Cataloging-in-Publication Data

Masada and the world of the New Testament / by John F. Hall, John W. Welch.
    p. cm. — (BYU studies monographs)
    Includes index.
    ISBN 0-8425-2344-8 (pbk.)
    1. Masada Site (Israel) 2. Palestine—History—To 70 A.D. 3. Excavations (Archaeology)—Israel—Masada Site. 4. Bible. N.T.—Criticism, interpretation, etc. 5. Bible. N.T.—Antiquities. I. Hall, John Franklin. II. Welch, John W., 1946- . III. Series.
DS110.M33M26 1997
933—dc21   97-4715
                                                    CIP

Printed in the United States of America
10 9 8 7 6 5 4 3 2 1

Table of Contents

Illustrations

Masada and Religion in First-Century Judea

The Romans in Judea

The End of Masada

Introduction

From March to September 1997, many of the artifacts excavated by Yigael Yadin at Masada in the 1960s will be on display at the BYU Museum of Art. That exhibition from the Hebrew University of Jerusalem will be supplemented by an adjoining exhibition of actual Dead Sea Scrolls and other ancient Jewish items. BYU Studies is one of the principal sponsors of these exhibits as these rare pieces come to the United States.

In connection with these exhibitions, which offer the opportunity to see original artifacts from the awe-inspiring fortress of Masada, which fell to the Romans in A.D. 73, and from nearby Qumran, BYU Studies offers two special publications. First is the English translation of the Hebrew catalog for the Masada exhibition. Edited by Gila Hurvitz of the Hebrew University, the catalog contains numerous color photographs and concise reports by leading scholars who have devoted their careers to excavating, preserving, and analyzing the archaeological remains of Masada. The second publication is this collection of studies, focusing on Masada and the world of the New Testament. This volume strives to take readers back into the first-century world of Herod, Josephus, Peter, and Jesus.

Every item from the ruins at Masada or Qumran suggests something about the broader setting in which early Christianity arose. For example, the sandals from Masada are no doubt similar to the sandals worn by John the Baptist, Jesus, and his disciples; the oil lamps found at Masada illustrate the kinds of lamps that may have been carried by the young women in the parable of the ten virgins; Herod's dinnerware evokes images of the parables of Jesus involving great aristocratic banquets; the Roman weapons found on that site remind us of the strength of Rome throughout the province of Judea; and so on. We hope that each ancient artifact and its modern explication will give the reader concrete images and new insights that will enrich the understanding of individual passages as well as the overall context of many details mentioned in the New Testament.

The following studies offer solid information about the material culture of first-century Judea. Even though the story of Masada itself has recently become significantly politicized and rightly reexamined in the scholarly literature, these developments do not diminish the importance of this archaeological site as a source of information about the world of the New Testament. Because our primary interests lie in discussing the ancient artifacts themselves, we have not attempted in this volume to homogenize the diversity of opinions that exist concerning the final hours at Masada or what motivated the overzealous people who died there.

In organizing and editing these materials, we have grouped them according to the main divisions of the Masada exhibition. The first section deals with Herodian times and culture. The essays in this section ask such questions as, What kind of person was King Herod the Great, the main builder of Masada and the king of the Jews mentioned early in the gospels of Matthew and Luke? How rich was he? How many construction projects did he undertake, and what was his influence in Judea and Galilee? What Hellenistic influences did he and others bring into Palestine around the birth of Christ?

The next two sections discuss the people who died at Masada and some of the artifacts from their daily life. Sometimes these Jewish rebels are called Zealots, but Josephus more specifically calls them the Sicarii (the "Dagger Men," from the Latin *sica,* which means dagger). Although the use of the latter term has recently become more politically and academically correct, it seems unlikely that the Sicarii called themselves by this pejorative Roman moniker. What they actually called themselves remains unknown. To be sure, this confusion only reflects the complicated political situation that existed in Palestine throughout the first century A.D. Many questions about these people remain to be explored: Who were these people? Were they outlaws, brigands, freedom fighters, or social heroes? How did they live? What daily artifacts did they use (keys, lamps, sandals, coins, wine jars)? How religious were these people? Where did they worship? Were their pools used for ritual immersion baths? What sacred texts did they use? What do the remains of their time at Masada tell us about the typical daily or religious life of people in this part of the world during the New Testament era?

Next, the Masada exhibition displays several Roman artifacts left from the Roman siege and conquest of Masada. These objects raise questions about the Roman presence in Judea: How, when, and why did the Romans establish control over Judea? How intrusive was the Roman military presence? How was the army organized? What weapons did they use? These details may remind the readers of references to Roman governors, soldiers, and weapons in the New Testament and of the disastrous end of the Jewish revolt, fulfilling the prophetic warning of Jesus to Jerusalem that "there shall not be left here one stone upon another" (Matt. 24:2).

The dramatic end of Masada as told by Josephus is borne out in large part by the archaeology. Yet, to the very end, questions remain: What was the role of lots and divination in the ancient world, and did Yadin find the actual lots drawn at Masada to determine the order of the final suicides? How reliable is Josephus in his history of Masada, and by implication in his records generally—all of which are very important in reconstructing the history of the world of the New Testament?

We hope the essays in this volume will provide interesting discussions of questions such as these. Our intention is to engage and explore these topics without being exhaustive or absolute. Also, because so much of our limited knowledge about Masada and the history of first-century Judea ultimately runs back to the accounts of Josephus, a certain amount of overlap exists from one study in this volume to the next. We trust that any repetition will be a friendly and helpful redundancy. Unless otherwise indicated, all citations of Josephus are to the Loeb Library edition.

We express great appreciation to the authors and editors who have responded promptly and enthusiastically to the tasks involved in producing this volume. Nancy R. Lund, managing editor of BYU Studies, has copyedited and coordinated the project as a whole.

Many interns and volunteers have assisted with source checking and formatting individual details. Karl F. Batdorff and Marny K. Parkin have gone the extra mile in typesetting. Executive editor Doris R. Dant has done the final copyediting, supervised the graphics, and provided numerous polishing touches.

BYU Studies is honored to collaborate with the Hebrew University in many aspects of the Masada exhibition. As a neighbor of the Hebrew University on Mount Scopus in Jerusalem and as a friend to many throughout the Middle East, Brigham Young University is pleased to be associated with the Hebrew University and the Israel Antiquities Authority as this fascinating and informative material comes from Masada to the United States.

John W. Welch
John F. Hall
February 1997

Masada:
A Forum Address at
Brigham Young University

Masada: Herod's Fortress and the Zealots' Last Stand
A BYU Forum Address

Yigael Yadin
Introduced and edited by S. Kent Brown

From 1963 to 1977, before Professor Yigael Yadin entered politics and became Deputy Prime Minister of Israel, he held the most distinguished chair of archaeology at the Hebrew University in Jerusalem, a chair which was established in the name of his father, Professor E. L. Sukenik, who was in his own right a noted archaeologist and linguist and who performed the initial work on three of the seven Dead Sea Scrolls discovered in Cave 1 at Qumran. An indication of the remarkable abilities of Professor Yadin can be seen in his notable military career. Without receiving any formal military training, he rose through the ranks of the Israel Defense Forces to become the Chief of Staff when Israel became a state. All that he learned about military affairs he learned on his own through reading and by practical experience, a remarkable record considering the fact that he retired from the army as a Lieutenant General.

Professor Yadin became Israel's foremost field archaeologist, having conducted extensive excavations at Hazor, Megiddo, and Masada. The last site forms the focus of the following forum address delivered in 1976. In addition, during his life he distinguished himself as one of the foremost scholars of the Dead Sea scrolls. He edited and published a number of these texts, including his three-volume work on the Temple Scroll, published in both Hebrew and English.

Yigael Yadin (1917–1984)

Dr. Yadin was the recipient of numerous awards; among them, he delivered the Schweich lectures of the British Academy and, just before coming to BYU, he delivered the prestigious Haskell lectures at Oberlin College. In addition, he received four honorary doctorate degrees.

The following piece I have edited with a light touch. Professor Yadin delivered this illustrated lecture at BYU on May 4, 1976.

I feel highly honored to speak in this forum on this day, which is also the memorial day for the fallen in Israel, on the eve of the Independence Day, tomorrow. I am happy to speak about a fortress situated on the other salt lake, on the Dead Sea, thousands of miles from here and thousands of feet below where we are standing, the lowest spot on earth. And the subject, as was said, is the rock fortress Masada and its story on the Dead Sea.

One of the strangest phenomena in human history is the struggle of the Jewish people for their spiritual independence, always the few against the many. And one of the most amazing, heroic, alas tragic episodes in this struggle is no doubt the story of Masada.

In A.D. 73, three years after the destruction of the temple of Jerusalem by Titus, when arches of triumph were erected in Rome to commemorate the great victory of Rome over Judea, when coins with the inscription the "Judaea Capta" were in currency throughout the Roman Empire, on one spot—and one spot only—960 Jewish zealots, patriots—men, women, and children—held that isolated rock fort near the Dead Sea in the Judean desert against the whole might of Rome headed by its crack Tenth Legion commanded by their famous General Silva. And when the inevitable and bitter end was near—they could not hold out anymore—they decided (and it is not for us to criticize them now) to take their lives with their own hands rather than to submit their spiritual and physical independence.

This amazing story, until recently, was in a way semilegendary because our sole source of information was the writings of Josephus Flavius, an unfortunate Jew, I would say, and a brilliant historian. He himself was a very important commander in this great war against the Romans in A.D. 66. But then for his own reasons, he defected to the Romans. When he sat in the court in Rome—maybe he had a guilty conscience—he repented perhaps and wrote his two major works, *The War of the Jews* and *The Antiquities of the Jews*. And it is only therein that we have a description of what happened in Masada on the eve of Passover, A.D. 73.

I cannot repeat what he says. This book is available today in paperback. I think that, because of his guilty conscience, this chapter of his, describing Masada, is the best. But what I would like to say is, that from my childhood—at that time I didn't ever dream that I would have the privilege to excavate Masada—I used to read like anyone in Israel the chapter on Masada.[1] And I used to visit Masada. Of the whole big speech which Josephus puts into the mouth of Eleazar ben Yair, the commander of these zealots,[2] I was particularly impressed by a few passages that always looked to me to be real and human. Ben Yair says to his fellows, as he's trying to persuade them to take their lives, "Do it quickly, before you hear your children crying, 'Daddy, Daddy,' and you won't be able to help them, before you see your wives being violated and you will be helpless." That, I imagined, could have happened then, could have happened anytime, anywhere. He says at the very end, when they decided to do that, they embraced each other and kissed—his wife, his children, everyone. They collected everything and set it on fire, lest it fall into the hands of the Romans. He says they drew lots as to who would be the last ten people to see that everybody complied with this order. These last ten or eleven people drew lots to see who was to be the last, and the last went to the palace and set the whole fortress on fire. These were the salient points of the description which were always in my mind from childhood. You can well imagine, therefore, that when in 1963 I was asked by the archaeological institutions of Israel to lead an excavation of that site, I considered myself rather privileged because Masada is not really just another archaeological site. For many of us it is a sort of mausoleum of the nation's martyrs.

Now, how to dig such a site, to hire labor? We had an idea. We thought that Masada and its story would appeal to people, and we asked for volunteers. The amazing response was that thousands of people from all religions, from all the continents, from all walks of life, from twenty-eight countries, flocked to help us. I said from all walks of life—from professors to hippies—although in those days it was impossible to distinguish who was who just by the look of it. The amazing thing was that, when we appealed for volunteers, we promised them three things. We promised them bad food, and we promised that they would sleep ten in a tent. We also promised them, or rather told them, that they had to pay their own fare. Needless to say, we kept all our promises. Nevertheless, all of them came and really helped us. It was because of these volunteers that we managed to excavate that site in eleven months of very hard work, which I reckon otherwise would have taken us twenty-five years in the normal procedures of excavating. They were volunteers, and you know very well that there is no one better than a volunteer to do any job. (I remember one industrialist was asked how many people worked in his plant. He thought for awhile and he said about 60 percent.) If I were asked, I would say 100 percent of our volunteers worked. Not all of them came, of course, for the same motives. Some said they came to slim down, to lose weight, and they were very successful, I must say. Nevertheless, when they left Masada, they all felt emotionally the way we did.

Now, I would like to take you to the top of Masada, not only to show you what we found there, but how we found it. This was part of an experience which for me was the greatest in my life. Before doing that, I must discuss two points. Otherwise I think it would be, perhaps, incomprehensible for some of you to understand what we found there. Josephus tells us that the first to fortify that rock was King Herod the Great, and he says that there were two motives. One, he was not really Jewish, but he became, with the help of Rome, the King of the Jews. Therefore he could not really rely on his citizens, so he built this rock fort in the desert as a potential asylum. Well, that made sense. The other reason, according to Josephus, was that Herod the Great was afraid of Cleopatra, who reigned in Egypt. As we know, she had some, shall we say, intimate relations with the great men of Rome at the time and coveted Judea. Herod, so said Josephus, was afraid that one day she would get what she wanted, so he built the fortress. (Now that was a bit difficult to grasp. I remember when I used to talk to each new batch of volunteers telling them that Herod the Great was afraid of Cleopatra. The youngsters, particularly, couldn't really understand that Herod the Great was afraid of Elizabeth Taylor.)

The more serious scholars thought that the first reason really was more correct. Whatever the reason, our excavations proved quite clearly that the Masada of Herod was not just a fort; it was really a royal fort built by a great king. Otherwise, we cannot understand why we found there on this isolated rock one palace after another, adorned with frescos and mosaics. He built it for himself, just in case, and, of course, also fortified it.

The second point is that we knew what happened on the Passover of A.D. 73, this great tragic deed of the zealots which turns Masada into Masada. Yet we asked ourselves what we were going to find archaeologically of these last events, which occurred within just a few days. Although we did not find mosaics or frescos of this period, the poor remains that we found of the zealots—their clothes, the women's sandals, the coins, and the stoves—for us these were really the greatest finds. These then are the two facets of Masada: the Herodian one and, if I might say, the heroic one.

First of all, I would like to acquaint you with Masada and how it looks. Looking at Masada from the south, the Dead Sea is on the right (to the east), the Judean Desert is on the left (to the west). Masada is a natural rock standing twelve hundred feet above the level of the Dead Sea. But since the Dead Sea is twelve hundred feet below the ocean level, the top of Masada is really at zero, so to say, from the ocean point of view.

Strange as it may sound, our first problem was to determine where to base our operation. The most natural spot would have been on the east, because there was a hostel, electricity, and a road. But that would have meant daily climbing what Josephus rightly calls the "snake path," a rise of twelve hundred feet. Although I was younger twelve years ago, it was too difficult for me to think of climbing twice daily from this side. More than that, we needed to use heavy equipment, and therefore we reluctantly decided to locate our operation on the western side. On the west was the huge ramp, the assault ramp which the Romans built and by means of which, in the end, they managed to reach Masada. The difference in altitude between the hill on the west and the top is only one hundred yards, or three hundred feet, in comparison to twelve hundred. I said "reluctantly" because on the west we were completely handicapped. There was no road, no water, no electricity.

However, the Israeli army helped us very much, and we were able to do everything that we needed.

There was another problem: where to put our camp. The whole desert was ours; nevertheless, the only good spot to pitch a camp had already been taken by Silva, the commander of the Tenth Legion. He was first to come, first to choose, and he chose well. He chose his place on the west, and one can still see how his camp looks even today, without excavating. It is remarkably well preserved, far from the maddening crowd. Silva was the destroyer of Masada. His camp today is a fine archaeological object, and we did not want to destroy it. So we pitched our camp nearby. We also had something which Silva didn't have. We had the bulldozers of the engineers of the Israeli army. They flattened the area, and we pitched our camp just to the south of Silva's. For many of us, it was symbolic. On the north was the camp of those who destroyed Masada two thousand years ago; on the south was the camp of newly born Israel, who was coming to reconstruct the ruins of Masada.

While working, we used to climb up to Masada along the top of the ramp. At the crack of dawn, we and all the volunteers used to climb this earthen ramp to the top. We installed a simple cable car for our equipment. But while we walked to the top of Masada and looked to the south, Masada took on a slightly different appearance for us. Although you can't see them easily, to the south of the ramp are two rows in the cliff of what look like little holes. Actually each of them is a huge water reservoir. A royal fort or no royal fort without water means nothing. Like today, in those days there was no spring of water at the site. Herod's engineer had an ingenious idea. In the desert, it doesn't rain—it pours. The idea was to build two little dams, collect the winter runoff water, and divert it by gravitation into big reservoirs. When you stand there today, in the heat, you dare not believe that such a thing could happen. There are about twelve of these reservoirs cut out of the rock, and as you stand there, as I said, in the scorching sun you won't believe that they can be filled.

When we were excavating, though, there were two terrible winters. Our tents were torn to pieces and blown about. But we were fortunate to see how the whole system would have worked were it not that the channels are now destroyed. A half an

The Masada Fortress. (1) Northern Palace, (2) Water Gate, (3) bathhouse, (4) storehouses, (5) synagogue, (6) Western Palace, (7) southern miqveh, or ritual immersion pool, (8) large underground cistern, and (9) aqueduct.

hour after the rain started, the deep, dry gullies were filled with gushing water. I managed to photograph a rare picture because the water currently falls off the cliffs of Masada in breathtaking waterfalls into the Dead Sea rather than into the reservoirs. We were also compensated by these rains: for two weeks afterward the whole desert blossomed, as the Bible said. Even the top of Masada looked briefly like a park. For a short time, everything was blossoming, but then returned to desert again.

Talking so much about the weather you would think I came straight from London. Maybe I'm giving you the wrong idea as if the main problem in Masada is the rain. Just the contrary. Eleven months of the year, it's the scorching sun. The volunteers, particularly the women who came from Scandinavia and the northern countries, found it extremely difficult to cope with the heat. Nevertheless, I want to tell you it was these men and women who did the work, the results of which I'm going to show you now.

Before the excavation, the stumps of the walls could be seen. One could also see the double wall of Masada, the casemate wall, as we call it. We shall have a word to say about that wall because it was here that we found the most interesting discoveries connected with the zealots.

Now our first problem was to locate Herod's fantastic palace. Josephus goes out of his way in his description to say that Herod built a hidden palace, with a hidden staircase, decorated with frescoes. Until our excavation, all scholars identified that building with the biggest structure on the site. However, there was one big fly in the ointment. The location of that large building did not tally with Josephus's description. He said it was in the north, but the large building was in the west. He said the palace was under the wall, but this structure was within the wall. He said there was a hidden staircase, but this building was flat. Unfortunately, as it happens with us scholars, when the theory does not tally with the facts, we come to the conclusion that the facts in the texts are wrong. This was how it was left for many years, until it was suggested by youngsters, in the early fifties, that the palace was not on the west but rather in an incredible spot. Two youngsters climbed Masada, not along the ramp or snake path, but up the narrow bluff on the north. When they climbed there, they saw three terraces: a lower, a middle, and an upper. Having read Josephus, one of them ventured to publish an article in a semiscientific journal suggesting that this was the palace that Josephus had described. And they were right. Therefore, the first real objective in our dig, you can well imagine, was to excavate this palace. We proved that this was the palace. However, I do not call it the palace; I call it the villa. Only the megalomaniac Herod— I mean he was a great king with great lust for building—could have built a villa on this narrow bluff, on these three terraces. It was a place only for himself or one of his nine known wives. All the rest was just for pleasure and luxury.

We started at the lower terrace and had removed only the top debris when a very crucial moment arrived: pillars began to appear. If Josephus was correct, then the wall paintings would appear from this point downwards. What we found in that spot, two weeks later, was the lower part of the wall covered with well-preserved wall paintings. They are not beautiful, perhaps, according to our modern taste, but that was the fashion in Rome in those days, including Pompeii and elsewhere. The idea was to imitate by painting the lower part of the wall as if it were built of marble panels. In fact, the desperate efforts of these artists can be seen in the inner peristyles, where the artist tried to imitate the veins of the marble. All was remarkably well preserved after two thousand years, and it showed that Josephus was right in his description of the luxury of the buildings which Herod built.

However, this was merely one facet. Before I was able to photograph that wall, we had to remove three meters of debris consisting of complete fire damage. In the fire level, we found coins with the inscription "The Freedom of Zion"[3] struck by these same zealots fighting Rome. We found many pieces of clothing, sandals, and jewelry belonging to the zealots. So we knew who built the latest structure, and we also knew who were the last to die here. And just to the left of this spot of wall, Herod built for himself a little bath—hot room, cold room, and a tepid room. Since this area was lower, it was covered by much more debris. When we removed the debris, even the most cynical members of our expedition could not go on working because, on the floor, there were three skeletons: a man who looked to be an officer and warrior, a young woman, and a child.

The man, as I said, was an officer, for we found near him hundreds of scales of armor and arrows with their wooden shafts. Because of the lack of humidity, everything was well preserved. The man must have been a very important commander. His young wife's scalp was found still intact, with the beautiful plats of hair and her kerchief stained with blood. These are things you don't normally find in excavations. But even if you do, you do not know the story behind them. We asked ourselves if it were possible that we had found the very last person, as Josephus tells us, who went down to the palace, killed his family, and set the whole palace on fire. Probably yes. Of course, we shall never be able to prove it, but I think the circumstances and the analogy to what Josephus said are really striking.

This was our first encounter with the two facets of Masada: the beautiful buildings of Herod and the poor remains of the zealots, as such, but with an amazing story behind them.

The other two parts of this villa are not very important for us. The lower villa includes the bath where we found the skeletons. There is a middle terrace with the circular kiosk or overlook, for pleasure. On the upper one, there were four rooms with a beautiful semicircular balcony. This was the bedroom. There were also some guest rooms. How many people were killed to build it, I don't know. But it is a fantastic villa.

To the south of that villa was a large complex. All the visitors who had came to Masada in the last one hundred years had identified these with the storerooms, because Josephus also talks about the storerooms which Herod built. Certainly they looked like storerooms. And we decided to excavate them—easier said than done. What one could see were the lower stumps of the wall. All the fallen stones—some of them weighing three or four hundred pounds—were lying on the ground. If it were not Masada, we would just take the stones and throw them away. But it was Masada, and we had to think about future visitors. So we decided to use a different technique: to restore first and excavate later.

In a typical area before excavation, one can see the lower walls and fallen stones. We recruited good masons and told them to take these stones and build them back into the walls. I cannot pretend that we put each stone in its exact spot. But amazingly, when they finished their work, all the walls were of the same height. This shows that we were not too far wrong in our reconstruction. Having removed the stones, we started to dig again. A few inches under the surface, we again encountered the terrible fire layer, which the zealots left behind them, sometimes with charred beams and thousands of broken jars. These were the signs of the last moments, as Josephus says, when ben Yair told them to set the whole fortress on fire lest it fall into the hands of the Romans. We didn't excavate all of the storerooms. I left a few for future archaeologists, as great as the temptation was to check everything.

If we move further to the west, we come to the building which was thought to be the palace described by Josephus. It was really the palace par excellence, not the villa which Josephus described, but the ceremonial building—four thousand square meters. We started our excavations in order to find the main court of the palace. It took a group of volunteers eleven months to clear the whole area, including the layers of ash. It turned out to be the central court of the palace, revealing two pillars upon a beautiful plaster floor of the court.

It was a big palace indeed, with its own court and its own storerooms. In fact, the longest storeroom is seventy meters in length. There were also workshops and administrative rooms. To prove that this was the great palace of a great king, we found the throne room of Herod, and nearby there was a room filled with stones about four or five yards deep. When we removed those, we were rewarded. It turned out to be the waiting room for the VIPs who came to see Herod. This was the only place which Herod bothered to pave with a beautiful mosaic floor—multicolored— the earliest mosaic floor ever found in the Holy Land. It's beautiful. The interesting thing is that, although it is the earliest, it's simple. Another interesting thing is that, although Herod was not a Jew, he married the last of the Maccabean queens. Even here on top of Masada, although the whole style is Hellenistic and pagan, instead of adopting pagan images as was normal throughout the Near East, he used the patterns that were popular in Jewish art, like the pomegranate and the vine leaf. So this really was a great palace. Nearby he had a bathroom (he had bathrooms everywhere, like a good Roman), and in the corridor leading to the bathroom, we also found a mosaic floor. Now it's not as nice as the floor of the waiting room, but I don't think too many of us can boast of having mosaic floors in corridors leading to our bathrooms.

When one looks at the mosaic floor, typically one does not notice the other rough stones. I left these in place. Every visitor can see them because they give the true picture of Masada. One sees the mosaics of Herod the Great and on top of them the few stones that are part of a bin or a stove which the zealots built. When they came, they had priorities other than just to admire the beautiful mosaics of Herod. They came as squatters. And this stone really tells a great story as in the Bible when Joshua placed the stones. He asked God why he should put the twelve stones near the Jordan River. God said, "When your children come they will ask what these stones mean, and then you will tell them" (Josh. 4:3-7). Today when people come to Masada, they ask what these stones mean, and the whole story is really there.

Now before we went to Masada, we asked ourselves if we were going to find the skeletons of the 960 Jews. We knew we had very little chance because we knew that the Romans had stationed a garrison there who must have disposed of the bodies for hygienic reasons. Nevertheless, we looked for them from the very beginning. One promising site was on the southeast sheer cliff of Masada. We could see a number of little caves from there. This was a sheer cliff of twelve hundred feet. We decided to explore some of them with the help of ladders and ropes. In the little cave on the south, when we removed the top fifteen or twenty inches, we were confronted by an ugly sight, a heap of skeletons. Were these the skeletons of the zealots? Were these skeletons of the Romans? Were these the skeletons of some Christian monks who lived at Masada in the sixth century? At that time I didn't know. But now all these skeletons have been examined. They are skeletons of men, women, children, and even an embryo that was found near its mother's skeleton. I believe this dismisses the possibility these were monks or that these were Roman soldiers. Whether these were of the zealots, I don't know.

In a different vein, I mentioned that there was this double wall surrounding Masada. From the air, we could see that it was a double wall. But on site it was one huge heap of stone, one thousand three hundred yards long. I decided to excavate one spot just to know how it was built. Once I started I couldn't stop. The excavation revealed two walls, the outer wall and the inner wall. And then occurred to me what I should have thought of before. Where did the zealots live with their families? Masada had been built with palaces, with storerooms. The one hundred and ten rooms within this double wall really were a blessing—I wouldn't say even in disguise—for the zealots. It was there that they lived. It was there that we uncovered the most moving discoveries related to the zealots because, unlike the public buildings which they set on fire, they did not burn the walls. Sometimes we had the feeling that we were entering rooms that had been lived in only yesterday. For example, we would enter a room, finding a clay stove with the soot still on the wall. In another case, we found the stove with unused faggots of wood, along with a jar for flour or oil. These scenes freeze the last moments before life came to a standstill.

Yet the most moving thing for us was that in the rooms themselves, which were not burned, there was a heap of ashes, but only in the corner. Then we remembered what Josephus said, how these people embraced each other and then took their belongings, their private belongings, and set them on fire. It was in these fire heaps that we found the jewelry and other things. A heap of ashes like that means nothing anywhere else, but the story at Masada, of course, was great. Further, on the floor we found a lot of objects. And because of the lack of humidity even objects made of organic matter were found in abundance. For example, we found clothing, the earliest pieces of clothing ever found in the Holy Land—tunics and other garments. We found, of course, many objects of daily life, like spindle whorls and spoons made of ivory. We even found a die. I'm ashamed to say that this die is loaded. I give the zealots the benefit of the doubt—I say they took it from the Roman soldiers—but who knows. We found, of course, a lot of metal objects on the floor: cosmetic objects of women, perfume bottles, a comb, a mirror, sticks to paint the eyes and the cheeks. (Human nature hasn't changed in the last two thousand years, I must say.) And of course we found metal buckles and other metal objects; the more precious ones we found buried under the floor. On the floor, we found huge quantities of food. We assumed that they did not die of hunger. There were nuts, dates, olives, cereal, pomegranates, and salt—huge, huge quantities.

When we went to Masada, we asked ourselves—we didn't ask, we just dreamt—whether we were going to find scrolls of the Bible or not. We knew it would be difficult, for there are no caves there. We also knew that the zealots wouldn't burn the holy scriptures, but where to look for them was hope against hope. Weeks passed, and we found nothing. And then one day a volunteer came and on his trembling palm was a black piece of leather. We couldn't see anything except for a few letters, but with the infrared photograph, this fragment turned out to be part of the book of Psalms, Psalms 82 and 85, beautifully written. These texts come from the oldest part of the biblical psalms. There can be no doubt about this manuscript's date, A.D. 73 at the latest, and it was obviously written before the destruction of Masada, perhaps sixty or seventy years before that date. The strength of tradition, the division into chapters, the spelling of the words are exactly like the Hebrew Bible which we all still use to this day. In all, we found fourteen scrolls.

One of the buildings looked suspicious to us. This was built into the casemate wall that was divided into rooms. From the very beginning we saw that one part of the wall protruded inward. When we excavated it, we found that this building had benches all around the inside of it. I immediately suspected that this was a synagogue. But I didn't dare utter that because, if I were right, this was not only the oldest synagogue known, but the only one ever discovered from the time of Second Temple or the time of Jesus. It was oriented toward Jerusalem, and on the day that we finished clearing it, we had a group of rabbis who came to inspect the ritual bath. The time for praying came, and I said to one, "You know, Rabbi, I found a building. Perhaps it is a synagogue, but I can't guarantee it. It's your responsibility if you want to pray there." And the rabbi said, " I don't care what you say, I'm going to pray. From now on it will be a synagogue." It was really quite an emotional sight for me because I knew that it was a synagogue. These Jews were praying again in this synagogue after two thousand years, looking towards Jerusalem.

The plan of the synagogue is very simple, with benches and an orientation toward Jerusalem. But the room at the back was suspicious. So we cut a section to see where the missing pillars were. When we cut into that section, a scroll fell into our hands. We looked carefully and we saw that there was originally a pit cut into the floor; the scroll had been buried and the pit filled in. Then we knew that this was a genizah, the hiding place in a synagogue where Jews used to hide their books. We decided to remove the whole floor, and I gave this task to a volunteer from our marines. When he removed the floor, another pit appeared. At that moment, he received an order to go back to his army camp for three days. He cried like a baby, this sturdy soldier, and said, "This is my pit." This was one of the most difficult decisions I had to make, but because he had worked very hard, I said, "I'll wait; it waited two thousand years, it'll wait another three days." When he came back, he cleaned the pit, and at the bottom there was a scroll. It was not well preserved, eaten by moths. It turned out to be the book of Ezekiel. The miracle—if you like, a coincidence—is that of all the pages that were preserved, only the page with the famous prophesy of Ezekiel about the resurrection of the dry bones of Israel was extremely well preserved (Ezek. 37:1-10).

Near this synagogue stood another building that was rather strange. We called it the apartment house because it was built with one big room and two small rooms. Maybe these were the apartments or flats of the officers of the administration. Of course, we decided to excavate it. While I was in the synagogue, taking out the remnants of Ezekiel, I saw that there was a commotion among the volunteers in the other buildings. I saw that all of them were looking at a girl with a bikini, and I thought this was the attraction. However, when I came nearer, I saw that she had been cleaning the floor of the two smaller rooms. (I wish her mother would have seen how thoroughly a cleaning job she did.) She overdid it, rather, and scratched a bit of the mud floor. Under the floor she found a cache of coins. This is what they were all watching. These coins were unusual because the patina indicated that these were silver coins. With a touch of cleaning in the laboratory, they turned out to be, so to say, brand new. They turned out to be sixty silver shekels, struck in this very war against the Romans, for the first time found in their pure archaeological context. Because they were not used, the zealots had buried them under the floor lest they fall into the hands of the Romans. They looked beautiful after cleaning. And they are the typical ones, with the holy chalice, saying year two, year three, year four, year five of the revolt, with the inscription "The shekel of Israel," and on the other side, "Jerusalem the holy." Unlike the silver coins, on top of the floor we found hundreds of thousands of pennies. The zealots simply threw them on the floor. They didn't care whether they fell into the hands of the Romans. These too were covered with holy symbols and with the Hebrew inscription "For the Freedom of Zion." The inscriptions said, "Year two" and on the other side they said, "For the Freedom of Zion." These were the coins that were struck by the Jews in the great war against Rome, so there was no doubt whatsoever who the last defenders of Masada were, as in fact Josephus tells us.

In conclusion, I want to tell you something that I was always asked when I had visitors at Masada and I showed them the palaces. There is always someone who will ask a very annoying question, "What is the most important thing that you discovered?" I'm not going to tell you what the most important thing is that I discovered because I don't know. I don't know whether one scroll is more important than the other, whether these coins are more important, or the frescos more than the mosaics. The whole thing is important.

But I would like to end with a find which perhaps, if not the most important, was definitely the one which electrified all of us there, archaeologists and lay workers. Between the storerooms and the villa, there were typical groups of volunteers working. When one group came to a layer of ashes, suddenly they found eleven small pieces of pottery, or sherds, each of them with an inscription of one name in ink, one name only. It was interesting to see the volunteers and us, without talking to each other, say, "Is it possible that we have found the actual lots of the last ten or eleven people, which Josephus described?" This possibility was strengthened when the names which we read there were nicknames, rather than proper names, names of commanders. For example, one was called "the hunter." Another was called Joab, like the commander-in-chief of David. One was called "the one from the valley" and so on. The possibility became a probability when, on one of these, we found the magic name of ben Yair, the very commander of the zealots—ben Yair, the one who, according to Josephus, was the head.

Now whether this is really the same ben Yair, as I believe, or not, it is because of ben Yair, it is because of the fire that the zealots left behind them everywhere on top of Masada, that Masada today, for many of us, for all of us in Israel, and for many of us in the world, is not just an archaeological site. It is a symbol, it is a challenge, and it is also a reminder. This is why to this very day,[4] three or four times a year, the recruits of the armored corps of the Israeli army take the oath of allegiance to the state of Israel on top of Masada, saying three times, "Masada shall not fall again." Thank you very much.

NOTES

[1]Josephus, *Jewish War* 7.252–406.

[2]For one use of the word *zealots* in reference to general sorts of rebels (*to tōn zēlōtōn klēthentōn genos*), which could include the Sicarii, see Josephus, *Jewish War* 7.268, 272. For a more specific analysis of the group that formally called themselves Zealots according to Josephus, *Jewish War* 4.161, see Kent P. Jackson, "Revolutionaries in the First Century," in this volume.

[3]The coins from the first through the third years of the revolt preserve this phrase, "the freedom of Zion." Coins from year four and year five read "for the redemption of Zion." See Yaakov Meshorer, "The Coins of Masada," in *Masada I: The Yigael Yadin Excavations 1963-1965, Final Reports,* ed. Joseph Aviram, Gideon Foerster, and Ehud Netzer (Jerusalem: Israel Exploration Society and Hebrew University of Jerusalem, 1989), 101-19; and Yaacov Meshorer, "The Coins of Masada," in *The Story of Masada: Discoveries from the Excavations,* ed. Gila Hurvitz (Provo: BYU Studies, 1997), 141.

[4]On the cessation of the swearing-in ceremonies on Masada in 1987, see Nachman Ben-Yehuda, *The Masada Myth* (Madison: University of Wisconsin Press, 1995), 159-60.

Herodian Times
and Historical Backgrounds

King Herod

Richard Neitzel Holzapfel

Introduction

Herod visited Masada, a Hasmonean mountain stronghold situated near the Dead Sea, on at least two occasions before he began
his remarkable career as king of the Jews.[1] Popularly known today
as Herod the Great, Herod eventually became connected with this
site when he indelibly placed his architectural mark on its isolated
rocky plateau. Standing at an elevation of about thirteen hundred
feet above the level of the Dead Sea, the fortress, now called Hor-
vot Mezada (Ruins of Masada),[2] is extremely difficult to access
because of its steep and sometimes vertical sides.

Herod's first recorded visit to Masada occurred during a fratri-
cidal war between two Hasmonean claimants to the Jewish throne,
Hyrcanus II and Aristobulus II.[3] Herod was sent by the Jerusalem
government in 42 B.C. to recapture the fortress from the rebels.[4]
The second visit occurred two years later in a completely different
setting: with support from the Parthians, who were Rome's chief
rivals in the East and the successors to the Persian Empire in
present-day Iran, Aristobulus's son Antigonus sought to depose
his uncle Hyrcanus and oust the Romans.

With his betrothed Hasmonean princess, Mariamme; her
mother, Alexandra; his mother, Cypros; his sister, Salome; his
youngest brother, Pheroras; and some servants, supporters, and
soldiers, Herod, a supporter of Rome, fled Jerusalem in an effort to
escape capture and certain death. He left his family and supporters
holed up at Masada while he continued on to Alexandria, Rhodes,
and eventually to Rome itself to gain additional support to oust the
Parthians and their appointed king, Antigonus (Mariamme's uncle).

In 40 B.C., during his visit to Rome—Herod's first to the imperial capital—the Roman senate, under the direction of the triumvirs Antony and Octavius, named him king of Judea, Galilee, Perea, and Idumea. Nevertheless, Herod took several years to secure his rule. This effort to stabilize his kingdom began upon his return to the region in the following year.

Herod landed at Ptolemais (present-day Acco) in early 39 B.C. to begin the difficult task of imposing order and authority over the nation. Following a successful Galilean campaign, Herod turned his face toward Masada once again. Taking the Via Maris down the coast, Herod captured the city of Joppa (present-day Yafo) and proceeded to Masada, bypassing Jerusalem. Herod eventually broke Antigonus's siege of Masada and freed his family and supporters.

The survival of Herod's entourage during the long siege was complicated by the lack of water. Their capitulation was averted only because a sudden rainfall filled their cisterns. As a result of this near disaster, Herod eventually added twelve huge cisterns to provide the fortress with a sufficient water supply. The cisterns were carved into the northwest side of the cliff and connected to the mountain's top by a system of paths.

During his reign, Herod built walls and other new structures— including the Northern Palace—at the remote site. Renowned for his palaces and fortifications, Herod's efforts to improve Masada made the Hasmonean stronghold his own.[5] Herod's ambitious efforts to transform Masada are symbolic of what he did to the religious, economic, and social landscape of the region during his reign as king of Judea.

Herod's kingdom had experienced repression, revolt, and turmoil for several hundred years. It had been ruled from Egypt by the Ptolemies for over a hundred years after the death of Alexander the Great in 323 B.C. It became part of the Seleucid kingdom around 200 B.C. and eventually achieved a considerable degree of independence for nearly a century under the Hasmoneans. However, from 63 B.C. onwards, the whole region (Judea and Syria) was effectively under Roman control as a client kingdom of Rome, although Judea and Samaria did not become organized Roman provinces until A.D. 6 and Galilee and Perea not until A.D. 44. While Herod was alive, his world was part of the Greco-Roman world.[6]

Herod's "Northern Palace." Sometimes called a villa, this complex was built on the northern tip of the Masada plateau and two lower terraces.

Although the influence of his life changed the history of his land and his people, in the broader historic fabric of this period Herod may be considered simply as a minor client king of the Roman Empire. Nevertheless, his life deserves consideration, not only in its own right but also for several other cogent reasons: First, Herod's life crossed the paths of many influential people (for example, Julius Caesar, Augustus, Mark Antony, Cleopatra, Marcus Agrippa, and Jesus of Nazareth).[7] Second, his descendants and relatives (such as Archelaus, Herod Philip, Herod Antipas, Herodias, Salome, Agrippa I, and Agrippa II) continued to occupy positions of power and influence into the second century A.D., and several made appearances in the New Testament.[8] Third, Herod left the modern world important cultural artifacts (including archaeological remains at Jericho, Hebron, Caesarea Maritima, Herodium, and Masada) that enable scholars to reconstruct the social setting of his world. Fourth, Herod's Judea occupied a critical position in the region, controlling the only land route between Syria and Egypt. Finally, Herod's life illuminates much about his world—the world that saw the birth and rise of Christianity.

Sources for Herod's History

Just as Herod's life reveals much about his age, his age elucidates much about his life. Surprisingly, the sources available to reconstruct Herod's life—literature, archaeology, numismatics, and inscriptions—may be better than those for Seneca or even for Paul. Louis Feldman argues, "There is no figure in all antiquity about whom we have more detailed information than Herod."[9]

Josephus. The primary literary source on Herod's life is Flavius Josephus (Yoseph ben Matatyahu in Hebrew).[10] His books *Jewish War,* published sometime between A.D. 75 and 79, and *Jewish Antiquities,* published between A.D. 93 and 94, contain a wealth of information about Herod.[11] Josephus virtually stands alone as the written witness of Herod and his times. While his reports in *Jewish War* and *Antiquities* are sometimes inconsistent and contradictory, Josephus's histories reveal much about this period of time and Herod's position in it.

The Herodian Dynasty

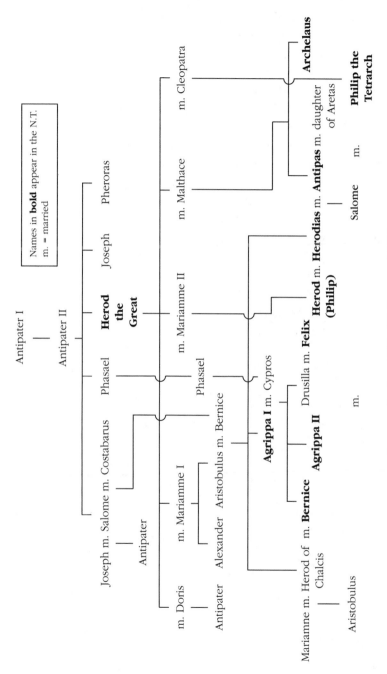

Names in **bold** appear in the N.T.
m. = married

Source: *Anchor Bible Dictionary*, 3:175

Apparently, Josephus's main source on Herod's life was the now nonextant writings of Nicholas of Damascus, a non-Jew and intimate friend of Augustus.[12] Nicholas not only tutored Herod in philosophy but acted as a court advisor and court historian. Josephus also had access to Herod's no longer extant *Memoirs,* which in all likelihood provided additional information.[13] Finally, most scholars agree that Josephus utilized archival sources in Rome, particularly in his later work, *Antiquities.*

Using Josephus to reconstruct historical events in Herod's life is somewhat problematic as already noted, since his assessment of the king is often contradictory.[14] Josephus was the descendent of a Hasmonean princess and was conscious of this pedigree. As a result of family pride, one could expect from Josephus a biased interpretation of the conflict between the Hasmonean side of Herod's family and the Idumean side.

Three basic questions arise when consulting Josephus on Herod: first, the reliability of his sources; second, Josephus's own reliability; and third, his historical balance in treating events in the life of Herod. Josephus's lack of balance is nowhere more evident than in his decision to dedicate in his writings three times more space to Herod's family problems than to other important events of his reign.

Furthermore, one may be puzzled by Josephus's access to speeches and private conversations, such as discussions between Herod and Octavian and remarks made by Herod and his wives in their bedroom. Certainly Josephus followed the practice introduced by the ancient Greek historian Thucydides. Thucydides stated that since it was impossible to always give a verbatim report of speeches, he put into the speaker's mouth the thoughts "given in the language in which, as it seemed to me, the several speakers would express, on the subjects under consideration, the sentiments most befitting the occasion, though at the same time I have adhered as closely as possible to the general sense of what was actually said."[15] Smallwood argues, with regard to the speeches in *Jewish War,* "those attributed to Herod need not be rejected as pure Josephan fantasy," since Herod's *Memoirs* and the writings of Nicolas of Damascus could have given intimate information that Josephus included in his works.[16]

Strabo and Other Ancient Writers. After Josephus, other ancient writers, such as Strabo, left information about Herod. Often writers, particularly Christians, portrayed Herod in a negative light. Fiction and legends created over time eventually were accepted as fact in many cases.[17]

Modern Sources. Just as it is difficult to find a coherent assessment of Herod's life and reign in ancient sources, people living two thousand years after Herod's death also vary in their points of view. Modern descriptions for Herod range anywhere from a genius to a lunatic and from a despot to a well-meaning king with his country's best interests at heart.

Stewart Perowne notes that Herod has been "for 2,000 years . . . detested as one of the most wicked men."[18] While Perowne's description of Herod varies somewhat from this commonly held view, he nevertheless concludes his biography with this observation, revealing the lenses by which many judge Herod's life and administration:

> [Herod] did not realize the spiritual world in which he lived. . . .
> Some centuries before Herod's day, the prophets had propounded a
> spiritual view of religion. . . . Herod perceived none of these things.
> He was bent solely on the affairs of this world. His great crime against
> Jewry, for which he had done so much, was not that he repressed
> nationalism, but that he never realized its spiritual destiny. Herod's
> tragedy was not that he saw the vanity of the dream, but that he
> never beheld the glory of the vision.[19]

Another perspective, a Jewish one, is found in the work of Samuel Sandmel. He states categorically that "Herod was hated, and he was cruel."[20] Yet, Sandmel attempts to place Herod in context and as a result softens some of the prevailing views of Herod, giving more depth to his portrait than has been done in the past.

David M. Rhoads assesses Herod as a "half-Jew from Idumaea, . . . [who] with the help of mercenary troops . . . conquered Jewish territory and succeeded in establishing himself as king of the Jews." He concludes, "The needs of the country were secondary to his efforts to maintain a place for himself within the empire. . . . Having forced his rule upon the nation, he reigned like a tyrant."[21]

A more recent account by Lee Levine begins to move beyond many earlier interpretations.[22] He states, "The Herodian period . . . was a distinct improvement over its predecessors [including

Hasmonean kings]." All in all, Levine continues, "Herod offered the Jews an unwavering political policy which advocated cooperation and integration within the *pax Romana*." He concludes that the consequences of the collapse of this policy seventy years later "proved to be catastrophic and tragic for the Jewish people."[23]

Peter Richardson offers another example in the shift from the old paradigm. To date, Richardson provides the most radical reassessment of Herod's life and reign. He argues that, far from being a "usurping alien" or "half-Jew," Herod was a "third-generation Jew who was attentive to his religion—a Jew, however, who was a Roman citizen and a Hellenist, who shared the religious outlook of most Roman citizens."[24]

The New Testament. Despite current scholarly reassessment, popular views of Herod are still primarily based on another ancient document, the New Testament book of Matthew. It presents a vivid, dramatic, and horrifying image of Herod—one that is found only in Matthew:

> After Jesus was born in Bethlehem in Judea, during the time of King Herod, Magi from the east came to Jerusalem and asked, "Where is the one who has been born king of the Jews? We saw his star in the east and have come to worship him." When King Herod heard this he was disturbed, and all Jerusalem with him. When he had called together all the people's chief priests and teachers of the law, he asked them where the Christ was to be born. "In Bethlehem in Judea," they replied, "for this is what the prophet has written: 'But you, Bethlehem, in the land of Judah, are by no means least among the rulers of Judah; for out of you will come a ruler who will be the shepherd of my people Israel.'" Then Herod called the Magi secretly and found out from them the exact time the star had appeared. He sent them to Bethlehem and said, "Go and make a careful search for the child. As soon as you find him, report to me, so that I too may go and worship him." (New International Version [NIV], Matthew 2:1-8)[25]

The Magi departed and found the house where Joseph, Mary, and the young child Jesus were living, and after presenting their gifts, they departed for home without informing Herod. Joseph, warned by an angel, left Bethlehem and fled into Egypt to escape a death decree similar to the one issued by Pharaoh (Ex. 1:22):

> When Herod realized that he had been outwitted by the Magi, he was furious, and he gave orders to kill all the boys in Bethlehem

and its vicinity who were two years old and under, in accordance with the time he had learned from the Magi. Then what was said through the prophet Jeremiah was fulfilled: "A voice is heard in Ramah, weeping and great mourning, Rachel weeping for her children and refusing to be comforted, because they are no more." (NIV, Matthew 2:16-18)[26]

The New Testament informs the reader that when Herod died "an angel of the Lord appeared in a dream to Joseph in Egypt and said, 'Get up, take the child and his mother and go to the land of Israel, for those who were trying to take the child's life are dead'" (NIV, Matthew 2:19-20).

This image of Herod and its subsequent fusing with the lives of other descendants with the same name mentioned in the New Testament only reinforce the stereotype so prevalent today.[27] The often-quoted statement supposedly made by Augustus, "I would rather be Herod's pig than his son," capsulizes the most prevalent attitude towards King Herod.[28] However, like most other historical figures of the past, the portrait of Herod is far more complex than is this superficial view.

Herod's Background and Rise to Power

Ancestry. Herod (*Herodes Magnus* in Latin and *Hērōdēs* in Greek) was the son of Antipater of Idumea. Idumea (called Edom in the Old Testament) was a relatively small area stretching approximately from the southern portion of the Judean hill country to the northern part of the Negev. To the east, Idumea bordered the Judean desert and the Dead Sea, and its territory reached west into the provinces of the port cities Gaza and Ashkelon. The area formed a vital power base for Herod's eventual rise to power.

Apparently, Idumea was annexed, not conquered, by the Hasmoneans in about 120 B.C., and the conversion of the inhabitants to Judaism was voluntary, not forced as has been traditionally argued.[29] Idumea shared the Jewish allegiance to the nation, religion, and Jewish culture as demonstrated in their unity with Judea against the Romans in war in A.D. 66. This is an important point that helps underscore Herod's own piety and will be discussed later.

During this period of conquest and annexation, the Hasmonean leaders established themselves as Greek-style absolute monarchs, eliminating opponents and adopting the Greek practice of crucifying political enemies. There were, of course, those who supported them and those who did not approve of their reign, particularly of their Hellenizing tendencies.

Herod's father and grandfather were men of experience and prominence and rose to importance during the reign of the Hasmonean queen Alexandra Salome. Herod's grandfather Antipas was appointed *stratēgos* (praetor or general) over Idumea by Alexandra Salome and Alexander Jannaeus, her husband. Salome and Alexander had two sons, the older Hyrcanus II and the younger Aristobulus II. Following Alexander's death, Salome retained the throne, but Hyrcanus was appointed high priest. When Salome died suddenly in 70 B.C., Hyrcanus was crowned king. Herod's father, Antipater, was a wealthy man, who eventually made his home in Jerusalem, where he advised the Hasmonean court of Hyrcanus. If Herod was born in Jerusalem while his father served in Hyrcanus's court, which is certainly possible, Herod would have been an ethnic Idumean only.

The integration of the Idumean nobility with the Hasmoneans is demonstrated in Hyrcanus's marriage to an Idumean and in Herod's later marriage to a Hasmonean princess. Most importantly, Josephus affirms many positive qualities possessed by Antipater and clearly blames the Hasmonean court for giving away its authority and power.[30]

Cypros, Herod's mother, apparently came from a distinguished Nabatean family (possibly the royal family of Aretas III or Obodas II). Whether or not Cypros was a converted Jew is unknown, and the extent of Herod's Jewish education is lost to us. However, at this period of time, identification of a child with Judaism came through the father, not the mother. Herod was therefore a third generation Jew, born into this aristocratic family in the late 70s B.C. (usually dated at 73 B.C.). He had three brothers, Phasael, Joseph, and Pheroras, and one sister, Salome. Two of his siblings (Joseph and Salome) had Jewish names—another indication of the family's close association with Judaism.

The Hasmonean (Maccabean) Dynasty

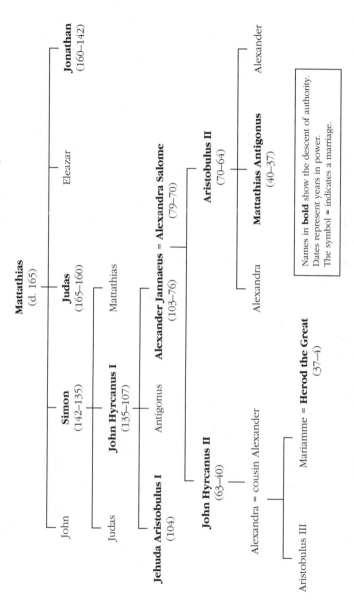

Mattathias
(d. 165)

John

Simon
(142–135)

Eleazar

Antigonus

Judas
(165–160)

John Hyrcanus I
(135–107)

Jonathan
(160–142)

Judas

Mattathias

Jehuda Aristobulus I
(104)

Alexander Jannaeus = Alexandra Salome
(103–76)   (79–70)

Alexandra

Aristobulus II
(70–64)

Alexander

John Hyrcanus II
(63–40)

Mattathias Antigonus
(40–37)

Alexandra = cousin Alexander

Aristobulus III

Mariamme = **Herod the Great**
(37–4)

Names in **bold** show the descent of authority.
Dates represent years in power.
The symbol = indicates a marriage.

All dates are before Christ. Source: *Anchor Bible Dictionary.*

Younger Years. Josephus suggests that as a young man Herod was athletic, agile, tall, and strong. As a member of the upper class, he played soldier, hunted, and learned to ride horses. Apparently, while Herod was still a young boy, the Essene Manaemos prophesied that Herod would eventually become king. Training, education, and family connections prepared Herod to serve his nation, but events beyond his control eventually gave him the throne.

A decade after Herod's birth, Aristobulus and Hyrcanus each struggled to establish himself as the legitimate successor to the throne and, in the process, instituted civil war in the land. The inability of the Hasmonean royal family to solve their civil, dynastic, and religious affairs led Roman general Pompey to take advantage of the situation by expanding Roman hegemony in the region.[31] Many Jews were relieved to have Rome intervene in what had become a chaotic situation, but there was some early resistance against the occupation government, particularly in Galilee, where many Gentiles had become enthusiastic converts to Judaism.

Pompey eventually sided with Hyrcanus and occupied Jerusalem in the autumn of 63 B.C.[32] The Roman general then appointed Hyrcanus high priest and ethnarch. Hyrcanus served basically from 63 to 40 B.C., with several periods of interruption. During this time, Aristobulus was captured twice and taken to Rome in both cases. Upon his second release in 49 B.C., Aristobulus headed towards Judea, desiring to depose his brother. However, his intercession in Judean affairs was halted when he was apparently poisoned under orders of Quintus Metelus Scipio, Governor of Syria.

Herod's father, Antipater, supported not only Hyrcanus, but also the Roman alliance. He demonstrated his loyalty to Rome by providing troops and paying for supplies, notably for a Roman campaign in Egypt. Rome gradually drew power away from the Hasmoneans, and while Hyrcanus retained his position as high priest, Antipater increasingly dominated the political life of Judea. Herod's own rise to prominence was greatly enhanced when his father was made a Roman citizen (an honor transmitted to Herod and his children) and appointed *epitropos* (procurator or governor) in 47 B.C. by Julius Caesar, three years before Caesar's assassination.[33]

Antipater asked his two sons to help in the difficult task of establishing order. Herod and his brother Phasael were soon there-after appointed governors, Herod of Galilee and his brother of Jeru-salem. The northern region was a difficult assignment since the borders were infested by brigands.[34] Herod was twenty-five years of age at the time but gained a reputation for his military and admin-istrative abilities when he imposed order in Galilee by putting down the revolt of Hezekiah (Ezechias in Greek sources). He was admired by the Galilean Jews and the Roman officials in Syria for his service.

At this young age, Herod succeeded in establishing order but was also challenged by some of Jerusalem's elite, who were appar-ently disturbed by Antipater's rise to power. When summoned to answer for his actions in summarily executing Hezekiah, Herod arrived in Jerusalem to stand trial before the Sanhedrin.[35] One of the Sanhedrin's fearless members, Samainas, told the gathering that if they did not check Herod now, some day he would be king. This was the second time this prediction had been made. Under pres-sure from Rome through Hyrcanus, the Sanhedrin cleared Herod of charges, and he continued serving in appointed positions.

Family and Marriages. During this period, Herod married Doris, one of his ten wives. This was a time when Jewish families, unlike their Roman and Greek counterparts, were endogamous community families, characterized by equality of brothers, cohabi-tation of married sons with parents, frequent marriage between children of brothers, and occasionally polygamy.[36] Throughout his life, Herod demonstrated intense family loyalty to his parents, brothers, and sister. Such fidelity and allegiance was a hallmark of Antipater's family that continued among his children even after he was murdered.

Arch rival Malichus poisoned Antipater in 43 B.C., an act that set back Herod's career. Eventually, with permission from his Roman patrons, Herod had Malichus killed. Even Hyrcanus was apparently relieved, fearing that Malichus wanted to depose him also. Herod made himself indispensable to Hyrcanus, thereby cementing his position in the kingdom as the successor to Antipater. In addition, loyalty to Antipater's memory and to Herod's own abilities kept the Romans from deserting Herod when members of the Jerusalem aristocracy tried to remove him from his position of power following his father's murder. In 42 B.C., Cassius reappointed Herod governor of Coele-Syria (the area around Damascus). Herod had been first appointed to this position in 46 B.C. by Sextus Caesar.

In the same year, Herod divorced Doris (also divorcing a niece and a cousin, both of whom he had apparently married before Doris). Following his divorces, he prepared to marry Mariamme I (a Hasmonean princess and granddaughter of both Hasmonean rivals, Aristobulus II and Hyrcanus II). While Herod certainly married Mariamme in an effort to connect himself with the Hasmonean family, he apparently truly loved her. Although approved by Hyrcanus, the marriage was not sanctioned by Mariamme's mother, Alexandra.

His marriage to Mariamme represents Herod's first attempt to connect himself to the royal family.[37] Later, he married a daughter of a Jewish temple priest, thus connecting himself to the important religious segment of his kingdom. The effort to make proper connections with other families was not limited to his own marriages. As Richardson demonstrated in his insightful construction of Herod's family tree, the Herodian family was intermarried in complex and multiple ways in a web of royal lineages—an attempt to provide some stability in the region.[38]

Herod, King of Judea

Aristobulus's son, Antigonus, joined forces with the Parthians in an effort to supplant Hyrcanus (and therefore Herod) and Roman influence in the region. Hyrcanus was captured and disfigured (preventing him from serving as high priest). Being warned of the impending attempt to capture him, Herod fled Jerusalem. Eventually he made his way to Rome in spite of the dangers of winter sea travel and the chaotic atmosphere in Rome at the time. Apparently his subsequent nomination in 40 B.C. by Marc Antony to become king of Judea was a complete surprise.

Josephus provides a dramatic picture of Herod walking out of the senate house in Rome between Marc Antony and Octavian Caesar: "The meeting was dissolved and Antony and Caesar left the senate-house with Herod between them, preceded by the consuls and the other magistrates, as they went to offer sacrifice and to lay up the decree in the Capitol. On this, the first day of his reign, Herod was given a banquet by Antony."[39] Herod was thirty-three years of age and faced a promising future as king of Judea.

The Struggle to Secure the Kingdom. Herod lived his life in a period when ambitious people were sometimes brutal and lacking in compassion. It was an era of fratricide, savagery, killing, conspiracy, civil disturbances, and international plots and counterplots. Most importantly, it was a period when security was often nonexistent.

During this period, Jews were defined by three separate and distinct categories: ethnic, political, and religious. Herod could claim the title "King of the Jews" by virtue of his religious adherence. Additionally, he could claim the title "King of Judea" by virtue of his political status as a resident of Judea.[40] However, because his ancestry was Idumean, he could not claim either title based on ethnicity.

Like others during this period, Herod apparently chose dependency on Rome as the best strategy for assuring the welfare of the nation and of Judaism in general. This may have been his most important and successful decision. As future events seem to prove, Herod's prudence in accepting the political realities of Rome's dominance in the first century was a better alternative to the irresponsibility and impulsiveness of the political and religious zealots that brought Judea in direct and open conflict with Rome in A.D. 66. His commitment to Rome and to Judaism penetrated his policies in various degrees.

After two and one-half decades of strife in the region, Herod sought to unify the people and establish tranquillity within the nation. For Rome's part, the region was important because it served as a buffer state between themselves and their nemesis, the Parthians. The Parthian Empire was the only remaining formidable threat to the extensive dominance of Rome in the Mediterranean world.

Following his landing at Ptolemais in 39 B.C., Herod secured Galilee, moved south and captured Joppa, Masada, and Orhesa (Khirbet Khoreisa, south of Hebron). His successes encouraged many to join his cause, enlarging his army considerably. His attempt to secure Jerusalem was halted, however. In the following year, he captured

Sepphoris and routed the rebels in the Arbela caves (in Galilee), demonstrating ingenious military strategy and callous effectiveness by lowering soldiers in cages from above the cave rather than attempting an attack from below.

However, his throne was not secure until he finally stormed Jerusalem with Roman assistance in 37 B.C. This time Herod prevented the Roman general from desecrating the temple and stopped the complete plunder of the city. Jerusalem was the most significant city in the region and was an important symbol. It became the capital of Herod's kingdom and continued to be the religious center for Jews, including Diaspora Judaism.

Often, Herod's reign is identified as beginning when Jerusalem was taken instead of when he was appointed three years earlier. Herod married Mariamme just before Jerusalem capitulated. In another important action taken at this time to help insure the stability of the fledgling regime, Marc Antony executed Antigonus, who was Aristobulus's last surviving son and Herod's chief rival.

Among Herod's efforts to secure his kingdom was an ambitious building program that included building walls and fortifications. Apparently Herod's first building effort in the Herodian capital was the Antonia Fortress (named in honor of Marc Antony, who had nominated him for the throne).[41] The Antonia was a combination of palace and fortress with high walls and towers, moat, courtyards, baths, and quarters for a large number of troops.[42]

Later, Herod built his largest, most impressive palace fortress at the western edge of the Upper City. Called the Central Palace, it was an architectural achievement as well as a strong fortress. It was comprised of the city fortification wall itself on the western side and an inner wall forty-five feet high in the south and east, with towers at regular intervals. On the north side was still a stronger fortress or citadel formed by three multistoried towers, named for a friend slain in battle (Hippicus), a son also killed in war (Phasael), and his Hasmonean wife (Mariamme).

Another defensive measure undertaken by Herod was the construction or reinforcement of Jerusalem's massive walls. Herod also sought to add to the security of his kingdom by building fortresses at Masada, Machaerus, Hyrcania, Cypros, Alexandrium, Jericho, and Herodium.[43] These efforts at security did not always

Ruins of Herod's Western Palace at Masada. Aerial view looking south.

Building ruins at Masada

prove successful, especially when territory was confiscated with consent of his Roman patrons.

In 26 B.C., Cleopatra, who desired to annex Arabia, Judea, and southern Syria into her own kingdom, gained Iturea, Samaritis, some independent coastal cities, and parts of Nabatea, further pressing Herod's control of the region. Court intrigues continued within the family, who utilized outside forces to help sway the balance. In 34, Cleopatra gained Jericho and parts of the coastal plain, increasing pressure on Herod's land claims again. She apparently associated with anti-Herodian forces in Jerusalem, which caused Herod more concern about increased political pressure from within and without the state.

Another apparent setback occurred when Herod chose to support Marc Antony against Octavian when a rift between the two Roman leaders escalated to open conflict. On September 2, 31 B.C., Octavian's forces defeated Antony and Cleopatra at Actium, making Octavian the sole ruler of the Roman Empire. During the following year, Herod succeeded in what might be considered a most remarkable comeback. The forty-three-year-old Herod proceeded to Rhodes, where Octavian had made public his decision to support, wherever possible, existing client kings. Herod risked everything on this one opportunity by placing his crown aside, dressing as a commoner, and appealing to Octavian personally. Josephus records Herod's defense:

> "I was made king by Antony, and I acknowledge that I have in all things devoted my services to him. Nor will I shrink from saying that, had not the Arabs detained me, you would assuredly have found me in arms inseparable from his side. I sent him, however, such auxiliary troops as I could and many thousand measures of corn; nor even after his defeat at Actium did I desert my benefactor. When no longer useful as an ally, I became his best counsellor; I told him the one remedy for his disasters—the death of Cleopatra. Would he but kill her, I promised him money, walls to protect him, an army, and myself as his brother in arms in the war against you. But his ears, it seems, were stopped by his infatuation for Cleopatra and by God who has granted you the mastery. I share Antony's defeat and with his downfall lay down my diadem. I am come to you resting my hope of safety upon my integrity, and presuming that the subject of inquiry will be not whose friend, but how loyal a friend, I have been."[44]

Octavian realized that the loyalty shown by Herod to his patron Antony, who had been the legitimate Roman ruler in the East, was not only natural, but commendable. Herod was Rome's most active proponent in the region, and Octavian believed Herod's loyalty could be transferred to him. Herod, therefore, emerged from the crisis stronger than ever.

Soon after Antony and Cleopatra's final defeat, Herod received Cleopatra's bodyguards (some four hundred Gauls) and the territory once confiscated by her in addition to the coastal cities of Gaza, Anthedon, and Joppa; Strato's Tower (future site of Caesarea); Samaria; and the Transjordanic cities of Gadara and Hippos. Herod thus advanced his nation from being a small landlocked state to one that rivaled the ancient Israelite kingdoms of David and Solomon.

The Struggle to Maintain the Kingdom. Both Octavian, who by this time was the emperor Augustus, and Marcus Agrippa made state visits to Judea. Herod also visited Italy on several occasions, helping cement the Herodian relationship with Rome, a relationship that spanned nearly two hundred years—from Antipater's assistance to Julius Caesar to Herod's grandchildren and great-grandchildren well into the early second century A.D.

Renewed in his determination to establish law and order in his kingdom, as Rome required and as he believed was in the best interest of Judea, Herod moved to eliminate all domestic opposition to his rule and control any institution which might threaten his ability to rule effectively. Herod carried out proscriptions of the leading Hasmonean courtiers. Forty-five notables of Antigonus's party were executed, and all others disappeared from the historical record. Herod made the Sanhedrin (whatever their function had been before) more like the privy councils of other Hellenistic kings—convened at his request and made up largely of family, friends, and close associates.

Herod appointed the high priest and ended the Hasmonean practice of uniting the political and religious authority in one person (the high priest had also been king). While certainly this move helped consolidate power into his hand, it may also suggest a respect for Jewish law and tradition, since he was not a descendent of Aaron and therefore could not assume the role of high priest.

Against his own wishes but under pressure from Antony, who was in turn pressured by Cleopatra, Herod had appointed his brother-in-law Aristobulus III as high priest. Entrusting the position of high priest to the surviving male member of the Hasmonean dynasty proved too destabilizing, and in 35 B.C. Herod had Aristobulus killed in Jericho. It had become obvious that Aristobulus was becoming the focus of an effort to reassert a Hasmonean claim to the throne. From that point forward, Herod appointed some six high priests who came from Alexandria and Babylonia, from families with no special connection with Judean politics. Their only qualification for office, it appears, came from the purity of their priestly lineage.[45] It must be recalled that the Hasmoneans had also controlled the office of high priest and were vocally criticized by the Essenes for this policy.

As attested by Josephus on numerous occasions, Herod did not fail to forestall any attempt to overthrow him—even if he had to execute family members,[46] including his wife's grandfather (Hyrcanus II); his mother-in-law (Alexandra), his brother-in-law (Costobar), and eventually his wife (Mariamme). Evidence suggests that Alexandra, Costobar, and Mariamme plotted against Herod. Instead of legitimizing his regime, Herod's marriage to Mariamme had revealed, reflected, and intensified strains within the political, cultural, and societal confines of his kingdom during this turbulent period of history. His marriage into the Hasmonean dynasty had been intended to transcend and relieve the stresses between religion and ethnicity, priesthood and kingship, insiders and outsiders, and between generations. Instead the marriage had become a source of nationalist intrigue and enmity.

His execution of Mariamme, however, was the beginning of a long downward spiral of trouble in his own family—a family paralyzed with rivalries and strains. He was vexed with her death until his own death in 4 B.C., demonstrating a persistent love-hate relationship with his young wife, but in light of Mariamme's capital offense against the state, Herod apparently felt he had no other choice but to execute her.

Later, Alexander and Aristobulus, his sons by Mariamme, were executed when accused by other family members of planning to assassinate their father. Tragically, another son, Antipater, was convicted of plotting against his father and was executed shortly before Herod's own death in 4 B.C. Far from being simply capricious acts based solely on anger or resentment (certainly these emotions were involved), his actions were calculated to preserve the stability of the region and in family matters were also based on a kinship system deeply rooted in the notions of honor and shame.[47] Betrayal by family members brought shame on the king and undermined his authority. Additionally, Jewish tradition gave him recourse against his rebellious sons.[48]

However, these incidents, as noted in Josephus, reveal the problematic nature of Herod's methods of maintaining security, particularly that of a widely used means of extracting information—physical torture.[49] Confessions given under duress could yield extremely questionable information, which created a vicious cycle that made it nearly impossible for Herod to clearly define the extent and exact nature of subversion within his realm and family.

Much like dynastic struggles in Rome and Ptolemaic Egypt, Herod's family seethed with infighting, as competing factions within the family sought to advance their cause for succession.[50] Of Herod's fifteen known children, ten were sons. Richardson argues:

> With ten wives and an embarrassment of male children as potential successors, the rivalry within the palace walls for precedence was

intense. . . . Along with the poisoned palace atmosphere that afflicted immediate family relationships, there were strong pressures to form alliances beyond the palace walls that would create a firm base for succession.[51]

Herod may have altered his will on six occasions, an indication of the struggle between family members vying for power and position. Certainly this betrays a regime plagued by chronic suspicion, as potential claimants to the line of succession accused each other of disloyalty to Herod and the state.

Josephus takes an inordinate amount of space reviewing the details of the infighting, obscuring other important events of Herod's reign. Yet even in his personal life, Herod tried to promote harmony, reconciling with wives and children on several occasions. He also attempted to prepare his sons to rule Judea following his death. For example, he sent several of them to Rome to be educated and prepared for future service to their nation. Even when Augustus chastened Herod for believing all the accusations brought against family members, he also censured family members regarding the actions that brought about such allegations.

Herod's Relationship with Rome and with Judaism. Through Herod's influence, Rome demonstrated a respect for Judaism and its institutions on numerous occasions. Sosius, the governor of Syria who captured Jerusalem for Herod in 37 B.C., gave gold to the temple before he left. In 15 B.C., Augustus's friend and son-in-law, Marcus Agrippa, sacrificed a hecatomb at the temple to the delight of the populace; and apparently all the Roman emperors welcomed and perhaps paid for sacrifices offered on their behalf in Jerusalem.

In 22–21 B.C., Herod remitted one-third of the taxes following the sabbatical year. Octavian, now known as Caesar Augustus, rewarded Herod by adding Gaulanitis, Hulata, and Panias to his territory. Herod was appointed epitropos of Coele-Syria for the third time. Herod received many honors, including such titles as a "friend and ally" as well as "friend of the Romans" and "friend of Caesar."[52] Also, Herod was given the rare opportunity to name his own successor, requiring only the confirmation of Caesar. With new titles, honors, and territory, Herod moved to expand Judea's influence in the region.

Having created the first Judean navy, Herod joined Marcus Agrippa (who was now coregent with Augustus) in an expedition to the Black Sea and Pontus. In 14 B.C., Herod again remitted taxes after the sabbatical year of 16/15 B.C. In 12 B.C., Augustus gave Herod half of the income of the Cyprus copper mines (and the management of the other half), thus facilitating Herod's building programs. That year, with his increased economic power, Herod apparently saved the Olympic games by providing badly needed funding. The trustees of the Olympic games appointed him president of the games, a post without precedent.[53] During the same year, the great architectural and engineering wonder, the Mediterranean seaport Caesarea, was opened.[54]

Another apparent contribution to the prosperity and security of the nation was Herod's effort to discourage sectarian strife and division by emphasizing Jewish worship at the temple in Jerusalem. Furthermore, Herod did much to protect Jews outside Judea, who were relatively more numerous in the Greco-Roman world than at present, representing as much as 10 percent of the population (seven million out of seventy million).[55] With Herod's help and influence, the Jews of the Diaspora were guaranteed freedom to worship, to follow their dietary and sabbatical laws, to send the temple tax to Jerusalem as prescribed in the law, and to avoid military service in the Roman army. Herod may have even helped finance a synagogue in the imperial capital itself; at least, the Jews there named a synagogue in his honor. Because Herod was a friend of Rome, the Jews of the Diaspora experienced an unprecedented time of prosperity and security in the empire. It seems obvious why Diaspora Jews were favorable to Herod. In addition, they, of course, were engaged in the same balancing act of trying to practice Judaism while living in the Roman world.

Herod's greatest achievement for his nation and for Judaism was the construction of the temple in the capital city.[56] Apparently, he paid the complete cost to train and support the priests doing the work of gathering the building materials from various parts of the region and rebuilding the temple. It was a magnificent structure, innovative in its design. For example, Herod's temple included provisions for women and Gentiles.[57]

Drawing of mosaic pavement at Masada. As is the case with all the mosaics at Masada, no images of animals or humans are worked into the design. This particular mosaic is multicolored and is located in the antechamber leading into the reception room of the Western Palace.

While Herod undoubtedly hoped this huge project would ingratiate himself to his Jewish subjects, he also hoped this monumental work project would stimulate the economy. Certainly it was a manifestation of his commitment to his Jewish faith. Other acts reflect his devotion; for example, he constructed memorials to the patriarchs and matriarchs at Hebron, to Abraham at Mamre, and to King David in Jerusalem.[58] The walls surrounding the ancient oak tree at Mamre and the Herodian buildings over the caves of Machpelah (located in Idumea) may also demonstrate Herod's belief that no fundamental contradiction existed between his Idumean heritage and his Judaism.

Another manifestation of Herod's commitment to his Jewish heritage is the absence of any animal or human representations on his coins and in his buildings.[59] In particular, the design of one coin minted during the third year of his appointment to kingship (the first year of his effective reign), utilizes motifs from the temple, symbolic of his deep-seated attachment to his heritage. Other symbols found on Herodian coins differ little from Hasmonean iconography.

Mosaic on the floor of room 449 at Masada. Post-Herodian inhabitants partially built over the mosaic.

Herod's sympathy with Jewish law and tradition is demonstrated by the favor Herod showed
the Essenes as a result of an Essene's prophetic blessing given
Herod in his youth. Some evidence
suggests that the Essenes reentered
Jewish life during Herod's reign[60]
as a result. Another evidence of
Herod's adherence to Jewish law
is that he required circumcision of
non-Jewish males who wanted to
marry members of his family.

Herod, like his father, would
have resented being identified as
"half-Jewish." He demonstrated his
loyalty to Judaism and to Judea on
many occasions. If one takes another position, many of Herod's
actions are unintelligible.

Masada mosaic

Economy, Culture, and Religion. Herod's construction projects throughout the region (walls, shops, towers, palaces, cisterns,
theaters, stadiums, aqueducts, fortresses, amphitheaters, and public buildings) strengthened Judea's economy. He improved trade
routes, enlarged harbors, and created new markets for dates, wine,
olive oil, asphalt, and opobalsam. Other industries such as glass,
pottery, and perfume expanded significantly during his reign.
Resettlement programs, agricultural development, and work relief
gave the nation an unprecedented era of productivity.

As noted, tax relief and gifts of grain to his subjects following
sabbatical years and natural disasters helped the citizens of Judea.
He apparently even melted his gold and silver jewelry into bullion
for trade during economic crises and allocated food supplies to
neighboring states in need. His concern was also directed to the
infirm and elderly. Herod's efforts to improve the quality of life in
his kingdom included efforts to enact new laws improving social
justice while encouraging the application of the Torah in everyday
life. Such actions gained him not only the support of his subjects

and the good will of his neighbors, but also an international reputation of generosity and innovation.

Moreover, Herod attempted to be fair to his non-Jewish subjects. He demonstrated that it was possible for a Jewish king to remain on friendly terms with local pagans in the Greek cities around and within Judea. The difficulties inherent in ruling two distinct groups of people within the region (Jews and non-Jews) cannot be overemphasized.[61] Hostilities between the Jews of the Judean and Galilean hills and the pagan inhabitants of the Greek cities on the coastal plan and in the Decapolis went back to Hasmonean times. In the second and early first centuries B.C., the aggressive Hasmonean state had expanded into surrounding areas and suppressed the freedom of city states such as Gaza and Ashkelon to such an extent that, when Pompey conquered the Jews and restricted their state to the hill country, the cities greeted him as a liberator. The Hasmoneans found their Greek subjects immutably alien: unlike the hill peoples of Galilee and Idumea, attempts to convert them to Judaism proved ineffective.

For Herod, attempts to steer a middle course between the competing cultural communities was challenging. His gentile subjects thought of him as a Jewish king; nevertheless, he supported non-Jewish citizens of the regions in their rights and furnished funds to build Greek cities and temples. Further, his army was composed of both Gentiles and Jews.[62] Assuming that this army was typical, it not only checked rebellion from within, but also protected the inhabitants of Judea from attack from without.[63]

Certainly, Herod encouraged the adoption of many aspects of Greek culture, even among his Jewish subjects.[64] Art and architecture were copied from the surrounding culture (Greek architecture adorned the entirely Israelite temple in Jerusalem). Greek was widely spoken, though doubtless more so in cosmopolitan Jerusalem than in the Galilean and Judean countryside. Hellenization had come about neither through imposition from outside nor through the spontaneous adoption of Greek culture wholesale nor through gradual assimilation, but through the deliberate integration of Greek elements to enrich the indigenous society and culture.[65] Apparently, Herod amassed a sizable Greek library and surrounded himself with competent individuals (including

Romans and Greeks) to help run the affairs of state and manage increasing resources.

"In the Hellenistic and Roman periods the leading families of the cities of Asia enjoyed greater wealth than ever" before.[66] The Herodian dynasty was one of these families. Herod used his resources to move beyond his own kingdom. Herod donated funds to build facilities for festivals and games at Berytus, Damascus, Delos, Ptolemais, Sidon, and Tripolis. Inscriptions and monuments in Herod's honor were located in Athens, Chios, Cilicia, Cos, Lycia, Pergamum, Phaselis, and Samos. He helped improve public buildings at Antioch, Balanea, Bybulus, Laodicia-on-the-Sea, Sparta, and Tyre. Herod built temples to Roma and Augustus in Caesarea, Panias (Caesarea Philippi), and Sebaste. He reconstructed a temple in Rhodes, and helped complete a temple in Si'a.

Many studies of Herod's life emphasize his building projects for the obvious reason that they have endured. They are observable by even the most casual tourist and are certainly the most easily appreciated aspect of his career, stunning in any way one chooses to categorize them—size, location, or purpose. He was a remarkable patron, matching even Augustus and Marcus Agrippa, his only two rivals. The significant absence of any references to architects suggests that Herod played a crucial architectural role in his building program.

Of course, like many other aspects of his life, the purposes of his massive building programs have been examined and reexamined on numerous occasions in an attempt to "reveal Herod's personality, fears, tastes, and ambitions."[67] Some believe that the palace and fortress complexes reveal Herod's paranoia; the Jewish projects, a crafty plan to ingratiate himself with the religious element of his nation; and the non-Jewish construction projects, his deep commitment to Hellenism (even paganism). Whatever purposes these structures were intended to fulfill, they represent an ambitious enterprise, superbly implemented.

Herod's Death and the Aftermath. In spite of these many successes, Herod's last year was difficult and full of confusion, betrayal, and stress. Apparently for the New Testament authors Luke and Matthew, Herod's last days were significant to early Christians as an important historical reference point. Luke sets the historical stage of his gospel by identifying the announcement of John the Baptist's birth: "In the time of Herod king of Judea, there was a priest named Zechariah, who belonged to the priestly division of Abijah; his wife Elizabeth was also a descendant of Aaron" (NIV, Luke 1:5). Matthew also identifies the historical setting of Jesus' birth in Judea: "After Jesus was born in Bethlehem in Judea, during the time of King Herod, Magi from the east came to Jerusalem" (NIV, Matt. 2:1).

Sometime between the events discussed in Matthew 2:1-18 and 19-23, Josephus records that it was rumored that Herod was about to die (in his seventieth year—about 4 B.C.).[68] Upon hearing this news, the rabbis Judas (Judah ben Zippori) and Mathias (Matthias ben Margalit) incited their students to tear down a Roman Eagle that had been placed—probably some ten to twenty years earlier—on the outside of what is now called Wilson's arch, an entrance to the temple complex.[69]

Herod was incensed at their apparent ingratitude—he had built the temple and made every effort to balance the demands of Jewish tradition and Roman requirements. On March 12, Rabbi Judas and Rabbi Matthias, the instigators and leaders of the action, and some of the students involved in the protest were executed. On the following night, there was an eclipse of the moon—a symbol of the changes that were to befall the kingdom. Shortly thereafter, Herod died at his winter palace in Jericho. His last struggles are vividly described by Josephus:

> From this time onwards Herod's malady began to spread to his whole body and his sufferings took a variety of forms. He had fever, though not a raging fever, an intolerable itching of the whole skin, continuous pains in the intestines, tumours in the feet as in dropsy, inflammation of the abdomen and gangrene of the privy parts, engendering worms, in addition to asthma, with great difficulty in breathing, and convulsions in all his limbs.[70]

As in life, Herod's last sickness is surrounded by controversy—various diagnoses have been suggested for his complaint, ranging from arteriosclerosis to syphilis. Whatever the cause of his last illness, Herod went to his winter palace at Jericho, where he distributed fifty drachmas[71] to his soldiers and greater gifts to commanders and friends.

According to Josephus, one of Herod's final acts was to gather Jewish leaders from throughout his kingdom into the hippodrome at Jericho. He then ordered that they all be killed when he died. Josephus suggests that Herod wanted his subjects to mourn at his death. Sandmel argues that this story, like the Matthean account regarding the "slaughter of the innocents," is nothing more than an attempt to malign him.[72] Ironically, both stories have largely shaped the artistic and popular view of Herod in modern Judaism and Christianity.

Certainly, of the two stories, the Matthean narrative is the most plausible, since Herod continually eliminated subversive or radical elements within the state in an attempt to assure continued stability in the region.[73] Such internecine struggles were paralleled in the Roman provinces and in Rome itself—it is just that Herod's life is better documented than the lives of many client kings of Rome, thus revealing the reality rather than an imagined ideal.

Whatever the truth may be about his last days and his death, Herod's body was taken "two hundred furlongs to Herodium, where, in accordance with the directions of the deceased, it was interred. So ended Herod's reign."[74] Ironically, the burial place of one of the best documented personalities in the ancient world remains hidden to archaeologists today.[75]

While Josephus often renders a harsh verdict on the life of Herod, another ancient source gives a more positive one. Strabo, a contemporary of Herod, notes that he was "so superior to his predecessors, particularly in his intercourse with the Romans and in his administration of affairs of state, that he received the title of king."[76] In all likelihood, Strabo was in Rome on at least two occasions when Herod was there, and he may have traveled through Judea during Herod's reign, thereby having a more personal view than that of Josephus.

While it is impossible to access Herod's inner motives (which were naturally complex and perplexing), external events do represent one means of understanding the meaning of his life and his career as king of the Jews. However one assesses his reign, Herod's death signaled the end of an era that witnessed Rome's most successful attempt to impose order on Judea.

Bronze coin from the reign of Herod (37 B.C.). The obverse, on left, shows a tripod with a basin; the reverse, a helmet with palm branches. The palm branches were a typical Jewish (Hasmonean) symbol. The absence of animal or human figures on the coin may also represent Herod's commitment to his Jewish heritage. The inscription around the obverse proclaims Herod the King, rather than Herod the Great, perhaps indicating how he referred to himself.

The Herodian dynasty sought to renew itself through the succession of the sons to the father's kingdom. When Herod died in 4 B.C., his kingdom was divided among three sons (Archelaus as king of Judea; Herod Antipas as tetrarch of Galilee; and Herod Philip as tetrarch of Trachonitis). This effort to maintain a family dynasty may be one of Herod's greatest failures. The following decades reveal the internal weakness within the fabric of the Herodian dynasty and the failure of Herod's successors to legitimatize themselves with their subjects and/or with Rome. The sporadic and often nonviolent manifestations of resistance to Herod's rule and to his patron, Rome, gradually increased and eventually engulfed the entire nation in war against the most powerful state in the Mediterranean world in A.D. 66.[77]

Conclusion

The fall of Jerusalem in A.D. 70 was the death knell to Herod's dreams, and to his efforts to bring peace and prosperity to Judea and establish his family securely upon the throne. The devastating result of the war included the consignment of the Judean ruling class to oblivion and the end of sacrificial worship of God in the temple. Many rich landowners were imprisoned, enslaved, or executed. Priests who surrendered when the temple was already on fire were put to death. Most of the Jews who escaped without physical punishment lost their land. Jews were required to pay the poll tax of two drachmas annually to Capitoline Jupiter, just as the tax had formerly been paid to the temple. This tax, the *fiscus Judaicus,* symbolized the deliberate destruction, not just of the Jewish nation, but of the religion and society of Judea.

Finally, Jewish rebels fleeing the formidable Roman army made their last stand at Masada in A.D. 70, after the fall of Jerusalem to Titus. The defensive infrastructure at Masada, so well implemented by the Hasmoneans but fortified mainly by Herod, was eventually breached by the Romans. Evidently, refusing to surrender to Flavius Silva and the Roman Legio X Fretensis, the defenders took their own lives on Masada, making it a symbol of Jewish nationalism and a popular tourist site today.

"To King Herod the Jew." Found at Masada, this inscription from an amphora, one of thirteen with similar inscriptions, specifies the destination for the jar of wine. The inscription can also be translated as "to the Jewish king Herod."

Among the many artifacts discovered by archaeologists at Masada were several jars from a shipment of wine apparently sent in 19 B.C. from southern Italy.[78] On the jars, which were found scattered in several locations on the mountain fortress, were thirteen Latin inscriptions that refer to "King Herod the Jew" or "the Jewish king Herod" (*regi herodi iudaico*), rather than "Herod King of the Jews." Not only do these inscriptions reveal how others viewed Herod, but they also represent his own self-definition: he was a Jewish king, king of Judea (including Jews and non-Jews).

Through his political acumen and his consummate diplomacy, Herod exercised considerable freedom in his country's internal affairs, promoting the well-being of his own subjects (Gentiles and Jews) and of Jews throughout the Roman Empire as he sought to make Judea the premier province in the Roman Empire.

Richard Neitzel Holzapfel is Assistant Professor of Church History at Brigham Young University.

NOTES

[1] Except where noted otherwise, all the information about Herod's life and activities comes from Josephus.

[2] Herod is the name of several members of a dynasty that were appointed to govern Jewish Palestine under Roman rule. Today, King Herod is known popularly as "Herod the Great," and even Jewish scholar Stephen Wylen argues, "He designated himself Herod the Great, and by this name he has gone down in history." Stephen M. Wylen, *The Jews in the Time of Jesus: An Introduction* (New York: Paulist, 1996), 70. However, no contemporary historical record accords him this title, and likewise no available data suggest that he ever wished to be so identified. Apparently, the title crept into usage after his death as a means to distinguish him from his descendants who shared his name. In that sense, it simply meant "Herod the *elder*," instead of the connotation suggested by the titles given to Macedonian leader Alexander (Alexander the Great) or to the Russian leader Peter (Peter the Great). See Peter Richardson, *Herod: King of the Jews and Friend of the Romans* (Columbia: University of South Carolina Press, 1996), 12.

[3] The Hasmoneans (Maccabeans) were a family of high priests and kings descended from Mattathias, the father of Judas Maccabeus. They influenced the political and religious life of Judea from 165 until 37 B.C. Under their political leadership (between 142 and 63 B.C.), Judea became, in the period of Seleucid decline and before the rise of Rome, an independent state. This rise to power

began in Mattathias's rebellion against the anti-Jewish decrees of Antiochus IV Epiphanes in 167 B.C., when he and his five sons fled into the hills, attracting a sizable guerrilla force and organizing an effective resistance to the Syrian occupation. The goal of achieving religious toleration eventually grew into a desire for national independence, which was eventually achieved. Scholars are divided about which Maccabean leader Josephus refers to as the one who established the fortress on the plateau and gave it the name Masada, "Mountain Stronghold": Jonathan, the brother of Judas Maccabeus (mid–second century B.C.) or Alexander Jannaeus, whose Hebrew name was also Jonathan.

4Most readers are accustomed to dating ancient events as either A.D. (*anno domini,* Latin for "year of our Lord") or B.C. (before Christ). Today, many scholars present an alternative designation of C.E. (the Common Era, meaning common to all people who utilize the traditional Western calendar) and B.C.E. (before the Common Era). In terms of the older abbreviation, then, C.E. corresponds to A.D., and B.C.E. to B.C.

5For example, noted Israeli archaeologist Yigael Yadin notes, "There was no controversy at all about the man who turned Masada into the formidable fort it became: King Herod the Great." Yigael Yadin, *Masada: Herod's Fortress and the Zealots' Last Stand* (New York: Random House, 1966), 11.

6The Greco-Roman world is a term used by scholars to describe the lands surrounding the Mediterranean from the time of Alexander the Great through the first three or four centuries of the Roman Empire.

7Gaius Julius Caesar was born on July 12, 100 B.C., in Rome; appointed dictator for ten years in 47 B.C. and for life on February 14, 44 B.C.; assassinated on March 15, 44 B.C.; and deified in 42 B.C. Gaius Julius Caesar Octavianus (Augustus) was born on September 23, 63 B.C., in Rome, a son of Julius Caesar's niece; was adopted by Caesar; effectively became emperor in 27 B.C.; extended his powers in 23 B.C.; died on August 19, A.D. 14; and was deified on September 17, A.D. 14. Marcus Antonius (Marc Antony) was born around 83 B.C.; was appointed with Lepidus and Octavian *tresviri rei publicae constituendae* (triumvirate); was defeated at Actium in September 31 B.C. (after an open breach with Octavian earlier); and eventually committed suicide on August 30 B.C. Cleopatra VII was born in 69 B.C.; became joint ruler of Egypt with Ptolemy XIII in 51; sided with Marc Antony against Octavian (Augustus); and committed suicide on August 10, 30 B.C. Marcus Vipsanius Agrippa was born in 64 or 63 B.C.; became *praetor urbanus* in 40 B.C.; was appointed *tribunicia potestas* (making him second only to Augustus) in 18 B.C.; and died in March 12 B.C. Jesus of Nazareth was born in 4 B.C. at Bethlehem (shortly before Herod's death) and began teaching throughout Galilee and Judea before being executed in Jerusalem in A.D. 30.

8Herodias was the daughter of Herod's son (Aristobulus) and Herod's niece (Bernice). She married Herod's son Herod Philip (who ruled as tetrarch from 4 B.C. to A.D. 33/34), and she later married another of Herod's sons, Herod Antipas (who ruled as tetrarch from 4 B.C. to A.D. 39), as noted and discussed in Mark 6:17–29; Matthew 14:3–12; and Luke 3:19–20. Agrippa I (identified simply as Herod in the New Testament) was the son of Herod's son (Aristobulus) and is discussed in Acts 12:1–23. Agrippa II and Bernice were children of Agrippa I and interviewed Paul at Caesarea as noted in Acts 25:13–26:32. Drusilla, third and youngest daughter of Agrippa I, was married to the Roman procurator of Palestine (Felix) and is mentioned in Acts 24:24. The Philip mentioned in Luke 3:1 was the son of Herod and Cleopatra of Jerusalem, and he founded the city of Caesarea Philippi (Mark 8:27). Salome (unnamed in the New Testament) was the daughter of Herodias and Herod Philip and stepdaughter of Herod Antipas and is mentioned in the story of Herodias noted above (Mark 6:17-29).

[9]Louis H. Feldman, "Josephus," in *The Anchor Bible Dictionary,* ed. David Noel Freedman, 6 vols. (New York: Doubleday, 1992), 3:989. Additionally, Mary Smallwood suggests that because of these same sources, we have more information about Herod's land "than we do about any other part of the Roman Empire" during this period of transition. E. Mary Smallwood, "Introduction," in *Josephus: The Jewish Wars,* rev. ed. (New York: Penguin Books, 1981), 18-19.

[10]He was a priest of royal descent and Pharisaic persuasion, born in Jerusalem in A.D. 37, just after Pontius Pilate was removed as provincial governor. Apparently he took a leading but reluctant part in the revolt of A.D. 66-73, and after he surrendered to the Romans in Galilee, he witnessed the last stages of the revolt from the Roman camp. Later Josephus attached himself to the Flavian family, obtained Roman citizenship, and spent the second half of his life at the imperial capital, where he composed his historical works, which were written mostly in Greek.

[11]Originally the titles of Josephus's works were in Greek, but modern scholarship regularly follows the convention of translating the titles of Greek works into Latin for reference purposes. An excellent English translation of *War* that is readily accessible to the general public is Josephus, *The Jewish War,* trans. G. A. Williamson, introduction by E. Mary Smallwood, rev. ed. (New York: Penguin Books, 1981).

[12]See S. Safrai and M. Stern, eds., "The Jewish People in the First Century," in *Compendia Rerum Judaicarum ad Novum Testamentum,* 2 vols. (Assen: Van Gorcum, 1974), 1:21 and following.

[13]Josephus, *Antiquities* 15.174.

[14]Some of the contradictions may indicate how Josephus's archival research in the imperial capital offered him an alternative interpretation of events other than Nicolas's and Herod's histories, which were Josephus's main sources in his earlier work.

[15]Thucydides, *Peloponnesian War,* ed. and trans. Charles F. Smith, Loeb Classical Library (Cambridge: Harvard University Press, 1980), 1.22.1.

[16]Smallwood, "Introduction," 24.

[17]For example, Eusebius, citing Julius Africanus, states that Herod burned the archives of Jewish families so that he would not be embarrassed by references to his own origins. See Eusebius, *Ecclesiastical History,* trans. Krisopp Lake, Loeb Classical Library (Cambridge: Harvard University Press, 1980), 1.7.13. Such an act is highly unlikely since Josephus indicates that the information was available. Josephus, *Against Apion* 1.31.

[18]Stewart Perowne, *The Life and Times of Herod the Great* (London: Hodder and Stoughton, 1956), 176.

[19]Perowne, *Herod the Great,* 179-80.

[20]Samuel Sandmel, "Herod," in *The Interpreter's Dictionary of the Bible,* 4 vols. (Nashville: Abingdon, 1962), 2:585-94; Samuel Sandmel, *Herod: Profile of a Tyrant* (Philadelphia and New York: J. B. Lippincott, 1967), 261.

[21]David M. Rhoads, *Israel in Revolution: 6–74 C.E.: A Political History Based on the Writings of Josephus* (Philadelphia: Fortress, 1976), 23–24.

[22]L. I. Levine, "Herod the Great," in *Anchor Bible Dictionary*, 3:161–69.

[23]Levine, "Herod the Great," 165, 169.

[24]Richardson, *Herod: King of the Jews*, xiii.

[25]"King of the Jews" is a political phrase which certainly would make Herod and Jerusalem's elite duly troubled. Later, after Herod's death, Joseph decided to go to Galilee and avoid Herod's son Archalaus, who was then ruling over Judea.

[26]The story would have sounded familiar to most of Matthew's Jewish readers. For Matthew, Jesus' life was a fulfillment of the stories of Moses. See Exodus 1–20.

[27]Herod's son Herod Antipas was responsible for the execution of John the Baptist and played a role in the passion narrative; and Herod's grandson Herod Agrippa I was responsible for the arrest of Peter and the execution of James. Agrippa I was apparently a devoted Jew and is still honored as "a genuinely pious Jew" whom his subjects "loved." See Wylen, *Jews*, 75. He is identified simply as "Herod" in the book of Acts. See Acts 12:1–11.

[28]This statement may reveal something about Herod's religious proclivities as it suggests that he observed Jewish dietary law, including abstinence from eating pork.

[29]A. Kasher, *Jews, Idumaeans, and Ancient Arabs* (Tübingen: J. C. B. Mohr, 1988), 46–47; see also Richardson, *Herod: King of the Jews*, 54–55.

[30]Most scholars agree that later legends making Antipas the son of a temple slave of Apollo at Ashkelon are mere fiction; see Sandmel, "Herod," 586.

[31]Even Josephus blames the two Hasmonean claimants as responsible for Roman intervention. See Josephus, *Jewish War* 1.19.

[32]In the process, the Holy of Holies in the temple was exposed, a desecration in the eyes of the Jews. Many defenders of the capital were killed, albeit mostly by Aristobulus's rebels. Even though Pompey ordered the cleansing of the temple and a resumption of rituals and worship, the occupation of Jerusalem may have initiated a hostility to Roman rule among some of the Jews.

[33]Additionally, he was exempted from taxes. These favors were a reward for despatching Jewish troops to help Julius Caesar at Alexandria. Apparently, the Jews were genuinely loyal to him, especially during the civil war which pitted Caesar against Pompey. Their support (through Antipater) was not forgotten as Caesar made Judaism a legal religion and offered them several concessions: excusing them from emperor worship, which he understood was impossible for monotheists. Instead, the Jews were to offer an additional morning sacrifice to God in honor of the emperor, and he excused them from agricultural taxes during the Sabbatical year (when the Jews neither planted nor harvested crops).

[34]See John W. Welch, "Legal and Social Perspectives on Robbers in First-Century Judea," in this volume.

[35]Herod's first reaction to the trial (which could have imposed the death penalty if the accused were found guilty of violating the law) was to inflict a retaliatory strike against Jerusalem. However his father and brother persuaded him to refrain, arguing among other things that it would be a violation of Jewish law. This is one example of the use of piety as a successful argument for or against an act, which may reveal Herod's personal commitment to Judaism.

[36]K. C. Hanson, "The Herodian and Mediterranean Kinship, Part I: Genealogy and Descent," *Biblical Theology Bulletin* 19, no. 3 (1989): 77.

[37]Apparently Herod arranged for his brother Pheroras to marry Mariamme's sister and his son Antipater to marry Antigonus's daughter. Richardson identifies many other such marriages. See Richardson, *Herod: King of the Jews,* 46-51.

[38]Richardson, *Herod: King of the Jews,* 46-51.

[39]Josephus, *Jewish War* 1.285.

[40]Jesus of Nazareth was a Jew because of his acceptance of Judaism (religious) and because of his ethnicity (Mary and Joseph were descendants of Judah), but he did not live in Judea. He was a Galilean.

[41]The Antonia Fortress was more of a major reconstruction and expansion of the existing Hasmonean fortress known as Baris (*bira,* Hebrew for fortress).

[42]For a detailed description of the Antonia Fortress, see Andrew Teasdale, "Herod the Great's Building Program," in this volume.

[43]Interestingly enough, this is the only site Herod named after himself. Herodium was a complex in the barren Judean hills south of Jerusalem and east of Bethlehem. When Herod fled Jerusalem as the Parthians prepared to attack the city, he met a group of rebels at this site in 40 B.C. This may explain why he later built the complex.

[44]Josephus, *Jewish War* 1.388-90.

[45]The longest serving high priest (about 24 through 5 B.C.) was Simon ben Boethus, who became Herod's father-in-law (Mariamme II).

[46]Familial rivalries also existed in the Hasmonean Dynasty; for example, Aristobulus I seized power from his mother and starved her to death. He also incarcerated several of his family members. Alexandra Salome, wife of Aristobulus I, arranged to kill her brother-in-law (Antigonus) as her husband lay dying. Following Aristobulus's death, she freed her other brothers-in-law and married the youngest, Alexander Jannaaeus. He killed one of his brothers and later his anti-Pharasis policy led to an unsuccessful rebellion in which some fifty thousand people were killed. Later, those assisting Alexander Jannaaeus in implementing his policies were executed or brutally murder with the consent of Alexandra. After their deaths, her two sons (Aristobulus II and John Hyrcanus) divided the nation into factions, causing a long and deadly civil war full of intrigue and political murders (including the murder of Herod's father).

[47]See K. C. Hanson, "The Herodians and Mediterranean Kinship, Part III: Economics," *Biblical Theology Bulletin* 20, no. 1 (1990): 20.

[48]Deuteronomy 21:18-21.

[49]Torture was commonly practiced in the ancient world. The ancient Greek practice of torturing slaves to obtain information influenced early Roman laws, in which torture gave the testimonies of slaves and those of low social status more validity.

[50]See Michael Grant, *From Alexander to Cleopatra: The Hellenistic World* (London: Weidenfeld and Nicolson, 1982), 196-98; see also Theodore John Cadoux, "Cleopatra VII," in *The Oxford Classical Dictionary* (Oxford: Clarendon, 1970), 251-52; Levine, "Herod the Great," 161-69; and Ben Witherington III, "Herodias," in *Anchor Bible Dictionary,* 3:174-76.

[51]Richardson, *Herod: King of the Jews,* 37.

[52]See Levine, "Herod the Great," 163.

[53]See M. I. Finley and H. W. Pleket, *The Olympic Games: The First Thousand Years* (London: Chatto and Windus, 1976), 99.

[54]Known today as Caesarea Maritima, the name *Maritima* was added by modern archaeologists to distinguish it from Caesarea Philippi. See Teasdale, "Building Program," for a complete discussion of Caesarea. See also Kenneth G. Holum and Robert L. Hohlfelder, eds., *King Herod's Dream: Caesarea on the Sea* (New York: W. W. Norton, 1988).

[55]Apparently, the same percentage of Jews existed in the Parthian Empire. See Wylen, *Jews in the Time of Jesus,* 42.

[56]There are numerous references to Herod's temple in the New Testament, Josephus's writings, the Mishnah, and the Dead Sea Scrolls. It is considered the most important monument and the most significant national and religious institution for Jews during this period (only the Essenes considered it less important).

[57]For further discussion of the temple complex, see Teasdale, "Building Program."

[58]Archaeological data, the type of stonework, and the dating connect these structures to Herod, but no epigraphic or literary evidence supports the conclusion that he built them as a measure of his devotion.

[59]Apparently, pagan temples were erected only for the non-Jewish population of Herod's realm.

[60]The Essenes were apparently a group begun by priests opposed to the Hasmonean attempt to usurp the high priest's office. They established their own institutions, lived in separate communes in towns and cities, and separated themselves from the temple. The identity of the Herodians mentioned in Matthew and Mark has always baffled scholars, but there is some evidence that the Herodians were Essenes, having been "nicknamed by the common people because of the protection and favor Herod showed them"; see Constantin Daniel, "Les Hérodiens du Nouveau Testament, sont-ils des Esséniens?" *Revue de Qumran* 6 (1967): 31–53; 7 (1970): 397–402.

[61]Hostilities between the two groups are no more evident than at the beginning of the war in A.D. 66, which saw appalling massacres in the cities around Judea—Jews killing Gentiles and destroying their property, while Gentiles killed Jews in a number of cities, most horrifically in Sycthopolis.

[62]Like the later Hasmonean kings and queens, whose power rested on their mercenary armies comprised mostly of non-Jews, Herod's army apparently also consisted of a large number of non-Jews, particularly within the officer corps.

[63]See Wilfried Nippel, *Public Order in Ancient Rome* (New York: Cambridge University Press, 1995).

[64]The Roman Empire itself arose in the context of the Hellenistic world and took full advantage of its unity, promoting the use of the Greek language and accepting aspects of Greek culture. The complex unity achieved culturally through Hellenization and politically through integration of territory made Rome a strong and viable power during this period. Apparently, Herod felt he could accomplish the same on a local level, precariously balancing the demands of Jewish tradition, Roman political influence, and cultural Hellenism.

[65]Apparently, most Jews enjoyed a completely relaxed attitude to the Hellenization of their society, even if some of them occasionally made rhetorical attacks upon particular manifestations of this process. This attitude is no more

difficult to understand than Roman attacks on Greek culture by Hellenized members of the Roman aristocracy.

[66]G. E. M. de Ste. Croix, *The Class Struggle in the Ancient Greek World* (London: Duckworth, 1981), 119.

[67]Holum and Hohlfelder, *King Herod's Dream,* 59.

[68]Josephus, *Jewish War* 1.651.

[69]Josephus, *Jewish War* 1.648-55; for the apparent location of the eagle, see Richardson, *Herod: Kind of the Jews,* 15-18.

[70]Josephus, *Jewish War* 1.656.

[71]See Nanci DeBloois, "Coins in the New Testament," in this volume.

[72]Sandmel, *Profile of a Tyrant,* 261.

[73]Nevertheless, Matthew's account is often rejected as a completely reliable historical source; see Samuel Sandmel, "Herodians," in *Interpreter's Dictionary,* 2:594-95. There are several reasons given. First, it was composed after the events it reports. However, the date of a text's composition is not necessarily a warrant against the possibility that it preserves accurate memories, if it was able to use earlier sources. The Homeric epics, Arrian's *Anabasis,* and Livy's histories are regularly used by scholars, even though they were composed centuries after the events they described. Second, there is no extrabiblical confirmation or corroboration. Likewise, many historians do not reject other historical narratives, just because there is little or no external verification, as in the case of Hannibal's fifteen-year campaign in Italy or Agricola's seven-year administration of Britain. Other New Testament scholars are less certain. W. F. Albright and C. S. Mann state, "The slaughter of infants two years old or less in a town of the size of Bethlehem (population ca. 300) at this time would not only have been a comparatively minor incident, and so probably unknown to Josephus, but also completely in line with Herod's known character." W. F. Albright and C. S. Mann, *The Anchor Bible Matthew* (Garden City, N.Y.: Doubleday, 1971), 19.

[74]Josephus, *Jewish War* 1.673.

[75]See Ehud Netzer, "Searching for Herod's Tomb," *Archaeology and the Bible: The Best of BAR, Volume Two: Archaeology in the World of Herod, Jesus, and Paul,* ed. Hershel Shanks and Dan P. Cole (Washington, D.C.: Biblical Archaeology Society, 1990), 136-57.

[76]Strabo, *Geography,* ed. and trans. H. L. Jones, Loeb Classical Library, 8 vols. (Cambridge: Harvard University Press, 1917-33), 16.2.46.

[77]Scholars have often characterized Herod's reign as seething with revolutionary fervor. A recent study, however, reveals a more complex picture. See Richard A. Horsley, *Jesus and the Spiral of Violence: Popular Jewish Resistance in Roman Palestine* (Minneapolis: Fortress, 1993), 59-145.

[78]Hannah M. Cotton and Joseph Geiger, "Latin and Greek Documents," in *Masada II: The Yigael Yadin Excavations 1963-1965, Final Reports,* ed. Joseph Aviram, Gideon Foerster, and Ehud Netzer (Jerusalem: Israel Exploration Society and Hebrew University of Jerusalem, 1989), 133.

Herod's Wealth

John W. Welch

Herod's construction of Masada and many other massive building projects leave no doubt that Herod the Great had access to large amounts of gold and silver. But where his wealth came from and how much he had is not entirely clear. Several clues, however, concerning the sources and relative amounts of Herod's immense wealth and his use of this money to achieve political ends can be found in the historical remains and from the records of Josephus Flavius.[1] This article briefly identifies the main financial information known about Herod, outlines his political uses and principal sources of income, and appraises his economic resources in order, ultimately, to shed light on certain sums of money mentioned by Jesus in the New Testament.

Herod's Political Uses of Wealth

King Herod was politically astute. His shrewdness is particularly visible in his uses of financial resources to achieve important political objectives.

For example, when Antony and Cleopatra entered Judea on their campaign against the Parthians in 34 B.C., Herod managed to escape from Cleopatra's plans against him by giving her large gifts and agreeing to lease back from her for two hundred talents each year the valuable lands that she had previously taken from his domain.[2] Then, as Octavius was securing control over the eastern Mediterranean, Herod provided generous assistance to him and his armies: "In short, there were no necessaries which the army lacked."[3] In return for this support, Herod was soon richly rewarded. When Octavius defeated Antony and Cleopatra, not only was Herod given back all of the lands Cleopatra had appropriated from him, but he also received several new territories ranging from Gaza in the south, to Joppa on the coast, to Samaria in the hill country.[4]

Later, in 23 B.C., in compensation for ridding the land around Damascus of robber infestation, Herod was awarded further territories north of Judea and Galilee, and a few years later, Caesar proclaimed Herod the procurator of Syria.[5] Each of these additions augmented Herod's political prestige, as well as his revenue sources and cash flows.

Besides using money to please the rulers in Rome, Herod expended vast amounts of money to enhance his local reputation. Each of his building projects created jobs and wages for numerous workers, and apparently Herod was prompt as a paymaster. Over eighteen thousand workers were employed for several years in constructing the great temple in Jerusalem, and Josephus reports that they were immediately paid for their daily labor: "If anyone worked for but one hour of the day, he at once received his pay."[6]

While much of this huge building growth in the tiny land of Israel benefited the king, as did his palaces in Jericho and Jerusalem and his various fortresses, Herod also built or rebuilt many cities, such as Caesarea, as well as paved the whole of Jerusalem with white stone; these projects directly benefited the populace as a whole. It was said that Herod renovated the temple at his own expense in order to ingratiate himself to his kingdom.[7] Josephus discusses Herod's motives in making these expenditures as follows:

> To the Jews he made the excuse that he was doing these things not on his own account but by command and order, while he sought to please Caesar and the Romans by saying that he was less intent upon observing the customs of his own nation than upon honouring them. On the whole, however, he was intent upon his own interests or was also ambitious to leave behind to posterity still greater monuments of his reign. It was for this reason that he was keenly interested in the reconstruction of cities and spent very great sums on this work.[8]

Whatever his intentions, the economic consequences of Herod's building projects must have had profound effects on the entire economy and society of all peoples under his dominion.

Herod also made use of his financial powers to establish political connections and win honor all around the eastern Mediterranean. He lavished grants on various cities and peoples around the region: he built public buildings and gymnasia for Tripolis in North Africa, for Damascus in Syria, and a wall for Byblus in present-day Lebanon, as well as "halls, porticoes, temples, and marketplaces for Berytus and Tyre, theatres for Sidon and Damascus, an aqueduct for Laodicea on sea, baths, sumptuous fountains and colonnades, admirable alike for their architecture and their proportions, for Ascalon."[9] His gifts of land, groves, food, money, tax relief, construction capital, shipbuilding financing, donations, temple refurbishings, and street pavings extended from Syria to Greece, from Cilicia in Asia Minor "to every district of Ionia," including Cos, Rhodes, Lycia, Samos, Nicopolis, Pergamum, and on into the mainland Greek cities of Athens and Sparta. He handsomely enriched the traditional venue of the Olympic games, over which he presided one year, endowing them "for all time with revenues" so that people would not forget his service as president.[10] No doubt this foreign aid improved political conditions for the thousands of Jews living in many cities abroad, each of whom paid a temple tribute back to the temple in Jerusalem each year (the Apostle Paul encouraged his converts to continue making payments to be taken to Jerusalem, 1 Cor. 16:3), which amounted to very large sums of money, attracting considerable attention and causing occasional problems.

While his munificence may have enhanced the reputation of Herod and the Jews of the Diaspora abroad, at home Herod was sometimes regarded as "the most cruel tyrant that ever existed," who crippled the cities under his dominion, "lavishing the lifeblood of Judea on foreign communities."[11] Some of this grousing, however, must have been overstated in light of the money that poured into Jerusalem from Jews and God-fearers all over the known world.[12] Moreover, when his kingdom was crippled with famine, Herod used his own moneys, including his artistic ornaments of gold and silver, to purchase grain from Egypt to relieve the suffering of his people.[13] Josephus claims that "there was no one who asked for aid in his need and was turned away without getting such help as he deserved," and at least once, because of this solicitude, the people changed their opinion of Herod.[14]

Jesus once said, "Make to yourself friends of the mammon of unrighteousness" (Luke 16:9). It would appear that no one around the time of Christ was more experienced than Herod the Great at using mammon to make friends and influence people.

Main Sources of Herod's Wealth

With all this wealth being used for construction and other purposes, one wonders where it came from. Herod skillfully exploited every available source of revenue common to his day and then some.

Of course, he collected taxes from his subject peoples. Were his tax policies oppressive? Upon Herod's death, one of the things his people clamored for was tax relief. While this outcry may indicate that Herod's tax rate was probably high, popular pressures for tax relief are virtually universal. Moreover, in one period of recovery from sharp crop failure and economic trouble, Herod "remitted to the people of his kingdom a third part of their taxes."[15] On another occasion, he remitted a fourth of their taxes for the previous year because he was in a good mood.[16] In the case of the colonists who settled in Batanea, he remitted the taxes completely. Thus, "the frequently-drawn picture of a kingdom tragically oppressed" by taxes does not appear to be entirely accurate. Moreover, "there is no evidence that Herod or his heirs paid any tribute to Rome after 30 B.C.E."[17]

Indeed, Herod's financial resources "did not come exclusively from the imposition of taxes on the kingdom."[18] Herod also collected tribute from other peoples. At one time, the king of Arabia paid a tribute to Rome of two hundred talents, which Herod was responsible to collect.[19] He also controlled important trade routes, from which he derived customs duties, including the Nabatean trade from Arabia and maritime commerce through Caesarea.[20]

Moreover, Herod brought considerable personal wealth to his kingdom. He owned valuable lands which he rented out. For a time the Arabs rented grazing land from Herod.[21]

He was also engaged in direct agricultural production on his lands. He owned large groves of date palms and balsam trees. On the latter crop, he held a monopoly, for balsam grows only at Jericho in nearby En Gedi, and it was "the most precious thing there."[22] This crop brought in a large income. In 34 B.C., Antony took the balsam groves near Jericho and presented them to his love, Cleopatra.

When confronted by the two, Herod "appeased their ill will," agreeing to take these lands back on lease "for an annual sum of two hundred talents."[23] In the end, these lands were restored to Herod by Octavian in 30 B.C. Moreover, Herod's personal estate included fertile lands in the Jezreel Valley that he acquired by appropriation from the Hasmoneans.[24]

In addition, money flowed from all over the known world into the temple in Jerusalem, and hence into the kingdom of Herod, by virtue of the annual half-shelek temple tax that every Jewish man over the age of twenty was required to pay. Large Jewish populations in Rome, Alexandria, Ionia, Babylon, and elsewhere, sent convoys each year transmitting these payments.

Perhaps most amazingly, Herod collected substantial royalties from the sale of copper on the island of Cyrus (which name in Greek means "copper"). The copper mines on that island produced high quality ore and provided a main source of copper for the entire Roman empire. Herod obtained these rights from Augustus Caesar, who was interested in strengthening the hand of Herod in the East so that he could stabilize that part of the world. In that connection, "Herod made a present of three hundred talents to Caesar, who was providing spectacles and doles for the people of Rome, while Caesar gave him half the revenues from the copper mines of Cyprus, and entrusted him with the management of the other half."[25]

Occasionally, Herod turned to confiscation and exercising royal powers of eminent domain. For example, in order to make his gifts to Antony, Herod confiscated valuable equipment or ornaments and generally "despoiled the well-to-do," killing forty-five of the leaders of Antigonus's party and placing guards to be sure that no silver or gold was taken out with the bodies.[26] On one occasion, Herod took 3,000 talents from the tomb of King David.[27] Apparently, Herod had no problem taking from the rich, or from anyone for that matter. Josephus tells, "In place of their ancient prosperity and ancestral laws, he had sunk the nation to poverty and the last degree of iniquity. In short, the miseries which Herod in the course of a few years had inflicted on the Jews surpassed all that their forefathers had suffered during all the time since they left Babylon to return to their country in the reign of Xerxes."[28] Herod's storehouses at Masada and elsewhere are evidence that this statement may well have considerable truth behind it.

Amounts of Money Involved in Herod's History

If the raw numbers given by Josephus can be trusted, even as approximations, Herod had large amounts of revenue coming in each year. In addition, he held in reserve substantial supplies of hard currency, especially in the temple treasury.

Josephus describes the contents of the temple early in Herod's reign as already including "the candelabrum and lamps, the table, the vessels for libation and censers, all of solid gold, an accumulation of spices and the store of sacred money [*hierōn chrēmatōn*] amounting to two thousand talents."[29] By leaving the utensils and wealth of the temple in place, Pompey garnered the goodwill of the people of Judea. Crassus, however, marched into Jerusalem and carried away all of the money in the temple, amounting to 2,000 talents, along with all of the gold, equal to 8,000 talents.[30] The total value of the wealth of the temple given by Josephus was thus at least 10,000 talents. When the Romans burned the temple in A.D. 70, Sabinus, one of many looters, "openly took four hundred talents for himself."[31]

In addition to those assets, it has been estimated that "the total annual fiscal yield that Herod drew from the kingdom was about 1,050 talents."[32] From Galilee alone, the tax output the year after Herod's death was 100 talents;[33] at the same time, the total revenue from Idumea, Judea, Samaria, Strato's Tower, Sebaste, Joppa, and Jerusalem was 400 talents;[34] and from Jamnia, Azotus, and Phasaelis, 60 talents.[35]

While no figures exist to document Herod's revenues from rents or from farming and mining activities, his profits must have well exceeded the 200 talent rent he received from Cleopatra on one tract of land alone, and the income from the mines in Cyprus would have been very significant indeed.

By Galilean and late Jewish definitions, a talent of gold or silver was at least 20.4 kilograms; a Tyrian talent was about 42.5 kilograms.[36] So 1,000 talents would have amounted to 45,000 or 93,500 pounds (22.5 or 46.75 tons), respectively.

If the recent estimates are anywhere near accurate in placing the total Jewish population in the Roman empire at this time at about five to seven million people, the annual temple tax from Jews all over the world could have easily yielded over a million shekels. At 15.126 grams of silver per shekel, this amount would equal 15,126 kilograms (33,347 pounds, or 16.7 tons) of silver.

What purchasing power all this wealth commanded is difficult to say. Much depended on the circumstances of supply and demand, need and desire. For example, the Persian Emperor Darius gave the Jews 50 talents for the rebuilding of the temple in the days of Ezra.[37] A son who managed 3,000 talents belonging to his father in Egypt spent 400 talents in an extravagant display to impress Ptolemy and Cleopatra.[38] A group of Jews paid 8 silver talents to Florus, the Roman procurator in Caesarea, in an attempt to protect the synagogue there;[39] and when Titus surrounded and attacked Jerusalem in A.D. 70, the cost of a single measure of grain in the face of starvation rose to the extraordinary price of 1 talent.[40]

Even after a lifetime of heavy spending, Herod still held several well-stocked treasuries when he died. Josephus points out that after the death of Herod, his sons got, along with land, significant amounts of hard currency. Augustus Caesar himself served as the executor of Herod's estate. The emperor awarded Perea and Galilee to Herod's son Antipas, "with a revenue of two hundred talents" annually.[41] In the north, Philip's annual revenue was one hundred talents; and in the south, Archelaus's income was four hundred talents according to one account,[42] six hundred talents according to another.[43] Salome's share was a total revenue of sixty talents, with various other gifts totaling 1,000 (or 1,500) talents going to other members of Herod's family.[44] Finally, Herod's legacy to Caesar was another 1,000 talents.[45]

Large Monetary Amounts in the New Testament

The vast wealth of King Herod and his dynasty helps to put various events and sayings from the life of Jesus into an historico-economic perspective.

Jesus concentrated his time in Jerusalem by spending it in or around the great Temple of Herod. The fabulous wealth and dominant economic functions of the temple[46] must have prompted

Jesus' warnings against the temple hierarchy and its money changing. As Jesus sat opposite the temple treasury watching people making contributions to the temple, "and many that were rich cast in much" (Mark 12:41), the enormous accumulations of wealth visible in that extravagant place must also have stood in grotesque and shocking contrast to the simple needs of the poor, making the scene even more poignant when "there came a certain poor widow, and she threw in two mites, which make a farthing" (Mark 12:42), which was all that she had.

Money also figures prominently in Jesus' parable of the talents. A man traveling abroad left his goods in the hands of three servants. To one "he gave five talents, to another two, and to another one" (Matt. 25:15). Five talents was obviously a sizable amount of gold or silver—either 102 or 212 kilograms (225 or 467.5 pounds), depending on which weight system was involved. Even the servant with one talent was given sufficient funds to enter into a significant commercial venture. In addition, the ratio of 1:2:5 might have reminded some of Jesus' listeners of the disposition of income streams under Herod's estate among three of his sons, Philip (100 talents), Antipas (200 talents), and Archelaus (400 or 600 talents).

Above all, in the parable of the unforgiving servant, a certain servant was brought to give an accounting to his king. The servant owed the king a debt of 10,000 talents (Matt. 18:24). When the servant begged for leniency and worshipped the king, the king was moved with compassion and forgave the entire debt. That same servant, however, went out and found one of his fellows who owed him 100 pence and demanded payment. When the king learned what had happened, he reinstated the debt in full. Not only does that large debt figure represent an impossible sum, worth perhaps several billion dollars in today's markets, but against the historical background of the Temple of Herod it is noteworthy that 10,000 talents was exactly equal to the value of the total temple treasury as stated by Josephus. Thus, the unforgiving servant may in fact represent the king or the temple high priest into whose hands God had entrusted the keeping of that huge amount of sacred wealth. No one else in Judea could conceivably have held that kind of money. Thus, the political upshot of the parable may well be this: despite the great debts and offenses of the rulers of the temple against God, they can be readily forgiven by God, so long as they beg his forgiveness and worship him. When asked, however, to be generous to a commoner in need of a small amount, the rich rulers of the temple will be unmoved, and as a consequence, they will be held personally accountable for the loss of the entire temple treasury.

John W. Welch is the Robert K. Thomas Professor of Law at Brigham Young University. Appreciation is expressed to Allison Welch for her research and assistance on this and other topics concerning Masada and the New Testament.

NOTES

[1]See generally, Emilo Gabba, "The Finances of King Herod," in *Greece and Rome in Eretz Israel,* ed. A. Kasher, U. Rappaport, and G. Fuks (Yad Ishak Ben-Zvi: Israel Exploration Society, 1990), 160–71.

[2]Josephus, *Jewish War* 1.362.

[3]Josephus, *Jewish War* 1.395.

[4]Josephus, *Jewish War* 1.396.

[5]Josephus, *Jewish War* 1.398–99, and Josephus, *Antiquities* 15.360, indicate that Herod was associated with the procurators of Syria, who were required to obtain Herod's consent to all their decisions.

[6]Josephus, *Antiquities* 20.220.

[7]Josephus, *Antiquities* 15.380.

[8]Josephus, *Antiquities* 15.330.

[9]Josephus, *Jewish War* 1.422.

[10]Josephus, *Jewish War* 1.423–27.

[11]Josephus, *Jewish War* 2.85.

[12]Josephus, *Antiquities* 14.110–11.

[13]Josephus, *Antiquities* 15.306–8.

[14]Josephus, *Antiquities* 15.313, 315.

[15]Josephus, *Antiquities* 15.365.

[16]Josephus, *Antiquities* 16.64.

[17]Gabba, "Finances of King Herod," 164.

[18]Gabba, "Finances of King Herod," 164.

[19]Josephus, *Antiquities* 15.107.

[20]L. I. Levine, "Herod the Great," in *The Anchor Bible Dictionary,* ed. David Noel Freedman, 6 vols. (New York: Doubleday, 1992), 3:164.

[21]Josephus, *Antiquities* 16.291.

[22]Josephus, *Antiquities* 15.96.

[23]Josephus, *Jewish War* 1.362.

[24]Levine, "Herod the Great," 3:164.

[25]Josephus, *Antiquities* 16.128.

[26]Josephus, *Antiquities* 15.5.

[27]Josephus, *Antiquities* 16.179–82.

[28]Josephus, *Jewish War* 2.86.

[29]Josephus, *Jewish War* 1.153; see also Josephus, *Antiquities* 14.72.

[30]Josephus, *Antiquities* 14.72, 105-9.

[31]Josephus, *Antiquities* 17.264.

[32]Gabba, "Finances of King Herod," 161.

[33]Richard A. Horsley, *Archaeology, History, and Society in Galilee: The Social Context of Jesus and the Rabbis* (Valley Forge, Penn.: Trinity Press International, 1996), 29.

[34]Josephus, *Jewish War* 2.96-97.

[35]Josephus, *Jewish War* 2.98.

[36]Marvin A. Powell, "Weights and Measures," in *Anchor Bible Dictionary*, 6:907. For further discussion, see Nanci DeBloois, "Coins in the New Testament," in this volume.

[37]Josephus, *Antiquities* 11.61.

[38]Josephus, *Antiquities* 12.209-215-18.

[39]Josephus, *Jewish War* 2.287, 292.

[40]Josephus, *Jewish War* 5.571.

[41]Josephus, *Jewish War* 2.95.

[42]Josephus, *Jewish War* 2:95-97.

[43]Josephus, *Antiquities* 17.320.

[44]Josephus, *Antiquities* 17.323; Josephus, *Jewish War* 2:98-99.

[45]Josephus, *Jewish War* 2.100.

[46]Magen Broshi, "The Role of the Temple in the Herodian Economy," *Journal of Jewish Studies* 38, no. 1 (1987): 31-37.

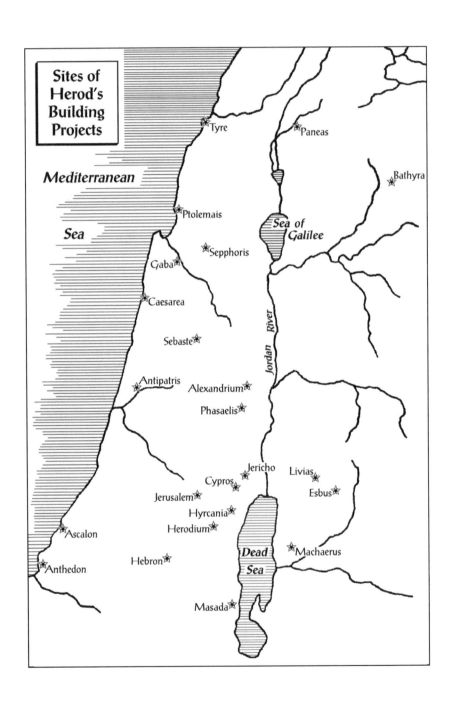

Sites of
Herod's
Building
Projects

Mediterranean

Sea

Tyre

Paneas

Bathyra

Ptolemais

Sea of
Galilee

Sepphoris

Gaba

Caesarea

Jordan River

Sebaste

Antipatris

Alexandrium

Phasaelis

Jericho

Livias

Cypros

Jerusalem

Esbus

Hyrcania

Herodium

Ascalon

Dead
Sea

Machaerus

Hebron

Anthedon

Masada

Herod the Great's Building Program

Andrew Teasdale

Herod the Great, although remembered principally in Christian circles for his slaughter of the infants as stated in Matthew's gospel, also left his mark on the world's memory as an ambitious builder. Herod finally consolidated power in 37 B.C. and immediately began an extensive building program—one perhaps unequaled in the history of ancient Israel. Ehud Netzer declares that "Herod the Great's building projects in W Palestine constitute the most prominent in the country, for any single specific period or personality." Herod's construction sites were located mainly in Western Palestine but also included places such as Antioch, Beirut, Damascus, and Rhodes.[1] The scope of his projects varied from simple monuments to public works, fortresses, palaces, and the magnificent temple in Jerusalem.

Our knowledge of Herod's building activities comes principally from archaeological remains, the writings of Flavius Josephus, and, in the instance of the temple in Jerusalem, the Mishnah. Several structures built by Herod are closely related to significant New Testament events, beginning with Zacharias's vision in the temple in Jerusalem and perhaps ending with Paul's departure to Rome from Herod's city of Caesarea.[2]

Herodium

Rising from the Judean wilderness and located just three miles southeast of Bethlehem is Herodium. Strategically placed at the apex of a small hill, Herodium is one of the palace fortresses Herod constructed as a security measure. The fortress was circular, just over two hundred feet in diameter. An exterior wall with four towers rose approximately one hundred feet above the original hill. The highest tower rose an additional fifty feet above the exterior wall. Huge quantities of soil were dumped around this exterior wall, creating a cone-shaped peak that gave the fortress the appearance of a volcano.[3]

This fortress dominated Bethlehem's skyline during New Testament times and remains a prominent feature of the region to this day. It certainly was, weather permitting, a landmark that Mary and Joseph would have looked for as they approached Bethlehem. Herodium may also have quartered the soldiers that carried out Herod's infant-extermination order.

Machaerus

Machaerus is another palace fortress with New Testament significance. It is located about twelve miles south and three miles east of the Dead Sea's northern shore. Upon Herod's death, Machaerus became the property of Herod's son Antipas, who ruled a split realm that included the area east of the Dead Sea and also the area around the Sea of Galilee's western shore. Sometime before Jesus began his ministry, Antipas fell in love with his niece, Herodius, who was also his half-brother's wife, and later married her—a flagrant breach of Jewish law. One outspoken critic of Antipas's action was John the Baptist. Matthew records that Herod Antipas imprisoned John and wanted to execute him, but he was worried about the reaction of the people who viewed John as a prophet. However, in the fortress palace of Machaerus, Antipas was finally persuaded to take action:

> But when Herod's birthday was kept, the daughter of Herodias danced before them, and pleased Herod. Whereupon he promised with an oath to give her whatsoever she would ask. And she, being before instructed of her mother, said, Give me here John Baptist's head in a charger. And the king was sorry: nevertheless for the oath's sake, and them which sat with him at meat, he commanded it to be given her. And he sent, and beheaded John in the prison. (Matt. 14:6–10)

Jericho

Jericho, another palace complex related to New Testament events, is located about thirteen miles from Jerusalem

Terrace of the Northern Palace. This impressive structure is just one of Herod's many building projects at Masada.

and approximately one mile southwest of the Old Testament Jericho. With its mild winters, Jericho served as a winter palace for Jewish rulers and also as a crossroads and an agricultural center.

Construction of this complex was initiated by the Hasmoneans, who built several grand estates, the beginnings of a palace, gardens, bathhouses, swimming pools, and multiple channels to conduct water from the nearby springs. Herod made improvements to the Hasmonean structures and added three palaces, a theater, a reception hall, a sunken garden, a horse and chariot racing course, and possibly a gymnasium.[4]

Although only thirteen miles from Jerusalem, Jericho is more than 3,200 feet lower in elevation. In fact, Jericho has the distinction of being the lowest city on the earth's surface—approximately 825 feet below sea level. This phenomenon gives added meaning to Jesus' statement introducing the parable of the good Samaritan: "A certain man went *down* from Jerusalem to Jericho" (Luke 10:30; italics added).

Jesus visited Jericho at least once. The synoptic gospels record that he visited Jericho on his final ascent to Jerusalem (Mark 10:46). It is recorded that there he healed a blind man, stayed with short-statured Zacchaeus, and delivered the parable of the pounds (Luke 18:35–19:27).

Caesarea Maritima

Another of Herod's projects was the city that he constructed and named Caesarea Maritima. He named it Caesarea in honor of Augustus Caesar; currently the qualifier *Maritima* is used to distinguish the city from Caesarea Philippi. Caesarea is located on the Mediterranean coast about fifty-five miles north-northwest of Jerusalem. It took from ten to twelve years to build the city, which was inaugurated in 10/9 B.C.[5] Caesarea was a large city (164 acres within the city wall) that included a theater, hippodrome, Roman temple, and more.[6] Josephus provides the best contemporaneous description of the city:

> And when he observed that there was a place near the sea, formerly called Strato's Tower, which was very well suited to be the site of a city, he set about making a magnificent plan and put up buildings all over the city, not of ordinary material but of white stone. He also adorned it with a very costly palace, with civic halls and—what was greatest of all and required the most labour—with a well-protected harbour, of the size of Piraeus, with landing-places and secondary anchorages inside.[7]

To supply water for the city, Herod constructed an aqueduct upheld by a six-and-one-half-mile line of arches. This aqueduct carried water from a spring near the base of the Carmel mountain range to Caesarea. However, the spring did not provide sufficient water for the city. Herod's solution to the fresh-water problem was to combine the water from two sources. To supply the additional water, a tunnel was constructed from the head of the aqueduct through six miles of limestone foothills to another source of fresh water creating a twelve-and-one-half-mile aqueduct—six miles tunneled and six and one-half miles over arches.[8]

Herod also put the tidal action of the Mediterranean Sea to good use. He constructed the city with a sewer system open to the

Aqueduct for Caesarea. The portion of the aqueduct supported by arches was six and one-half miles long. To supply water to Caesarea, Herod also tunneled six miles through limestone hills. The Mediterranean Sea is in the background of this view.

sea and used the high tides to flush the sewer. This measure certainly cut down on the city's appeal as a seaside swimming resort but was an effective and labor-saving way to keep the city clean.

The harbor constructed at Caesarea was, like many of Herod's projects, massive as well as innovative. It was entirely artificial—the first of its kind in the ancient world. It extended some fifteen hundred feet into the Mediterranean Sea and actually consisted of a smaller harbor nested inside a larger one. The southern and northern breakwaters were approximately two hundred feet wide and one hundred fifty feet wide respectively. The sixty-foot-wide entrance was located at the northwestern portion of the harbor.[9]

Josephus records that the breakwaters were constructed by submerging massive stone blocks.[10] Archaeological excavations have revealed that in addition to large blocks forms and underwater concrete were used in the breakwaters' construction. One form thus far examined was forty-nine feet by thirty-nine feet by five feet. After the form was built, a type of underwater concrete was used to fill the form. As each section was raised above sea level, the next section further out to sea was undertaken.[11]

Caesarea is the location of several significant New Testament events and has the distinction of being the first city where it is recorded that the gospel was preached to the Gentiles. Cornelius, the Roman centurion, was stationed in Caesarea when he had the vision that directed him to send for Peter. Peter responded by visiting Caesarea, preaching the gospel, and baptizing Cornelius and several of his associates (Acts 10).

There is an additional feature of Caesarea that is significant. Just to the south of the previously mentioned harbor, Herod built a seaside palace atop a small peninsula. Surrounded on three sides by water, this palace had a fresh-water pool as its central feature. The water for this nearly Olympic-sized pool (115 feet by 59 feet) was provided by channels cut into the rock at its eastern end. In the pool's center was a pedestal that probably supported a statue. A dining room was situated just east of the pool. This room had a beautiful multicolored tiled floor and an apse with a semicircular fountain. The palace also featured a Roman-style bath, colonnaded halls, and various serving rooms.

It is possible that this palace was the location of an important episode of Paul's life—his encounter with Agrippa.[12] After Paul's arrest in Jerusalem, he was brought to Caesarea. Several days later, Paul and his Jewish accusers met there before Festus, where Paul successfully defended himself against their charges and testified of Jesus' resurrection (Acts 25:18–19). Festus then offered Paul the opportunity to return to Jerusalem and defend himself there. But Paul, knowing of the Jewish plans for his murder and also knowing that he should go to Rome (Acts 23:11), asked to have his case tried before Caesar. Festus related these events to Agrippa, who was intrigued by what had happened and commanded that Paul appear before him:

> Then Agrippa said unto Festus, I would also hear the man myself. To morrow, said he, thou shalt hear him. And on the morrow, when Agrippa was come, and Bernice, with great pomp, and was entered into the place of hearing, with the chief captains, and principal men of the city, at Festus' commandment Paul was brought forth. . . . Then Agrippa said unto Paul, Thou art permitted to speak for thyself. Then Paul stretched forth the hand, and answered for himself. (Acts 25:22–23; 26:1)

Paul then gave a stirring account of his vision and missionary labors and of the persecution he received at Jewish hands. Paul's testimony was such that Agrippa was convinced of his innocence (Acts 26:32) and even professed, "Almost thou persuadest me to be a Christian" (Acts 26:28). Paul then embarked from the harbor at Caesarea for Rome.

The Temple Complex at Jerusalem

Without doubt, the greatest of Herod's construction projects was the temple complex in Jerusalem and the platform on which it rested. The temple platform was a massive structure that dominated Jerusalem in New Testament times and was the largest structure of its kind in the Roman world.

The Platform. The temple platform rests at the top of a ridge that runs north-south through Jerusalem. The Kidron Valley borders on the east, and the Tyropoeon Valley on the west. The ridge slopes down to the south and has a gentle rise as it continues to the north. The platform as originally constructed by Solomon was nearly square and about 861 feet on each side. A later addition, added by the Hasmoneans in the second century B.C., extended the platform roughly 130 feet to the south.[13]

Herod constructed an enormous expansion of this platform. Due to the precipitous drop of the Kidron Valley, Herod did not extend the platform to the east. He did, however, extend the platform in all other directions. When completed, it measured approximately 172,000 square yards.[14] The extensions to the south and west required the most effort because in these areas the hill's downward slope required the construction of massive retaining walls and a series of arches to support the platform. The retaining walls "towered more than 80 feet above the roadways . . . and reached over 50 feet below street level."[15] It is generally thought that one of these corners is the pinnacle of the temple where the second temptation occurred (Matt. 4:5-7).[16]

Many New Testament events occurred on this platform including Simeon and Anna's identification of the Messiah (Luke 2:25-38), Jesus' teaching of the doctors (Luke 2:46-49), many events of Jesus' ministry, and Peter and John's healing of the lame man (Acts 3:1-8).

The Royal Portico. Across the southern end of the platform, Herod built a royal portico, or stoa. There are no archaeological remains of this structure, as it was completely destroyed by the Romans in A.D. 70.[17] However, Josephus did provide an excellent description of this building:

> The fourth front of this (court), facing south, also had gates in the middle, and had over it the Royal Portico, which had three aisles, extending in length from the eastern to the western ravine. . . . Now the columns (of the portico) stood in four rows, one opposite the other all along—the fourth row was attached to a wall built of stone,—and the thickness of each column was such that it would take three men with outstretched arms touching one another to envelop it; its height was twenty-seven feet, and there was a double moulding running round its base. The number of all the columns was a hundred and sixty-two, and their capitals were ornamented in the Corinthian style of carving, which caused amazement by the magnificence of its whole effect. Since there were four rows, they made three aisles among them, under the porticoes. Of these the two side ones corresponded and were made in the same way, each being thirty feet in width, a stade in length, and over fifty feet in height. But the middle aisle was one and a half times as wide and twice as high, and thus it greatly towered over those on either side. The ceilings (of the porticoes) were ornamented with deeply cut wood-carvings representing all sorts of different figures. The ceiling of the middle aisle was raised to a greater height, and the front wall was cut at either end into architraves with columns built into it, and all of it was polished, so that these structures seemed incredible to those who had not seen them, and were beheld with amazement by those who set eyes on them.[18]

This building possibly served as a meeting place for Jewish leaders and may have been a regrouping area after their verbal forays with Jesus. It is also probable that this building was the banking center for the temple and the location of the money changers; hence it was presumably through this building that Jesus stormed with his scourge and overturned the money changers' tables.[19]

The Antonia Fortress. At the northwestern corner of this platform, Herod constructed the Antonia Fortress. Because this building was also destroyed by the Romans, once again Josephus provides the details about the building.[20] The fortress was roughly rectangular in shape and built upon a rock escarpment. Its appearance was "that of a tower with other towers at each of the four corners; three of these turrets were fifty cubits high, while that at the south-east angle rose to seventy cubits, and so commanded a view of the whole area of the temple."[21] The Antonia provided the Roman soldiers garrisoned there an excellent view of the platform and the crowds that often assembled below. As the temple platform was an assembly place for the Jewish people, there were many skirmishes there between the Roman soldiers and the Jewish crowds. One of these skirmishes involved Paul.

> And all the city was moved, and the people ran together: and they took Paul, and drew him out of the temple: and forthwith the doors were shut. And as they went about to kill him, tidings came unto the chief captain of the band, that all Jerusalem was in an uproar. Who immediately took soldiers and centurions, and ran down unto them: and when they saw the chief captain and the soldiers, they left beating of Paul.
>
> Then the chief captain came near, and took him, and commanded him to be bound with two chains; and demanded who he was, and what he had done. And some cried one thing, some another, among the multitude: and when he could not know the certainty for the tumult, he commanded him to be carried into the castle. And when he came upon the stairs, so it was, that he was borne of the soldiers for the violence of the people. For the multitude of the people followed after, crying, Away with him. And as Paul was to be led into the castle, he said unto the chief captain, May I speak unto thee?
>
> Who said, Canst thou speak Greek? Art not thou that Egyptian, which before these days madest an uproar, and leddest out into the wilderness four thousand men that were murderers?
>
> But Paul said, I am a man which am a Jew of Tarsus, a city in Cilicia, a citizen of no mean city: and, I beseech thee, suffer me to speak unto the people.
>
> And when he had given him licence, Paul stood on the stairs, and beckoned with the hand unto the people. And when there was made a great silence, he spake unto them in the Hebrew tongue. (Acts 21:30-40)

Paul, standing on the stairs of the Antonia, then proceeded to tell his conversion story. The Jews were enraged by his words, and the uproar prompted the chief captain to bind Paul and deliver him into the Antonia to be scourged. At this point, Paul played his trump card and informed the captain that he was a Roman citizen. A short time later, Paul was removed from the Antonia and taken to Caesarea.

It is possible that the Antonia served as the location of another significant New Testament event. Although Caesarea was the official residence for the Roman procurator, many times he governed directly from Jerusalem during the Jewish holidays, which were often marked by violent outbursts against the Romans. While visiting Jerusalem, Pilate resided at Herod's palace in the upper city or, when there was concern of a possible outbreak, in the Antonia. It is therefore possible that Pilate lodged in the Antonia during the Passover season just days after Jerusalem welcomed a new Jewish king.

Late Thursday night or early Friday morning before that fateful Passover, Jesus was arrested by the Jews in a garden just east of the temple. He was taken to Caiaphas's palace and there found guilty of blasphemy and worthy of death (Mark 14:64). Jesus was subsequently delivered to Pilate, and it may have been at the Antonia, just beyond the temple's shadow, that Pilate declared, "I find no fault in this man" (Luke 23:4). Later, Pilate offered the people the choice of freeing either Jesus or Barabbas, and the temple courtyard rang with the cry, "Crucify him" (Luke 23:21).

The Temple. The showpiece of the complex certainly was the Jewish temple. It was a massive structure, rising over 200 feet above the surrounding platform with an exterior at least partially covered in gold.

Computer-generated model of Herod's Temple, southern view

> The exterior of the building wanted nothing that could astound either mind or eye. For, being covered on all sides with massive plates of gold, the sun was no sooner up than it radiated so fiery a flash that persons straining to look at it were compelled to avert their eyes, as from the solar rays. To approaching strangers it appeared from a distance like a snow-clad mountain; for all that was not overlaid with gold was of purest white.[22]

The temple's front facade was about 172 feet high and 172 feet broad—the same as the length of the temple. The entrance was ornamented with golden vines and oversized grape clusters.[23] In front of the doors to the temple hung a "Babylonian tapestry, with embroidery of blue and fine linen, of scarlet also and purple, wrought with marvelous skill."[24]

This tapestry hung in front of two sets of double doors that opened into the holy place. The holy place was just over thirty-four feet wide, sixty-nine feet long, and sixty-nine feet high (twenty cubits by forty cubits by forty cubits) and contained three items: the golden lampstand (or menorah), the table of shewbread, and the altar of incense.

The holy place was separated from the Holy of Holies by two veils. The Holy of Holies was empty during New Testament times. In Solomon's temple, this room held the Ark of the Covenant, but by the time of Christ the Ark had been lost.

Around the Holy of Holies and the holy place were storage rooms, a water drain, and a stairway that provided access to the upper floor. The upper floor contained two rooms with the same dimensions as the holy place and Holy of Holies.

Although Jesus never entered the temple,[25] he initially recognized it as his father's house (John 2:16) and later claimed it as his own (Mark 11:17). The temple was the location of the first recorded New Testament event:

> There was in the days of Herod, the king of Judaea, a certain priest named Zacharias, of the course of Abia: and his wife was of the daughters of Aaron, and her name was Elisabeth. And they were both righteous before God, walking in all the commandments and ordinances of the Lord blameless. And they had no child, because that Elisabeth was barren, and they both were now well stricken in years. And it came to pass, that while he executed the priest's office before God in the order of his course, According to the custom of the priest's office, his lot was to burn incense when he went into

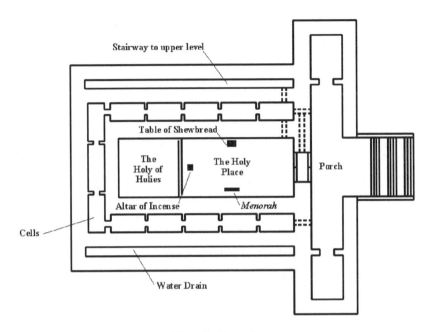

Herod's Temple

the temple of the Lord. And the whole multitude of the people were praying without at the time of incense. And there appeared unto him an angel of the Lord standing on the right side of the altar of incense. (Luke 1:5-11)

When the angel visited him, Zacharias was standing before the altar of incense in the holy place of the temple that had been built under Herod's direction.

Conclusion

From the angel's visit to Zacharias until Paul's departure from Caesarea to Rome, Herod's buildings provided the setting for many New Testament events. Netzer observes, "No doubt Herod had a deep understanding for building and architecture. The wide range of original ideas, the buildings' outstanding locations, and the unique combination of functions (such as at Herodium and Jericho's hippodrome) are clear evidence of Herod's personal role in the initiative as well as the implementation of these vast building activities."[26] Herod's architectural skill ensured that his buildings would endure for many ages, and it is entirely possible that some of these structures will yet provide the setting for significant future events for Israel and Christendom.

Andrew Teasdale is a graduate student at Utah State University.

NOTES

[1]See Ehud Netzer, "Herod's Building Program," in *The Anchor Bible Dictionary,* ed. David Noel Freedman, 6 vols. (New York: Doubleday, 1992), 3:169-72.

[2]For a complete listing of other structures built by Herod, see Josephus, *Antiquities* vol. 8, appendix D, 579.

[3]See Ehud Netzer, "Herodium," in *Anchor Bible Dictionary,* 3:176-180.

[4]See Ehud Netzer, "Jericho," in *Anchor Bible Dictionary,* 3:723-40.

[5]Josephus, *Antiquities* 15.341.

[6]See Robert J. Bull, "Caesarea Maritima: The Search for Herod's City," *Biblical Archaeology Review* 8 (May-June 1982): 27.

[7]Josephus, *Antiquities* 15.331-32.

[8]Bull, "Caesarea Maritima," 29.

[9]See Robert L. Hohlfelder, "Caesarea beneath the Sea," *Biblical Archaeology Review* 8 (May-June 1982): 44.

[10]Josephus, *Jewish War* 1.411-12.

[11]See Linley Vann, "Herod's Harbor Construction Recovered Underwater," *Biblical Archaeology Review* 9 (May-June 1983): 10-14.

[12]Barbara Burrell, Kathryn Gleason, and Ehud Netzer, "Uncovering Herod's Seaside Palace," *Biblical Archaeology Review* 19 (May-June 1993): 50-57, 76.

[13]See Leen Ritmeyer, "Locating the Original Temple Mount," *Biblical Archaeology Review* 18 (March-April 1992): 24-45, 64-65.

[14]Approximately 1,550 feet (north-south) by 1,000 feet.

[15]Ehud Netzer, "Temple, Jerusalem" in *Anchor Bible Dictionary,* 6:365. Netzer also points out that the platform's retaining walls were made of stone blocks varying in size. The largest block discovered thus far measures more than forty feet long. It is estimated that this stone weighs more than 100 tons (for comparison, the largest stone at Stonehenge weighs 40 tons).

[16]Traditionally, the southeast corner has been identified as the location for the second temptation. I believe the argument is stronger for the southwest corner. Since a possible focus of the second temptation was that of worldly recognition, the southwest corner makes better sense. An individual falling without harm from this corner would have been in full view of all the people in the busiest areas surrounding the temple platform, whereas the same event happening at the southeast corner would have been seen by a much smaller population.

[17]The royal portico rested atop Herod's extension of the platform's southern end. Although the portico was completely destroyed, much of Herod's extension remains to this day. Ritmeyer believes that his study of this extension has

provided sufficient information to determine the longitudinal axis of the three rows of pillars (the fourth row was part of the portico's southern wall) that supported the portico's roof. See Leendert Petrus Ritmeyer, "The Architectural Developments of the Temple Mount in Jerusalem" (Ph.D. thesis, University of Manchester, 1992), 237–52.

[18]Josephus, *Antiquities* 15.411, 413–16.

[19]It is interesting to note that the animals were probably held at the north end of the temple platform as the pools in which the animals were washed were located just to the north of the platform. The cleansing of the temple was not a small incident. It could have ranged across the entire length of the platform.

[20]Due to political sensitivities and the fact that buildings have been constructed over the previous location of the Antonia Fortress, it is not possible to conduct any archaeological excavations in the area. However, Michael Burgoyne has located what he believes to be a wall (over thirteen feet thick) remaining from the Antonia Fortress. See Michael Hamilton Burgoyne, *Mamluk Jerusalem: An Architectural Study* (London: Published on behalf of the British School of Archaeology in Jerusalem by the World of Islam Festival Trust, 1987), 204.

[21]Josephus, *Jewish War* 5.242.

[22]Josephus, *Jewish War* 5.222–23.

[23]Josephus, *Jewish War* 5.210.

[24]Josephus, *Jewish War* 5.212.

[25]There are several reasons for presuming that Jesus did not enter the temple itself. First, according to Jewish law, Jesus did not hold the proper priesthood office to enter the temple. If he had entered the temple, mention of this event and the corresponding outrage by the Jewish leaders probably would appear in the Gospels. Second, two Greek words with significant differences in meaning have been translated simply as "temple" in the King James Version. The Greek word *naos* most often refers to the actual temple structure. The Greek word *hieron* refers to the "temple at Jerusalem, including the whole temple precinct w.[ith] its buildings, courts, etc." Walter Bauer, *A Greek-English Lexicon of the New Testament and Other Early Christian Literature,* trans. William F. Arndt and F. Wilbur Gingrich, 2d ed. (Chicago: University of Chicago Press, 1979), s.v. "*hieron.*" For example, in Luke 1:9, Zacharias burned incense in the *naos.* In Matthew 21:12, Jesus went in to the *hieron* to cast out those who "sold and bought," meaning he did not enter the temple itself but the surrounding precinct. The word *hieron* is used in the references to Jesus being in the temple.

[26]Netzer, "Herod's Building Program," 3:172.

Alexander the Great Comes to Jerusalem: The Jewish Response to Hellenism

Cecilia M. Peek

When Alexander the Great defeated the forces of Darius III near Gaugamela in 331 B.C., he became heir to the Persian empire.[1] Palestine was among those territories acquired after his victory over the last Achaemenid ruler. For the first twenty years after Alexander's death, this region was hotly contested.[2] The territory was assigned to Laomedon in the initial division of responsibilities in 323 B.C.; he held it until Ptolemy Soter acquired it in 320. In 315, Antigonos One-Eye seized all of Palestine; Ptolemy retrieved it from Antigonos's son Demetrius in 312. Antigonos recaptured the area in 311, but he was killed at the Battle of Ipsus in 301. Seleucus, who then held Palestine, yielded it to Ptolemy. Ptolemy and his heirs held Judea for the next century. In 200, Antiochus III's decisive victory over the Ptolemies in the Fifth Syrian War made Jerusalem and its environs the concern of the Seleucid monarchs.[3] The Seleucids enjoyed political supremacy until Antiochus IV Epiphanes' persecution of the Jewish faith in the 160s B.C. incited the Hasmonean revolt, laying the foundation for the eventual independence of Judea.[4]

For a century and a half, Palestine had continued under the jurisdiction of one or another Hellenistic monarch. Jews came into regular contact with Hellenistic culture in the persons and policies of its rulers (however shifting) and the Greco-Macedonian settlers who penetrated the region.[5] Interaction between Jews and Greeks became more regular and sustained than ever before. It would be surprising indeed, if there were no signs of Hellenization (Greek cultural influence) in the Jewish community throughout the Second Temple period.[6]

One may argue, indeed many have argued, about the degree to which Greek models affected Jewish society. An enormous body of scholarship has been devoted to the study of Hellenism and the Jews, with particular attention given to the period of the reign of Antiochus IV Epiphanes (beginning in 170 B.C.) and the ensuing Hasmonean revolt down to the high priesthood of Simon, last of the Maccabean brothers, in 140.[7]

The initial encounter between Hellenism and Judaism has been variously treated by scholars. One view holds that "two opposing parties" existed within Judaism. On one hand were the "devout" Jews—usually linked in the first centuries with the Pharisees and the Essenes—who were pious observers of the law and naturally, if not always successfully, opposed to Greek influences. On the other hand were the "Hellenists"—Jews who accepted and promoted Greek culture, which was energetically championed by Antiochus IV Epiphanes. The devout Jews gained a decisive advantage when the Selucid king tried to substitute Greek rites for traditional Jewish worship. The Jewish faith, previously giving way to Greek practices, was ironically preserved by the king's overzealous attempt at Hellenization. The sponsors of Hellenistic culture suddenly met with the active resistance of the monotheistic Jews.[8] For those who view this resistance as successfully prevailing, the Jewish community "was and remained in political institutions, in observances and in its culture and literary products" markedly "un-Hellenistic."[9]

Another view claims that the Greek influence in Palestine was profound and pervasive, originally meeting no resistance and influencing everything from politics and economics to literature and philosophy. According to this school, there was a process of assimilation and understanding that resulted in a decidedly Hellenized Palestinian Judaism, not notably distinct from the Judaism of the Diaspora. The process of assimilation in the period of initial encounter was interrupted only by the nationalistic uprising of the Maccabees.[10] The main proponents of cultural assimilation and accommodation, in time, became known as the Sadducees.

Evidence of Jewish Reception of Greek Culture

Jewish sources themselves suggest that at least some Jews were receptive to Hellenistic culture and that Jewish involvement with Greek traditions was not always considered a threat to religious piety. The writer of 1 Maccabees, himself critical of the corrupting influences of Greek culture, admits a widespread, Jewish-initiated desire to participate in some of the forms of Greek life in the second century B.C. After a cursory summary of the career of Alexander the Great and his political successors, he records:

> From them came forth a sinful root, Antiochus Epiphanes, son of Antiochus the king; he had been a hostage in Rome. He began to reign in the one hundred and thirty-seventh year of the kingdom of the Greeks. In those days lawless men came forth *from Israel,* and misled many, saying, "*Let us go and make a covenant with the Gentiles round about us,* for since we separated from them many evils have come upon us." This proposal pleased them, and *some of the people eagerly went to the king.* He authorized them to observe the ordinances of the Gentiles. So they built a gymnasium in Jerusalem, according to Gentile custom, and removed the marks of circumcision, and abandoned the holy covenant. They joined with the Gentiles and sold themselves to evil. (1 Macc. 1:9–15; italics added)[11]

The language is strongly biased, being that of an author whose own life postdated the events he describes here by a generation[12] and who viewed the Jewish involvement with the "ordinances of the Gentiles" as a departure from the sacred traditions of the fathers. The only thing one can say with any certainty about the actions of these unnamed Jews, apart from the author's interpretation of those actions, is that they approached the Seleucid king and requested and received authorization to build a gymnasium, the traditional site for Greek education. The interest in this Greek custom in Jerusalem originated with the Jews themselves, although in time this development admittedly became problematic for some Jews.[13]

A more precise account is given in 2 Maccabees. This book describes a dispute over the high priesthood between a certain Simon and the high priest Onias. Jason, the brother of Onias, is said to have gone to the king, Antiochus IV, and obtained the high priesthood for himself by promising the king 80 talents more tribute than he had hitherto received. Jason offered an additional 150 talents, over and above the 80 talents already proffered, for permission to establish by his (Jason's) authority a gymnasium, a body of youth to attend it, and the right to register Antiochenes in Jerusalem.[14] The king assented; Jason took office and "shifted his countrymen over to the Greek way of life" (2 Macc. 4:7–10).

This account likewise attributes the impetus for a gymnasium and perhaps other Greek cultural practices to certain Jews themselves—in this case to Jason. There is no evidence of resistance to the gymnasium in Jerusalem. The author of 2 Maccabees regards the response in Jerusalem as a dangerous rejection of the laws of God, for which the Jews would be punished (2 Macc. 4:16–17), but such a view is interpretive. Of the admittedly few contemporaneous sources, none characterizes the gymnasium or Jason and his Hellenizing reforms as an evil destined to bring on God's wrath.[15] At the time the gymnasium was established, it seems to have been very popular, and the priests seem to have participated enthusiastically.[16] The Jewish high priest was, however, careful to secure the activity under priestly control—Jason specifically requests that it might be established under *his* authority, perhaps to be free from any non-Jewish management in the regulation of the enterprise.

The story of Jason establishing a gymnasium describes just one Jewish response to Hellenistic culture. Elements of Greek society other than the gymnasium and periods other than the Maccabean could serve as further case studies for the Jewish relationship to Hellenistic culture in intertestamental and New Testament times. In other subjects and other times, it is also possible to see Jewish acceptance and appropriation of Greek traditions. Two examples may be mentioned—the writings of Jewish historians and the work of Jewish artisans.

Jewish writers sometimes adopted the historiographic methods of Greek historians of the Hellenistic era. Writing in Greek, Jewish historians claimed the non-Greek origin of Greek culture. This practice was by no means limited to Jewish authors: one of the earliest known examples of this kind of nationalistic apologetic comes from Hecataeus of Abdera, who was commissioned by King Ptolemy of Egypt to write a history of that country. His *Kulturgeschichte,* which represented Egypt as the original source for the great cultural achievements of Greece, served as a model for several Hellenistic Jewish authors.[17]

The Jew Eupolemus calls Moses the first wise man, using the Greek term *sophos*. Moses is, therefore, not just the conduit of God's commandments to Israel, but the first *philosopher*, the originator of Greek wisdom.[18] Artapanus, writing in the second century B.C., portrays Abraham, Joseph, and Moses all as cultural benefactors. Abraham taught astrology to the king of the Egyptians. Joseph instituted successful farming innovations and discovered measures as well. Moses is credited with a variety of practical inventions, including ships, devices for lifting stones, as well as Egyptian weapons, fighting techniques, and philosophy. Besides these, he is supposed to have had a hand in organizing Egyptian worship, to have been a great military leader, and to have had virtually magical powers.[19]

By fashioning Moses and his patriarchal predecessors as cultural benefactors of Egypt, Artapanus indirectly asserts Jewish superiority over the Greeks. According to Hecataeus, on whose history Artapanus strongly relied, the Greeks derived their wisdom and learning from the Egyptians; according to Artapanus, the Egyptians derived theirs from the Jews.[20]

Jewish artisans likewise imitated Greek styles, utilizing Greek architectural and mythological motifs in the ornamentation of their own religious and secular structures. Archaeology has yielded some interesting finds in Palestinian synagogues. Jewish symbols sometimes coexist with Greco-Roman mythology. The synagogue at Hammath-Tiberias from around the third and fourth centuries A.D. preserves a mosaic of Helios with globe and whip in hand.[21] The third-century synagogue at Chorazin has a frieze representing

Corinthian capital from Masada. Reflecting the influence of Hellenistic traditions upon Herod's architecture, this engaged capital (specifically the upper drum) is from the banqueting hall of the Northern Palace.

Hercules, the Medusa, a centaur, and some decidedly Dionysiac humans.[22] Whatever the motivation for such depictions, we must assume by their presence in the centers of Jewish religious life that they were aesthetically acceptable to some pious Jewish audiences.

The Reception of Alexander as a Prototype

In antiquity, individual Jewish attitudes to Hellenism likely varied as much as modern interpretations of them. There can be little doubt that the introduction of Hellenistic rule gave rise to recurring and energetic discussions concerning the appropriate Jewish response to the policies of Hellenistic monarchs in Palestine and the cultural forms that accompanied them.

Consider the visit of Alexander the Great to Jerusalem after his conquest of Tyre in 332 B.C. Greek historians make no mention of this visit; in

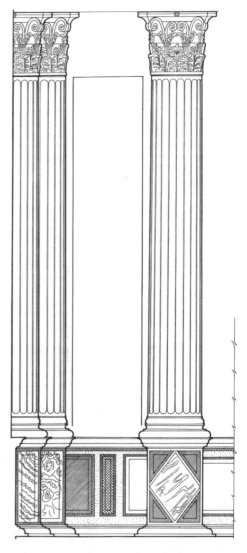

Restored section of the Northern Palace's banqueting hall. The Corinthian capitals combined with the painted pedestals reflect a mix of styles.

fact, no surviving non-Jewish source mentions any connection between Alexander and the Jews. The Jewish historian Josephus is the earliest extant author to record a visit by Alexander to Jerusalem.[23] The tradition behind Josephus's narrative is obscure at

best.[24] It is possible that Alexander visited Jerusalem, but the preserved descriptions of his visit are almost certainly fictional, "mere
ex post facto legends."[25] This is not to say that Josephus's account
is therefore without historical value. Albeit untrustworthy in
reconstructing the facts of history, it does offer valuable insight
into at least one Jewish view of the appropriate relationship between
the Jews and a Greek ruler.

According to Josephus, Alexander, while engaged in the siege
of Tyre, sent a letter to the Jewish high priest Jaddus. Alexander had
already defeated Persian forces at the Granicus and taken Damascus
and Sidon. The siege of Tyre was proving more arduous and time-
consuming than he had anticipated.[26] In his letter to Jaddus, Alexander demanded assistance, provisions, and the tribute that had
formerly been paid to the Persian king Darius. The high priest
refused to violate his oath to Darius as long as the king remained
alive. Jaddus's refusal enraged Alexander, and he vowed to attack the
high priest and make an example of him once he had subdued Tyre.[27]

After the Macedonian forces took Tyre and Gaza, Alexander
became anxious to go to Jerusalem.[28] When the high priest heard
of his approach, he was naturally frightened, and he joined the
people in offering sacrifice and praying to their God to protect and
deliver them. Jaddus was commanded by God in a dream to deco-
rate the city with wreaths, to open its gates, and to go out and
meet the approaching force. The people were to be dressed in
white garments; the priest himself in his priestly regalia. Jaddus
was assured that they would suffer no harm.[29] Alexander's arrival is
the dramatic moment of the account:

> When [Jaddus] learned that Alexander was not far from
> the city, he went out with the priests and the body of citizens,
> and . . . met him at a certain place called Saphein. This name, trans-
> lated into the Greek tongue, means "Lookout." For, as it happened,
> Jerusalem and the temple could be seen from there. Now the Phoeni-
> cians and the Chaldaeans who followed along thought to themselves
> that the king in his anger would naturally permit them to plunder the
> city and put the high priest to a shameful death, but the reverse of
> this happened. For when Alexander while still far off saw the multi-
> tude in white garments the priests at their head clothed in linen, and
> the high priest in a robe of hyacinth-blue and gold, wearing on his
> head the mitre with the golden plate on it on which was inscribed
> the name of God, he approached alone and prostrated himself
> before . . . the high priest.[30]

Upon seeing this, all the Jews shouted greeting to Alexander and surrounded him. Alexander's men were amazed at their leader's behavior, and his general Parmenion asked him why he, to whom others do obeisance, had bowed down to the high priest of the Jews.[31] Alexander explained that he had prostrated himself not before Jaddus, but rather before the God whom Jaddus served and whose name appeared on the high priest's mitre. He claimed that he had previously seen Jaddus in a dream, dressed in the very attire in which they now beheld him. In Alexander's dream, the high priest urged him "not to hesitate but to cross over [into Asia] confidently, for he himself would lead [Alexander's] army and give over [to him] the empire of the Persians."[32] Encountering the living version of the apparition in his dream assured Alexander of divine guidance and future success.[33]

Alexander then gave the high priest his hand, and the whole multitude proceeded into the city, which stood open to receive him. Alexander offered sacrifice to the God of Israel in the temple,[34] honored the priests, and bestowed gifts on the inhabitants of the city. He was shown a copy of the book of Daniel,[35] in which the fall of Persia at the hands of a Greek was prophesied, and Alexander took this Greek to be himself. Perhaps most importantly, he granted the high priest's request that the Jews be free to observe their country's laws and be exempt from tribute every seventh year. He even extended the free observance of their laws to the Jews in Babylon and Media. Those who wished could join his army, and we are told that many did.[36]

The tale in Josephus has been characterized as "two substories." The ceremonial reception of Alexander upon his arrival in Jerusalem constitutes the first part; the miraculous preservation of the Jewish people and their temple because of divine dreams, the second.[37]

It is said that the account of Alexander's arrival and that of his epiphany must originally have been two distinct narratives, which are thematically irreconcilable: the former demonstrates Jewish submission to Alexander, while the latter demonstrates Alexander's submission to the God of the Jews.[38] However, is it not the very disjunction between the narratives that accurately characterizes the tension in the relationship between Alexander and the

Jewish people? The story as a whole represents an effort to clarify and relieve that tension by defining the Jewish place in a world dominated by the Hellenistic world-conqueror. The hard fact is that the Jews must acknowledge the *temporal* overlordship of the victorious Alexander and, by extension, whichever of his successors should control Palestine. But their lives are also governed by their God and the laws established by Him, and He takes precedence. The superiority of God's claims must be upheld, while Alexander must be satisfied.

The *adventus* and epiphany aspects of the story combined achieve the desired effect; together they define the proper relationship: God's chosen people are prepared, under certain circumstances, to open their city, serve in the army, and render other signs of temporal submission to an earthly king. The earthly king must in turn submit, literally or figuratively, to their God. Alexander bows to the God of Israel; he offers sacrifice to Him in His temple. In addition, he bestows gifts on the Jews and agrees to allow them freedom to observe their traditional laws unmolested. As Alexander favored the Jews, so the God of the Jews would favor Alexander. Jewish prophetic predictions of Alexander's success and Jewish fidelity to him are at one with Alexander's acknowledgment of God. Their submission is possible precisely because Alexander does bow to their God, who is Lord over all. Here is a worldly king they may recognize.

Fanciful though Josephus's account of Alexander the Great's visit to Jerusalem may be, it is powerful metaphor. It commemorates and contemplates the introduction of Hellenism to Judea. Greeks and Jews were aware of each other before Alexander conquered the Persian empire, but the imposition of Hellenistic rule in Palestine that accompanied Alexander's conquest brought more lasting contact and the possibility for a more profound influence between these cultures. The relationship that developed was often friendly, sometimes violently strained, and always complex.

Josephus—or, better stated, his source—appropriately chose to describe the very inception of this relationship as the model for it. Alexander is the type of the Hellenistic ruler, the first and the best of them. His favor for and warm reception by the Jews symbolize the ideal interaction between the Jewish people and a foreign sovereign. Interaction with Hellenistic overlords and their Roman replacements would continue for many years after Alexander's lifetime, and the story of his visit to Jerusalem was perhaps in part *ex post facto* justification of the political reality of Hellenistic and Roman rule in Judea. Foreign kings did hold sway in Palestine, but submission to their authority could be explained and justified.

The *quid pro quo* of the Jewish exchange with Alexander is mythical assurance that the Jews are favored and protected by their God and that there is no shame in accepting the government of a great man who recognizes that Israel's God is greater still.[39] This concept was not only metaphor; it also illustrated genuine sentiment. Jewish fidelity to any ruler depended on that ruler's respect for their religion, as Antiochus IV Epiphanes discovered to his sorrow. When he threatened Jewish religious independence, the Jews jeopardized foreign control over Palestine—a situation that Herod the Great and his successors continued to confront, down to the time of Masada.[40]

Cecilia M. Peek is Instructor/Lecturer of Classics at Brigham Young University.

NOTES

[1]On Gaugamela and its aftermath, see Arrian, *Anabasis* 3.7-22; Diodorus Siculus, 17.54-73; Quintus Curtius, 4.9-5.13; Plutarch, *Alexander* 31-43; and Justin, *Epitome* 11.13-15. Although there had been conquests in abundance before this encounter and Darius himself escaped this one, Alexander considered Gaugamela decisive. After this battle, he adopted the official title of the ruler of the Persian empire—"king of kings." See Plutarch, *Alexander* 34.1.

Alexander and his Hellenistic successors have traditionally been described as intentionally initiating and effecting the infiltration of Hellenistic culture—the language, philosophy, art, and customs of Greece—into the non-Greek world. This view is sometimes still perpetuated in textbooks of Greek history. John B. Bury and Russell Meiggs, *A History of Greece to the Death of Alexander the Great* (New York: St. Martin's, 1980), 446, refers to "the expansion of Hellas and the diffusion of Hellenic civilization which destiny had chosen [Alexander] to accomplish." It is now widely recognized that there was more of cultural exchange than of infiltration. Two examples: the Seleucids depended largely on styles of governance put in place by their Achaemenid predecessors to manage their extensive realm. The Ptolemies eagerly adopted and adapted the ancient

Phaoronic traditions of Egypt to confirm their rule of that territory. On the Seleucids, see Susan Sherwin-White, "Seleucid Babylonia: A Case-Study for the Installation and Development of Greek Rule," in *Hellenism in the East,* ed. Amélie Kuhrt and Susan Sherwin-White (Berkeley and Los Angeles: University of California Press, 1987), 1–31. For the Ptolemies, see Dorothy Thompson, *Memphis under the Ptolemies* (Princeton: Princeton University Press, 1988), 106–54.

[2]The area was strategic for its proximity to Coele-Syria. See Peter Green, *From Alexander to Actium: The Historical Evolution of the Hellenistic Age* (Berkeley and Los Angeles: University of California Press, 1990), 497.

[3]Diodorus Siculus, 18.3; 19.59.2; 19.80–86; 19.93.4; 21.1.4; 39.6; Quintus Curtius, 10.10.2; Justin, *Epitome* 13.4.12; 31.1.1–2; Polybius, 16.18–19. For discussion of the Fifth Syrian War and its outcomes, see Frank W. Walbank, *A Historical Commentary on Polybius,* 3 vols. (Oxford: Oxford University Press, 1967), 2:523–25, 546–47.

[4]Epiphanes' baffling behavior has been sensibly reconsidered by Erich S. Gruen, "Hellenism and Persecution: Antiochus IV and the Jews," in *Hellenistic History and Culture,* ed. Peter Green (Berkeley and Los Angeles: University of California Press, 1993), 238–64. Epiphanes' Seleucid predecessors had been markedly supportive of Jewish traditions in Palestine. See Josephus, *Antiquities* 12.138–46; and 2 Maccabees 3:2–3 for Antiochus III and Seleucus IV. Hasmonean rule of Judea lasted approximately from 165 to 35 B.C.

[5]Greek *poleis* (city states) were eventually spread across Palestine, as noted by Gruen, "Hellenism and Persecution," 240, and 241, figure 38.

[6]Indeed, the politics, personal tastes, and architecture of King Herod the Great that are reflected at Masada are only a few of the evidences of Hellenistic influences in the world of the Jews leading up to the time of the New Testament. As Masada testifies, Greek influences in Palestine were strong, but they were neither universal nor unproblematical.

[7]Samuel K. Eddy, *The King Is Dead: Studies in the Near Eastern Resistance to Hellenism, 334–31 B.C.* (Lincoln: University of Nebraska Press, 1961), 183. Eddy rightly observes that Hellenistic Judaism is "virtually a separate field."

[8]Emil Schürer, *The History of the Jewish People in the Age of Jesus Christ (175 B.C.–A.D. 135),* ed. and rev. Geza Vermes and Fergus Millar, 2 vols. (Edinburgh: T. and T. Clark, 1973–79), 1:145–46.

[9]Fergus Millar, "Background to the Maccabaean Revolution: Reflections on Martin Hengel's *Judaism and Hellenism,*" *Journal of Jewish Studies* 29–30 (spring 1978): 1–21.

[10]Martin Hengel, *Judaism and Hellenism: Studies in Their Encounter in Palestine during the Early Hellenistic Period,* vols. 1–2 (Philadelphia: Fortress, 1974), 6–106. Hengel speaks of the "repudiation" of Hellenism after the Hasmonean rebellion.

[11]The anti-Gentile, anti-Antiochus bias of the author is obvious. Compare Jonathan Goldstein, "Jewish Acceptance and Rejection of Hellenism," in *Jewish and Christian Self-Definition,* ed. Ed P. Sanders, A. I. Baumgarten, and Alan Mendelson, 2 vols. (Philadelphia: Fortress, 1981), 2:75, where he discusses the Jewish "desire for closer association with the Greeks and for the establishment of a gymnasium."

[12]Jonathan Goldstein, *I Maccabees* (New York: Doubleday, 1976), 62–63.

[13]These buildings "were decorated with representations of various gods and . . . the students in these classrooms were expected, even compelled, to take part in pagan religious festivals"; moreover, in their physical exercises, "athletes performed in the nude," all of which "helps explain the negative attitude of traditional Jews toward the gymnasium." John T. Townsend, "Education (Greco-Roman)," in *The Anchor Bible Dictionary,* ed. David Noel Freedman, 6 vols. (New York: Doubleday, 1992), 2:313.

[14]What precisely is meant by "registering Antiochenes in Jerusalem" is debated. The prevailing views are summarized by Gruen:

> Scholars have interpreted it either as the installation of a Greek *politeuma* of Hellenized Jews within the city of Jerusalem or as a wholesale conversion of Jerusalem into a Greek *polis,* a new "Antioch-at-Jerusalem." It is hard to imagine just what would be meant by the latter. Certainly Jerusalem did not adopt a full panoply of Greek political institutions, nor did she abandon her traditional structure of governance. The "Antioch-at-Jerusalem" comprised, at most, a select body of individuals keen on the promotion of Hellenism. The discernible consequences lie in the sphere of culture rather than politics. (See Gruen, "Hellenism and Persecution," 243, with n. 13)

[15]Goldstein, "Jewish Acceptance," 81, mentions the books of Jubilees, Enoch, Daniel, and the Testament of Moses. The book of Jubilees expresses some misgivings about the Jewish relationship to Greeks but does not criticize the establishment of a gymnasium. Neither Enoch nor Daniel refer to Jason's reforms as much of an event. The Testament of Moses partially blames the sins of Israel for the persecution under Antiochus, but the sins described have nothing to do with participation in the gymnasium.

[16]2 Maccabees 4:13–14; Goldstein, "Jewish Acceptance," 79–80. Goldstein attributes more interest in these activities to Antiochus IV than the account seems to justify. He also surprisingly assumes that the reforms sponsored by Jason and approved by the Seleucid king "provided that Greek law rather than the Torah was to be followed in at least some aspects" (78, 79), but there is no good evidence for this conclusion, and it is, at best, guesswork. On priestly participation in the gymnasium, see also Gruen, "Hellenism and Persecution," 243.

[17]It became commonplace "for eastern writers to dispute (in Greek!) the claim that the Greeks with their gods and heroes had been civilizers of mankind." Arthur J. Droge, "The Interpretation of the History of Culture in Hellenistic-Jewish Historiography," *Society of Biblical Literature: Seminar Papers,* no. 23 (1984): 135–36, 139. Compare Phillip Sigal, "Manifestations of Hellenistic Historiography in Select Judaic Literature," *Society of Biblical Literature: Seminar Papers,* no. 23 (1984): 161–85.

[18]Carl R. Holladay, *Fragments from Hellenistic Jewish Authors,* vol. 1, *Texts and Translations,* no. 20 (Chico, Calif.: Scholars, 1983), 113. See also Droge, "Interpretation," 140.

[19]Holladay, *Fragments,* 205–25; Droge, "Interpretation," 154.

[20]Droge, "Interpretation," 151.

[21]Joseph M. Baumgarten, "Art in the Synagogue: Some Talmudic Views," *Judaism* 19 (spring 1970), 196-206, especially 197.

[22]Baumgarten, "Art in the Synagogue," 197. What precisely is to be inferred from such decoration is debated. Some argue that it was standardized ornamentation and that it says nothing about the theology of the artists or those who commissioned them. Others view it as evidence for "a syncretistic kind of Jewish mysticism."

[23]Josephus, *Antiquities* 11.317-20, 325-39. See also Victor Tcherikover, *Hellenistic Civilization and the Jews,* trans. S. Shimon Applebaum (Philadelphia: Jewish Publication Society of America, 1961), 41-42 and following; Hengel, *Judaism and Hellenism,* 6 and following; Schürer, *History of the Jewish People,* 1:138 n. 1.

[24]Shaye J. D. Cohen, in "Alexander the Great and Jaddus the High Priest according to Josephus," *Association for Jewish Studies Review* 7-8 (1982-83): 65-67, does not believe that Josephus originated the story, although he does credit him with the form it takes in *Antiquities.* He characterizes it finally as a Palestinian piece of the pre-Maccabean period, sharing "concerns and motifs" of "the literature of Palestine of the second half of the second century B.C.E." Adolphe Büchler, in "La relation de Josèphe concernant Alexandre le Grand," *Revue des études juives* 36 (1898): 1-26, and scholars who followed his lead concluded an Alexandrian anti-Samaritan origin for the Alexander stories as retold in Josephus. Josephus refers, in *Against Apion* 2.43, to a reference by a certain Hecataeus to benefactions granted by Alexander to the Jews. Was this historian perhaps the source for Josephus's account of Alexander's visit to Jerusalem as well?

[25]Green, *Alexander to Actium,* 499.

[26]The siege of Tyre spanned several months beginning in early 332 B.C.

[27]Josephus, *Antiquities* 11.317-320.

[28]Non-Jewish sources for this period of Alexander's life take him to Egypt almost immediately after he takes Gaza.

[29]Josephus, *Antiquities* 11.325-328.

[30]Josephus, *Antiquities* 11.329-331. The Greek verb used in 11.331 and translated "prostrated" is προσκύνησε; it describes an act of obeisance traditionally performed by subjects of the Great King of Persia when in his presence. It can likewise refer to a gesture of submission and humility toward a god.

[31]Such a question would have been anachronistic. While Alexander was destined to receive this form of homage from his Persian subjects, he had not by this time been acknowledged and therefore treated as the great king. For the introduction of *proskynesis* (prostration) at the court and the complexities attending it, see Arrian, *Anabasis* 4.12; Quintus Curtius, 8.5; Justin, *Epitome* 12.7; and Plutarch, *Alexander* 54.

[32]Josephus, *Antiquities* 11.334.

[33]Josephus, *Antiquities* 11.335.

[34]There would be nothing surprising, had Alexander actually visited Jerusalem, in his offering sacrifice to the local deity. He displayed similar respect to local religions and cult practices elsewhere. In Egypt, for example, he sacrificed to the sacred Apis bull and other gods in the city of Memphis. Arrian, *Anabasis* 3.1.2-3. See Thompson, *Memphis under the Ptolemies,* 106.

[35]This claim is, like the supposed query of Parmenion, anachronistic if the book of Daniel can, as most scholars agree, be dated to the 160s B.C. On the date of Daniel, see Louis F. Hartman and Alexander A. DiLella, *The Book of Daniel* (New York: Doubleday, 1978), 9–18.

[36]Josephus, *Antiquities* 11.335–39.

[37]Cohen, "Alexander the Great," 45, 49 n. 24, rightly characterizes the reception as an *adventus* story, of which many examples survive in ancient literature, especially from the Roman Empire. The parallels between Josephus's story of Alexander's arrival and the traditional *adventus* ceremony can readily be seen in Cohen's description of an *adventus*. See also Sabine MacCormack, "Change and Continuity in Late Antiquity: The Ceremony of *Adventus*," *Historia* 21 (1972): 721–52; and Fergus Millar, *The Emperor in the Roman World* (Ithaca: Cornell University Press, 1992), 31–40. The miraculous preservation of the people and their temple is called an "epiphany" story, and it too fits into a literary tradition.

[38]Cohen, "Alexander the Great," 54.

[39]A similar sentiment is presented in 3 Maccabees, wherein Jewish fidelity to the Ptolemaic ruler is affirmed and the warning issued that God will support only a ruler who favors His people.

[40]L. I. Levine, "Herod the Great," in *Anchor Bible Dictionary*, 3:167–68.

A Historical Sketch of Galilee

Andrew C. Skinner

By the first century A.D., much of Palestine, the area known to the Israelites as the "land of promise," was divided under the Romans into five areas of provincial or semiprovincial status: Galilee, Idumea, Judea, Perea, and Samaria. Only Judea was overwhelmingly Jewish, while the other provinces, although mostly Jewish, also supported mixed populations of Jews, Greeks, and Syrians. This ethnic background and many historical factors become significant when one seeks to understand the elements that contributed to Jewish rebellion and to Galilee as a seedbed of revolt, including the Jewish War against Rome.

Galilee in Old Testament Times

Galilee, the northernmost region of Palestine, encompassed villages and small towns made up mainly of Jewish inhabitants, as well as larger towns composed of Jews and many Gentiles, some of whom were remnants of peoples imported by the Assyrians after their conquest of the district around 732 B.C. Galilee's diverse ethnicity may be the reason Isaiah referred to "Galilee of the nations" as an area filled with a people who "walked in darkness," but who would see "a great light"—presumably referring to a future time when the region would be repopulated by Jews and the Messiah would arise from that re-Judaized area (Isa. 9:1-2).[1] The name "Galilee" (Hebrew *galil*) seems to be derived from Northwest Semitic languages (Canaanite or Hebrew) and may have meant something like "circuit," "circle," or "ring" and by extension, the "district" that surrounded the great inland sea, the Sea of Galilee.[2]

Evidence suggests that the initial appearance of the name in a text comes from Pharaoh Thutmose III's fifteenth-century B.C. town list. He was the great warrior-pharaoh of the New Kingdom, who first conquered Megiddo in northern Israel in 1468 B.C. and subsequently participated in some twenty campaigns in that region.[3]

Mention of Galilee occurs infrequently in the Hebrew Bible (Christian Old Testament) for at least two reasons. First, in Old Testament times the names of the Israelite tribes who had inherited a particular area of the promised land were used to reference that specific geographical locale more often than other designations. The territory of Galilee was divided between Asher, Issachar, Naphtali, and Zebulun. Second, because the Galilee region was so distant geographically from Jerusalem—the legitimate center of religious, economic, and literary activity in the land—Galilean events were not given great space in the Hebrew Bible.[4] However, the term *Galilee* as a proper name was familiar among scribes and writers relatively early, as indicated by six clear attestations in the Old Testament, including Isaiah 9:1 and other passages mentioning different cities "in the land of Galilee" (see 1 Kgs. 9:11; Josh. 20:7; 21:32; 2 Kgs. 15:29; and 1 Chr. 6:76).

By the close of the Old Testament period, the region of Galilee had long been associated with war and invading armies. The Jezreel Valley (usually included as part of Galilee, though sometimes regarded as simply the border between Samaria on the south and Galilee on the north) was the classic warpath and battlefield of empires in the ancient Near East. Famous non-Israelite warrior-kings who traversed the Jezreel Valley and other parts of Galilee include the Egyptians Amenhotep II, Thutmose III, Seti I, Rameses II, and Necho; the Assyrians Tiglath-pileser III, Shalmaneser V, Sargon II, and Sennacherib; and the Babylonian Nebuchadnezzar II. The list of later, postbiblical military leaders who fought in the area includes the Macedonian Alexander the Great, Seleucid Antiochus IV, Ptolemaic Cleopatra VII, and the Romans Pompey, Antony, Vespasian, and Titus.

Israel also turned Galilee into a battleground. Joshua's northern campaign took the conquering Israelites right through the heart of Galilee, as the tribes under Jehovah's direction fought major battles against the great Canaanite coalition (Josh. 11). Later,

Deborah and Barak won a stunning victory over Jabin, Sisera, and the Canaanites under the shadow of Mount Tabor (Judg. 4–5). Once the people of Israel had become settled in the region, Galilee was devastated by Benhadad of Damascus (1 Kgs. 15:20) and again by Hazael (2 Kgs. 12:18). It was reclaimed by King Jeroboam II of the Northern Kingdom of Israel around 826 B.C. (2 Kgs. 13:22).

The greatest blow leveled against the region of Galilee in preexilic Israelite times came in 733–732 B.C., when Tiglath-pileser III advanced on the area, struck it with full force, captured it, and turned it into an Assyrian province. According to Assyrian inscriptions and 2 Kings 15:29, all Israelite lands in Galilee and Transjordan were overrun, portions of the population deported, and numerous cities destroyed.[5]

Not a great deal is known about Galilee during the Assyrian and Persian periods that followed the final capture of Samaria and the deportation of thousands more Israelites by the successors of Tiglath-pileser III. At Megiddo structures manifesting clearly discernible Assyrian characteristics have been unearthed, indicating that those buildings were part of an administrative capital. In fact, in Assyrian documents the area was called the satrapy of Megiddo. Artifacts found at the village of Cana, north of Nazareth, have provided additional evidence of a strong Assyrian presence in Galilee. Through the Persian period, apparently Galilee and Samaria were a single district.[6]

Galilee in Hellenistic Times

Galilee came under the control of Alexander the Great following his conquest of Jerusalem in 332 B.C. Upon Alexander's death, his empire was carved up among his generals and their families. The Ptolemies inherited Egypt and Palestine, including Galilee, while the Seleucids received Syria and Mesopotamia. Royal agents of the Ptolemies traveled far and wide in search of commodities desired by Egypt. One such official was Zenon, whose personal archives, discovered at Philadelphia in the Fayum, tell of his travels to Galilee in 259–258 B.C. and of the competent rule of the Ptolemies in that region.[7]

However, the Ptolemaic and Seleucid factions constantly warred over control of Palestine during the third century B.C., and several of the campaigns were conducted in the Galilee region.[8] After a seventy-five-year period, events in upper Galilee arrived at a point of crisis in 198 B.C. At Panias (Banyas) near Dan, the area in the north near Caesarea Philippi of the New Testament, the Seleucid Greek rulers of Syria led by Antiochus III (the Great) soundly defeated the Ptolemaic Greek rulers of Egypt, who were led by Scopas. Domination of the entire region, including Galilee, passed to the intensely Hellenizing Greeks of Syria.[9] This set the stage for the conflict between Hellenism and Judaism that eventually resulted in a revolt of the Judean Jewish priestly family named the Hasmoneans (also known as Maccabees). The Hasmoneans, using the issue of Hellenization as a pretext, inaugurated a war against the Seleucids not only to free the Jews from Hellenistic influences by seizing power, but also to establish themselves over their previous rivals among the Jewish nobility. Under the leadership of the third son of the Hasmonean family, Judah Maccabee, the Jews began to throw off the shackles of Seleucid domination and rededicated their once-desecrated temple at Jerusalem in 165 B.C.

As the war proceeded, a Seleucid general named Bacchides was dispatched to Judea with an army to quell the revolt. On his march from Damascus, he passed through Galilee, wreaking vengeance on the Jewish citizens and the inhabitants of Arbela, located immediately west of the Sea of Galilee.[10] More than one hundred years later, the caves of Arbela would again become the site of great carnage, only this time at the hands of one of the Jews' own leaders—Herod the Great.

Several more costly battles, led by Judah Maccabee's brothers and successors, ultimately won independence for the Jews. One of the more famous of these campaigns occurred in western Galilee. It is significant not only because it cost the life of Jonathan Maccabee, leader of the revolt after Judah, but also because it shows that major Jewish resettlement had begun in Galilee by 143–42 B.C.[11]

After Jonathan's brother Simon was treacherously slain in 134 B.C., rule in Palestine devolved to Simon's son John Hyrcanus I. He set about to bring all of Palestine under Hasmonean Jewish control. Hyrcanus succeeded in connecting Galilee with Judea (thus further opening up Galilee to Jewish resettlement) by conquering an intermediate string of Hellenized cities that had prevented such a union. Hyrcanus's successors, Aristobulus and Alexander Janneus, completed the conquest of almost all of Palestine. Under Janneus, the Hasmonean (or Maccabean) state reached its apogee.[12]

Jewish independence came to an abrupt end when Pompey (later a member of Rome's first triumvirate) annexed Palestine to Syria in 63 B.C. In Judea, Perea, Idumea, and Galilee, the Romans continued the local Jewish administration then in place, under the jurisdiction of the Roman governor of Syria. The Samaritans became independent, and the Jezreel Valley (plain of Esdraelon as it is known in Greek) was detached from Galilee.[13]

Though the Romans reinstated Hyrcanus II as high priest in Jerusalem, under Hyrcanus much political influence was eventually gained by a man named Antipater. He was the son of a rich Idumean also named Antipater, who had been appointed *stratēgos* (a type of governor) by the Hasmoneans in the days of Alexander Janneus (103–76 B.C.). Apparently, the younger Antipater's political career began as governor of Idumea under the tutelage of his father. But his own power base was greatly strengthened when he aided Julius Caesar with additional troops during Caesar's occupation of Alexandria. In 52 B.C., Cassius captured Tarichaeae (southwest shore of the Sea of Galilee) and put Peitholaus to death for rallying partisans against Antipater. Cassius then enslaved thirty thousand Galileans.[14] By 47 B.C., Antipater was effectively in control of Judea, and he gave his sons Phasael and Herod (later Herod the Great) the tasks of governing Jerusalem and Galilee respectively.[15] Soon another vivid lesson "in what the consequences would be of opposing Roman rule" came in 43 B.C., when Judea was slow in paying tribute to Rome; Jewish city officials and villagers were sold into slavery.[16] Beginning his administrative career in Galilee, Herod eventually established a powerful monarchy that exercised tight control over the entire country until his death in 4 B.C.

Herod's Impact on Galilee

The name of Herod the Great and the district of Galilee are intricately intertwined. Virtually each time mention is made in the sources about the early life of the Idumean-born ruler, Galilee is also mentioned. When Herod was appointed governor (*stratēgos*)

of Galilee, he was twenty-five years old.[17] He immediately began to
establish his reputation as an aggressive ruler who would tolerate
no challenge to his authority. Inheriting a Galilee known for its
brigands and rebels who occupied numerous caves in the region,
Herod moved against them swiftly and ruthlessly. The first to be
captured was one Hezekiah, a Jewish bandit-chief operating between
Galilee and Syria and the father of Judas the Galilean, who later led a
revolt against the Roman-backed regime after Herod's death in 4 B.C.[18]

Herod's execution of Hezekiah and his rebel followers without due process, based solely on his own authority, was greatly
admired by the Syrians[19] but led to his arraignment before the Sanhedrin. Herod intimidated and manipulated the Jewish senate by
appearing with a heavily armed guard. Ultimately, he escaped to
Syria, was given added authority from the Roman governor of Syria,
and returned with great zeal to Judea to exact heavy taxes from the
Jews.[20] In 43 B.C., Herod's father was murdered by a Jewish oppo-
nent of the family. The following year found Herod again engaged
in military action in Galilee against Antigonus II, a rebellious Hasmonean leader who challenged the authority of the ruling Hasmonean Hyrcanus, whom Herod supported. After this time, Herod's
goal of imposed unification became all the more difficult due to
the opposition of some Galileans.

The Antigonid faction continued their rivalry with Hyrcanus
by enlisting the aid of Parthians to invade Judea and support their
cause. Herod escaped from the invaders and fled to Masada and
subsequently to Rome, where, on the recommendation of Marc
Antony, he was appointed by the Roman senate a client king for
Judea and surrounding territories, even though the area was still in
the hands of his rival, Antigonus. When he returned to consolidate
his rule in Palestine, he began his campaign in Galilee. From there
he proceeded to capture Joppa on the Mediterranean coast, continued on to Masada where he freed his family, and tried to besiege
Jerusalem but had to break off the attack when his Roman support
left for their winter camp on the coast.[21]

In the winter of 39–38 B.C., Herod went back to Galilee and
set out for Sepphoris in a driving snowstorm, only to find that
Antigonus's soldiers had abandoned the city. Herod then turned
towards the task of eliminating some of his other opponents at

the village of Arbela, which stood below the caves of a mountain precipice to the west. Josephus tells us Herod stormed their strongholds and "pursued them, with slaughter, to the Jordan and destroyed large numbers of them; the rest fled across the river and dispersed. Thus was Galilee purged of its terrors, save for the remnant still lurking in the caves, and their extirpation took some time."[22]

In a very famous incident, Herod completed the task of cleaning out the caves by devising a brilliant, but ruthless and gruesome strategy. He had his soldiers lowered in cages from atop the cliffs (rather than attacking from below), where they used grappling hooks to extract the enemy and then hurled them to their deaths on the valley floor far below.[23]

Josephus refers to these cave-dwelling resistance fighters as brigands or bandits. But the deaths of entire families who were holed up in the caves, including women and children, makes the episode seem excessively vicious and unrestrained, a point not irrelevant to the thoughts of the men, women, and children later at Masada. Josephus also describes a closely related subsequent action undertaken by Herod against certain rebels who had overwhelmed the contingent of troops Herod had left stationed in the area after the Arbela incident. This group of bandits fled to marshes and fortresses around Lake Huleh. Herod dealt with them and subsequently fined some nearby towns that were believed to have been supporting bandits.[24] Herod rounded out his Galilean campaign of 38 B.C. by quelling a revolt of Galileans who had attacked nobles and Herodian supporters and had drowned them in the Sea of Galilee.[25]

In 37 B.C., Herod gained de facto military power over the land when he captured his Hasmonean rival, Antigonus. He then destroyed the political power of the Sanhedrin by executing forty-five of its members who had supported this faction of the divided Hasmoneans. The heavy hand of Herod's control then came to Galilee as it did elsewhere in Palestine, but evidence indicates that Galilee appears to have become relatively stable after Herod's successes. In 20 B.C., Augustus Caesar came to Syria and met with Herod. As a result of this meeting, certain districts in the Huleh Valley (Paneas and Ulatha) were transferred to Herod's vast kingdom.

In the years that followed, Herod turned his attention to building programs. Therefore, it is surprising that there was little monumental Herodian construction in Galilee, considering that Herod's early career and reputation were made there. As pointed out, he might have called attention to his military prowess and his "glory days" in Galilee through the construction of monuments and buildings at noteworthy sites. He did not. Even Sepphoris, the capital of Galilee during the first century, benefited little, according to the literary and archeological records. Thus some have argued that the common view of Galilee as a hotbed of dissent requiring tight control through constant enforcement is contradicted by the fact that there is no evidence of great fortresses or major fortifications being built there.[26] For whatever reason, Judea and Samaria received almost all of Herod's attention and money, while Galilee received little or nothing and remained relatively impoverished.

Galilee in New Testament Times

As events immediately following the death of Herod demonstrate, underneath the surface Galilee was anything but calm. The picture provided by the New Testament fits well the notion of a whole class of socially and economically disadvantaged Galileans, disinherited and disenchanted, who had lost lands and livelihood under Herod's Roman-backed overlordship. Soon after Herod's burial, several popular outbreaks occurred in virtually every quarter of the land. These uprisings included demands for tax reductions, relief from economic and political oppression, and cries for religious reform.

The most significant revolt during that time of transition came in Galilee where one Judas, son of Hezekiah, raised an army to attack the royal arsenal at Sepphoris and sought to become king. There was almost certainly an element of personal vengeance in these actions, since years earlier (47 B.C.) Herod had first made a name for himself by launching a fierce attack on Hezekiah, who was waging a guerrilla war in the north of Galilee—part of Herod's early stewardship.[27] At this point, Varus, governor of Syria, entered Palestine with two powerful Roman legions and four regiments of cavalry to crush the revolt decisively. Galilee was the first to be subdued because many of its Greek inhabitants had been murdered by rebeling Jews.[28] Although the Romans treated friendly provinces benevolently, "they became unusually brutal" in putting down repeated rebellions and, if necessary, "maintained the *pax Romana* by terror."[29] After Varus's successful action, the emperor Augustus divided the country among Herod's sons; they were each to oversee much smaller districts than their father had ruled, and they "ruled" under the jurisdiction of Rome. Herod Antipas governed Galilee and Perea from 4 B.C. to A.D. 39.

One of the most famous residents of Galilee during this period was Jesus of Nazareth. He set a number of his parables in Galilean surroundings (for example, Matt. 20:1-15 and Mark 12:1-11). Some of the characters in the parables are large landowners. On the basis of evidence from the Mishnah and from archaeology, it has been argued that individual ownership of small tracts of land gave way at this time to ownership of large tracts of land by a wealthy few. Whole villages sometimes came to be owned by one person. Farmers and their sons became dayworkers.[30] This situation was nowhere more keenly felt than in Galilee, where agriculture was always the mainstay of existence. "The impoverishment of the farmers resulted in an enormous exodus from the country. Galilee was particularly affected by this because most of the villages were there."[31]

Galilee in New Testament times was apparently viewed by some as being filled with "unlearned" men who clashed with Jewish leaders in Jerusalem (Acts 4:13). This was another source of tension in Galilee and Judea that took its toll on the peace of the Jewish nation.

The volatile atmosphere of Galilee now intensified even more. It seems clear from the New Testament that during this period there were many debtors, many beggars, and numbers of slaves whose situation was dire. This seems to be verified by Josephus, who reports that during the time of the First Jewish Revolt (A.D. 67-70), Simon bar Gioras, a leader of one of the rebel factions, demanded the freeing of all Jewish slaves as part of his plan.[32]

Jewish resistance to Herodian and Roman rule is extremely complex, but it seems clear that Galilee was a critical focal point of this resistance from 4 B.C. to A.D. 66. In fact, Josephus traces the origins of the Zealot movement (or "Fourth Philosophy") in A.D. 6

to Saddok the Pharisee and Judas the Galilean—a man from Gamla. They called for armed revolt, saying that such heavy tax assessments amounted to slavery and that only God was master of the Jewish people.[33] It is possible that Jesus was tarred in some minds by the reputation of his native area.

After the death of Herod Agrippa I (Acts 12:20-23), Emperor Claudius made the whole of Palestine a Roman province and appointed Cuspius Fadus (A.D. 44-46) as governor. During the governorship of his successor, Tiberius Julius Alexander (46-48), the sons of Judas the Galilean were crucified.[34] In 46 they had emerged to initiate some program of resistance against Rome in Galilee and the Transjordan.[35]

In 52 a conflict erupted between Galileans and Samaritans when Galileans were murdered in Samaria while on their way to a festival in Jerusalem. When the Roman governor Cumanus failed to take action, Galilean instigators promoted a punitive expedition into Samaritan territory by appealing to the Zealot watchwords of "freedom from foreign control." Hostility broke out and spread to Jerusalem. It was resolved by Claudius.[36]

Cumanus was succeeded by Antonius Felix (52-60), Porcius Festus (60-62), Albinus (62-64), and Gessius Florus (64-66), under whom the first revolt against Rome began. An example of their venality is found in Acts 24:24-27, which recounts Felix's attempt to extort a bribe from the Apostle Paul, who was under house arrest at Caesarea.

The Jewish War was sparked by the perceived injustices of Florus in Caesarea,[37] and soon hostilities were unleashed. By 66 the Sanhedrin had been invested with executive powers for the Jews, and they appointed Flavius Josephus as one of the commanders of Jewish troops in Galilee. His assignment was to fortify the cities in Galilee including Jotapata, Tarichaeae, Tiberius, Sepphoris, and Gischala. He reports that he was able to mobilize one hundred thousand men and train them for battle.[38] This seems an exaggeration, but there is no doubt that Josephus performed a difficult task. It was made more so by opposition from another Galilean leader of a rebel faction, John of Gischala. Josephus also says that there was additional opposition in Galilee stemming from intense disagreement between the Jewish population living in the countryside and those in the larger towns. In his writings, the country folk are cast as far more nationalistic than the city dwellers.[39]

All of this played into the hands of the Roman general Vespasian, who was sent by Nero to crush the revolt and who advanced first on Galilee. Strategically, this was probably a wise move, since from the point of view of Galilean geography many of the important rebel areas were clustered in Galilee, especially upper Galilee.

> If we look at Upper Galilee as an excellent area of refuge set apart by reasons of topography . . . then we can better understand why certain events took place there and not elsewhere. For example, it was in these rocky hills that Jesus the brigand chief was hired to wrest the Galilean command from Josephus; that John of Gischala plundered much of Galilee; that Varus sent troops from Ptolemais to subdue rebellious groups; that Cestius, governor of Syria, marched into the area.[40]

In the face of Vespasian's expected onslaught, the main part of Josephus's army fled to the fortress of Jotapata, where Josephus himself took personal charge of its defense. Vespasian laid siege to the fortress for forty-seven days, after which it fell into Roman hands through treachery. All the inhabitants were either killed or taken into slavery, and the city razed to the ground. With this victory, the Romans gained one of the most important strongholds in Galilee. Soon thereafter the Romans conquered Tarichaeae, Gamla, and Mount Tabor. By the end of 67, the Romans had the entire Galilee region under their control. Thus, the Jewish War that ended at Masada began in Galilee, where the dissatisfactions that led to the Jewish rebellion were more seriously exacerbated than in Judea itself. In light of the historical character of this region, it is not surprising that strong feelings, toward war on the one hand, but also for peace on the other hand, should emerge onto the world's stage from the land called Galilee.

Andrew C. Skinner is Associate Professor of Ancient Scripture at Brigham Young University.

NOTES

[1]For a fascinating discussion, see Bargil Pixner, *With Jesus through Galilee according to the Fifth Gospel* (Rosh Pina, Israel: Corazin, 1992), 16–17. Father Pixner, who has spent much of his career in Galilee, maintains that the Assyrian-dominated region of Galilee around Nazareth was repopulated sometime around 100 B.C. by a Davidic Jewish clan from Babylon and that the name Nazareth (which does not appear in the Old Testament, Josephus, or the Talmud) was derived from the Hebrew word for branch or offshoot, *netzer,* in fulfillment of Isaiah's messianic prophecy (Isa. 11:1).

[2]On the Northwest Semitic meaning, see Frances Brown, S. R. Driver, and C. A. Briggs, *A Hebrew and English Lexicon of the Old Testament* (Oxford: Clarendon, 1976), 165.

[3]On the name of Galilee in Thutmose's list, see Jan Jozef Simons, *Handbook for the Study of Egyptian Topographical Lists Relating to Western Asia* (Leiden: Brill, 1937), list I, no. 80. On Thutmose and his campaigns, see James B. Pritchard, ed., *Ancient Near Eastern Texts Relating to the Old Testament* (Princeton: Princeton University Press, 1969), 234–43.

[4]Rafael Frankel, "Galilee," in *The Anchor Bible Dictionary,* ed. David Noel Freedman, 6 vols. (New York: Doubleday, 1992), 2:879.

[5]Pritchard, *Ancient Near Eastern Texts,* 283. For the summary of the episode see John Bright, *A History of Israel,* 2d ed. (Philadelphia: Westminster, 1976), 273.

[6]Avraham Negev, ed., *The Archaeological Encyclopedia of the Holy Land,* 3d ed. (New York: Prentice Hall, 1990), 149.

[7]Yohanan Aharoni and Michael Avi-Yonah, *The Macmillan Bible Atlas,* rev. ed. (New York: Macmillan, 1977), map 177.

[8]Josephus, *Antiquities* 12.132.

[9]Josephus, *Antiquities* 12.133–46; Aharoni and Avi-Yonah, *Bible Atlas,* map 180.

[10]Josephus, *Antiquities* 12.420–22; Aharoni and Avi-Yonah, *Bible Atlas,* map 195.

[11]Aharoni and Avi-Yonah, *Bible Atlas,* map 205. For primary sources see 1 Maccabees 12:39–54; and Josephus, *Antiquities* 13.187–212.

[12]Menahem Stern, "Hasmoneans," in *Encyclopedia Judaica,* ed. Cecil Roth, 16 vols. (Jerusalem: Keter, 1972), 7:1456.

[13]Aharoni and Avi-Yonah, *Bible Atlas,* maps 214 and 216.

[14]Josephus, *Jewish Antiquities* 14.120; Josephus, *Jewish War* 1.180. See the discussion in Richard A. Horsley, *Jesus and the Spiral of Violence—Popular Jewish Resistance in Roman Palestine* (Minneapolis: Fortress, 1993), 43–58.

[15]Henk Jagersma, *A History of Israel from Alexander the Great to Bar Kochba* (Philadelphia: Fortress, 1986), 97, 99–100.

[16]Josephus, *Jewish War* 1.219–20; Horsley, *Spiral of Violence,* 43.

[17]Josephus, *Jewish War* 1.199-200; Josephus, *Jewish Antiquities* 14.143. The later specifies that Herod was fifteen years old, but this must be corrected since he died about age seventy. See Peter Richardson, *Herod: King of the Jews and Friend of the Romans* (Columbia: University of South Carolina Press, 1996), 108 n. 52.

[18]Josephus, *Jewish War* 1.204-6; Josephus, *Antiquities* 14.159-60.

[19]Josephus, *Jewish War* 1.205.

[20]Josephus, *Antiquities* 165-84.

[21]See the succinct summary in Aharoni and Avi-Yonah, *Bible Atlas,* map 219 and accompanying text.

[22]Josephus, *Jewish War* 1.307.

[23]Josephus, *Jewish War* 1.309-13; Josephus, *Antiquities* 14.421-30.

[24]Josephus, *Jewish War* 1.314-16; Josephus, *Antiquities* 14.431-33.

[25]Josephus, *Jewish War* 1.326; Josephus, *Antiquities* 14.450.

[26]Richardson, *Herod,* 175.

[27]Josephus, *Antiquities* 14.159.

[28]Josephus, *Antiquities* 17.286-98; Josephus, *Jewish War* 2.66-79.

[29]Horsley, *Spiral of Violence,* 43.

[30]Jagersma, *History of Israel,* 119.

[31]Jagersma, *History of Israel,* 120.

[32]Josephus, *Jewish War* 4.508.

[33]Josephus, *Antiquities* 18.4-5, 23; Josephus, *Jewish War* 2.433.

[34]Josephus, *Antiquities* 20.102.

[35]Rhoads, *Israel in Revolution,* 57.

[36]Josephus, *Antiquities* 20.118; Josephus, *Jewish War* 2.232.

[37]Josephus, *Jewish War* 2.285-92.

[38]Josephus, *Jewish War* 2.572-75.

[39]Jagersma, *History of Israel,* 141.

[40]Eric M. Meyers and James F. Strange, *Archaeology, the Rabbis, and Early Christianity* (Nashville: Abingdon, 1981), 40.

Masada and Life in First-Century Judea

Revolutionaries in the First Century

Kent P. Jackson

Zealots, terrorists, freedom-fighters, bandits, revolutionaries—who were those people whose zeal for religion, for power, or for freedom motivated them to take on the Roman Empire, the greatest force in the ancient world, and believe that they could win? Because the books of Flavius Josephus are the only source for most of our understanding of the participants in the First Jewish Revolt, we are necessarily dependent on Josephus for the answers to this question.[1] His writings will be our guide as we examine the groups and individuals involved in the Jewish rebellion.[2]

In some popular literature today, all the revolutionaries who participated in the rebellion and war against the Romans are lumped together under the title *Zealots.* Although this use of the term *Zealots* is widespread, it is an erroneous identification. Josephus discusses five distinct groups of revolutionaries and applies the name *Zealots* to only one of them.[3] From his writings, we can see that each of the five groups had independent origins, objectives, and histories. In some instances, they shared common beliefs and even worked together. But more often they are described as independent and motivated by different goals. They were frequently at odds—and even at war—with each other. The five groups were the Sicarii, the Zealots, John of Gischala and his followers, the Idumean militia, and Simon bar Giora and his followers.

The revolt against Rome broke out in the summer of A.D. 66 when lower priests, in defiance of the high priests, ceased the sacrifices that had been offered at the temple in behalf of the Roman emperor.[4] A civil war erupted in Jerusalem for control of the Jewish state. Those lower priests, joined by many from the disgruntled urban populace and others from the countryside, fought against the national leadership—the high priests and their confederates—who governed the land as clients of Rome. The rebels initially seized the temple and the lower city while the government remained in control of the upper city. Eventually, the rebels were able to remove the government from power and take control. Afterwards, they slaughtered the Roman garrison, even though they had promised the soldiers safe passage out of the city.[5]

In response to those overt acts of rebellion against Rome, the governor in Syria, Cestius Gallus, marched to Jerusalem with an army in October 66. After a short siege, he abandoned his design to retake the city. As he retreated, the rebels attacked his forces, driving them out of the country and seizing large quantities of weapons and supplies. This decisive victory seems to have been what the rebels needed to gain popular support for their cause. Most of the Jews, both in Jerusalem and throughout the country, now favored revolution and joined the effort. Even the high priests and the traditional leadership supported the rebellion. A new provisional government was established with the high priest, Ananus, at its head. The traditional rulers were once again in power, this time to guide the revolution against Rome.[6]

The Sicarii

Josephus, strongly critical of those who participated in the civil wars and the revolt against Rome, reports that the revolutionaries were involved in "every kind of wickedness"—to the point that no one could imagine a vice that they had not tried. "First to begin this lawlessness and this barbarity" were those who belonged to the group called the Sicarii.[7]

The Sicarii were led by a man named Menahem and other descendants of Judas of Galilee, who had incited rebellion against Rome in A.D. 6. They were motivated theologically by Judas's belief that Jews should acknowledge no overlord but God.[8] Putting that philosophy into practice, the Sicarii received their name from the *sica*, a dagger that they employed in the murder of fellow Jews—hence the name *Sicarii*, or "dagger-men."[9] In the fifties and sixties, these terrorists used assassination as a political tool to spread discontent against the Roman occupation and to incite the people to revolution.

In 66, near the time when the revolution against the high priest's government broke out, Menahem and his followers captured Masada from the Romans. They killed the small garrison of Roman troops there and took possession of the supplies and armaments that Herod, and later the Romans, had stockpiled.[10] Some of the Sicarii stole into Jerusalem and fought with the revolutionaries against the Jewish government, enabling the revolutionaries to prevail.[11] Menahem arrived in Jerusalem and for a time took control of the revolutionary efforts, waging war against wealthy Jews and continuing the work of political assassination. When Menahem entered the temple dressed in the clothing of a king, the other revolutionaries wanted no part of him, so they killed him. His followers were then driven out of Jerusalem and forced to retreat to their stronghold at Masada, where they stayed for the duration of the war.[12]

While the Sicarii were at Masada, they did not participate in the defense of Jerusalem or assist other Jews in the war against Rome. Josephus tells us that they instead raided and plundered

"A[nani]as the High Priest, ᶜAquavia his son." A probable reference to the Ananias who was son of Nedebaus and high priest in Jerusalem. Ananias was murdered by the Sicarii under Menahem when they took control of Jerusalem during the rebellion against Rome. This murder provided one of the motives behind the assassination of Menahem himself.

Jewish villages in the countryside, taking the spoils to Masada.[13] After Jerusalem had fallen and the war was over, the Roman clean-up operation brought the army of the procurator, Flavius Silva, to Masada. Masada was militarily insignificant, but it had been a continuing source of terrorist activity. In a siege, the stronghold fell. Some Sicarii had already fled to Alexandria, where they continued their terrorism, mostly in the form of the assassination of highly placed Jews who were friendly toward Rome. In due time, the Jews in Egypt were able to eradicate them.[14]

After its destruction by the Romans, Masada lay virtually untouched until the twentieth century. Excavations there in the 1960s revealed the remarkable palaces and auxiliary buildings of its Herodian period. They also revealed evidence of the occupation by the Sicarii, as well as of the Roman siege.[15] Sadly, however, Masada's history and the character of its inhabitants have been distorted since the late 1940s for modern political purposes. The terrorist assassins, who preyed on Jewish victims and who for the most part were feared and despised by their Jewish countrymen, were transformed into a national symbol of freedom. Fortunately, a clearer understanding of Masada and the Sicarii has prevailed and is becoming more widely known.[16]

The Zealots

Josephus is our source for the term *Zealot* in the context of the First Jewish Revolt. He uses the word in a few instances to mean "fanatic,"[17] but he does not apply it to a revolutionary group or individual revolutionaries until 68, midway through the revolt. At that point, a group named Zealots was organized to contend for power against the provisional government in Jerusalem.

Josephus tells us that a man named Eleazar bar Simon, a priest, gained popularity among the citizens of Jerusalem during the time of the provisional government. Claiming that the rulers were traitors who sought reconciliation with Rome, in the winter of 67–68 he lead a group of followers in a coup against the government and took control of the temple. This revolutionary group is the one that Josephus calls the Zealots.

The Zealots appear to have continued some of the aims of those who started the revolt in the summer of 66. Among their number were lower priests and revolutionaries from Jerusalem's lower classes. But most appear to have been from outside Jerusalem—refugees from Vespasian's conquests of the land and bandits from the countryside. The Zealot agenda was militantly religious and militantly nationalistic. It was also decidedly antiaristocratic. They chose their own high priest by lot to lead the state, a man whom Josephus characterizes as ignorant and totally unfit.[18]

From the temple, which served as their fortress, the Zealots preyed on their opponents in Jerusalem, imprisoning or killing many of the aristocracy and committing outrages against the people of the city, particularly those whom they suspected of antirevolutionary sympathies. In his disdain for extremists, Josephus tells us that the Zealots were zealous not for anything good, but instead "for all that was vile—vile beyond belief."[19] In their "utter lawlessness," "no one could equal the Zealots; . . . there was no crime in the records that they did not zealously reproduce."[20]

Before long the people of Jerusalem grew tired of the Zealots' atrocities and laid siege to the temple to oust them. But, with the help of a revolutionary army from Idumea, Eleazar and his followers were able to break the siege and conquer all of Jerusalem. The city was looted and thousands were killed, including Ananus, the high priest, and others of his government. In due time, the Idumeans could no longer abide the Zealot terror, so they withdrew from the city. The Zealots stayed in Jerusalem and continued the purge against their enemies.[21]

The Zealots were engaged in constant civil war while they were in Jerusalem, fighting against Simon bar Giora, the Idumean militia, and John of Gischala. Eventually, however, they were persuaded to fight under John's command.[22] As a result of this constant warfare and shifting loyalties, they gradually decreased in number. By the time of the Roman siege of Jerusalem, they were a fairly small group. Though they fought through the duration of the war against Rome, they did not play a major role. Josephus notes their final fate when the conquerors took Jerusalem: "Each of them found a fitting end, God sentencing them all to the penalty they deserved. Every torment mankind can endure fell upon them to the very end of their lives. . . . Yet it would be true to say that they suffered less misery than they had caused: to suffer what they deserved was impossible."[23]

John of Gischala

Josephus viewed John of Gischala as a rival, and thus our information about him must be viewed as containing some bias. Even so, John's motives and actions in Josephus's writings appear to be less extreme than those of either the Sicarii or the Zealots, although Josephus classifies him as worse. Unlike the Sicarii and the Zealots, John seems not to have been motivated by religious zeal. Instead, at least in Josephus's description, personal ambition seems to be what drove John. Still, it is clear that he was fiercely nationalistic and believed that God would vindicate the Jews' cause.[24]

John led a revolutionary bandit army in Galilee at the time Josephus was trying to consolidate his own position as commander of the Jewish forces there. When the provisional government in Jerusalem sided with Josephus, John withdrew to Gischala, his hometown, until the Romans took that city. John and his followers fled to Jerusalem, where they were welcomed as needed reinforcements. Soon they became embroiled in the politics of the city.[25]

John sided with the provisional government of the high priest Ananus. When the Zealots broke from the government and tried to take over the city, John professed outward loyalty to the government but secretly conspired with the Zealots to overthrow it. John and the Zealots conquered Jerusalem, and John's Galilean soldiers joined the Zealots in the killing and looting. When Simon bar Giora entered the city to remove John and his Zealot allies, John broke with the Zealots, defeated them in battle, and soon took control of them.[26]

During the siege of Jerusalem, the Zealots fought under John's command against the Romans. When the city fell, John was taken by Titus to Rome, where he was sentenced to imprisonment for life for his participation in the revolt.[27] Josephus's summation is that John, who had a "morbid craving for a fight,"[28] was more wicked than even the Sicarii and "subjected his country to countless woes."[29]

The Idumean Militia

Idumea was the territory south of Judea and west of the Dead Sea that included the southern half of the Judean Hills. Since the Babylonian exile, it had been inhabited by a combination of Edomites, Arabs, Jews, and others. Conquered by John Hyrcanus in 129 B.C., Idumea's non-Jewish population converted to Judaism, and the territory was added to the Hasmonean kingdom.[30] Beginning in A.D. 6, Idumea was part of the Roman province of Judea.[31]

By the time of the First Jewish Revolt, the Idumeans were thoroughly Judaized and zealous for the independence of the Jewish state. In Josephus's writings, they are characterized as fiercely nationalistic and ready to fight against any foe who promoted appeasement with Rome. That characteristic made them important contributors to the war effort, but it also made them susceptible to extremism.

In the winter of 68, the Zealots were confined in their temple fortress in Jerusalem and were under siege from the government and the populace of the city. They appealed to the Idumean militia for help by telling them that the high priests and the government were traitors who wanted to surrender Jerusalem to Rome. Believing that the Zealots were the true "champions of liberty,"[32] the Idumeans came to their assistance and liberated them.[33] "We Idumaeans will defend the House of God and fight for our common country," said one of their leaders, "firmly resisting both the enemy from without and the traitors within."[34] They then joined the Zealots in the looting and killing that followed their victory. Josephus tells us that it was the Idumeans who killed Ananus, the high priest.[35]

But the Idumeans soon became suspicious of the Zealots' objectives and disbelieved their claim that the high priests had intended to betray the city. So they abandoned the Zealots, liberated two thousand persons held in Zealot prisons, and left Jerusalem to ally themselves with Simon bar Giora.[36] Some of the Idumean militia remained in Jerusalem, first to become allies of John of Gischala and then to fight against him. Having come to Jerusalem to overthrow the high priests and the government, the Idumeans now joined them and invited Simon bar Giora into Jerusalem to remove the Zealots and John.[37] The Idumeans then allied themselves with Simon and fought under his command for the rest of the war.[38]

Simon bar Giora

As the social and economic order in Palestine began to unravel midway through the first century A.D., lawlessness became rampant and both the Romans and the Jewish central government began to lose control. Among other things, the fragmentation of society invited opportunists to gather followers and even to create small armies. Motivated more by personal ambition than by religious fervor, these militia groups were able to sustain themselves by acts of banditry and terrorism.[39]

Simon bar Giora was the leader of a militia group prior to the outbreak of the war. Josephus first mentions him as attacking the retreating army of Cestius Gallus and capturing large quantities of Roman supplies.[40] Simon became successful conquering the countryside and taking booty from the wealthy. When Ananus sent out an army to capture him and end his banditry, Simon fled to Masada and sought temporary refuge with the Sicarii there. After Ananus's death and the fall of the provisional government, Simon left Masada and continued his conquests. He soon gained control of other areas, including Idumea.[41]

Simon presented himself as a champion of the lower classes, attacking the rich and proclaiming "liberty for slaves and rewards for the free."[42] In his actions, some have seen messianic overtones.[43] As he gained territory and popularity, Simon attracted an ever-growing army of loyal followers, which now included freed slaves, the remnants of other bandit groups, and also "many respectable citizens who obeyed him like a king."[44] As upper-class persons fled from the Zealot terror, they flocked to Simon and sought his leadership to remove the Zealots and John of Gischala from their strongholds in Jerusalem. The Idumeans who had quit their alliance with the Zealots and left Jerusalem joined Simon and became a major part of his army from that point on. In the spring of 69, Idumeans still in the city, who were now at war against John and the Zealots, joined with the remnants of the provisional government and let Simon's forces into the city. There he was hailed as their "deliverer and protector" and "master of Jerusalem."[45]

Simon set about to eradicate John and his Zealot allies so he could rule the nation by himself and lead the revolt against Rome. The civil war that ensued involved armies with thousands of men fighting in city streets. It lasted more than a year and even continued after the Roman siege began.[46] Simon gained the upper hand and controlled most of Jerusalem, but he was never able to dislodge his enemies. The toll of this conflict was extremely heavy, with thousands of civilian casualties and the deliberate destruction of most of the supplies that had been laid in store to sustain the city during the Roman siege.[47] As usual, both sides in the conflict terrorized the civilian population.[48] Josephus reports, "The entire City was the battleground for these plotters and their disreputable followers, and between them the people were being torn to bits like a great carcase. Old men and women, overwhelmed by the miseries within [the city], prayed for the Romans to come, and looked forward to the war without, which would free them from the miseries within."[49]

As the Roman siege was underway, Simon and John belatedly suspended their civil war and fought to defend Jerusalem. Josephus characterizes Simon as a strong and decisive leader who ruled as a dictator. He commanded an army of fifteen thousand men, including ten thousand of his own troops and five thousand from the Idumean militia. John had six thousand of his own soldiers and over two thousand Zealot allies under his command.[50] When Jerusalem had fallen and the city was destroyed, Simon, dressed in white robes, came out from hiding and surrendered to the Romans.[51] Viewing him as the leader of the Jews, the conquerors took him to Rome as the chief trophy in Titus's triumph. After the celebration, he was executed.[52]

The Revolutionaries and the New Testament

Since Jesus and his earliest "zealous" followers lived in the generation that preceded the revolt against Rome, in order to avoid confusion it is appropriate to ask whether there are connections between them and the other revolutionary movements of the first century. The New Testament mentions a Galilean revolutionary named Judas (Acts 5:37), who presumably was the same who incited rebellion in A.D. 6 and whose descendants and followers founded the Sicarii. But nothing of what we have seen regarding the revolutionaries and their actions during the Jewish War bears any resemblance to the teachings or actions of Jesus and the early Christians as depicted in the New Testament.

Both Judaism and Early Christianity had an appreciation for those who demonstrate zeal for righteous causes. Old Testament figures such as Phinehas (Num. 25:11) and Elijah (1 Kgs. 19:9–10) served as models for later believers by being "zealous" (*qn'*) in God's cause. Thus it should not surprise us that Paul describes himself in his preconversion days as "exceedingly zealous of the traditions of my fathers" (*zēlōtēs;* Gal. 1:14) and "zealous toward God" (*zēlōtēs;* Acts 22:3). One of Jesus' twelve Apostles, named Simon, is surnamed *zēlōtēs,* "zealous," in Luke (Luke 6:15; also Acts 1:13). In Matthew and Mark, Simon is surnamed *ho Kananaîos,* "the Canaanite" in the KJV (Matt. 10:4; Mark 3:18). The word *Kananaîos* actually transliterates the original Aramaic term *qan'ānā',* "zealous."[53] The text gives us no indication as to why Simon was called "zealous," and there is no reason to believe that it had anything to do with revolutionary things, especially given the New Testament doctrine of submission to civil authority (see Luke 20:22–25; and Rom. 13:1–7). More likely, "zealous" characterizes his commitment to his calling as a servant of Christ.[54]

Kent P. Jackson is Professor of Ancient Scripture at Brigham Young University.

NOTES

[1]Josephus's account of the First Jewish Revolt, including the events that led to it, is found in three sources: *Jewish Antiquities, The Jewish War,* and *Life of Josephus.* An accessible English translation of *The Jewish War* is G. A. Williamson, trans., *The Jewish War* (Harmondsworth, England: Penguin, 1980). English translations in this article will be from Williamson.

[2]Josephus's work is of indispensable value for our knowledge of the war and of those involved in it. Yet most historians today recognize that his writing was not without bias and self-interest. He was a participant in the war and thus was contemporary with the events he describes and in several instances knew personally (and had strong feelings about) the principal characters. Since what we know about those persons comes from Josephus, ours is undoubtedly an incomplete

view of them. Two recent studies that have dealt responsibly with the historiographic issues are David M. Rhoads, *Israel in Revolution: 6-74 C.E.: A Political History Based on the Writings of Josephus* (Philadelphia: Fortress, 1976); and Richard A. Horsley and John S. Hanson, *Bandits, Prophets, and Messiahs: Popular Movements at the Time of Jesus* (San Francisco: Harper Collins, 1985).

[3]See Morton Smith, "Zealots and Sicarii: Their Origins and Relations," *Harvard Theological Review* 64 , no. 1 (1971): 1-19; and Marc Borg, "The Currency of the Term 'Zealot,'" *Journal of Theological Studies* 22, no. 2 (1971): 504-12.

[4]Those sacrifices had been instituted in the days of Augustus and Tiberius as a compromise in lieu of sacrifices *to* the deified emperor that were offered elsewhere in the Roman world. See Josephus, *Jewish War* 2.197.

[5]Josephus, *Jewish War* 2.417-56.

[6]Josephus, *Jewish War* 2.499-565.

[7]Josephus, *Jewish War* 7.259-62; Williamson, *Jewish War,* 380-81.

[8]Josephus, *Jewish War* 2.118.

[9]Josephus, *Antiquities* 20.186.

[10]Josephus, *Jewish War* 2.408-9.

[11]Josephus, *Jewish War* 2.425-32.

[12]Josephus, *Jewish War* 2.433-48. For more on Menahem's messianic aspirations, see Richard A. Horsley, "Menahem in Jerusalem: A Brief Messianic Episode among the Sicarii—Not 'Zealot Messianism,'" *Novum Testamentum* 27, no. 4 (1985): 334-48.

[13]Josephus, *Jewish War* 4.399-405.

[14]Josephus, *Jewish War* 7.407-19. For Sicarii terrorism in general, see Richard A. Horsley, "The Sicarii: Ancient Jewish 'Terrorists,'" *Journal of Religion* 59, no. 4 (1979): 435-58.

[15]Yigael Yadin, *Masada: Herod's Fortress and the Zealots' Last Stand* (New York: Random House, 1966).

[16]For example, Nachman Ben-Yehuda, *The Masada Myth: Collective Memory and Mythmaking in Israel* (Madison: University of Wisconsin Press, 1995).

[17]For example, Josephus, *Jewish War* 2.444, 564.

[18]Josephus, *Jewish War* 4.155; see also Josephus, *Jewish War,* 4.130-61.

[19]Josephus, *Jewish War* 4.161; Williamson, *Jewish War,* 236.

[20]Josephus, *Jewish War* 7.268-70; Williamson, *Jewish War,* 381.

[21]Josephus, *Jewish War* 4.193-235, 283-365.

[22]Josephus, *Jewish War* 4.577-84.

[23]Josephus, *Jewish War* 7.271-72; Williamson, *Jewish War,* 381. Horsley provides a detailed overview of the Zealots in Richard A. Horsley, "The Zealots: Their Origin, Relationships, and Importance in the Jewish Revolt," *Novum Testamentum* 28, no. 2 (1986): 159-92.

[24]Josephus, *Jewish War* 6.99.

[25]Josephus, *Life* 43-194, 304-8; Josephus, *Jewish War* 4.84-120.

[26]Josephus, *Jewish War* 4.121-28, 208-32, 389-97; 5.98-105.

[27]Josephus, *Jewish War* 5.278-79, 439-41; 6.15-110, 432-34.

[28]Josephus, *Jewish War* 6.95.

[29]Josephus, *Jewish War* 7.263. Josephus accuses John of various sacrilegious acts. Josephus, *Jewish War* 7.264. See Rhoads, *Israel in Revolution,* 134, and the references cited there.

[30]Josephus, *Antiquities* 13.257-58, 395-96.

[31]Josephus, *Jewish War* 3.52-55.

[32]Josephus, *Jewish War* 4.272.

[33]Josephus, *Jewish War* 4.228-309.

[34]Josephus, *Jewish War* 4.281; Williamson, *Jewish War,* 246.

[35]Josephus, *Jewish War* 4.310-17, 326-44.

[36]Josephus, *Jewish War* 4.345-53.

[37]Josephus, *Jewish War* 4.566-76.

[38]For example, Josephus, *Jewish War* 6.92.

[39]See Horsley and Hanson, *Bandits, Prophets, and Messiahs,* 48-87.

[40]Josephus, *Jewish War* 2.521.

[41]Josephus, *Jewish War* 2.652-54; 4.503-37.

[42]Josephus, *Jewish War* 4.508; Williamson, *Jewish War,* 264. See Josephus, *Jewish War* 2.652; 5.439-40.

[43]See Horsley and Hanson, *Bandits, Prophets, and Messiahs,* 119-27.

[44]Josephus, *Jewish War* 4.509-10; Williamson, *Jewish War,* 264.

[45]Josephus, *Jewish War* 4.575, 577; Williamson, *Jewish War,* 268. See Josephus, *Jewish War,* 4.353, 566-76.

[46]Josephus, *Jewish War* 5.255.

[47]Josephus, *Jewish War* 5.21-26.

[48]Josephus, *Jewish War* 5.27-35, 251, 439-41; see Josephus, *Jewish War* 5.1-38.

[49]Josephus, *Jewish War* 5.27-28; Williamson, *Jewish War,* 278.

[50]Josephus, *Jewish War* 5.248-50.

[51]Josephus, *Jewish War* 7.28-29.

[52]Josephus, *Jewish War* 7.153-55.

[53]See Joseph A. Fitzmyer, *The Gospel according to Luke (I-IX),* Anchor Bible, ed. William Foxwell Albright and David Noel Freedman (Garden City, N.Y.: Doubleday, 1981), 619; and John Nolland, *Word Biblical Commentary, Volume 35A: Luke 1-9:20* (Dallas: Word Books, 1989), 271.

[54]For an overview of the issues relevant to Jesus and revolutionary movements, see Edwin Yamauchi, "Christians and the Jewish Revolts against Rome," *Fides et Historia* 23, no. 2 (1991): 11-30.

Legal and Social Perspectives on Robbers in First-Century Judea

John W. Welch

Robbers, bandits, zealots, Sicarii, and other groups operating outside of normal legal channels were prominent features on the political landscape in and around the Roman province of Judea in the first century. To an extent, the Jewish insurgents who died at Masada can be viewed as robbers or bandits within the ancient meaning of those terms. Knowing something about the prevailing laws concerning robbery and the typical characteristics of social banditry helps modern people to understand these "outlaws" and to imagine how typical Roman rulers or average Jewish citizens in that day probably viewed both the group of dissidents who died at Masada and others like them mentioned in the New Testament.

There are two viewpoints concerning such rebels. As robbers or bandits, they appear very different from one perspective than from the other. Government officials, who generally favor law and order, see robbers as an extremely negative element in society. Legally, they perceive robbers as violent, destructive criminals, whose very existence threatens the public order. Not surprisingly, Josephus, who wrote his histories to please his Roman patrons, presents a very negative view of antiestablishment operators. The average citizen in the city or village however, probably viewed these bands of fighters much more favorably. To the oppressed or disempowered, social bandits like Robin Hood can become sympathetic folk heroes who set out at all cost to right what they and many of their fellow citizens perceive to be fundamental wrongs. Without understanding both sides of this explosive social and political phenomenon, observers will never come to grips with the essence of the dynamics behind Masada and its world.

The Legal Establishment's View

Considerable evidence allows us to reconstruct a profile of what it meant to be a robber under most legal systems in the ancient world. Especially interesting is the distinction between being a thief and being a robber. In ancient times, a thief was a fairly innocuous person, primarily perceived as a local person who worked alone and stole in secret from his neighbor. He was dealt with judicially; he was tried and punished civilly (usually by monetary fines), most often by a court composed of his fellow townspeople. Robbers, on the other hand, were typically outsiders, brigands or highwaymen who attacked in groups with open and deadly force. When possible, robbers were dealt with militarily. In most instances, the army was responsible to rid the countryside of robbers, and such outlaws could be executed summarily without any legal recourse.

The legal concepts of theft and robbery in the ancient world have been analyzed most thoroughly by Bernard S. Jackson.[1] The following summary draws largely on his findings, supplemented with the studies of others.[2] Jackson recognizes, of course, that legal terms in the ancient world are not defined precisely, and thus one must "resort to etymology and semantics,"[3] together with social context and historical data, to detect the ancient meanings of such words. From that evidence, the following characteristics and legal treatment of robbers in the ancient world can be identified.

In Hebrew, the terms *gazal* (to rob) and *gazlan* (robber) normally mean taking property openly and blatantly, while the words *ganab* (to steal) and *gannab* (thief) usually connote stealing in secret.[4] Similarly, the Greek term *kleptes* "is used to describe a stealthy person who, without violence, deprives another person of his property," whereas by contrast, "in the Old Testament and Apocrypha, a λῃστής [*lēstēs*] is always a brigand, a marauder, a member of a gang whose activity takes place out of doors. He belongs to a troop that attacks caravans or settlements with weapons and robs them of their goods."[5] According to Jackson, this distinction between secret and open taking became a "firmly distinguished" and "clearly established" point of law in rabbinic Judaism in the first and second centuries A.D.[6]

A gazlan is typically an outsider, whereas a gannab is an insider who belongs to and lives within the same community as his victim.[7] The terminology might change from culture to culture, but ancient languages regularly used two different words to convey the persistent social and legal distinction between neighborhood thieves and outside bands of robbers.[8]

Robbers normally acted with force and violence, while thieves were usually unseen and did not harm their victims.[9] Indeed, robbery was "usually committed by a group"; the Hebrew word *gedud*, meaning "bandit" (literally, "band"), conveys the collective character of these groups.[10] In early Roman law, the use of a gang was vital to the definition of brigandage.[11] The laws of some peoples even provided numerical tests for distinguishing thieves (acting alone or in very small groups) from robbers (working in a group large enough to be considered a band).[12]

Some of these groups were organized as "professionals," with recognized leaders and rules of the pack. Achilles Tatius describes one very large militant band with a leader called "king."[13] Where the men in these bands had come from is not often clear, but Lutz speculates they were dissidents, foreigners, descendants of foreign mercenaries, and social outcasts—groups begotten especially by "political, economic, and social conditions [that] made for a distinct class of human dross."[14]

Robbers bound themselves together with oaths and clothed themselves with religious ritual. "The robbers lived under their own code, sanctioned by their own religious views and practices. They had their own priests."[15] Josephus reports that one band had an oath that they all swore.[16] According to Dio Cassius, another band, which under the leadership of the priest Isidorus nearly threw all of Egypt into revolt in A.D. 172–73, sacrificed the companion of a Roman centurion and "swore an oath over his entrails and then devoured them."[17] It is said that they would sacrifice and eat these victims to purify their camp.[18] Still, Josephus says these brigands were not above robbing from one another.[19] Diodorus takes plundering to be a full-time occupation for robbers.[20]

An important obligation of these robbers was to keep secret their identity and also the whereabouts of their hideout. Their camps were usually located in the mountains,[21] where, according to Josephus, the brigands whom Herod conquered lived in caves with their families.[22] Josephus gives a graphic account of the caves opening onto mountain precipices.[23]

The mode of operation of these robbers often involved swooping down out of their mountain roosts in raids on villages.[24] On occasion, however, they could also work within large cities. For example, in Jerusalem during the time of Felix (around A.D. 51), bandits committed a wave of murders, one of Jonathan the High Priest, in broad daylight. The Sicarii, one of the most notorious bands, would mingle among the crowds at festival times, carrying daggers and stabbing their enemies, after which they would join in the cries of indignation and alarm.[25] One robber butchered his seven sons and wife and then committed suicide before the eyes of Herod.[26] Josephus gives the following account of the operations of several of these groups, including Sicarii based at Masada in A.D. 67:

> These assassins, eluding under cover of night those who might have obstructed them, made a raiding descent upon a small town called Engaddi. Those of the inhabitants who were capable of resistance were, before they could seize their arms and assemble, dispersed and driven out of the town; those unable to fly, women and children numbering upwards of seven hundred, were massacred. They then rifled the houses, seized the ripest of the crops, and carried off their spoil to Masada. They made similar raids on all the villages around the fortress, and laid waste the whole district, being joined daily by numerous dissolute recruits from every quarter. Throughout the other parts of Judaea, moreover, the predatory bands, hitherto quiescent, now began to bestir themselves. And as in the body when inflammation attacks the principal member all the members catch the infection, so the sedition and disorder in the capital gave the scoundrels in the country free licence to plunder; and each gang after pillaging their own village made off into the wilderness. Then joining forces and swearing mutual allegiance, they would proceed by companies—smaller than an army but larger than a mere band of robbers—to fall upon temples and cities. The unfortunate victims of their attacks suffered the miseries of captives of war, but were deprived of the chance of retaliation, because their foes in robber fashion at once decamped with their prey.[27]

Robbers would take any action possible to harass the highways or weaken the local government.[28] Indeed, the robber bands in Egypt described by Lutz were always on the verge of "immediately flaring up again whenever the government showed the least signs of political or economic weakness."[29] Josephus expressly correlated the rise of robbers with "sedition and disorder in the capital."[30] Thus the action of these robbers was often political in nature,[31] and it was common for robbers to claim or dispute the throne.[32]

Robbers' raids sometimes involved large-scale destruction;[33] other times they attacked solely to restock their supplies or supplement their meager income off the land.[34] The military strength of some of these groups cannot be doubted: one nearly captured the city of Alexandria from the Romans.[35] They were more threatening than foreign invaders.[36]

In lieu of ransacking, robbers would often demand ransom or extort money from towns. One text suggests that robber leagues were so well established in Egypt that they became entitled by custom to demand ransom equal to one fourth of the property seized or threatened.[37] In addition, they might bribe local officials. Josephus accuses Albinus of taking kickbacks from brigands.[38]

The task of clearing the countryside of the menace of these robber bands was typically the responsibility of the local governmental authorities. Considerable pressure was exerted on local authorities if a robber was not caught. Indeed, many ancient kings left inscriptions boasting that they had successfully eradicated the robbers from their territory.[39] Under the law, a shepherd or carrier was liable for loss from theft but not for loss to robbers, against whom he was *de jure* considered powerless.[40]

If caught, a robber was not entitled to the protections of law and therefore could be dealt with by military force and martial law.[41] The severity of punishment seems to have corresponded directly with the seriousness of the problem robbers presented at a particular time and with the central government's ability to do something about them.[42] Robbers would be put to death,[43] "often executed summarily."[44] The mode of punishment, at least in one case, was crucifixion;[45] decapitation by the sword probably also occurred.[46]

The leaders of these robber bands attracted the attention of higher officials. Josephus reports that Herod put to death a robber-chief named Ezekias, who headed a "large horde,"[47] and records the arrest of another brigand-chief, Eleazar, who was sent to Rome for trial, even though he was not a Roman citizen.[48] Perhaps he was displayed as part of a triumph.

Because of their ominous threat to society, plagues of robbers were viewed in some circles as instruments of divine justice. The wicked were beset with the violent attacks of these brigands as a manifestation of God's judgment. For example, Hosea 7:1 reads: "When I would have healed Israel, then the iniquity of Ephraim was discovered . . . and the troop of robbers spoileth without."

From this brief summary of the legal view of robbery in the ancient eastern Mediterranean, the modern reader can begin to appreciate the intense concern and mortal terror that all ancient rulers, whether Roman or Jewish, undoubtedly felt in the face of any serious threat from robbers.

The Social Activist's View

While legal administrators and government authorities consistently and vehemently branded robbers as criminals and outlaws, not everyone in society would view them so negatively. Robin Hood episodes show that social banditry may be viewed positively in certain circles. Richard A. Horsley and others have shown that the phenomenon of social banditry often took the form of popular defiance against situations that many common people viewed as unjust.[49]

It oversimplifies matters, Horsley argues, to conclude that Josephus used the idea of banditry merely to pass a polemical moral judgment against Jewish rebels, and he demonstrates that Josephus presents "no consistent castigation" of these fighters in terms of banditry. Instead, on closer inspection, Josephus clearly presents the insurgents as a coalition of actual bandit groups and other leaders.[50]

Drawing on anthropological and sociohistorical studies, Horsley then paints a portrait of social banditry, noting that "the conditions which produce [banditry] are basically similar for most traditional (pre-industrial) agricultural societies."[51] In particular, "social banditry emerges from circumstances and incidents in which what is dictated by the state or the local rulers is felt to be unjust or intolerable."[52]

Banditry often arises in the countryside as a preemergent condition before the time when the poor reach "effective methods of social agitation."[53] Urban unrest and city mobs may also serve as a seedbed for urban banditry, as Donaldson has shown.[54] Factors typically contributing to the rise of banditry include administrative inefficiency, the presence of sharp social divisions, times of economic crises, famines, prolonged wars, and other such elements that "can bring banditry to epidemic proportions."[55]

Moreover, such bandits usually "enjoy the support of their village or of the people in general. They have no difficulty rejoining their community periodically or permanently."[56] Sometimes local people even protect these social bandits, who give the poor hope that they may finally overcome their oppressive situation.[57]

To the poor and the oppressed, social brigands are frequently heroes, functioning "as defenders and champions of the common people."[58] As a result of their grass-roots origins and support, social bandits often "share the basic values and religion of the peasant society from which they arise (and of which they remain a marginal part), and are in fact themselves quite devout, defenders of the faith as well as of (the) right."[59]

Obviously, these general conditions apply precisely to the rise of robbers and social bandits in the eastern Roman territories, as can be fully documented from many historical Roman sources.[60] This social typology fits precisely the Jewish rebels under Hezekiah and the fighters who made their last stand at Masada. Each of these factors is clearly present in connection with the phenomenon of robber-rebels in first-century Judea.

In Galilee during the decades just before the episode at Masada, widespread opposition to the institutional rulers was felt. Previous revolts had led to violence.[61] Events such as one in which a Roman soldier tore up and burned a copy of the sacred book of the law and another in which some Samaritans killed a Galilean on his way to Jerusalem encouraged ransacking and disorder.[62]

In the middle of the first century, prolonged famines made life very difficult for the Jewish common folk. The local villagers did not seek to stop or arrest the robbers but rather provided them supplies and cover. These "oppressive and ever tightening political and economic circumstances, further aggravated by such incidents, drove increasing numbers of the people into banditry."[63] The situation was exacerbated when Albinus adopted a policy of allowing imprisoned robbers to be ransomed by their relatives. Many were released from prison, and they became leaders of the eventual full revolt against the Romans.

Finally, these social brigands evidently shared the basic religious values of the common Jewish population. At one point in the revolt, they took control of the temple in Jerusalem, and they "looked to the central Jewish symbols and institutions . . . as their own . . . and as something to be defended against foreign incursions."[64]

Seen from the perspective of the local rank-and-file townspeople, the activities of these daring robbers take on a much different hue than when seen through the eyes of government officials and powerful administrators. Thus, the position of the militant band at Masada was precariously ambiguous in the world in which they lived.

Robbers in the New Testament

This information about ancient law and society sheds light not only on the gallant behavior of the Jewish rebels and on the determination of the Romans in capturing Masada at all costs, but also on several passages in the New Testament. The original biblical terminology consistently assumes that the reader understands the ancient legal concepts of theft and robbery, and the New Testament narratives interestingly reflect the ambiguity of first-century politics and society toward robbers.

Indeed, even though the King James translators used the words *theft* and *robbery* interchangeably, the Greek New Testament uses these separate terms accurately and meaningfully. For example, the English word *thieves* is rightly used in translating Matthew 6:19, "where thieves break through and steal." The Greek word rightly rendered as "thieves" is *kleptai*. Likewise, Judas is suitably described as a "thief" (*kleptes*) in John 12:6. But the translators settled on a weak rendition of Matthew 21:13, where Jesus is made to say, "Ye have made [my house] a den of thieves." The Greek word here is *lēston*, and it should have been translated "robbers." Thieves do not have dens, but robbers do. Nevertheless, in Matthew 21:13 Jesus is actually quoting from Jeremiah 7:11, which was rightly translated in the King James Version as "a den of robbers."

Robbers were obviously well known in New Testament times. Paul speaks of having journeyed "in perils of waters, in perils of robbers" (2 Cor. 11:26). In the parable of the Good Samaritan, Jesus makes use of this terrifying social problem to impress his Jewish audience. Nothing could be worse than to be attacked by bloodthirsty outlaws. Although the English translation reads, "A certain man went down from Jerusalem to Jericho, and fell among thieves" (Luke 10:30), it is evident that one does not fall among thieves out in the desert but among robbers. Indeed, the unfortunate traveler fell among robbers; the Greek word in this parable is *lēstais,* "robbers." The message of the parable becomes even more emphatic when one realizes that robbers were in the area. By stopping to care for the victim, a wealthy person made himself an easy and likely target for the robbers who were probably still lurking not far away.

Among the final words of Jesus, thieves and robbers also figure prominently. In his lament over Jerusalem, Jesus said, "If the goodman of the house had known in what watch the thief would come, he would have watched" (Matt. 24:43), and thus his disciples expected his return to occur "as a thief in the night" (1 Thes. 5:2; 2 Pet. 3:10); in each case the Greek word is *kleptes,* as one should expect. But when the soldiers came to arrest Jesus in the Garden of Gethsemane, he asked them "Are ye come out as against a thief?" (Matt. 26:55); here the word is *lēstēs.* Indeed, why would soldiers come out against an ordinary citizen. By apprehending Jesus in this way, his opponents have already effectively condemned him to be treated as a robber, whose legal rights then became inconsequential. Being so characterized, however, would not have been viewed as a negative in all circles of society, especially among Jesus' Galilean followers.

Finally, the King James translation says that Jesus was crucified between two "thieves" (Matthew 27:38). In actuality, we can now appreciate the fact that he was put to death between two robbers (*lēstai*), also called evil-doers (*kakourgoi,* Luke 23:33), who were being put to death as public spectacles. Indeed, the word *lēstēs* was correctly translated as "robber" in the part of the story that speaks of the prisoner who was released instead of Jesus: "Now Barabbas was a robber" (John 18:40). That one word alone speaks volumes about why a crowd of people could possibly have expressed their preference in favor of such a figure, a bandit, and consequently against Jesus.

John W. Welch is the Robert K. Thomas Professor of Law at Brigham Young University and Codirector of the Masada Exhibition Project.

NOTES

[1]Bernard S. Jackson, "Some Comparative Legal History: Robbery and Brigandage," *Georgia Journal of International and Comparative Law* 1, no. 1 (1970): 45-103; *Theft in Early Jewish Law* (Oxford: Clarendon, 1972); "Principles and Cases: The Theft Laws of Hammurabi," in *Essays in Jewish and Comparative Legal History,* ed. Jacob Neusner, vol. 10 of *Studies in Judaism in Late Antiquity* (Leiden: Brill, 1975), 64-74.

[2]For example, Henry F. Lutz, "The Alleged Robbers' Guild in Ancient Egypt," *University of California Publications in Semitic Philology* 10, no. 7 (1937): 231-42; and Richard A. Horsley with John S. Hanson, *Bandits, Prophets, and Messiahs: Popular Movements at the Time of Jesus* (Minneapolis: Winston, 1985; reprint, San Francisco: Harper and Row, 1985).

[3]Jackson, *Theft in Jewish Law,* 1.

[4]Jackson, *Theft in Jewish Law,* 1-5. See generally, G. Johannes Botterweck and Helmer Ringgren, eds., *Theological Dictionary of the Old Testament,* trans. John T. Willis, 7 vols. (Grand Rapids, Mich.: Eerdmans, 1974-1995), 2:456-58; 3:39-40. See also Francis Brown and others, *A Hebrew and English Lexicon of the Old Testament* (Oxford: Clarendon, 1952), 159-60, 170.

[5]George Wesley Buchanan, "Mark 11.15-19: Brigands in the Temple," *Hebrew Union College Annual* 30 (1959): 173.

[6]Jackson, *Theft in Jewish Law,* 20, 26. Jackson suggests that this development was influenced by the Greek concepts of *klope* (secret theft) and *lopodusia* (robbery by violence), described further in David Cohen, *Theft in Athenian Law* (Munich: Beck, 1983), 79-83.

[7]Jackson, "Robbery and Brigandage," 46; Jackson, *Theft in Jewish Law,* 6. Jacob Milgrom, taking issue with Jackson, has argued that Jackson's insider/outsider distinction between *ganav* and *gazlan* is not always demonstrable, while a violence/nonviolence distinction is. See Jacob Milgrom, "The Missing Thief in Leviticus 5:20ff.," *Revue internationale des droits de l'antiqûité* 22 (1975): 71-85, and "The Priestly Doctrine of Repentance," *Revue biblique* 82, no. 2 (1975): 186-205, esp. 188 discussing Leviticus 19:13 (rob a neighbor).

[8]The persistence of this distinction is seen in the fact that it has endured down to modern times in the Near East. In Arabic, *sirka* (theft; compare *saraqu* in the Code of Hammurabi 6–10, 14) occurs "wenn ein Beduine einen Stammesgenossen bestiehlt" (that is, if a Bedouin steals from a kinsman), whereas *ghazu* (robbery) is "wenn zwei Stämme in Feindschaft sind" (that is, if two tribes are hostile enemies) and one attacks the other to take their animals. Gustav Dalman, "Aus dem Rechtsleben und religiösen Leben der Beduinen," *Zeitschrift des deutschen Palästina-Vereins* 62 (1939): 53.

[9]R. Laird Harris, Gleason L. Archer Jr., and Bruce K. Waltke, eds., *Theological Wordbook of the Old Testament,* 2 vols. (Chicago: Moody, 1980), 1:150, 157–58, 168.

[10]Jackson, *Theft in Jewish Law,* 6, 9, 14, 33. Similarly, *shod, peshat, bazaz,* and *pariz.* Harris, *Theological Wordbook,* 1:150.

[11]Jackson, "Robbery and Brigandage," 45, 64; Jackson, *Theft in Jewish Law,* 6.

[12]For example, Ulpian required more than three or four to constitute a group of rioters. Anglo-Saxon law defined a band as ranging from seven to thirty-five. Jackson, "Robbery and Brigandage," 77, 90.

[13]Lutz, "Robbers' Guild," 233.

[14]Lutz, "Robbers' Guild," 241; see also 234, 236. In Rome, 76 B.C., domestic upheavals, according to Cicero, "resulted in armed bands of slaves running wild in the countryside," a condition leading to the edict of Lucullus against gangs of brigands (*hominibus coactis*). Jackson, "Robbery and Brigandage," 70.

[15]Lutz, "Robbers' Guild," 240.

[16]Josephus, *Jewish War* 4.408 (*synomnymenoi kata lochous*). The Greek here probably means more than simply that they "swore together" (*synomnymenoi*) but also that their oath was peculiar to or customary with their band (*kata lochous*).

[17]Dio Cassius, 72.12.1, cited in Lutz, "Robbers' Guild," 242. Other such oath swearing was accompanied by drinking the blood of slaughtered human victims; compare Lutz, "Robbers' Guild," 240 n. 48.

[18]Lutz, "Robbers' Guild," 240.

[19]Josephus, *Antiquities* 15.348. For a colorful analysis of the writings of Josephus in this area, see David M. Rhoads, *Israel in Revolution: 6–74 C.E.: A Political History Based on the Writings of Josephus* (Philadelphia: Fortress, 1976), esp. 159–62.

[20]Lutz, "Robbers' Guild," 239–41.

[21]Jackson, *Theft in Jewish Law,* 6–7.

[22]Josephus, *Jewish War* 1.311; Jackson, *Theft in Jewish Law,* 34, n. 7; see also Lutz, "Robbers' Guild," 233, commenting on the savagery of robbers.

[23]Josephus, *Jewish War* 1.309–16; Josephus, *Antiquities,* 14.421–22.

[24]For example, the raid of the town of En Gedi, Josephus, *Jewish War* 4.403 and following.

[25]Josephus, *Antiquities* 20.160–65; Josephus, *Jewish War* 2.254.

[26]Josephus, *Jewish War* 1.312.

[27]Josephus, *Jewish War* 4.402–9.

[28]Jackson, *Theft in Jewish Law,* 15.

[29]Lutz, "Robbers' Guild," 234.

[30]Josephus, *Jewish War* 4.406–7.

[31]For this reason, the Roman government and not the Sanhedrin kept jurisdiction over brigandage in Palestine. Jackson, *Theft in Jewish Law,* 251-60.

[32]Jackson, *Theft in Jewish Law,* 35, discusses the story told by Rabbi Meir in Tosefta Sanhedrin 9.7 and the characterization of pretenders to the throne as robbers in Roman rhetoric. See Ramsay MacMullen, "The Roman Concept of Robber-Pretender," *Revue internationale des droits de l'antiquite* 10 (1963): 221-25.

[33]Lutz, "Robbers' Guild ," 234.

[34]Jackson, *Theft in Jewish Law,* 14-15; Lutz, "Robbers' Guild," 234; 1 Samuel 25.

[35]Lutz, "Robbers' Guild," 242.

[36]Lutz, "Robbers' Guild," 238.

[37]Lutz, "Robbers' Guild," 232.

[38]Josephus, *Jewish War* 2.274.

[39]Jackson, *Theft in Jewish Law,* 15-16; Lutz, "Robbers' Guild," 235.

[40]Jackson, *Theft in Jewish Law,* 13-14, 39; Exodus 22:9, 11; Code of Hammurabi 103.

[41]Jackson, "Robbery and Brigandage," 63. "Against them the laws of war operated." John Michaelis, *Commentaries on the Laws of Moses,* trans. A. Smith (London: Rivington, 1814), iv, 280, cited in Jackson, *Theft in Jewish Law,* 16, see also 180, 251.

[42]Jackson, *Theft in Jewish Law,* 153.

[43]See, for example, Code of Hammurabi, section 22. In Egypt, the death penalty applied if a person could not prove that he had acquired his wealth in an honest livelihood. Lutz, "Robbers' Guild," 232. In early Roman law, the penalty for robbery was "the interdict of fire and water"; under Tiberius the penalty became deportation; and for ordinary *grassatores* (highwaymen) the punishment was sometimes death. Jackson, "Robbery and Brigandage," 79, 86.

[44]Jackson, *Theft in Jewish Law,* 38, 252, listing examples; Jackson, "Robbery and Brigandage," 86.

[45]Josephus, *Jewish War* 2.253; see also the two robbers (*kakourgoi,* Luke 23:32; *lēstai,* Matthew 27:38 and Mark 15:27) crucified with Jesus.

[46]See Abimelech's slaying of the Shechemite band in Judges 9:45 and Josephus, *Jewish War* 2.260. Later, Maimonides prescribes decapitation for murderers, Sanhedrin 15.12, and robbers are often associated with murderers. Compare Jackson, *Theft in Jewish Law,* 186.

[47]Josephus, *Jewish War* 1.204; Josephus, *Antiquities* 14.159, in Jackson, *Theft in Jewish Law,* 252.

[48]Josephus, *Jewish War* 2.253; Josephus, *Antiquities* 20.161, in Jackson, *Theft in Jewish Law,* 253-54.

[49]Richard A. Horsley, "Josephus and the Bandits," *Journal for the Study of Judaism* 10, no. 1 (1979): 37-63; Eric Hobsbawm, *Primitive Rebels: Studies in Archaic Forms of Social Movement in the Nineteenth and Twentieth Centuries* (1959; reprint, New York: Norton, 1965); Eric Hobsbawm, *Bandits* (New York: Delacorte, 1969); Anton Blok, "The Peasant and the Brigand: Social Banditry Reconsidered," *Comparative Studies in Society and History* 14, no. 4 (1972): 494-503, with Eric Hobsbawm, "Social Bandits: Reply," 503-5.

[50]Horsley, "Josephus and the Bandits," 38.

[51]Horsley, "Josephus and the Bandits," 43.

[52]Horsley, "Josephus and the Bandits," 43.

[53]Hobsbawm, *Primitive Rebels,* 23, quoted in Horsley, "Josephus and the Bandits," 44.

[54]T. L. Donaldson, "Rural Bandits, City Mobs, and the Zealots," *Journal for the Study of Judaism* 21, no. 1 (1990): 30-40.

[55]Horsley, "Josephus and the Bandits," 44.

[56]Horsley, "Josephus and the Bandits," 45.

[57]Hobsbawm, *Primitive Rebels,* 14.

[58]Horsley, "Josephus and the Bandits," 46; Hobsbawm, *Primitive Rebels,* 24.

[59]Horsley, "Josephus and the Bandits," 46.

[60]See the discussion in Horsley, "Josephus and the Bandits," 49-52.

[61]Josephus, *Jewish War* 1.304-13.

[62]Josephus, *Jewish War* 2.229.

[63]Horsley, "Josephus and the Bandits," 57.

[64]Horsley, "Josephus and the Bandits," 60.

"The Keys of the Kingdom": Keys from Masada

Marti Lu Allen

At least six keys were recovered at Masada from levels the excavators apparently associated with the occupation of the Sicarii.[1] Would a small group of people living close together and uniquely bound by a common cause feel the need for security from each other—even as they defended themselves on an isolated mesa in the middle of the desert? What do these keys tell us about the people who used them on Masada, and what significance do they hold for the modern observer? This chapter explores the types and functions of typical locking devices in the ancient Mediterranean world from 2000 B.C. down to Byzantine times and sets the cultural backdrop for their use at Masada.[2]

Latches and Bolts

Latches provided a simple means of locking in antiquity. Wood and metal latches were probably affixed to doors or crate lids in such a way that they could be rotated and then hooked to a stationary feature (door jamb, body of crate). A wood pivot door excavated at Karanis, Egypt, preserves a latch (see fig. 1). In its locked state, the door latch rested in an L-shaped bracket attached to the interior wall of the building. A person standing outside the building could unlatch the door by pulling on a string fed through a small hole in the door. Once the latch cleared the bracket, the door could be opened. The pull string was knotted at one end so that it could not be pulled all the way out.

Bolts afforded one of the earliest means of locking up in antiquity. Bolting a door, for example, entailed simply drawing a bolt

Fig. 1. Wood door with latch. From Kara-nis, Egypt, first century–fourth century A.D.

from a socket or channel in the threshold across a door, thereby preventing the door from being opened (see figs. 2, 3). Bolts were used singly or in pairs and sometimes in conjunction with door bars to block doors, thereby constituting a form of lock. Door bolts were often situated near the base of the door rather than being medially placed.

Wood Locks and Keys

The earliest locks in the Mediterranean world were made of wood and worked according to the law of gravity. When the wood lock was in an unlocked state, moveable pins (tumblers) stored inside it were held in suspension above the bolt. When the bolt was thrown, the tumblers liter-ally "tumbled" downward into corresponding receptacles within the bolt. Thus lodged within the bolt, the tumblers obstructed its withdrawal, providing an effective lock. Locking devices based on this principle go back as far as four thousand years in Egypt, whence they spread to other areas of North Africa. Such devices have continued in Egypt most likely without interruption right up to the present day. In the mid–nineteenth century, American Linius Yale "rediscovered" them and patented the design; the so-called Yale cylinder lock remains in popular use today.

Fig. 2. Threshold for double-bolted door. Karanis, Egypt, first century–fourth century A.D.

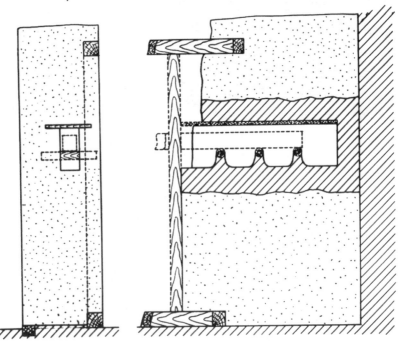

Fig. 3. Diagram of bolt and bolt channel. Door between house C50A and C51B at Karanis, Egypt, first century–fourth century A.D.

Ancient wood lock cases were of two principal types, the two-hand, in which two hands were required to engage and release the locking mechanism, and the one-hand. The number of hands required to operate a lock depended on whether or not the prongs of the key had to pass through the bolt in order to displace the tumblers. In the two-hand lock case (see fig. 4), the key displaced the tumblers without ever coming into contact with the bolt itself. Therefore, while one hand operated the key, a second was needed to withdraw the bolt. In the single-hand version (see fig. 5), the prongs of the key had to pass through the bolt in order to dislodge the tumblers. With the key thus engaged within the bolt, the same hand that had inserted the key could then use the key as a handle to withdraw the bolt. A palm pivot door from Karanis preserves a one-hand lock located near the door's base (see fig. 6). The lock is still fully functional, but since its key has not survived, the lock can be activated only by turning the entire door upside down.

A striking feature of the ancient wooden lock system was the "key hole." Considerable wrist action was required in order to maneuver the key into the lock channel, and the wrist needed room to perform these actions. Therefore, in the case of door locks, the key hole, that is, an aperture actually cut through the door, had to be large enough to accommodate not only the key, but the hand holding it (see figs. 4–6). A person standing outside a locked door would insert both hand and key through this hole in the door and then guide the key into the lock channel to disengage the tumblers.

By modern standards, ancient keys were large and awkward, particularly wooden ones. Actual wood keys from Karanis range between about six and twelve inches in length (see fig. 7). According to the evidence of ancient vase paintings depicting keys and on the surviving artifacts themselves, keys could be in excess of twenty inches in length. Generally equipped with carrying ropes, large keys were borne over the shoulder either singly or in bunches.

The secret to the ancient wooden lock lay in the number and pattern of its tumblers and tumbler holes. More complex tumbler systems required more particularized keys and theoretically afforded a greater degree of security. However, design potential in

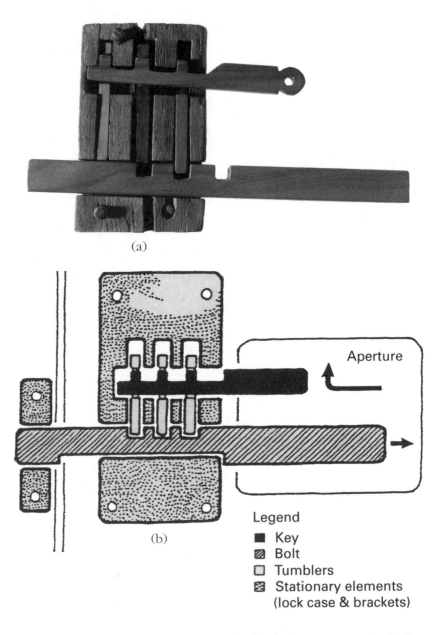

Fig. 4. (a) Two-hand wood lock. Only the lock case is original; the other parts have been reconstructed. **(b) Cross section of a two-hand lock.** To operate, (1) with one hand insert key through aperture in door, (2) engage tumblers with prongs of key to lift them from bolt, and (3) leaving the first hand in place, with the other hand withdraw bolt. Key cannot be removed while lock is unlocked.

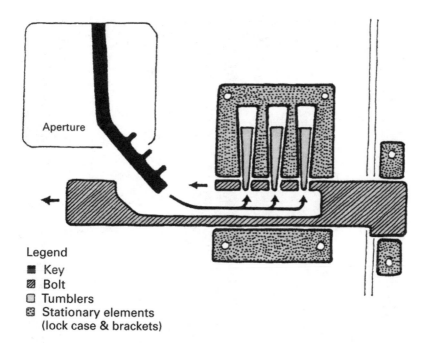

Fig. 5. Cross section of a single-hand wood lock. To operate, (1) insert key through aperture, (2) engage bolt with prongs of key (action will expel tumblers), and (3) use key (still engaged in bolt) to withdraw bolt from bracket. Key can then be removed.

wooden locks seems never to have been fully exploited. In theory, each tumbler or tumbler hole (and the corresponding prong on the key) could be uniquely shaped to make disengagement of the tumblers as difficult as possible. In fact, tumblers and tumbler holes are almost always uniform in shape, the prongs of any one wooden key always of equal size. Perhaps such precision was difficult to achieve in wood. Or, perhaps the principle that a little deterrent goes a long way prevailed in antiquity even more than it does today.

Metal Locks and Keys

Locks and keys made of metal offered a number of advantages over wooden locking devices. Notably, the mechanisms of metal locks could be smaller and stronger; their keys, smaller, stronger.

Fig. 6. **Door preserving single-hand lock.** From Karanis, Egypt, first century–fourth century A.D. The latch was placed quite low by modern standards. *Left:* exterior side. *Right:* interior side.

Yet, wooden locks and keys continued to be used side by side with their superior metal counterparts due at least in part to economic factors. Not only was metal more expensive than wood, but one also had to contract the services of artisans skilled in metallurgy and the forge to produce them. Wooden locks and keys, on the other hand, could be fashioned by common laborers out of materials readily available.

The use of metal in the construction of locks may well go as far back as the use of wood. As a rule, bronze and iron were used together in the construction of metal locks. The key itself and the

Fig. 7. **Wood keys.** From Karanis, Egypt, first century–fourth century A.D.

visible elements (those on the exterior) of the lock case were usually made of bronze, a durable and precious material that could be brought to a handsome polish. The internal mechanisms (bolt, tumbler system, casing, etc.) were made of less costly but highly corrosive iron. Thus, while many metal lock cases have survived from antiquity, they are usually too corroded to allow close analysis of the internal mechanisms.

On the basis of the evidence that has survived (mainly the keys alone), we know that metal locks operated on the same general principle as the wooden types described above and most likely developed directly out of these earlier versions. Metal locks were of two principal types, those operated by slide keys (fig. 8) and those operated by turn keys. The former were typical of Roman society and most likely continued in use through early Byzantine times. The latter were also used by the Romans but became most popular in Byzantine times.

Slide keys (see figs. 9, 10) were commonly shaped like an L and required an L-shaped key hole. The foot of the L, or the bit, as this extension is called, was equipped with raised teeth, which, when passed in a sliding motion through the key hole, displaced from a hidden bolt a series of pins (tumblers) held in position by a spring (see fig. 8). Once engaged, the key itself was used to move the bolt out of its seating, and it remained engaged as long as the

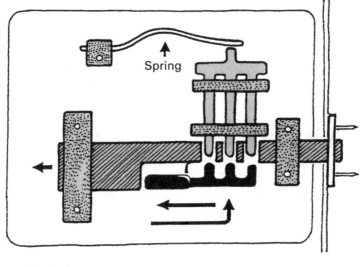

Legend
■ Key
▨ Bolt
▢ Tumblers
▩ Stationary elements
   (lock case & brackets)

Fig. 8. **Cross section of a slide-key-operated spring lock.** To operate, (1) insert key through L-shaped aperture in lock plate, (2) engage bolt with prongs of key, which will expel spring-guarded tumblers, and (3) use key (still engaged in bolt) to withdraw bolt from bracket. Key cannot be removed while lock is unlocked.

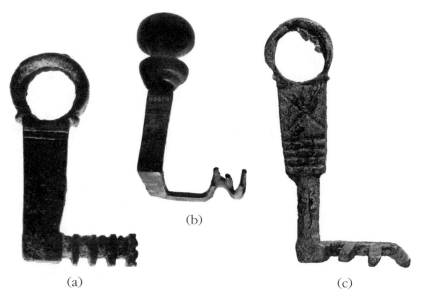

Fig. 9. **Bronze slide keys**. Roman period, first century–fourth century A.D. (a) from Seleucia-on-the-Tigris, Iraq; (b) from Egypt; and (c) from Rome (?), Italy.

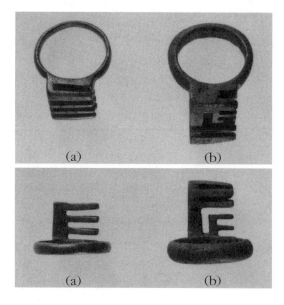

Fig. 10. **Slide keys from Masada**. As can be seen from the two views, both are of the finger-ring type, a design that enabled the owner to carry a key conveniently by wearing it as a ring.

bolt was in the unlocked position. Locks that worked on the slide-key principle were therefore not effective for locking doors. Rather, they were useful only for boxes, crates, cabinets, and other small furnishings. The remains of several wooden crates and boxes, some with their locks intact, were excavated at Karanis (see fig. 11).

How long slide keys continued in use is unknown. Slide keys are commonly found at Pompeii, the Roman town destroyed by the eruption of Mount Vesuvius in A.D. 79. They have been recovered in Roman contexts in many other parts of the empire, and it is likely that they did not die out until the early Byzantine period.

Turn keys are the ancient equivalent of skeleton keys (see fig. 12). They differ in appearance from slide keys in that the shaft, or barrel, is more rodlike, they typically have wider, panel-like bits, and these bits usually bear open recesses rather than solid projecting teeth. Typically, a turn key with a bit of the proper height and length was inserted through a vertical slit in the lock plate and rotated until it engaged the bolt. The bolt could then be lifted and released.

Both slide keys and turn keys had the capacity to employ either weighted or spring-guarded tumblers and even spring-triggered bolts. These features would have obviated the cumbersome wrist movements necessary to operate wooden locks and would have permitted smaller key holes. Sometimes the internal works of such locks were equipped with restraining features called wards that would obstruct the wrong key. Only a key with a correctly shaped channel or recess could clear the wards and successfully engage the lock. Ancient locksmiths also made frequent use of obstructions in or around the key holes that would prevent entrance of the wrong key. For example, a key hole might bear a notch that would admit only a key with a corresponding groove.

Facing page:

Fig. 11. Wood "trick" box. *Top:* the lid has been slid partially off. *Middle:* the secret compartment is visible. *Bottom:* the secret compartment has been opened and its contents, two beads, revealed. From Karanis, Egypt.

In most turn keys, however, the sole features of design that enabled the key to engage the bolt were the dimensions of the barrel and bit. The careful latticework that often characterized the panels of unwarded turn keys (see fig. 12) served no function save decoration. Thus, as was the case with skeleton keys, many turn keys would have been interchangeable. Although the turn key was by far the most popular type of key used in Byzantine times, their standard of security was generally inferior to the earlier slide keys preferred by the Romans. Indeed, security-minded people of Byzantine society deemed it necessary to use turn keys in conjunction with other security devices, such as seals and stamps. Being unique to each owner, seals and the impressions made by them were used to maintain the integrity of documents, vended products, and other property.

The Keys from Masada

In design, style, and type, the keys found at Masada are purely Roman, consistent with Roman design preference and with Roman locking standards of the first century. They may originally have been brought to the site by Herod or by the First Roman Garrison and then retained by the Sicarii to operate locks on the site. They are all made of bronze and all appear to be slide keys (see fig. 10). They were not door keys but, rather, would have been used to activate metal lock cases securing crates, boxes, or portable furnishings such as might have held precious documents, currency, or jewelry. The doorways at Masada, if they were secured at all, were most likely fitted with simple latching and bolting mechanisms or with one- or two-handed locks made of wood.

Keeping track of keys in an age before clothing was designed with pockets posed a challenge in antiquity. Three of the keys from Masada are finger-ring keys (see fig. 10): their design would have enabled the owners to wear them on their fingers. Sometimes keys were designed with a hinge, such that the bit could be folded over and cupped in the palm of the hand (see especially fig. 12c). No examples of this so-called swivel ring key were found at Masada.

Virtually all bronze keys in Roman and Byzantine times were designed with a ring at the head of the shaft or barrel to admit a

Fig. 12. Byzantine turn keys. Notice their similarity to skeleton keys. These keys also swivel, as can be seen in the view of (c). (a) The key chain and seal of "Basil."

carrying thong or chain (compare figs. 7, 9, 12). A fragmentary key from Masada still preserves both part of a leather thong and a chain.[3] Reference has already been made to the chore of carrying large wooden keys. Indeed, the keys controlled by one person could be so numerous as to require the services of a key bearer. The number of an individual's keys normally corresponded to the number of properties owned (houses, granaries, strong rooms, and so forth). Conversely, one's wealth was evident in the numbers of keys carried. Therefore, keys were a status symbol and sporting them in public, a statement of personal wealth.

The function of a key, inasmuch as it gives access to something of value that is worth guarding, is deliberate and symbolically profound. Keys have been used in legal, literary, and religious analogies since they were first invented. The reference to having the "key to a problem" goes back to the ancient Greeks.[4] In Greek mythology, Hecate held the key of Hades.[5] Since the time of the Twelve Tables,[6] giving or taking back the keys to the household storage room was a Roman form of divorce,[7] and the Latin phrase *claves tradere* meant to deliver up a household for possession or oversight.[8] In the Old Testament, Isaiah prophesied, "And the key of the house of David will I lay upon his shoulder; so he shall open, and none shall shut; and he shall shut, and none shall open" (Isa. 22:22; see also Rev. 3:7). In the New Testament, Christ gave his Apostle Peter the keys to the kingdom of heaven (Matt. 16:19), and in Luke 11:52, he speaks of "the key of knowledge." The book of Revelation speaks of "the keys of hell and of death" (Rev. 1:18) and "the key of the bottomless pit" (Rev. 9:1; 20:1). Since Byzantine times, the act of extending the "key to the [gates of the] city" has symbolized submission to authority. If the keys from Masada carry any symbolism for the contemplative reader, their use in metaphors of authority and the granting of access to enlightenment (or dread) may well be the most poignant images.

Marti Lu Allen is Associate Director of the Museum of Peoples and Cultures at Brigham Young University and Codirector of the Masada Exhibition Project.

NOTES

[1]*The Story of Masada* exhibition inventory numbers 93-629, 93-630, 93-611, 93-617, 93-616, and 81-2089. I am grateful to Ehud Netzer for photographs of some of these; see my fig. 10.

[2]See generally, T. K. Derry and Trevor I. Williams, *A Short History of Technology from the Earliest Times to A.D. 1900* (New York: Oxford University Press, 1961); W. M. Flinders Petrie, *Tools and Weapons: Illustrated by the Egyptian Collection in University College, London* (London: British School of Archaeology in Egypt, 1917); E. M. Husselman, *Karanis Excavations of the University of Michigan in Egypt, 1928–1935: Topography and Archaeology,* Kelsey Museum of Archaeology Studies 5 (Ann Arbor: University of Michigan Press, 1979); Albert Neuburger, *The Technical Arts and Sciences of the Ancients,* trans. Henry L. Brose (New York: Barnes and Noble, 1969); Charles Singer and others, eds., *A History of Technology,* vol. 2, *The Mediterranean Civilizations and the Middle Ages c. 700 B.C. to c. A.D. 1500* (Oxford: Clarendon, 1956); and Gary Vikan and John Nesbitt, *Security in Byzantium: Locking, Sealing, and Weighing* (Washington, D.C.: Dumbarton Oaks Center for Byzantine Studies, 1980).

[3]*Masada Exhibition* inventory number 93-629.

[4]Vett. Val. 179.4.

[5]*Oxford Classical Dictionary,* 3d ed. (New York : Oxford University Press, 1996), s.v. "Keys and Locks."

[6]The Romans' first written laws, drawn up in 451 B.C., were inscribed on twelve tablets and dealt with marriage customs, criminal punishments, property rights, and legal procedures.

[7]Cicero, *Orationes Philippicae in M. Antonium* 2, 28, 69.

[8]*Digesta, Libri Pandectarum* 18, 1, 74; 31, 77, 21.

The Virgins' Lamps: *Shine Beautiful!*

Marti Lu Allen

The light of Christ shines beautiful for all of us.
[Anonymous quote inscribed
on a Palestinian lamp of the fourth–fifth century A.D.]

In the ancient Mediterranean world, hand-sized lamps made of baked clay were used to light one's way after dark. The equivalent of the modern-day light bulb, clay lamps were also an essential part of the ancient household and are among the most common articles found during archaeological excavations (see figs. 1–9). Their nozzles held a burning wick fueled by oil, and they cast a dancing, flickering light like a candle or lantern. The essential parts of the lamp structure were a reservoir or cavity to hold the fuel, usually olive oil, and a wick rest or feature to anchor the wick, which could be a length of tightly twisted flax or other fiber. The reservoirs held sufficient oil to keep the lamp burning throughout an entire night, although the wick had to be shifted every few hours.[1]

The Bible makes many references to lamps, most frequently in association with offerings made at an altar and in connection with a golden candelabra.[2] They may not have been the earthen lamps in common usage in antiquity. In at least one instance, however, the Bible almost certainly refers to hand-sized clay lamps. Jesus relates the parable of the ten maidens who needed oil lamps to light their way to a midnight marriage.[3] Only five of the young girls witnessed the spectacle, as Jesus relates:

> Then shall the kingdom of heaven be likened unto ten virgins, which took their lamps, and went forth to meet the bridegroom. And five of

them were wise, and five were foolish. They that were foolish took
their lamps, and took no oil with them: But the wise took oil in their
vessels with their lamps. (KJV, Matthew 25:1-5)

What would these lamps carried by the five wise "virgins"
have looked like? Were they *beautiful?* Or were they ordinary,
everyday things? How would they have compared to lamps used
by other people in the Holy Land? Were similar lamps used at Masada? Did pagans, Christians, and Jews use the same kinds of lamps?

This article will enable the patient reader to ponder these
questions for him- or herself. It attempts to condense a very large
body of (sometimes esoteric) literature on the topic of lamps in
the Holy Land from about 2000 B.C. through the first century A.D.[4]
An examination of lamp-making techniques, shape, and decoration
will sharpen the eye for this mission. Reflecting upon the meanings of their decoration and how these relate to the beliefs of their
users will lighten the heart. Special attention will be accorded
lamps found at Masada, because some of them are on display in
The Story of Masada: Discoveries from the Excavations, and
because the contexts of their discovery often have much to teach
us. Indeed, in postulating a theory on what the virgins' lamps
looked like, the reader will have to exercise the same sort of inves-
tigative thinking that archaeologists do when faced with their complex heaps of dirt and ruins.

History of Technique, Shape, and Decoration
in Palestinian Lamps

The study of ancient Mediterranean lamps is a veritable disci-
pline unto itself. These ubiquitous artifacts are long-lived in the
archaeological record, and they experienced an intricate and complicated evolution in technique of manufacture, shape, and decoration. For these reasons, clay lamps can often be dated rather
closely, making them very useful to the archaeologist for dating
other things found with them. Chemical analyses of the clay fabric
by neutron activation analysis (NAA) aid specialists in determining
the sources of the clays used in lamp manufacture. This information can help identify the output of workshops and trace patterns
of distribution. The subject matter used in decorating the lamps,

moreover, sheds light on the beliefs and concerns of their users. Thus, lamps are a particularly worthy class of artifacts to examine in detail.

Technique and Shape. Ancient lamp makers used three principal techniques to make clay lamps, and all three are represented in the Palestinian repertoire. The makers could form lamps by hand, use a potter's wheel, or cast them in molds. The technique of manufacture greatly influenced the shape a vessel would take.

The earliest varieties of lamps were hand formed. These were not necessarily lamps by design but bowls adapted in a makeshift fashion to serve this function. Plain, hand-formed bowls with telltale wick burns on their rims have been recovered from contexts as early as the fourth and third millennia B.C.

Wheel-thrown lamps designed specifically for that function were made in Palestine by the late third millennium B.C. The so-called saucer lamp consists of a shallow wheel-thrown bowl, the rim of which was folded to form four corners that served as wick-slots (see fig. 1a). Lamps with just one folded corner became the most usual kind (see fig. 1b), a shape which persisted almost without change for nearly two thousand years in Palestine and indeed throughout the Mediterranean once the Phoenicians had colonized its coasts.

Beginning in the seventh century B.C., Greek lamps were imported to Palestine for the first time. These are technically different from the locally made saucer lamps, being bowl-shaped but with a separately made nozzle for the wick. Eventually the wheel was used to shape these lamps (see figs. 2a–c).

In the fifth and fourth centuries B.C., the Greek wheel-thrown lamp cornered the market in Palestine and even inspired local imitations. Yet, the old saucer lamp continued in use alongside it and elsewhere throughout the Persian period (587–333 B.C.). It finally died out at the end of the period but enjoyed a revival in the form of the so-called pinched lamp in the late Hellenistic repertoire of Palestine (second–first century B.C.).[5]

A fragment of a lamp from Masada dated to the late Hellenistic (Hasmonean) period or early in the reign of Herod represents this revived pinched type, although one has to be imaginative to recognize the type from the lamp's sole surviving fragment.[6] An

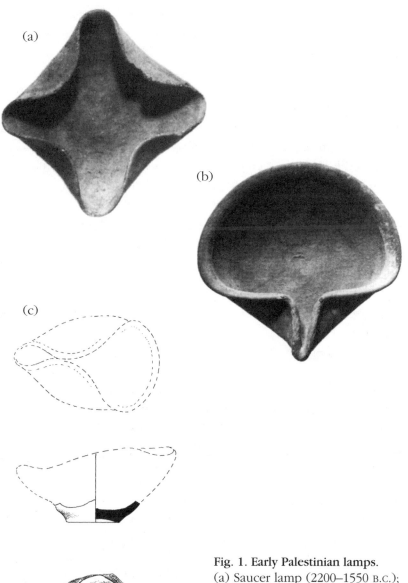

Fig. 1. Early Palestinian lamps.
(a) Saucer lamp (2200–1550 B.C.);
(b) saucer lamp (1550–1200 B.C.);
(c) Hellenistic pinched lamp (late 2nd century B.C.–early 1st century B.C.).

artist's reconstruction shows its folded lip and its bowl-like structure (see fig. 1c). It is smaller than the saucer lamps of earlier
times. According to the NAA results reported by Dan Barag and
Malka Hershkovitz,[7] the Masada pinched lamp is made of clay from
the area of Jerusalem. It is therefore a local imitation of the imported Hellenistic type.

The conquest of Persia in 333 B.C. by the Macedonian Greek
Alexander the Great brought substantial changes to Palestine and
the Near East. The great Persian empire was divided up into administrative centers that cultivated strong connections with Greek culture. In this Hellenized culture of the Greek East, the third technique
of lamp manufacture was first practiced—molding.

The craft of molding clay was an industry unto itself and required an expertise significantly different than that of wheel technology. To make a molded lamp, the artisan formed a two-part
mold off an original model or existing lamp or carved a negative
from scratch in a soft stone. One valve of the mold held the features of the top part of the lamp, which might include various decorations. The other valve was impressed or carved with plainer
features for the lower half.

From here lamp makers could easily mass-produce replicas.
The artisan pressed strips of clay into each of the two valves and
allowed them to dry to the leathery-hard state. While drying, the
clay would shrink, so that the impressions would easily come out
of the mold. The next step was to cut the wick hole and filling hole
into the top half of the impression and join the two halves along
their seams, using a solution of liquid clay or slip. The artisan used
a sharp tool to pare down the seam lines and to freshen or add
details, making each impression unique.

The lamp was then fired into permanence along with, poten-
tially, tens of mold duplicates. Since an existing lamp could serve
as the original from which new (clay or plaster) molds could
be made, artisans could easily copy any lamp that came on the
market—a plagiarism of sorts. And plagiarize they did—even at
the expense of producing dulled images as the mold generations
wore on. Many artisans began signing their wares or impressing
their "maker's mark" on the underside of the lamp, thus spreading their fame wherever the lamps were distributed.

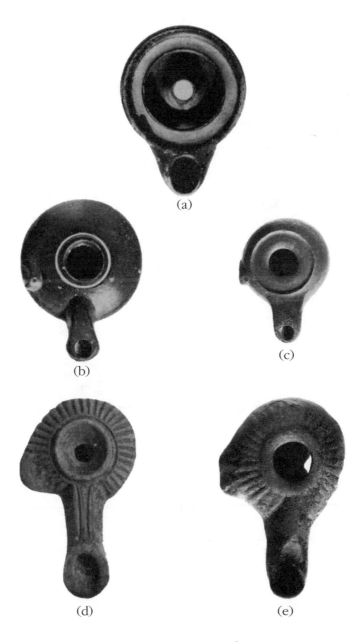

Fig. 2. Hellenistic lamps. (a) Wheel thrown (6th century B.C.); (b) wheel thrown (late 4th century B.C.–second quarter 3rd century B.C.); (c) wheel thrown (late 4th century B.C.–second quarter 3rd century B.C.); (d) molded (mid-2nd century B.C.–first half 1st century B.C.); (e) Palestinian copy of Hellenistic radial lamp, from Masada (late 2nd century B.C.–1st century B.C.).

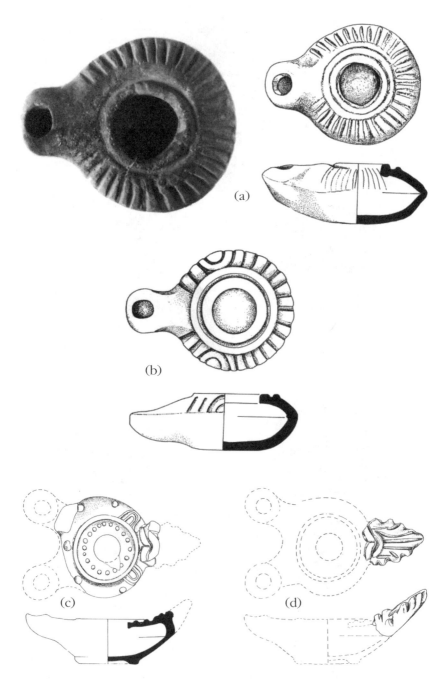

Fig. 3. Lamps from Masada (1st century B.C.). (a) Judean radial; (b) Judean radial with concentric circles; (c) two-nozzled with palmette handle; (d) two-nozzled with palmette handle.

The Greeks practiced the craft of molding lamps as early as the third century B.C. By the second century B.C., mold-made lamps were the norm throughout the Mediterranean, and Rome led the industry.[8] The characteristic early Roman lamp has a round body with a distinct spout terminating in a triangular or rounded nozzle (see figs. 4–5). The body of the lamp rests on a flat base or a pronounced ring-shaped foot. A kind of Roman lamp popular in the late first century B.C. and early first century A.D. has a tall delta- or crescent-shaped handle and one or two nozzles (see fig. 4a–c). Both a single-nozzled and a two-nozzled example found their way to Masada.[9] Their shape and their crisp, carinated features indicate they had metal prototypes.

A distinctive feature of the typical Roman lamp is the wide field around the filling hole called the discus (see figs. 4–5). Excess oil or spills could pool here and be funneled into the reservoir. This flat or depressed area was typically the focus of decoration (see below). The filling hole itself is consequently smaller than in Hellenistic and earlier lamps. Most types of early Roman Imperial pictorial lamps persisted with minute (and, to the specialist, noticeable!) changes well into the second century A.D.

Around the end of or just after the reign of Herod the Great, probably in response to the demand for late Hellenistic and Early Roman lamps, an interesting development took place in Palestine. Palestinian lamp makers invented (or re-introduced) a wheel-made oil lamp (see fig. 6a–b). This type of lamp bears the misnomer "Herodian," for when specialists first studied it, they believed it dated concurrently with Herod's reign. This type of lamp has a circular, wheel-made body to which a separate, hand-formed nozzle was joined. In contour, right down to their knife-pared, triangular nozzles, "Herodian" lamps resemble their imported molded contemporaries (compare fig. 5a). The filling-holes are significantly larger, however. This was a cheaper lamp, for its production did not require the kind of expertise needed to make the molded lamps, an advantage that spared consumers the costs of importation markups.

By the second half of the first century A.D., local Palestinian lamp makers had fully embraced mold technology into their practice. Nabatean lamp makers also capitalized upon the technology.

Notably, two new types of molded lamps were introduced (1) a round lamp with a discus, and (2) a round lamp with a decorated shoulder, called a Southern or Judean molded lamp. Round lamps with the discus have a flat reservoir with a petite nozzle and lack a handle (see fig. 7a–b). Their bases are flat, usually with an imitation ring base and, commonly, potters' marks. They are decorated both on the shoulder and in the discus. Although clearly inspired by Roman lamps, this type of lamp was fairly restricted in distribution to Syria-Palestine, being found in Jerusalem in levels predating A.D. 70, as well as in contexts dating to the third century.

In contour, Judean molded lamps imitate the shape of the contemporary "Herodian" lamp, right down to the flare of the nozzle (see fig. 7c–e). Fin-shaped motifs flanking the nozzle give the impression of knife paring like the "Herodian" lamps, and the filling hole is the same size. Here the comparison ends, for Judean molded lamps always have handles and incorporate a wide variety of decorations. Judean molded lamps were a local phenomenon, as is indicated by their chemical "fingerprints." Analysis of two examples by NAA point to clay sources in the Shephela of western Judea. A third sample is chemically similar to clays found in the Jerusalem area.[10] This type of lamp came onto the market after the destruction of Jerusalem in A.D. 70 and continued into the second century.

In the third and fourth centuries, Palestinian lamp makers developed regionally distinct varieties of lamps. Molded lamps were the rule. Existing types were expanded upon and there were new developments in shape. Notably, the nozzle tended to lose its discreteness, and, as a result, the body became pearshaped, ovid, and conical.

Preferences in Decoration. Early Palestinian wheel-made lamps as well as the earliest Greek molded lamps are almost purely utilitarian in nature and sparsely decorated if at all (see figs. 1–2). Even as late as the mid-second–early first century B.C., the favored ornamentation of Hellenistic molded lamps consisted only of nodules or closely set lines disposed radially about the shoulder (see fig. 2d). The single, pre-Herod lamp from Masada is apparently a local copy of one of these (see fig. 2e).[11] Compared to earlier Greek issues of the type, the Masada example is quite degenerate, being dulled and uninspired in character. As a local copy of the imported Hellenistic type, it could well be several mold generations removed from the original Greek series.

Fig. 4. **Early Roman lamps** (Augustan-Flavian). (a) With delta handle, plain discus; (b) with delta handle, Medusa in discus; (c) with crescent handle, arms and weapons in discus; (d) ovolo on rim, plain discus.

The modest character of the designs in these and many other types of Hellenistic lamps would have made them acceptable to a Jewish market. A large group of lamps from Masada dubbed "Judean Radial" by Barag and Hershkovitz take their inspiration from both Hellenistic and Roman contemporary lamps but were probably drawn from molds created locally (see fig. 3a–c).[12] Eighty-seven lamps from Masada or fragments thereof exhibit radial decorations on the shoulder, and some have a simple circle of dots in raised relief in a narrow discus. Some lamps from Masada with these decorations also have two nozzles as well as handles in the shape of palmettes (see fig. 3c–d).[13] In these respects, they clearly draw upon Roman lamps of the Augustan period (compare fig. 4a–b). While samples analyzed by NAA are inconclusive as to the location of the clay source used in these lamps, these lamps are paralleled primarily in Judea, and abundantly so. These particular lamps from Masada are believed to date to the reign of Herod.

The so-called "Herodian" lamp type described above was in high demand in the first century A.D. A major difference between "Herodian" lamps and their molded competitors is their decoration. "Herodian" lamps are plain in aspect and almost entirely void of decoration (see fig. 6a–b). They neither have a discus nor is the shoulder used for decoration. A few incised or rouletted lines and a few punched circle designs on the nozzle suffice.

"Herodian" lamps circulated within a restricted geographical area, being most common in Judea and rarer in north Judea and Transjordan. Visually acceptable to Jewish sectors of the population, they had a lengthy popularity, continuing in circulation through the first half of the second century A.D. Most of the lamps from Masada are of the common "Herodian" type and date to the period of Sicarii occupation.

Facing page:

Fig. 5. Early Roman imperial lamps. (a) Triangular nozzle, plain discus (Augustan/early Tiberian century A.D.–2nd century A.D.; (b) rounded nozzle, amphora in discus (1st century A.D.–2nd century A.D.); (c) small nozzle scored at base, potter's signature CATILVEST on base (second third of 1st century A.D.–2nd century A.D.); (d) small nozzle scored at base, potter's mark on base (second third of 1st century A.D.–2nd century A.D.); (e) factory lamp, potter's signature FORTIS on base (from circa A.D. 79–3rd century A.D.); (f) sketch of discus of Roman lamp imported to Masada (A.D. 40–80).

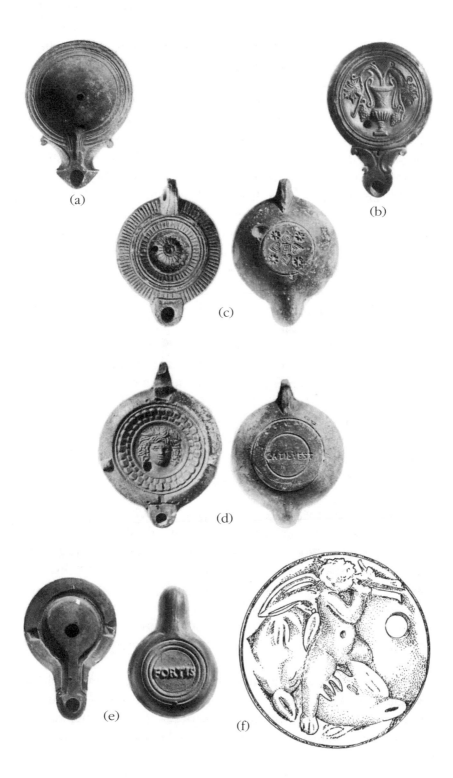

(a)

(b)

(c)

(d)

(e)

(f)

Lamp makers of first-century A.D. Judea offered a Jewish clientele alternatives to the plain "Herodian" lamp. Floral and geometric designs, permissible within Jewish religious restrictions, did occur. After the destruction of Jerusalem in A.D. 70, many Jews moved south in search of safer havens. The lamp makers who catered to them broadened their repertoire of decorations, as observable in the Southern or Judean molded lamps (see fig. 7c–e). They used, in addition to floral and geometric motifs, a range of articles such as vases and domestic paraphernalia. This shift marks a slight relaxation in the standard against pictorial representations, although lamps with deliberately defaced ornamentation raise the eyebrows (see fig. 7d, motifs defaced on shoulder).[14] The motifs include volutes, double axes, ovolos, darts, triangles, and leaves, as well as a wide range of pictorial subjects.

Varda Sussman points out that these pictorial subjects—candelabra, baskets of fruit, myrtle, palm branches, etc.—express a "longing for the Temple and its rebuilding and the memory of [Jewish] festivals."[15] In keeping with the Jewish prohibition against making true-to-life representations of the menorah, none of the candelabra depicted on the lamps have seven branches.[16] In addition, figural representations remained taboo for the most part. Clearly, Judean molded lamps were designed primarily for Jews. Lamps of this type were recovered from the caves in the Judean Desert, where people fleeing the Bar Kokhba War (A.D. 132–35) took refuge.

In sharp contrast to Hellenistic and "Herodian" lamps, Roman lamps had from their inception a manifestly decorative aspect, an aspect that no doubt greatly enhanced their appeal and marketability. The area favored for decorations in the earliest Roman lamps was the discus. In the disk of the lamp, decorations of all sorts were molded in relief, first at the expense of the size of the filling-hole (see figs. 4–5). In later developments, however, the shoulder of the lamp became the focus of designs at the expense of the discus (see fig. 8).

The repertoire of decorations on Roman relief lamps include geometric and floral designs, human figures and gods, and animals as well as scenes from the hunt, the circus, everyday life, and so on. A curious Roman convention of early Roman lamps is the pair

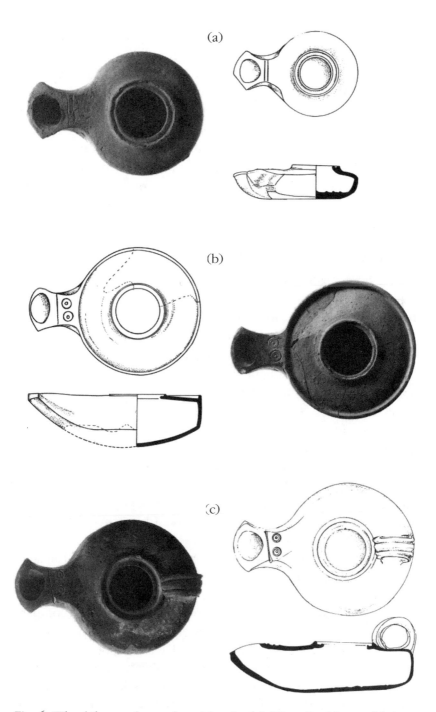

Fig. 6. **Wheel-thrown lamps from Masada.** (a) "Herodian" lamp; (b) "Herodian" lamp; (c) plain grayware with handle.

of volutes that flank the nozzle (see figs. 4, 5b). Rendered in pronounced relief, the volutes have a sculpturesque quality.

The decorative motifs of most Roman lamps are deployed away from the lamp user's perspective; that is, they face the nozzle and not the filling hole (see figs. 4b, 5b, 5d).[17] It stands to reason, therefore, that if one commonly held the lamp with the wick side away from the body, the motifs would have been best appreciated by people who met the lamp holder in passing or by anyone after the lamp had been placed in the destination of its use, that is, on a table or in a wall niche. In many Palestinian lamps, the opposite perspective was employed for the motifs (see figs. 7d, 8a).[18] Thus, lamp users typically had the benefit of viewing the motifs right-side up both while walking and after setting the lamp down. It would have made for a more personal experience for the user, especially if the motifs had a special significance for the user rather than being purely ornamental in character.

There was a tremendous demand for Roman decorated lamps; they were exported and widely copied throughout the empire. An imported example brought to Masada by a Roman soldier preserves in its discus the scene of Eros playing the double flutes and riding a dolphin (see fig. 5f). Roman discus lamps served as the prototypes for the class of Palestinian round lamps with the pictorial disci already discussed (see fig. 7a–b). The linear rendering of the conventional Roman volutes on the nozzles of one example (see fig. 7a) betrays the copyist's uninspired hand. The pictorial subject matter on these lamps would have been offensive to Jewish sectors of the society. Roman pictorial lamps would have appealed most to pagan markets and to Hellenized Jews.

The demand for Roman discus lamps was curbed in Palestine perhaps by their high cost and by the offensive content. Cosmopolitan Jews of the first century A.D. would still have been able to choose from a selection of plain, imported Roman lamps (compare fig. 5a). One particularly innocuous possibility was the so-called Factory lamp (see fig. 5e), the brainchild, it seems, of a lamp maker named Fors (see the Latin signature FORTIS, "of or belonging to Fors" on the base of fig. 5e). They hit the market before A.D. 79, having been found in the ashes of Pompeii, and persisted into the third century A.D. These lamps were purely utilitarian and had no

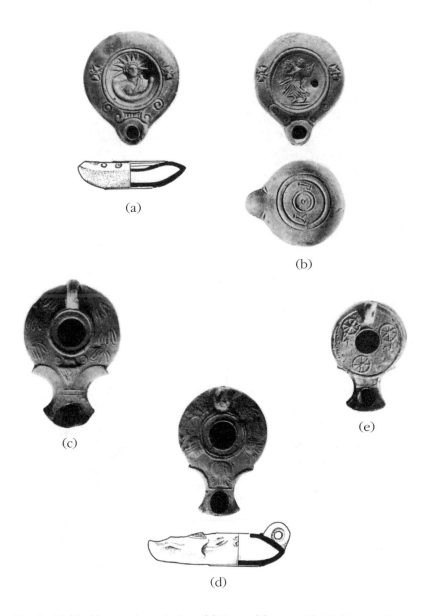

Fig. 7. **Molded lamps from Judea.** (a) Round lamp with Helios in discus (second half of 1st century A.D.–3rd century A.D.); (b) round lamp with Victory(?) in discus (second half of 1st century A.D.–3rd century A.D.); (c) Southern or Judean lamp, myrtle and amphora on shoulder (second half of 1st century A.D.–2nd century A.D.); (d) Southern or Judean lamp, motifs defaced except for three amphorae (second half of 1st century A.D.–2nd century A.D.); (e) Southern or Judean lamp, spoked wheels on shoulder (second half of 1st century A.D.–2nd century A.D.).

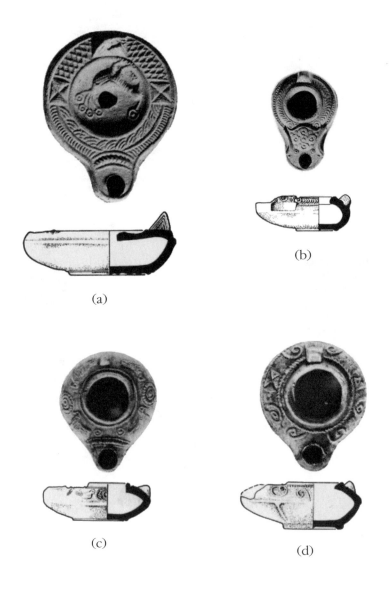

Fig. 8. Palestinian molded lamps (3rd century A.D.-4th century A.D.).
(a) Round lamp of the South, double axes and geometric motifs on
shoulder, peacock in discus; (b) bow-nozzled lamp, herringbone motifs
on shoulder, quatrefoil loop on nozzle; (c) ovoid lamp of the South,
confronted doves on shoulder; (d) ovoid lamp of the South, double axes
and half-volutes on shoulder.

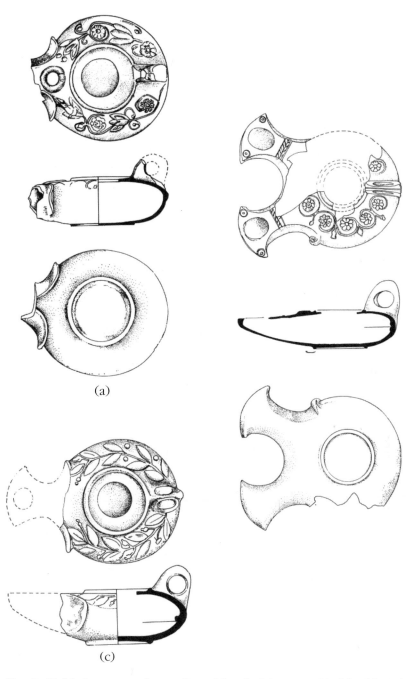

(a)

(c)

Fig. 9. Molded grayware lamps from Masada (circa A.D. 50–66). (a) Stylized flower, plantain leaves and garland on shoulder; (b) garland of flowers on shoulder; (c) olive leaves and fruit on shoulder.

decorations at all. Sterile to the point of being boring, they never-theless had a wide circulation in Rome's western empire. Perhaps they functioned exceptionally well—a tiny hole in the nozzle may have enabled the insertion of a pin to shift the wick, or it may have been an air vent. Few such lamps were imported to the eastern provinces. The contemporary "Herodian" lamps offered equivalent features for a local price.

Beginning in the third century, decorations varied regionally along with lamp types, and the prohibition against depicting the menorah relaxed somewhat, making it difficult to determine which religious groups patronized a given lamp type. In Byzantine times (later fourth–seventh centuries), lamp makers sometimes added inscriptions on lamp shoulders in various languages. Examples of Greek inscriptions translate as "The light of Christ shines for all," "Beautiful little lamps," and "The Mother of God."[19] Lamp makers also used fairly generic symbols, indicating little about the religious leanings of the user. Although the beautiful little lamps themselves have endured, the hands that lit them remain invisible to us.

Lamps from Masada and the Significance of Their Contexts

An Additional Type: Luxury Grayware. Over 1,100 lamps and fragments of lamps have been excavated at Masada.[20] Special-ists Barag and Hershkovitz identified seven classes of locally made lamps in addition to one class of imported lamps and copies thereof. Generally speaking, the lamps from Masada fall within the late Hel-lenistic and early Roman types discussed above. They were fired various shades of buff, reddish-brown, and brown, the color range most common in late Hellenistic and early Roman lamps.

A series of lamps from Masada are gray with a black slip. They may have been inspired by imported lamps.[21] Barag and Hershkovitz, noting their high quality and rarity in the Masada lamp assemblage, suggest they were a luxury ware.[22] Yet they are clearly a local phe-nomenon: they were confined largely to Judea and the central coastal plain. Analyses by NAA point to a clay source near Jerusalem or to a source on the north coast.

Grayware lamps from Masada were both wheel thrown and molded. The wheel-thrown types resemble "Herodian" lamps in form, and both types are probably contemporaneous (see fig. 6c).[23]

However, the grayware lamps were brought to completion more expertly, and some varieties have high-quality stamped, rouletted, and incised decorations on their nozzles.

Another series of grayware lamps was made from molds.[24] In shape these lamps resemble the lamps just discussed, although some have a looped handle. They differ in decoration, exhibiting typically a volute or finlike decoration flanking each side of the nozzle. In this respect, they follow early Roman Imperial lamp makers in a well-established convention. In lieu of a discus of any note, these lamps were decorated on their shoulders with rich floral motifs—olive twigs with leaves and fruits, myrtle twigs, oak leaves and acorns, plantain, caper, mallow, ivy, and acanthus. No complete specimens of these lamps survived at Masada, but drawings of the fragments help the mind's eye (see fig. 9). The floral lamps from Masada that could be dated are thought to belong to the years ca. A.D. 50–66, just prior to the period when the Sicarii occupied the site.[25]

Significantly, the decorations on all the grayware varieties would have been acceptable and—in the case of the floral lamps—of particular interest to a Jewish clientele. The myrtle, with its clusters of three leaves, is a species that grows in Galilee, the Golan Heights, and on Mt. Carmel and that is considered ritually purest by rabbinic sources.[26] The species of oak depicted is also common to the Judean Hills.[27] Barag and Hershkovitz see parallels to this floral mode of decoration in "the un-iconic art of Jerusalem in the century before the destruction of the city" (in A.D. 70).[28]

Contexts. When Yigael Yadin's excavations began at Masada in the early 1960s, the excavators gazed upon what might be described as a giant jigsaw puzzle whose intriguing pieces had to be sorted and put back together into a meaningful whole. For six decades after Herod had quitted Masada, the First Roman Garrison occupied the site (A.D. 6–66). They felt no obligation to tiptoe around so as to make it easy for future archaeologists to discover the sequence of events that had and would transpire at Masada. After the defeat of the First Roman Garrison, the Sicarii took up habitation. They wreaked their own special havoc as they adapted the site to suit their needs, building ritual baths, superimposing mud tubs over fine mosaic floors, and throwing up makeshift households within Herod's palaces and the casemate walls. The

Sicarii, in a last-ditch effort to save themselves, probably grabbed everything in sight to bolster the wall against the Roman battering rams. The siege ended in flames. Silva's troops cared even less for maintaining an air of orderliness. Following a second occupation by a Roman garrison, Masada lay fallow for almost four hundred years. Masada's Byzantine inhabitants had their own plans for the site (fifth century A.D.—circa 635–38).

Despite successive rounds of construction, occupation, renovation, destruction, and reoccupation, the excavators of Masada were able to reconstruct the sequences of events on the site. However, many structures saw a continuous inhabitation from Herod's time through the abandonment of the site by the Second Roman Garrison in about A.D. 115. The excavators could not usually discern whether a given patch of debris in a room had been formed exclusively by people of Herod's time, the Roman soldiers, or the Sicarii. Accordingly, the contexts or *loci* of artifacts (sing. *locus*) were very broadly defined, consisting generally of entire rooms and whole courtyards.[29] For example, lamps (and fragments thereof) were found in many places on the site, but with a few possible exceptions,[30] no lamps were definitely found "in situ," that is, in the place of their original use. Rather, they were recovered from debris piles, backfill from renovation activities, and the like. Thus, the lamps may have been kicked about or otherwise "redeposited" after their users set them down or discarded them.

Most of the lamps at Masada belong to the period of eight years of Sicarii occupation, A.D. 66–74. The wheel-made "Herodian" lamps were extremely common at Masada, constituting 80 percent of the assemblage, counting fragments. These modest, undecorated lamps were most abundant in contexts associated with the Sicarii occupation. While some of them may have been brought to the site by the soldiers of the First Roman Garrison, it stands to reason that many were used by the religiously strict Sicarii.

Archaeologists recovered many "Herodian" lamps as well as luxury molded lamps in the grayware from stratified contexts in buildings 11, 12, and 13. Many "Herodian" lamp nozzles turned up in a single courtyard of building 10.[31] All of these buildings were originally constructed as palaces by Herod, but the Sicarii later adapted them to serve as residences. The Sicarii took up household in them, adding new walls, blocking off doorways, and adding others. Within these reformulated spaces the Sicarii commonly installed cooking stoves and ovens (tabuns) made of mud, built small silos or bins for storage purposes, and added small niches in the wall to hold lamps or serve as shelves. The lamps from buildings 11, 12, and 13 all seem to date to the period of the Sicarii occupation.

A study of the imported lamps found at Masada yields equally interesting information. Donald Bailey reports that 64 imported lamps and fragments thereof have been found at Masada, all mold-made.[32] His tally included 31 apparently made in Italy, 6 in Asia Minor, 2 in the Phoenician part of the province of Syria, 14 of Nabatean origin, and 11 from unknown sources.

Significantly, the majority of imported lamps (52) date to the period when the First Roman Garrison occupied Masada (A.D. 6-66) and were likely imported for use by them.[33] The ones recovered at the site proper may have been found by the Sicarii and discarded.[34] An imported lamp found in Roman camp F (at the base of the mesa) undoubtedly belonged to a Roman soldier who participated in the siege (see fig. 5f).[35] Four others may have been brought to the site for use by the Second Roman Garrison (A.D. 74—circa 115).[36]

Sometimes archaeology is just vague enough to at once tantalize and nag the mind. Of intriguing note, for example, are the large groups of "Herodian" lamp nozzles found in *loci* 1047 and 1054.[37] Both of these *loci* are near the synagogue. How did they come to be there? One's imagination can be richly employed in attempts to explain the phenomenon—did evening activities in the vicinity of the synagogue consume lamps at an unusual rate? Did the men of the synagogue commonly "burn the midnight oil," as it were, immersed in their sacred texts? Were lamps used in the reading of texts particularly susceptible to defilement, or did the lamps need to be replaced more frequently to maintain the ritual purity of holy tasks? Were the lamps deliberately destroyed to keep them from falling into unholy hands? Or did they fall into "unholy" hands and meet their demise during or after the siege? A wholly mundane explanation may apply: were these *loci* garbage heaps?

The fact is, any speculation is simply that, as closer inspection reveals. *Locus* 1047 was a kind of corridor contingent with (but not communicating with) the north wall of the synagogue. The passage originally gave access to two long, partially subterranean rooms in the casemate wall (*loci* 1045 and 1046). These latter were back-filled during renovations prior to the Sicarii occupation. During the time when the Sicarii used the area, a pool was added, and the door-way leading to one of the casement rooms was equipped with a lamp niche. Unfortunately, the excavators could not distinguish be-tween the finds from the early and later stages of renovations. The lamp fragments may have been part of the backfill.

Locus 1054 was not a room at all but an open area to the immediate south of the synagogue. The Sicarii had constructed a niche in the synagogue's south wall at this point. Many whole ves-sels were found here as well as a hoard of about one hundred coins. The excavators concluded that the area had served as a dump.[38]

The Maidens' Lamps

What would the lamps carried by the five wise maidens in Matthew's story have looked like? Were they beautiful or ordinary? How would they have compared to lamps used by other people in the Holy Land? Were similar lamps used at Masada? Did pagans, Christians, and Jews use the same kinds of lamps?

To answer these questions, one must define a time frame for the lifetime of the maidens who, clearly, would not have been able to choose from hundreds of years of lamp varieties. The real ques-tion is, What did Jesus have in mind? It is his story, after all.

Jesus undoubtedly had a certain oil lamp in mind when he related his parable. The lamps must have been types he was famil-iar with. Therefore, the reader must establish the religious prefer-ences, personalities, and economic status of the maidens or, more accurately, these traits as assigned to the young women by Jesus. Perhaps his maidens had an eye for luxury—was he thinking of an especially unusual variety on sale in the market, a Roman discus lamp or copy thereof? Or were the lamps a more humble, mun-dane kind, such as the plain and less expensive "Herodian" type? Perhaps Jesus observed the lamps in use by others and used the same kind himself.

Finally, consider the purely practical matters. If you were involved in a midnight ritual in Jesus' time, what style of lamp would best have suited your needs as you sat or walked long hours in the sidelines of such an event?

For the most part, in antiquity lamps were so common a household item as to be taken for granted. Because the lives of everyday folk in antiquity were not normally the stuff of novelists and historians, theirs are the ones most difficult to reconstruct. Putting lamps in the hands of the five wise maidens two thousand years after the fact is not unlike the challenge Masada's excavators faced when first they tackled the jigsaw: it tantalizes and nags.

Marti Lu Allen is Associate Director of the Museum of Peoples and Cultures at Brigham Young University and Codirector of the Masada Exhibition Project.

NOTES

[1]Compare Varda Sussman, "Lighting the Way through History: The Evolution of Ancient Oil Lamps," *Biblical Archaeology Review* 11, no. 2 (1985): 48, who writes that the chore of keeping the lamps burning through the night was consigned to women. She cites Proverbs 31:18, "Her lamp does not go out at night."

[2]Mentions of lamps associated with a golden candelabra that the Lord ordered made for use on an altar are in Exodus 25:31, 37; 30:7-8; 35:14; 37:23; 39:37; 40:4, 25; Leviticus 24:2, 4; Numbers 4:9; 8:2-4; and 1 Kings 7:49. In a few instances the eyes or mouths of supernatural beings or creatures are likened to the light of burning lamps: Daniel 10:6; Ezekiel 1:13; and Job 41:19. Other symbolic uses of the word *lamp* are found in 2 Samuel 22:29; Psalms 119:105; Proverbs 6:23; 13:9; and 20:20.

[3]The full parable is related in Matthew 25:1-13. The ritual alluded to by Jesus may have consisted of escorting the bride and bridegroom to the nuptial chamber, where the virgins perhaps left their lamps as a blessing of light. Compare also the lights used by Gideon's army in Judges 7:16, 20, to fool the enemy at night, but these may have been torches rather than clay lamps. Other references to oil lamps are Genesis 15:17; 15:20; 1 Samuel 3:3; 1 Kings 15:4; Job 12:5; Isaiah 62:1; and Revelation 8:10.

[4]In this task, I am preceded by scholars far more authoritative than myself on the subject and their years of study and work form the foundation of my humble summary. In particular, I relied throughout this article on chapter 7, "Palestinian Lamps," in Renate Rosenthal and Renee Sivan, *Ancient Lamps in the Schloessinger Collection*, vol. 8 of *Qedem, Monographs of the Institute of*

Archaeology (Jerusalem: Hebrew University of Jerusalem, 1978), 75-139. Sussman, "Lighting the Way," 42-56, provides a good general article written for the lay person. For more technical details, I relied on the section on lamps from Masada written by Dan Barag and others, "Lamps," in *Masada IV: The Yigael Yadin Excavations 1963-1965, Final Reports,* ed. Joseph Aviram, Gideon Foerster, and Ehud Netzer (Jerusalem: Israel Exploration Society and Hebrew University of Jerusalem, 1994).

[5]Specialists disagree on whether or not these Late Hellenistic pinched or folded lamps could continue the saucer lamp tradition after a 150-200-year gap in production. They have been referred to both as "revivals" and "survivals" of the earlier saucer lamps. See Barag and others, "Lamps," 12 n. 6.

[6]This is type A, no. 1, discussed in Barag and others, "Lamps," 11-13.

[7]Barag and others, "Lamps," 11.

[8]The Roman lamps discussed in this article are standard types in the publications of lamp specialists. To get started, the reader may consult Rosenthal and Sivan, *Ancient Lamps;* O. Broneer, *Corinth,* 4, part 2, *Terracotta Lamps* (Cambridge, 1930); O. Broneer, *Isthmia,* 3, *Terracotta Lamps* (Princeton, 1977); D. M. Bailey, *Catalogue of the Lamps in the British Museum,* 3 vols. (London, 1975-83); or John W. Hayes, *Ancient Lamps in the Royal Ontario Museum,* vol. 1 (Toronto, 1980).

[9]These are nos. 153 and 155, discussed in Barag and others, "Lamps," 82-83, plate 4, both of which have been heavily restored and are in *The Story of Masada* exhibition.

[10]This is interesting, given the fact that Jerusalem lay in ruins after A.D. 70. Apparently, Jerusalem clays continued to be harvested even though the population had been decimated. See Barag and others, "Lamps," 77-78, where the authors also report the results of NAA on Judean molded lamps from Masada, Aroer, and the Cave of Horror.

[11]This is type B I, cat. no. 2, discussed in Barag and others, "Lamps," 13-14.

[12]These are type B II, cat. nos. 3-14, and type B III, cat. nos. 15-20, discussed in Barag and others, "Lamps," 19-24.

[13]These are type B IV, cat. nos. 21-25, discussed in Barag and others, "Lamps," 24.

[14]Compare type F, discussed in Barag and others, "Lamps," 77-78; and Rosenthal and Sivan, *Ancient Lamps,* 82-85, nos. 335-44, which are referred to as "Southern" lamps. On the defacement of lamps by zealous Jews, see, among others, Varda Sussman, "Early Jewish Iconoclasm on Pottery Lamps," *Israel Exploration Journal* 23, no. 1 (1973): 46-47.

[15]Sussman, "Lighting the Way," 54.

[16]Sussman, "Lighting the Way," 54-55, where she also notes that some of the stricter Jews would disfigure molds bearing representations of doves and fish so that the impressions lifted from them would not violate the prohibition against image making.

[17]Compare Barag and others, "Lamps," 75; Rosenthal and Sivan, *Ancient Lamps,* 83, no. 337, who note the existence of exceptions; and A. Levy, "An Observation on the Direction of Decorations in Palestinian Oil Lamps," *Israel Exploration Journal* 23, no. 1 (1973): 48-49.

[18]Figs. 7a-c are distinct exceptions.

[19]Joseph Naveh, "Lamp Inscriptions and Inverted Writing," *Israel Exploration Journal* 38, nos. 1-2 (1988): 36-43.

[20]About one-fifth of these lamps have been catalogued in the fourth volume of the recently published excavation reports (see above, note 4). This section of my article relies heavily upon the chapters written by Dan Barag and others.

[21]Barag and others, "Lamps," 53; Rosenthal and Sivan, *Ancient Lamps,* 12.

[22]Barag and others, "Lamps," 54.

[23]These are type C VIII and type C IX, discussed in Barag and others, "Lamps," 54-55.

[24]These are types D I-VI, discussed in Barag and others, "Lamps," 59-66.

[25]Barag and others discuss the dating in "Lamps," 67-69.

[26]As pointed out by Barag and others, "Lamps," 64, who cite the following in their notes 63-64: Babylonian Talmud, Sukkah 32b (London: Soncino, 1938, III, 144); and Michael Zohary, *Flora Palestina* II (Jerusalem: Israel Academy of Science and Humanities, 1972), 371, plate 542.

[27]As pointed out by Barag and others, "Lamps," 64, who cite the following in their note 65: Michael Zohary, *Flora Palestina* I (Jerusalem: Israel Academy of Science and Humanities, 1966), 33, plate 32.

[28]Barag and others, "Lamps," 70-71.

[29]For discussions on the architectural sequences and description of *loci* at Masada, see Ehud Netzer, "The Buildings: Stratigraphy and Architecture," in *Masada III: The Yigael Yadin Excavations 1963-1965, Final Reports,* ed. Joseph Aviram, Gideon Foerster, and Ehud Netzer (Jerusalem: Israel Exploration Society and Hebrew University of Jerusalem, 1991).

[30]An example of these exceptions is *locus* 1092, located in the central unit of the storeroom complex, in which a lamp and two pottery vessels were discovered sitting on an area of back-fill: see Netzer, *Buildings,* 70.

[31]Barag and others, "Lamps," 43; Netzer, *Buildings,* 311, *locus* 503.

[32]Barag and others, "Lamps," 79-99. Some of these are local copies of imported lamps.

[33]Barag and others, "Lamps," 79-99, nos. 138-59, 161-68, 172, 174-90, 195-98.

[34]See Barag and others, "Lamps," 79: "It is possible that all this [imported] material was dumped during the Zealots' occupation of the site." Donald M. Bailey's section of chapter 2 points out that there is nothing about the imported lamps that forces an exclusive date in the Sicarii period (A.D. 66-74).

[35]Barag and others, "Lamps," 98.

[36]Barag and others, "Lamps," 86-87, 92-93, nos. 173, 199-201.

[37]Netzer, *Buildings,* 399-401, 413.

[38]Netzer, *Buildings,* 413.

Loosing a Shoe Latchet: Sandals and Footwear in the First Century

Shane A. Baker

During the 1964 season of excavations at Masada, archaeologists made a stunning and emotionally compelling discovery while working in the area of the elaborate palace complex built by Herod at the north end of the fortress.[1] Located beneath a pile of heavy rubble covering the ruins of a small Roman-style bathhouse, excavators found the only physical remains of Masada's Jewish defenders discovered at the site itself. Sprawled upon the steps leading to the cold-water pool of the baths and on the ground nearby were the skeletal remains of three individuals—a young man in his twenties, a young woman about eighteen, and an eleven-year-old child.[2]

Surprisingly, each body was accompanied by perishable organic artifacts that gave a rare glimpse into the Masada rebels' daily lives. Close by the man lay silvered armor scales, arrows, the remains of a prayer shawl, and an *ostracon.* The dry atmosphere of the Judean desert had preserved the braided hair of the woman's scalp and several pairs of sandals, including a pair of nearly complete, delicately fashioned lady's sandals.[3] In stark contrast to the rather delicate sandals found with the body of the woman were the remnants of a Roman *caliga,* a type of heavy leather shoe with iron hobnails. These Roman shoes were found elsewhere in the fortress and are direct evidence of the Roman conquest and occupation of the site. These rare finds provide insight into the style of footwear that was common for both the Jewish inhabitants of Masada and the Roman army.

Grecian Footwear

During the Hellenistic period, Greek footwear developed variations that are likely predecessors of the types of footwear worn at Masada in the first century. The composite sandal, which had features of both shoes and sandals, appeared at this time.[4] Also during this time, the tongue first appeared, usually on composite sandals but also occasionally on shoes. The tongue is a flat piece of shaped leather that covered the top of the instep, over or through which the sandal lacings crossed. The tongue was usually bent down over the knot near the ankle and covered the instep in an ornamental flap that was fringed or scalloped at the lower edge.[5]

The shape of sandal soles also varied. By about 300 B.C., a style of shaped sole became popular that curved inward between the first two toes where the thong attached at the front of the foot. In its earliest form, this indentation appears as a shallow notch with abrupt edges, but later became deeper and more rounded, flowing into the outline of the rounded and gracefully shaped soles. Occasionally, the entire outer edge of the sole was repeatedly notched to follow the shape of all the toes, producing an almost scalloped appearance.[6]

Subtle changes are evident as well in the style of lacing that accompanied changing styles of soles on Greek sandals. By the late fourth century, many sandals were made with loops on the side of the foot near the base of the toes so that the thong from between the toes was fed through these side loops and then back across the instep and the rear of the foot. The heel of the foot was often surrounded by an elaborate network of crossed straps that formed a latticework that enclosed much of the rear of the foot. Special gilded sandals were worn by persons of high rank, and sandals for women were sometimes constructed with special ornamental pieces on the instep.[7]

Roman Footwear

Except for slaves, who were forbidden to wear sandals or shoes altogether, most Romans generally wore foot coverings both indoors and out, taking them off only before retiring to bed. The normal footwear could consist of either sandals or shoes, depending upon the demands of specific circumstances. Three types of sandals were commonly worn, each being adapted to a specific purpose. *Soleae* were simple, hobnailed, leather-soled sandals that had a thong between the toes that tied at the instep.[8] *Crepidae* were heavier, thick leather-soled sandals fastened with leather straps that passed through eyelets on the upper portion of the sandal.[9] A *carbatina* was a sandal made with a soft leather sole and an open decorative upper that was fastened with ribbons or a lace. Both crepidae and carbatina had leather uppers that covered much of the foot but still left the toes bare.[10]

Along with sandals, a variety of boots and shoes were worn. *Calcei* were common, ankle-high, closed-toe boots that laced around the ankle. They were the forerunners of most of the shoes worn in Europe during the Middle Ages.

Buskins, higher boots that reached to midcalf, were worn by the more wealthy Roman citizens and exhibited a great deal of variety. These boots were usually partially open along the front and were held on with a system of cross-lacing. Buskins were frequently lined with the skins of small animals, the heads and claws of which were allowed to hang down over the tops as ornament.

Soccei were shoes constructed with a leather sole without hobnails and with a separate leather upper. Heavy, leather, military-style boots often fitted with hobnails, such as the examples found at Masada, were called *caligae.*[11] The Romans also introduced *gallicae,* heavy wooden shoes with coarse rawhide uppers that were used in wet weather and on muddy ground. These are the ancestors of modern overshoes. Both shoes and sandals were sometimes worn with loose cloth wrappings that protected the lower leg (*fascia*) but are not stockings in the modern sense.

Footwear served as a definite status indicator for the Roman empire, with colors and styles that were differentiated according to both sex and social rank. As noted, slaves were forbidden to wear shoes, except in unusual circumstances where their assigned tasks necessitated additional protection for the feet. Patricians' sandals were red with a moon-shaped ornament on the back. A special tall, boot-type shoe was reserved for depictions of persons who were not mortals. This category included gods, demons, and other allegorical figures, as well as human beings shown after death.

Thus on some sarcophagi the deceased is represented twice, once as a living man wearing normal footwear and once as a deceased person shod in the footgear of immortality.[12]

The widespread influence of the Romans guaranteed that many of these shoe and sandal types saw extensive distribution, and much of the world's footwear in succeeding periods derived from Roman shoes. The concept of enclosed footwear, especially military boots modeled after the caliga, was carried by the Roman legions to distant lands, and closed shoes appeared throughout the Middle East during the first century.

The Footwear of Masada

Despite the wide variety of footwear developed and used by the Romans, the sandal remained the most common and widely worn type of footwear in the Middle East during the first century A.D. The vast majority of people, unable to afford shoes, probably used sandals almost exclusively. Scriptural references to footwear in both the Old and New Testament frequently make reference to sandals rather than shoes, and in many instances, sandals are probably the referent when the generic term *shoe* is used.

The archaeological excavations at Masada uncovered several relatively well-preserved examples of sandals and shoes worn by both the Sicarii and the men of the Roman siege forces. The exceptional conditions for preservation that prevailed in the area of the small Roman-style baths on the east end of the site permitted the excavations there to yield some of the best-preserved specimens at Masada. These included several pairs of sandals found near the skeleton of the woman. All of these associated materials, found in the vicinity of the baths, were dated to the period of the Masada incident.

The finds included one very finely made pair of women's sandals with a light leather sole and a leather thong for attachment. The soles of these sandals have a unique shape that is rounded at the heel but is squared and blunt at the front, a style apparently common to the period.[13] A rather delicate thong attachment of dual leather strips originates between the first and second toes and sweeps back to tie near the ankle and fasten to two leather tabs running up

a. Child's shoe

b. Scalloped sandal sole

c. Woman's sandal

Fig. 1. Sicarii footwear from Masada

from the sole on each side of the ankle. (See fig. 1c.) This type of sandal has also been found at sites in the Hever caves.[14]

A second type of sandal, represented by a much smaller pair also found near the body of the Sicarii woman, had a light, elegantly tapered leather sole with a scalloped edge outlining the area of the toes. This scalloped sole is similar to the earlier Greek style of shaped soles.[15] Because the straps are missing from these sandals, the manner of attachment cannot be determined, but they were probably attached by a light system of leather thongs like the other sandals found nearby. (See fig. 1b.)

Excavators found only one single example of an enclosed shoe associated with the Sicarii occupation. The specimen, although now somewhat shriveled and distorted, measures less than twelve centimeters in length and therefore is thought to have been made for a child. It is constructed with a heavier, layered leather sole and an ankle-high, full leather upper that enclosed most of the foot. (See fig. 1a.)

Evidence for shoes and sandals belonging to the Roman army came from several locations near the casemate wall and other various localities. A near-perfect example of a caliga was found with an intact strap and metal hobnails on the sole. The leather sole is rather stiff and is attached to the foot by a single strap across the instep. The leather upper enclosed the toes but was rather low cut so as to leave most of the top of the foot exposed. This specimen from Masada is lower cut and not as heavy as many other known examples. (See fig. 2.)

Fig. 2. **Roman caliga.** Notice the metal hobnails on the sole.

The fragmentary remains of a number of sandal straps were found throughout the site. These include a number of straps that are made of fancy openwork leather from various parts of the sandal. This type of elaborate strapping was common on many of the Roman sandals of the day and originated with the more complex, composite-style sandals developed by the Greeks.

The examples of footwear found at Masada give a glimpse of the styles worn by the Sicarii and the rank-and-file members of the Roman army. The woman's sandals appear to be a common, simple style that was utilized by people throughout the region. No examples of footwear worn by the Sicarii men were found, but they probably also wore simple sandals with leather bottoms and straps.

The Jewish inhabitants of Masada probably wore sandals most of the time when outdoors, but in accordance with well-established traditions took them off when entering the home. Children probably also wore sandals, although simple shoes were not unknown, as the Masada finds indicate. However, children likely usually went barefoot when playing outside. Roman soldiers were furnished with the bootlike caligae common to the army during this period, but they probably wore shoes most of the time as was the custom elsewhere in the empire. Undoubtedly, additional varieties of shoes and sandals similar to those already discussed were common to both groups during this period and were worn at Masada, but they have not been preserved or discovered.

Biblical Symbolism Involving Footwear

From the very earliest times, feet and footwear were selectively imbued with symbolic meaning and surrounded by prescribed symbolic behavior on specific occasions.[16] In the book of Exodus, when God spoke from the burning bush, he gave Moses this injuction: "Draw not nigh hither: put off thy shoes from off thy feet, for the place whereon thou standest is holy ground" (Ex. 3:5). Likewise, when Joshua met the "captain of the Lord's host" near Jericho, he was similarly commanded to remove his shoes for he stood on holy ground (Josh. 5:15).

The practice of going unshod as a mark of reverence and respect for holy places seems to have been widespread in antiquity and persists even today in many parts of the world. Moslems still remove their shoes before entering a mosque or when praying; in similar fashion, Latter-day Saints remove street shoes before entering the sacred areas of modern temples.

Although the scriptures make it clear that the practice of removing one's shoes in consecrated or holy places dates at least as early as the Exodus, it probably has origins long before that first recorded example in the Bible. Already by this early point in history, the practice of taking off one's shoes while inside a home appears to have been well established among Semitic peoples. Accordingly, the Israelites were instructed specifically during the first Passover to eat standing and *with their shoes on* (Ex. 12:11) as a symbol of their flight out of Egypt. Whereas today it might seem odd for us to be told to eat with our shoes on, apparently cultural mores on the matter were already so set that the Israelites would not have left their shoes on without being ordered by the Lord to do so.

It appears that going without shoes was also sometimes used as a symbol of mourning (Ezek. 24:17, 23) or of distress or humiliation[17] (Deut. 25:7-10; 2 Sam. 15:30; Isa. 20:2-4). By the time of the Judges, it was a common practice to seal or "confirm" certain important legal obligations or transactions by taking off a shoe or sandal and giving it to the person with whom the transaction was made. This action was considered to be a sign or "testimony in Israel" that sealed the arrangement, particularly in transactions involving real estate (Ruth 4:7).

Throughout the biblical period, it was a mark of hospitality to wash the feet of visitors or at least provide water and a basin so that the guests could wash their own feet. Since most people wore sandals and the climate was relatively hot and dusty, frequent foot washing became not only a luxury, but a necessity. Feet were routinely washed after a long journey and before going to bed (Gen. 19:2; 2 Sam. 11:8). The custom is described as early as the period of the patriarchs and continued into the early Christian era (see Gen. 18:4; 24:32; 43:24; 1 Sam. 25:41; Luke 7:44; and John 13:4-15).

The act of washing the feet of a guest carried the connotation not only of hospitality, but also of humility and subservience. The actual washing was often performed by servants, and so the Savior chose this example as a way to teach his followers the need to serve one another (Luke 13:4–15). A servant would pour water over the guest's feet into a basin or bowl, washing them with his or her hands, and then drying the feet with a cloth towel.

By the first century A.D., this almost ritualized washing of the feet had become closely affiliated with several other related practices. As already noted, sandals were always removed upon entering a house. Frequently, a servant was detailed with the responsibility of removing the visitor's or master's sandals, washing the feet, and then taking care of the footwear until its owner was in need of it again. If a master were to be simply passing through a home or walking barefoot on smooth ground or grass, the servant would follow, carrying the sandals in hand in order to supply them again when they were needed. This job of carrying the master's sandals was considered to be the most menial and lowly responsibility that could be performed.[18]

John the Baptist uses the symbolism surrounding the act of removing and carrying sandals to show his subordination and deference to Jesus Christ. In trying to help his followers understand the significance of the Savior's role and John's relationship to him, John pursues this figurative example in several different ways. At one point he states, "He that cometh after me is mightier than I, whose shoes I am not worthy to bear" (Matt. 3:11). Aside from simply indicating that he was not worthy to carry Christ's shoes, John also states that he not even worthy to loose or take off the shoes of Jesus. The Gospel writers Mark, Luke, and John all record John the Baptist as having said, "There cometh one mightier than I after me, the latchet of whose shoes I am not worthy to stoop and unloose" (Mark 1:7; Luke 3:16; John 1:27; see also 1 Ne. 10:8). The shoe latchet here is actually the long leather thongs or laces used on many first-century-style sandals to fasten them to the foot. As previously noted, leather straps or thongs were used by both the Greeks and the Romans and appeared in several styles throughout the biblical region. The use of the term "latchet" suggests a more elaborate sandal lace than the simple thong-type tie sometimes used.

John attempted to highlight the transcendent role that Christ would play in contrast to John's own humble ministry by reaffirming his unworthiness to untie the Savior's sandals in order to perform the humble service of washing His feet or carrying His sandals. John drove home his point by couching it in terms of common cultural practices that would have been familiar and important to his audience.

Conclusion

Though dried, shrunken, and curled by the dust and weather of the centuries that have passed since they were buried at Masada, the examples of footwear found at the site convey the essence of Middle Eastern footwear. The Roman caligae uncovered at the site undoubtedly look much like the footwear worn by the Roman legionaries of the time and impart some sense of the strength, determination, and organization of an empire that then ruled most of the known world. The sandals and shoes found at Masada differ little from those that would have been worn by Jesus Christ, Mary Magdalene, John the Baptist, Matthew, Peter, or any of the disciples.

Shane A. Baker is Collections Manager and Staff Archaeologist of the Museum of Peoples and Cultures at Brigham Young University.

NOTES

[1]Gideon Foerster, "Art and Architecture," in *Masada V: The Yigael Yadin Excavations 1963–1965, Final Reports,* ed. Joseph Aviram, Gideon Foerster, and Ehud Netzer (Jerusalem: Israel Exploration Society and Hebrew University of Jerusalem, 1995), 193–205.

[2]Yigael Yadin, *The Excavation of Masada 1963/64: Preliminary Report* (Jerusalem: Israel Exploration Society, 1965), 16–17.

[3]Yadin, *Excavation of Masada,* 16–17.

[4]Mary Wallace, "*Sutor Supra Crepidam,*" *American Journal of Archaeology* 44 (1940): 215.

[5]Wallace, "*Sutor,*" 215.

[6]Wallace, "*Sutor,*" 215–216.

[7]Wallace, "*Sutor,*" 217.

[8]Lesley Adkins and Roy A. Adkins, *Handbook to Life in Ancient Rome* (New York: Facts on File, 1994), 345.

[9]Jerome Carcopino, *Daily Life in Ancient Rome: The People and the City at the Height of the Empire* (New Haven: Yale University Press, 1940), 153.

[10]Adkins and Adkins, *Handbook,* 345.

[11]Carcopino, *Daily Life in Ancient Rome,* 153.

[12]A. L. Frothingham, "The Footgear of Immortality in the Redating of Roman Sculptures," *American Journal of Archaeology,* 2d ser., 22 (1918): 67.

[13]Yigael Yadin, *Masada: Herod's Fortress and the Zealots' Last Stand* (New York: Random House, 1966), 54.

[14]Yadin, *Masada,* 17.

[15]Wallace, *"Sutor,"* 215–216.

[16]See James M. Freeman, *Manners and Customs of the Bible* (reprint, Plainfield, N.J.: Logos International, 1972); and Fred H. Wight, *Manners and Customs of Bible Lands* (Chicago: Moody, 1953).

[17]Freeman, *Manners,* 115.

[18]Freeman, *Manners,* 333.

The Fruit of the Vine: Wine at Masada and in the New Testament

Jo Ann H. Seely

Blessed art Thou, O Lord, our God, King of the Universe
who created sweet wine, good must from grapevines,
that is pleasing to a person and good for man,
that gladdens the heart and makes the face shine.
It is consolation to mourners, and those of bitter spirit forget their misery.
It is medicine to all who drink it. (to him who drinks it sensibly).
It is heart's joy, gladness, and great delight to its drinkers.
He, our God, created it of old for pleasure,
among the works established from the beginning,
so that all who drink it shall bless God,
and praise the Author of understanding,
who prepared the delicacies of the world,
and formed the sweet things of the earth.[1]

This ancient Jewish benediction preserved from the Cairo Genizah is an expanded version of the one sentence blessing required by rabbinic law before wine could be drunk.[2] It extols the virtues of the fruit of the vine, acknowledges the goodness of God as provider, and cautions the overindulgent. The poem also reveals the broad spectrum of life in which ancient peoples partook of wine—from mere pleasure drinking to comfort for those in mourning. Wine was highly valued in antiquity. It was a common table drink, a desirable trade item, a gift to kings, a medical aid, a ritual offering, and part of nearly every aspect of life as it was shared by family, friends, priests, and kings to celebrate happiness and sorrow, worship and covenant.

This article will consider the use of wine in ancient Palestine, focusing primarily on its use in the first century A.D. The wine stores at Masada demonstrate that an effort was made to make wine available even in difficult circumstances. What can be learned from the wine kraters found at Masada? How was wine produced and what types of wine were available in ancient Palestine? What insight does the Old Testament provide, and how is wine viewed during New Testament times? Wine was more than just a staple of life; the "blood of the grape" became a rich symbol encompassing the blessing of God as well as his wrath and the ultimate passion of the Lord himself as he trod the winepress.

Wine at Masada

The excavations at Masada provide a small window into first-century Israel, and although the inhabitants were living under extreme conditions, the basic staples of life were present. Josephus describes the stores thus: "The stores laid up within would have excited still more amazement, alike for their lavish splendour and their durability. For here had been stored a mass of corn, amply sufficient to last for years, abundance of wine and oil, besides every variety of pulse and piles of dates."[3] Josephus writes that the rebels at Masada supplemented their supplies by vicious attacks on the nearby villages. On a night raid to En Gedi, they "rifled the houses, seized the ripest of the crops, and carried off their spoil to Masada. They made similar raids on all the villages around the fortress, and laid waste the whole district."[4] Both Josephus's account and the archaeological data indicate that there was plenty of food and wine on Masada.

One particular storeroom at Masada was thought to have been designed specifically for the storage of wine (or a liquid of some type). It had plastered walls and three well-plastered circular pits or depressions in the floor spaced across the length of the room. Scholars suggest that this room was for stocking wine and the pits were used to either facilitate pouring the liquid from the large storage jars into smaller vessels or to contain any wine that spilled during transfer. Most of the wine jars found seem to be of the Herodian period as indicated by their shape, but many had inscriptions in ink or charcoal with the new owners' names on them.[5] Of particular interest were the wine jars recovered bearing the inscription "To King Herod of Judea," which were apparently sent to Herod from Italy.[6] This was the first time the name of Herod had been found in an inscription. Also noted on the jars was the name of the Roman consul, C. Sentius Saturninus, who was in office in the year 19 B.C., providing an exact date for the archaeologists.[7]

Perhaps the most interesting inscription found on some of the jars was the Hebrew letter *tav*, which has been suggested to represent the word *tərûmāh*, or priestly due. The people at Masada may have been attempting to live according to the law as outlined in Numbers 18, which commanded them to bring to the Levites "all the best of the oil, and all the best of the wine, and of the wheat, the firstfruits of them which they shall offer unto the Lord, them have I given thee" (Num. 18:12). The Levites were then to give a tenth of this offering to the priests for their use (Num. 18:26–28). Certain of the jars may have been set aside for those of either the priestly or levitical lineage or even just separated from the stores in an effort to fulfill the commandment.[8]

Wine in Ancient Palestine

Vitis vinifera L. (the grape vine) has been cultivated in Palestine from the Early Bronze Age and is found in nearly every section of the country from the north to the south. Ample archaeological evidence demonstrates the widespread cultivation of grapes, including agricultural terracing, stone towers associated with vineyards, and thousands of winepresses, dating from the Early Bronze Age to the Byzantine period. The stone towers, often referred to as watchtowers, were used not only to guard the vineyards at harvest time, but also to store the grapes and protect them from the heat until they were transported to the winepresses.[9]

Production. Harvesting of the grapes occurred in September and October. Care was to be taken to not gather all of the fruit, as grapes are specifically mentioned to be left for the poor to glean (Lev. 19:10; Deut. 23:24). Harvesting and treading the grapes was a happy time of community comradeship and singing. The scriptures describe times of sorrow when "gladness is taken away, and joy out of the plentiful field; and in the vineyards there shall be no singing, neither shall there be shouting: the treaders shall tread out no wine in their presses; I have made their vintage shouting to cease" (Isa. 16:10).

Most winepresses were hewn out of solid rock, but some were built and plastered. A typical winepress would include a vat large enough for several men to tread the grapes. Sometimes a beam was placed overhead with ropes suspended to help support the treaders. As the grapes were pressed, the expressed juice would flow through a connecting channel, which contained a filter of thorns, from the first vat to a lower, smaller vat, where the juice would sit, allowing the lees to settle to the bottom. From this second vat, the juice would be poured into containers and moved for storage. The grape skins left in the first vat would often be pressed again to produce an inferior wine that could be used to make vinegar. At times a wooden beam with either weights or a screw attached was used to press the grapes. Winepresses were also occasionally used to crush olives after the grapes were pressed and to serve like cisterns to catch the winter rains.

Wine was stored either in earthenware pots or wineskins (*askoi*). The skins were usually made from goat or lamb hides with the neck and legs tied. The skins were able to stretch as the wine fermented and gases formed. Once the skins had already been used and stretched, new wine could not be poured into them or they would burst (Matt. 9:17). Earthenware jars, or amphorae, were sealed with clay, but a small hole was left by the handle to release the gases as fermentation took place. Eventually this hole was sealed with clay and stamped with the owner's name or seal. The softer rock beneath limestone so prevalent in Palestine allowed the digging of storage cellars all over the country. The wealthy had cellars in their own homes, and the pointed ends of amphorae were buried in the ground to keep the wine cool.

Words for Wine. The Mediterranean world has a rich vocabulary related to viticulture; here we will consider only the most common scriptural terms for wine.[10] Although the words have varying meanings, they are often used as synonyms in the text, where they all seem to suggest wine that was fermented and not simple grape juice.[11]

Yayin: The most prevalent of all the words for wine in Hebrew is *yayin*. It has a very wide distribution with cognates found in both Semitic and Indo-European languages, including

Amphorae from Masada. These two-handled jars with narrow necks were used to carry and store wine. The pointed ends could be buried in the ground to keep the wine cool.

Greek (*oinos*) and Latin (*vinum*). Scholars have argued that *yayin* does not have a Semitic etymology but probably came from Hittite or an Anatolian origin.[12] *Yayin* refers to wine in general and is used 141 times in the Old Testament in many different contexts.

Tirosh: On a few occasions, *tirosh* is translated as "new wine," but most often it is translated simply as "wine." It occurs thirty-eight times in the Old Testament. *Tirosh* should not be confused with grape juice when translated as "new wine," as the context in this passage shows: "New wine take[s] away the heart," or understanding (Hosea 4:11). *Tirosh* later becomes the expression for ritual wine and is used instead of *yayin* in the Qumran texts.[13]

Asis: This term appears only five times in the Old Testament and is derived from a root meaning "to press, crush," from which it takes the meaning of juice. It is used in poetry as a synonym for *tirosh* and was also considered intoxicating. In Isaiah we read that Israel's oppressors "shall be drunken with their own blood, as with sweet wine [*asis*]" (Isa. 49:26).

Oinos: This term is the common Greek word translated as "wine" in the New Testament. Out of thirty-seven occurrences of "wine" in the New Testament, thirty-three are translated from the word *oinos*. *Oinos* designates wine that is fermented and is used in references in which warnings are given concerning intoxicating effects of wine (see Eph. 5:18).

Gleukos: This term is usually translated from Greek as "white," but in one case in Acts *gleukos* is translated as "new wine." It was considered an intoxicant—those who heard the Apostles speaking in tongues at Pentecost accused them of being "full of new wine (*gleukos*)" (Acts 2:13).

Additional vocabulary relating to wine includes *must*—the juice from freshly pressed grapes, *lees*—that which is strained out after the wine has been left to sit and ferment, *dibs*—a thick syrup made from boiling the wine down and used to spread on bread or to mix with water as a beverage, and *wormwood*—a bitter herb (*Artemisia absinthium*) that was sometimes added to wine and that was used to make a strong tea used as a folk remedy for intestinal ailments. In the Bible, wormwood is often referred to symbolically as sorrow or bitterness (Deut. 29:18; Jer. 9:15; Rev. 8:10–11).

Types of Wine. In the ancient world, varieties of wine were made from prunes, raisins, cherries, dates, apples, and pomegranates, but the wines of Palestine were almost entirely made from fermented grape juice.[14] (There is one mention of pomegranate wine in Song of Solomon 8:2.) Once the grapes were pressed, the juice would begin to ferment within six to twelve hours.[15] The quantity of alcohol in the wine is uncertain, but scholars explain "the amount of alcoholic content which could be achieved by fermentation was not high when compared with what can be attained through modern methods of distillation, unknown in the ancient world."[16] Wines that were a year old were still considered new wine, and tradition held that a man could not drink old wine while giving his Jewish slaves new wine because of its inferiority.[17] Although wine improved over time, wines were generally consumed within three or four years. Modern pasteurization or containers that would allow longer storage periods were not available.[18]

Wines available in Palestine in the first century include red, white, clear, and dark wine.[19] Sorek (bright red) was thought to be very choice wine. Wines were also classified by taste including sweet, bitter, sour, smoked,[20] and boiled or cooked. Spices and scents were added not only to enrich the flavor, but also to help enhance wine that was spoiling due to storage conditions. The Talmud describes some of the spices or other substances added to wine, listing balsam, honey, pepper, myrrh, *sapa* (a sweet syrup used by the Romans), capers, and wormwood.[21]

In addition to wine, vinegar was produced by allowing either the wine or the lees of the wine to sour, causing a fungus (*Mycoderma aceti*) to develop and turn the alcohol into an acetic acid. Vinegar was also prepared from wine made of the grape skins after the new wine had been pressed. Vinegar had several functions—it was used as a dressing for salads and a sop in which to dip bread (Ruth 2:14) and on occasion in a diluted state as a drink. Vinegar was also used as a solvent for herbs and drugs and utilized for medicinal reasons. Vinegar mixed with myrrh was what was offered to Jesus on the cross just before he died (Matt. 27:34; Mark 15:23; John 19:28-30).

Wine in the First Century

Temple, Ritual, and Offerings. Wine played a significant part in the ritual at the temple during the New Testament period, not only as a libation accompanying the daily sacrifices, but also as an offering brought by individuals. At the conclusion of the morning and evening sacrifices, a priest poured out the drink offering of wine—called a libation—on the base of the altar (like the blood of other offerings), at which time the Levites began to sing, pausing for the trumpets blown by the priests, which signaled the people to bow down in worship.[22] The individual sacrifices (burnt, trespass, peace—but not sin[23]) could be accompanied by a meal offering and a drink offering. The peace offering was always followed by a shared meal which included wine. Each of the sacrifices was accompanied by a specified drink offering: for a lamb, 1/4 hin of wine (one hin is about five liters); a ram, 1/3 hin; and a bull, 1/2 hin (Num. 15:5-10).[24] Traditionally the offerers ate and drank together afterward.

The daily sacrifices and offerings were doubled on the Sabbath, and additional sacrifices and drink offerings were made on new moons and feast days, all of which were in addition to the individual votive and freewill offerings.[25] The Feast of Tabernacles in particular characterized by extra offerings of wine and water, perhaps because of its harvest connections.

The temple stored large amounts of wine from the offerings and tithes of the people. Three obligations could involve bringing wine to the temple: firstfruits, priestly due, and tithes. A harvest's firstfruits required a donation from the seven crops listed in Deuteronomy 8:8, including grapes. The priestly due (or *tərûmāh*) was taken from the best of all the fruit of field and tree—"whatsoever is used for food and is kept watch over and grows from the soil is liable to tithes."[26] In some cases, wine was donated for each of these offerings because it was easier to store. Altogether there

Inscription from a wine (or oil) vessel. Part of this inscription reads "suited for the purity of hallowed things." The inscription was probably written on a jar that stood at the head of a row in a Masada storeroom. After the jar had been emptied, it was destroyed to prevent storing contents in it that were not ritually clean—that, in other words, did not fit the description on the jar (Yigael Yadin and Joseph Naveh, "The Aramaic and Hebrew Ostraca and Jar Inscriptions," in *Masada I: The Yigael Yadin Excavations 1963–1965, Final Reports,* ed. Joseph Aviram, Gideon Foerster, and Ehud Netzer [Jerusalem: Israel Exploration Society and Hebrew University of Jerusalem, 1989], 35).

was a considerable amount of wine to take care of at the temple, and it was put in the care of a treasury officer who was presumably a Levite. Also among the priests serving their turn at the temple was a drink officer who was chosen by casting lots.[27] Another of the priests was responsible for the vessels on the shewbread table, which many believe contained wine (Num. 4:7), and for the twelve loaves or bread of the presence.[28]

The most obvious symbol of wine at the temple was the large sculpted vine that twisted above the front entrance. Josephus says that above the temple doors "spread a golden vine with grape-clusters hanging from it, a marvel of size and artistry to all who saw with what costliness of material it had been constructed."[29] Josephus also describes the vine as having "grape-clusters as tall as a man" hanging from it.[30] This vine caused some in antiquity to mistakenly believe that the cult of Dionysos had become part of Israelite worship.[31] The cult of Dionysos (the Greek wine god) was evident in some of the more Hellenized cities in Palestine such as Caesarea and Beth Shean (Nysa Scythopolis) in the north and Rafiah in the south. In Beth Shean, Dionysos was the principal deity, and there is literary, epigraphic, archaeological, and numismatic evidence of his cult there.[32]

Common Table Drink. "The ordinary table beverage of the Mediterranean world in Roman times was wine mixed with water."[33] This mixture was not only preferred for reasons of taste and custom, but mixing water with wine also helped to purify the water. The wine was poured through a strainer (to remove lees and insects) into a large bowl, where it was mixed with various amounts of water. From there it was poured into individual cups or bowls. Jewish literature before and after the first century records mixing wine with water: "It is harmful to drink wine alone, or again, to drink water alone, while wine mixed with water is sweet and delicious and enhances one's enjoyment" (2 Macc. 15:39). Rabbi Eliezer (circa A.D. 100) is quoted in the Mishnah: "They do not say the Benediction over the wine until water has been added to it."[34] The ratio is thought to be one part of wine to two parts water, but later Talmudic sources record a one to three mixture.[35]

Feasts and Special Occasions. Wine was served at festivities, such as circumcisions, engagements, and weddings, and especially on Sabbath, when the customary blessing (*kiddush*) on the wine was pronounced. Wine was particularly important at feasts, such as the four cups required at the Passover.[36] Those in mourning were offered wine as a "cup of consolation" (Jer. 16:7) not only to help lift their spirits, but also because food could not be properly prepared in a home where a death had caused a state of uncleanness.

The celebration Purim included an admonition to drink in great quantities. The Talmud says, "It is the duty of a man to mellow himself (with wine) on Purim until he cannot tell the difference between 'cursed be Haman' and 'blessed be Mordecai.'"[37] In Jewish custom, this was probably the only case in which excessive drinking was appropriate. Drunkenness was regarded negatively and denounced on numerous occasions in the Old Testament.[38] The New Testament says drunkards are not prepared for the kingdom (Luke 21:34; and 1 Cor. 6:10), bishops and deacons are not to be drunkards (1 Tim. 3:3, 8), and Christians are to be filled with the Spirit rather than with wine (Eph. 5:18). Paul suggests that Christians not drink any wine at all if it causes a weaker brother to stumble (Rom. 14:21).

Abstinence. Several groups and individuals abstained from drinking wine. Priests during their course of service at the temple were forbidden to partake of wine (Lev. 10:8–9; Ezek. 44:21). Nazirites (those who took on a special personal vow) were prohibited from any product of the vine including grape juice, wine, grapes, vinegar, or raisins (Num. 6:3). Nazirite vows were still very much in practice during the first century. At least temporarily, John the Baptist may have been a Nazirite (Luke 1:15), and Acts 18:18 suggests that Paul was completing a Nazirite vow.

The Rechabites also proclaimed total abstinence from wine,[39] while the drinking habits of the Essenes are debated. Because of Josephus' description of Essene meals, some scholars believe that the Essenes did not partake of wine: "It is in fact due to their invariable sobriety and to the limitation of their allotted portions of meat and drink to the demands of nature."[40] Others argue that the Essenes were merely circumspect in their use of wine and did not become intoxicated.[41] Yadin suggests that the only day the Essenes drank wine was on the Feast of New Wine, which occurs fifty days after Pentecost, as recorded in the Temple Scroll.[42]

Medicinal Uses. The scriptures record several instances of medicinal applications of wine. Paul suggests to Timothy that he "drink no longer water, but use a little wine for thy stomach's sake and thine often infirmities" (1 Tim. 5:23). One explanation of this passage is that mixing wine with water killed "the numerous bacteria and organisms [in the water] that still are troublesome in the Middle East."[43] The most celebrated instance of the medicinal use of wine is the story of the Good Samaritan and his compassion on the man who fell among thieves: "And [he] went to him, and bound up his wounds, pouring in oil and wine, and set him on his own beast, and brought him to an inn, and took care of him" (Luke 10:34). Wine and oil were sometimes mixed together for dressing wounds and at other times administered separately.[44] Though not as effective as modern medicine, the wine was probably helpful in reducing infection and was the only antiseptic that was readily available to the Samaritan.

Wine is accorded numerous medicinal properties by some first-century writers. Pliny the Elder provides a list of ailments and poisons for which wine is to be administered[45] and prescribes wine mixed with water for cardiac disease and stomach disorders.[46] Resinated wine (wine with pine resin added for either enhancement or as a preservative) was thought to be effective for a variety of illnesses:

> Dioscorides Pedanius, a first-century A.D. army physician, explained in his *De Materia Medica* (v. 34) that although resinated wine might cause headaches and dizziness, it aided digestion, was diuretic, and good for people with colds, coughs, intestinal pains, dysentery, dropsy, and other ailments. Indeed, Dioscorides made it sound like a wonder drug.[47]

In later centuries, wines produced in Gaza and Ashcalon were considered good for stomach distress, fever, colic, kidney diseases, and liver ailments. The wines also were mixed with various herbs for making eye salve.[48]

Old Testament

Symbol of Fruitfulness and Fertility. Viticulture is first mentioned in the Old Testament when Noah built an altar to offer sacrifice, and then he "began to be an husbandman, and he planted a vineyard" (Gen. 9:20). Vineyards, vines, and grapes became symbols of fruitfulness and of the Lord's gracious care of his children.

The spies sent by Moses into the promised land returned with a cluster of grapes so large that "they bare it between two upon a staff" (Num. 13:23). The enormous bunch of grapes represented the bounty and fertility of the land prepared by the Lord for the Israelites. Descriptions of the promised land always include the vine: "A land of wheat, and barley, and vines, and fig trees, and pomegranates; a land of oil olive, and honey" (Deut. 8:8). Psalms says, "Thy wife shall be as a fruitful vine by the sides of thine house" (Ps. 128:3), using the vine again as a symbol of fertility. However, the metaphor of the grape as a symbol for abundance and fertility appears only in references to the land prepared by the Lord for Israel—the vine of the enemy "is of the vine of Sodom, and of the fields of Gomorrah: their grapes are grapes of gall, their clusters are bitter: Their wine is the poison of dragons, and the cruel venom of asps" (Deut. 32:32-33).

An important example of the figurative use of the vine is the allegory of the vineyard in Isaiah 5. Israel is compared to a vineyard that has been carefully developed and tended in order to produce good fruit (and by extension good wine) but does not.

> Now will I sing to my wellbeloved a song of my beloved touching his vineyard. My wellbeloved hath a vineyard in a very fruitful hill: and he fenced it, and gathered out the stones thereof, and planted it with the choicest vine, and built a tower in the midst of it, and also made a winepress therein: and he looked that it should bring forth grapes, and it brought forth wild grapes. . . . What could have been done more to my vineyard, that I have not done in it? wherefore, when I looked that it should bring forth grapes, brought it forth wild grapes? (Isa. 5:1-2, 4)

Israel not only produced wild grapes, but also participated in the evil overindulgence in wine: "Woe unto them that rise up early in the morning, that they may follow strong drink; that continue until night, till wine inflame them" (Isa. 5:11), and "woe unto them that are mighty to drink wine, and men of strength to mingle strong drink: which justify the wicked for reward, and take away the righteousness of the righteous from him" (Isa. 5:22-23).

Symbol of the Atonement of Christ and Final Judgment.
Warnings against the wickedness of intoxication are mild compared
with the images of wine as blood and the pain of being trodden as
grapes in a winepress. The first appearance of the symbol of the
winepress in reference to the Messiah arises in the blessing given
to Judah by his father Jacob: "Binding his foal unto the vine, and
his ass's colt unto the choice vine; he washed his garments in wine,
and his clothes in the blood of grapes: His eyes shall be red with
wine, and his teeth white with milk" (Gen. 49:11-12). In the book of
Isaiah, the reapplication of these images helps us understand both
the suffering of the Savior and the judgment upon the sinners:

> Wherefore art thou red in thine apparel, and thy garments like him
> that treadeth in the winefat? I have trodden the winepress alone; and
> of the people there was none with me: for I will tread them in mine
> anger, and trample them in my fury; and their blood shall be sprin-
> kled upon my garments, and I will stain all my raiment. For the day of
> vengeance is in mine heart, and the year of my redeemed is come.
> And I looked, and there was none to help; and I wondered that there
> was none to uphold: therefore mine own arm brought salvation unto
> me; and my fury, it upheld me. And I will tread down the people in
> mine anger, and make them drunk in my fury, and I will bring down
> their strength to the earth. (Isa. 63:2-6)

The unrepentant will be trodden down like the grapes in the press
as the Lord executes his judgment, but as their blood stains his garments (just as the grape juice stains the garments of the treaders),
he will redeem them. The Lord will tread the press alone; it will
not be a time of singing and joy in the vineyard. Even the beam
overhead that lends support to those treading the grapes will not
be there to uphold him; he will bring salvation by his own arm
to the people.

Jeremiah employs the metaphor of the cup of fury to demonstrate the wrath of the Lord that will come upon all nations in judgment: "Take the wine cup of this fury at my hand, and cause all the
nations, to whom I send thee, to drink it. And they shall drink, and
be moved, and be mad, because of the sword that I will send among
them. Then took I the cup at the Lord's hand, and made all the
nations to drink, unto whom the Lord had sent me" (Jer. 25:15-17).

There follows a list of Israel and all her neighbors that will
partake in this terrible drink: "Drink ye, and be drunken, and spue,

and fall, and rise no more, because of the sword which I will send among you" (Jer. 25:27). Lamentations specifically mentions Israel as one to reap this punishment: "The Lord hath trodden under foot all my mighty men in the midst of me: he hath called an assembly against me to crush my young men: the Lord hath trodden the virgin, the daughter of Judah, as in a winepress" (Lam. 1:15).

Symbol of Covenant. Wine is also an integral part of covenant in the Old Testament. Abraham partakes of the bread and wine blessed by Melchizedek, the priest of the most high God, before he pays his tithes (JST, Gen. 14:18–20). Jacob offers wine and oil at the pillar he erected to commemorate the Lord's renewal of the covenant of Abraham with him at Bethel (Gen. 35:9–15). Wine as a drink offering becomes a significant part of the system of sacrifices and offerings in the Mosaic covenant (see details of this in the section above concerning temple, ritual, and offerings).

The writings of the rabbis and the apocryphal literature have many references to wine—more than can be accommodated within the scope of this paper. An example of the centrality of the symbol of the vine and the wine it produced can be found in the Jewish traditions concerning the Garden of Eden. These traditions suggest that a river of wine flowed through the Garden for the use of its inhabitants[49] and that the Tree of Knowledge was a grapevine.[50] The grapevine planted by Noah following the flood was also thought to have come from the Garden.[51]

New Testament

The Wedding at Cana and Other Social Situations. The miracle of turning water into wine was an appropriate way for Jesus to begin his ministry, during which he elevated wine as both a symbol of the gospel and a symbol of the blood of the new covenant. The wedding at Cana was a celebration in which wine would have played a very typical part.

Before the miracle at Cana occurred, the disciples had manifested their faith in Christ and had made the commitment to follow him. Just prior to visiting Cana, the disciples said, "We have found him, of whom Moses in the law, and the prophets, did write," and spoke in terms such as "Messias" (or Christ), "Son of God," and "King of Israel" (John 1:41, 45, 49). They then attended the wedding with Jesus and his mother and were witnesses to the miracle. After his account of the event, John tells us, "This beginning of miracles did Jesus in Cana of Galilee, and manifested forth his glory; and his disciples believed on him" (John 2:11).

On other occasions, Jesus participated with common people in their local customs and was censured by the Pharisees for doing so. Jesus describes John the Baptist as "neither eating nor drinking," to which his opponents said, "He hath a devil," but, Jesus continues, "the Son of man came eating and drinking, and they say, Behold a man gluttonous, and a winebibber" (Matt. 11:18–19).

When Jesus ate at the house of Levi, the scribes and Pharisees questioned his disciples, "How is it that he eateth and drinketh with publicans and sinners?" (Mark 2:16). Jesus' response was plain: "They that are whole have no need of the physician, but they that are sick: I came not to call the righteous, but sinners to repentance" (Mark 2:17). Jesus further explained that while the bridegroom is with them, they are not to fast; it is a time of joy. "But the days will come when the bridegroom shall be taken away from them, and then shall they fast in those days" (Mark 2:20). The problem was not the substances Jesus was eating and drinking, but the people with whom he was eating and drinking.

Wine and the Vineyard as Symbols. Following this interchange with the Pharisees, Jesus explains that his message is like new wine—it must be put in new bottles. Old bottles or used wineskins filled with new wine will burst when the wine begins to ferment and gases form because the containers have no flexibility or room for expansion. The gospel cannot be constricted to the forms and limitations of the old law, just as old wineskins cannot hold the new wine (Mark 2:22).

Later Jesus refers to Isaiah and appeals to the metaphor of the vineyard to confront the chief priests and Pharisees:

> Hear another parable: There was a certain householder, which planted a vineyard, and hedged it round about, and digged a winepress in it, and built a tower, and let it out to husbandmen, and went into a far country: And when the time of the fruit drew near, he sent his servants to the husbandmen, that they might receive the fruits of it. (Matt. 21:33–34)

The chief priests and Pharisees may not have understood the true significance of this parable, but from the story it became clear that the vineyard of Isaiah (the house of Israel) had not been tended carefully; when the servants of the householder were sent to it, they were turned away, and even the Son himself was slain when trying to go unto the vineyard. The Pharisees "perceived that he spake of them" and "when they sought to lay hands on him, they feared the multitude, because they took him for a prophet" (Matt. 21:45–46).

Nowhere does the image of wine have more impact than in the final days and moments of the life of the Savior. The fourth cup of Passover wine at the Last Supper was offered by the Lord to the Apostles as a replacement for the sacrificial blood under the Mosaic covenant: "For this is my blood of the new testament [or covenant], which is shed for many for the remission of sins" (Matt. 26:28).

Following this introduction of the sacrament, the Lord proceeded to Gethsemane, a garden with an appropriate name—the *gat* meaning press, of *shemen* or oil.[52] Here Jesus prayed, "O my Father, if it be possible, let this cup pass from me: nevertheless not as I will, but as thou wilt" (Matt. 26:39). The Savior partook of the cup (an allusion to the cup of wrath from the Old Testament) and suffered all the agonies of the world. In Luke one reads that as Jesus suffered in the garden "his sweat was as it were great drops of blood falling down to the ground" (Luke 22:44). One can almost visualize the grapes being trodden and the "blood of the grapes" pressed out as the Lord was alone in the press at Gethsemane. Finally, as he hung upon the cross, Jesus was offered vinegar, an inferior type of wine, for his thirst. Jesus told his disciples that he would partake of wine again only "when I drink it new with you in my Father's kingdom" (Matt 26:29).

John in Revelation tells us that, before the expected marriage supper of the Lord and the joy of drinking the wine together, the wicked (Babylon) will "drink of the wine of the wrath of God, which is poured out without mixture into the cup of his indignation" (Rev. 14:10). The wine of wrath will be full strength—not diluted with water, the form to which the Israelites were accustomed. It is a gruesome scene.

> And the angel thrust in his sickle into the earth, and gathered the vine of the earth, and cast it into the great winepress of the wrath of God. And the winepress was trodden without the city, and blood came out of the winepress, even unto the horse bridles, by the space of a thousand and six hundred furlongs. (Rev. 14:19-20)

The Lord's clothing will appear as a "vesture dipped in blood," and "he treadeth the winepress of the fierceness and wrath of Almighty God" (Rev. 19:13, 15). The mercy of God was extended to all his children as the Savior suffered in the press for all in the meridian of time, and now the justice of God will be meted out as the Lord treads the winepress to execute judgment on the wicked who would not accept his offering.[53]

Conclusion

The fruit of the vine gave many gifts to ancient Israel. It provided nourishment to both body and soul as beverage and offering. In times of plenty, it was a sign of righteousness; in times of sickness it was a healing agent for the wounded. It was imported by King Herod and was stored by the people at Masada. Wine became a symbol of grace and wrath, but the terrible scenes of judgment are not the final images of wine in the scriptures. In the end, wine will again represent the happiness and blessings poured out by the Lord upon his people. Zechariah describes the joy the Lord will bring, "And their heart shall rejoice as through wine: yea, their children shall see it, and be glad; their heart shall rejoice in the Lord" (Zech. 10:7). Amos says of those days, "The mountains shall drop sweet wine" (Amos 9:13). Wine is a symbol of fellowship—in celebration with family, in communion with God at the temple and with the Sacrament, and in the covenant for all who will join in the great marriage supper of the Lord.

> And also that a feast of fat things might be prepared for the poor; yea, a feast of fat things, of wine on the lees well refined, that the earth may know that the mouths of the prophets shall not fail; Yea, a supper of the house of the Lord, well prepared, unto which all nations shall be invited. First, the rich and the learned, and the wise and the noble; And after that cometh the day of my power; then shall the poor, the lame, and the blind, and the deaf, come in unto the marriage of the Lamb, and partake of the supper of the Lord, prepared for the great day to come. (D&C 58:8–11)

At the Last Supper, the Savior taught the Apostles about their relationship to him, touching on the imagery of the vineyard: "I am the vine, ye are the branches: He that abideth in me, and I in him, the same bringeth forth much fruit: for without me ye can do nothing"

(John 15:5). This statement of Jesus may, perhaps, have been motivated by the great temple decoration of the vine, as well as by Christ's personal love for the land and agriculture of Judea and Galilee. The branches derive their life from the vine, and as disciples they are enjoined to transmit that life into bearing good fruit. The fruit of the vine is a testimony of their lives and bears witness of the only "true vine" (John 15:1).

Jo Ann H. Seely is Instructor of Ancient Scripture at Brigham Young University.

NOTES

[1]Quoted in Arnold A. Wieder, "Ben Sira and the Praises of Wine," *Jewish Quarterly Review* 61, no. 2 (1970): 155–66.

[2]The blessing over the wine found in the Mishnah, "[Blessed art thou . . .] who createst the fruit of the vine" (Berakoth 6.1), was expanded by certain groups on Passover and on the Sabbath, but the full text of this version was referred to only in Rabbinic writings and was unknown until its discovery in the Cairo Genizah. See Naphtali Wieder, "Birkat Yean 'Asis,'" *Sinai* 10 (1947): 43–48, for the modern publication.

[3]Josephus, *Jewish War* 7.295–97.

[4]Josephus, *Jewish War* 4.404–5.

[5]Yigael Yadin, *Masada: Herod's Fortress and the Zealots' Last Stand* (Jerusalem: Steimatzky's Agency, 1966), 96, 100.

[6]Palestine was known for its viticulture, and there is considerable evidence that wine was exported for many centuries, so it is interesting to note the evidence of imported wines. See Magen Broshi, "Wine in Ancient Palestine—Introductory Notes," *Israel Museum Journal* 3 (spring 1984): 21–40, for a summary of importing and exporting wine in ancient Palestine. See also Shemuel Ahituv, "Economic Factors in the Egyptian Conquest of Canaan," *Israel Exploration Journal* 28, nos. 1–2 (1978): 93–105; and Y. Dan, "The Foreign Trade of Palestine in the Byzantine Period" (in Hebrew), *Cathedra* 23 (April 1982): 17–24.

[7]Yadin, *Masada,* 189.

[8]See John A. Tvedtnes, "The Priestly Tithe in the First Century A.D." in this volume for a review of this topic.

[9]Research on towers has shown that temperatures inside could be 11.5 degrees centigrade (20 degrees Fahrenheit) lower than the outdoors during July, and the humidity 24 to 39 percent higher than outside, which helped to prevent spoilage. See Z. Y. D. Ron, *Stone Huts as an Expression of Terrace Agriculture in the Judean and Samarian Hills* (in Hebrew), 1–2 (Tel Aviv: n.p., 1977), 69–87.

[10]For a lengthy, although not exhaustive list of the terms related to wine and viticulture in Hebrew, see A. van Selms, "The Etymology of *Yayin,* 'Wine,'"

Journal of Northwest Semitic Languages 3 (1974): 76-84. Also for a comparison of terms related to wine in the Mediterranean cultures, see John Pairman Brown, "The Mediterranean Vocabulary of the Vine," *Vetus Testamentum* 19, no. 2 (1969): 146-70.

[11]It may be noted, however, that one scholar has recently argued at length that the words for wine in the Bible may refer either to fermented or *unfermented* grape juice. Samuele Bacchiocchi, *Wine in the Bible: A Biblical Study on the Use of Alcoholic Beverages* (Berrien Springs, Mich.: Biblical Perspectives, 1989), 30. Bacchiocchi argues that the process of preserving unfermented juice was actually surprisingly simple and that the positive references to wine in the Bible "have to do with unfermented and unintoxicating grape juice" (30-31). He also states that the Bible is "consistent in teaching moderation in the use of wholesome, unfermented beverages and abstinence from the use of intoxicating fermented beverages" (35).

[12]See Brown, "Mediterranean Vocabulary," 147-48; see also van Selms, "Etymology," 76-84, where he suggests a possible Semitic etymology for the term *yayin*.

[13]It has been suggested that *tirosh* in many cases should be translated as "grape," particularly passages speaking of growth and harvesting of the tirosh. See S. Naeh and M. P. Weitzman, "*Tirosh*—Wine or Grape? A Case of Metonymy," *Vetus Testamentum* 44, no. 1 (1994): 115-19.

[14]For a discussion of wine making in the ancient Near East, see R. J. Forbes, *Studies in Ancient Technology,* 9 vols. (Leiden: Brill, 1955), 3:70-83. For a survey of wine in ancient Palestine, see Broshi, "Wine in Ancient Palestine," 21-40.

[15]W. Dommershausen, *"Yayin,"* in *Theological Dictionary of the Old Testament,* ed. G. Johannes Bolterweck and Helmer Ringgren, trans. David E. Green, 7 vols. (Grand Rapids, Mich.: Eerdmans, 1990), 6:61.

[16]Everett Ferguson, "Wine as a Table-Drink in the Ancient World," *Restoration Quarterly* 13 (1970): 144-45; see also Forbes, *Ancient Technology,* 3:60 and following, and 3:70-83.

[17]Broshi, "Wine in Ancient Palestine," 26.

[18]Forbes, *Ancient Technology,* 3:118.

[19]N. Avigad suggested this term, *yayin cchl,* referred to the place where the wine was produced. N. Avigad, "Two Hebrew Inscriptions on Wine-Jars," *Israel Exploration Journal* 22, no. 1 (1972): 4-5. A. Demsky has argued that the inscription refers to "dark wine" and cites the mention of dark-colored wine in the Mishnah. A. Demsky, "'Dark Wine' from Judah," *Israel Exploration Journal* 22, no. 4 (1972): 233-34.

[20]A reference to smoked wine was discovered at Lachish. See David Ussishkin, "Excavations at Tel Lachish—1973-1977," *Tel Aviv* 5, nos. 1-2 (1978): 83-84.

[21]See Broshi, "Wine in Ancient Palestine," 26-27, where he lists the names and additives of seven different types of wine along with the references from the Talmud for these wines.

[22]Mishnah Tamid 7.3. A wonderful description of this is preserved in the writings of Ben Sira, who lived in the second century B.C., but it is most likely very similar to the ceremony many years later as recorded by the Mishnah. See Sirach 50.1213-21.

[23]For more information on these sacrifices, see the LDS Bible Dictionary, s.v. "sacrifices."

[24]For a discussion of measures used in the Bible, see Roland de Vaux, *Ancient Israel,* 2 vols. (New York: McGraw-Hill, 1961), 1:199–203. The measurements for liquids included a hin, which was 1/6 of a bath. De Vaux gives several different possibilities for the capacity of a bath, varying from 4 gallons 7 pints (22 or 23 liters) to 10 gallons (45 liters).

[25]See Numbers 28 and 29 for a list of the sacrifices and offerings given on these occasions.

[26]Mishnah Maʿaseroth 1.1.

[27]A more detailed discussion of the priestly courses and their activities is found in Emil Schürer, *The History of the Jewish People in the Age of Jesus Christ,* rev. and ed. Geza Vermes, Fergus Millar, and Matthew Black, 2 vols. (Edinburgh: T. and T. Clark, 1979), 2:275–91.

[28]For a discussion of these vessels and their contents, see Menahem Haran, *Temples and Temple-Service in Ancient Israel* (Oxford: Oxford University Press, 1978), 216–17.

[29]Josephus, *Antiquities* 15.395.

[30]Josephus, *Jewish War* 5.210.

[31]"The Hellenes say that . . . in the *adyton* of the temple in Jerusalem from both pillars there were once vines made of gold which held up the hangings of purple and scarlet; and so they concluded that the temple was of Dionysos." J. Lydus, *On Months,* ed. R. Wuensch (Leipzig: n.p., 1898), 4:53, quoted in Brown, "Mediterranean Vocabulary," 170 n.

[32]Broshi, "Wine in Ancient Palestine," 30–31, gives a brief summary of the Dionysos cult and also refers to G. Fuks, *Scythopolis—A Greek City in Eretz Israel* (in Hebrew) (Jerusalem: n.p., 1983) for the archaeological evidence.

[33]Ferguson, "Wine as a Table-Drink," 141–53.

[34]Mishnah Berakoth 7.5.

[35]Forbes, *Ancient Technology,* 3:148.

[36]Prior to settlement in Canaan (and the tending of vineyards), water may have been used in the Passover service and in the drink offerings. Before proscribing the drink offerings to accompany burnt sacrifices, the Lord specifies the time of implementation as *"when ye be come into the land* of your habitations, which I give unto you"* (Num. 15:2; italics added; also Lev. 23:10) The Samaritan Passover still does not have wine as part of the ritual.

[37]Babylonian Talmud, Megilah 7b.

[38]See Isaiah 5:11; 28:7; 56:11–12; Habakkuk 2:5; Hosea 4:11; Proverbs 20:1; 21:17; 23:20–21, 31–35.

[39]The Rechabites were first established in the eighth century B.C., separating themselves from Israel and living a nomadic life. Jeremiah records this about them: "We will drink no wine for Jonadab the son of Rechab our father commanded us, saying, Ye shall drink no wine, neither ye, nor your sons for ever: Neither shall ye build house, nor sow seed, nor plant vineyard, nor have any: but all your days ye shall dwell in tents" (Jer. 35:6–7).

[40]Josephus, *Jewish War* 2.133.

[41]For the argument concerning this, see D. Rokeah, "Essene Notes," in *Shnaton: An Annual for Biblical and Ancient Near Eastern Studies* 4 (1980): 263–68.

[42]Yigael Yadin, *The Temple Scroll,* 3 vols. (Jerusalem: Israel Exploration Society, 1983), 1:88–90.

[43]This must have been based on observation rather than scientific theory as they did not have microscopes. See William L. Coleman, *Today's Handbook of Bible Times and Customs* (Neptune, N.J.: Bethany House, 1984), 68.

[44]Coleman, *Handbook of Bible Times,* 67.

[45]Pliny, *Natural History,* trans. H. Rackham and W. H. S. Jones, Loeb Classical Library, 10 vols. (Cambridge: Harvard University Press, 1926-65), 23.23, 43.

[46]Pliny, *Natural History* 23.25, 50 and following.

[47]James Wiseman, "To Your Health!" *Archaeology* 49, no. 2 (1996): 27.

[48]Philip Mayerson, "The Use of Ascalon Wine in the Medical Writers of the Fourth to the Seventh Centuries," *Israel Exploration Journal* 43, nos. 2-3 (1993): 169-73.

[49]Louis Ginzberg, *The Legends of the Jews,* 7 vols. (Philadelphia: Jewish Publication Society of America, 1983), 1:20.

[50]Ginzberg, *Legends,* 5:97 and following; see note 70 for references concerning the traditions of the forbidden fruit.

[51]Ginzberg, *Legends,* 1:167; see also Pirkei de-R. Eliezer, 23, Targum Yerushalmi to Gen. 9:20.

[52]The word *gat* by itself is translated as winepress. See Francis Brown, S. R. Driver, and Charles A. Briggs, eds., *A Hebrew and English Lexicon of the Old Testament* (Oxford: Clarendon, 1951), s.v. *"gat"* on p. 178 and *"shemen"* on p. 1032.

[53]See also the description of the winepress in Doctrine and Covenants 133:46-52.

Hebrew, Aramaic, Greek, and Latin: Languages of New Testament Judea

Roger T. Macfarlane

A trilingual inscription placed by Pontius Pilate upon the cross proclaimed "Jesus of Nazareth the King of the Jews." This *titulus* was able to be read by many of the Jews, John says, not only because of Golgatha's proximity to the city, but also because the text was written in Hebrew, Greek, and Latin.[1] Pilate's declaration addressed the multilingual population of Jerusalem, both its residents and also its visitors, who were filling the city during the Passover. Weeks later, on the day of Pentecost, Peter and some Apostles addressed Jews, residents of Jerusalem who had gathered from every nation, and for a moment the polyglot assembly communicated in one language. Miraculously, "every man heard them speak in his own language" (Acts 2:6). It was cause for amazement that these Galileans were able to be understood by Parthians, Medes, Elamites, Mesopotamians, Judeans, Cappadocians, Pontians, Asians, Phrygians, Pamphylians, Egyptians, Cyrenians, Cretans, Arabians, and proselytes and Jews from Rome (Acts 2:1–13).

Not only the Jerusalem of these anecdotes, but all of Roman Judea in the first century A.D. was a place of tremendous linguistic diversity. Centuries of political and religious change had resulted in the establishment of a culture in which Hebrew, Aramaic, Greek, and Latin were written, read, and especially spoken by a multilingual group. This included governors and subjects, scholars and laymen, missionaries and proselytes, buyers and sellers, clients and kings. The rock of Masada, having yielded from its rubble Latin, Greek, Aramaic, and Hebrew texts, exemplifies the societal internexus of New Testament Palestine.

Linguistic History of Judea

Latin was the language of Rome and was a relative newcomer to the linguistic hodgepodge in Judea. At the time of Pontius Pilate's prefecture, Roman presence in Palestine was scarcely a century old. After centuries of Persian and Hellenistic influence, the arrival of Rome made no dramatic impact on the linguistic environment of the area, though the nature of her arrival under the direction of Pompey the Great in 63 B.C. left an indelible political mark. A passage in the Palestinian Talmud states that "four languages have come into the world to be used, Greek for singing, Latin for warfare, Aramaic (*sursi*) for lamentation, Hebrew (*ivri*) for speaking."[2] This limited view of Latin's utility reflects an animosity toward Rome's military occupation of the region. Roman prefects and governors communicated in Latin with their peers on issues of military administration; Latin was also the official language of the Roman troops among the occupying force, as is manifest by scraps of Latin texts littered about Masada after its fall. One noteworthy papyrus, a document pertaining to the pay and kit of a member of the Roman garrison, records the presence of C. Messius C. f. Fabia Berutensis, a legionary soldier.[3]

As in other eastern provinces of the Roman empire, communication between Romans and the inhabitants of Palestine was conducted, pragmatically, in Greek. The language had enjoyed growing currency in the region for generations, with the result that, by the time of the Roman occupation, Greek was securely fixed as the *lingua franca*. Introduced formally at the time of Alexander's conquest of the area—of course there is evidence for very ancient trade between Greece and the Middle East—Greek remained the administrative language of Alexander's empire long after his early death in 323 B.C.

Classical Greece accommodated many dialects of the Greek language, with both subtle and deep differences existing among the various regions of Greece. The dialect of Attica, as spoken and written in Athens during the fifth century, came to be regarded as the standard of classical Greece. The consolidation of independent city-states into larger political units, coincident with the demise of Athens and the arrival of Macedonian supremacy, forged a new dialect of Greek that combined and blurred the peculiarities of various constituent dialects into one "common" dialect, the so-called *Koiné.* Koiné was the language that was exported with Alexander's conquests. Koiné Greek is Hellenistic Greek; the term applies to Greek spoken and written between the rise of Alexander until the advent of Byzantium, around A.D. 550. To be sure, a language spread over myriad peoples throughout nearly a millennium could hardly remain constant. And, indeed, Koiné was by no means static, but its relative stability was remarkable.

Alexander's legacy of Hellenistic culture survived the division of his realm by his successors. The Jews, like other nations in the vast territory of Alexander's conquests, remained under the influence of Greek-speaking dynasts for much of the next three centuries. When Ptolemy I Soter secured himself finally as Alexander's successor in Palestine and Cyprus in 304 B.C., he persisted in the use of Greek as the language of his administration. Under the watch of Ptolemy V Epiphanes, Ptolemaic control of Palestine was yielded in 200 to the Seleucid Antiochus IV, who conspired with pro-Hellenistic elements to convert Jerusalem into a Greek city and actually dedicated the temple there to Olympian Zeus. The ensuing Maccabean revolt produced an attitude of nationalism and allowed the remedy of many recent changes, especially the rededication of the temple to Israel's god in 164. Yet the influence of Greek language in Palestine remained strong, as many Jews had become bilingual.

From the second century before Christ, Jewish literature was both translated into Greek and written originally in Greek. Eupolemus (active between 158 and 150 B.C.) was a Palestinian Jew with a Hellenistic education, whose Greek account of the kings of Judea seems to have harmonized the Hasmonean claims to Jewish cultural sovereignty with Hellenism.[4] Josephus was also of Jewish aristocratic descent, a priest with a Pharisaic education and a political leader before Jerusalem's fall to Rome. When Josephus composed his history of the Jewish War, he wrote one account, no longer extant, in Aramaic for the Jews in Mesopotamia and another account, which survives, in Greek. He comments in the *Jewish Antiquities* on the tension that existed in his day between conservative Jews who would retain the use of Hebrew and those who sought to refine their use of Greek: "Our people dislike those who speak Greek well."[5]

Remarkable in its own right, but also noteworthy here because of its connection to Masada, is the apocryphal Ecclesiasticus or Wisdom of Ben Sira, which was written originally in Hebrew at Jerusalem in about 180 B.C. This book manifested a certain tolerance of Hellenism, provided it could be fitted to Judaism. The author, known as Ben Sira, is identified as a sage named Jesus, son of Eleazar, son of Sira.[6] Ben Sira proposed a way of life that reconciled fidelity to the faith of one's fathers with the difficulties of contemporary life. Hellenism was acceptable, provided it did not interfere with the functions of Jewish traditions.[7]

Ben Sira's grandson translated the book into Greek probably about the same time Eupolemus was writing. The Greek version, written for a readership that was not conversant in Hebrew, gave the book's teachings a wider audience and greater popularity. In his preface, the translator admits the difficulty of translating from Hebrew to Greek—clearly favoring the former, but his effort suggests that his grandfather's book would be less widely read in Hebrew than in Greek, at least among the Jews of the Diaspora. Fragments of the original Hebrew text of the Wisdom of Ben Sira have come to light in the last century, including a lacunulose scroll found at Masada. Containing portions of chapters 39:27–44:20, the Masada scroll is apparently the oldest surviving Hebrew manuscript of the text.[8]

Languages in First-Century Palestine

The Hellenization of Judea, which continued after the Seleucids under the Hasmoneans and then the Herodians, was reflected in secular and religious affairs. The dispersion of Jews among various cultures decentralized not only their political, but also their cultural unity. In the Diaspora, Greek came to be used as the *lingua franca*. At Jerusalem also, Israel became more accustomed to Hellenism and increasingly used Greek more commonly. The Passover and other feasts brought to Jerusalem an annual, if temporary, influx of Hellenized Jews. In Jerusalem members of the political and priestly elite sought advantage in the adoption of Hellenistic

culture and the use of Greek.[9] This is reflected in the surprising
fact that of all Jewish funerary inscriptions recorded at Jerusalem
before A.D. 70, 40 percent are in Greek.[10] It became so common for
Jews to use Greek that the invention of a Jewish historiography—
providing a readable record not just for Gentiles, but also for Jews
who knew little Hebrew—in the Greek language seems natural.

It would appear that members of all socioeconomic levels of
the community could use Greek, as suggested by a papyrus letter
found at Masada. The letter records the correspondence sent by one
Abascantos to a person, perhaps his own brother, named Judah.[11]
The contents of the letter could not be more mundane: the discussion pertains to the supply of liquids and lettuces. Yet the document is a valuable cultural artifact, demonstrating the casual and
practical use of Greek among the Jews at Masada.[12]

Abascantos's letter to Judah is indicative of commonplace use
of Greek in first century A.D. Palestine. In addition to the numerous
funerary inscriptions and the prohibitive inscription on the Jerusalem temple, further evidence is found in a decree on tomb robbery set up at Nazareth, the scroll of the minor prophets and other
Greek fragments from Qumran, and numerous books of both secular and religious importance to Jews, Christians, and pagans.[13]

Indeed, one need not look far for evidence that Greek was
commonplace in the multilingual society of first-century Palestine.
At this crossroads of the Middle East, Greek found common use
beside Hebrew and Aramaic. At the time of Masada's siege, Hebrew
and Aramaic each had enjoyed a long history in the region of
Judea. Classical Hebrew flourished throughout the history of the
Kingdom of Israel, around 1000–587 B.C. During this time, all formal prose was written in classical biblical Hebrew. The nature of
the language that was spoken at the time in the Southern Kingdom, however, is uncertain,[14] and with the captivity of Israel the
native language of the Jews suffered corruption. The exile of Israel's
educated elite necessitated their learning the language of Babylon,
where, by 587, Aramaic had replaced Akkadian as the spoken language. Cyrus made Aramaic the administrative language of the vast
Persian empire and thus assisted in the proliferation of that language. It had already been introduced into Palestine in the eighth
century (2 Kgs. 17:24).

There is no doubt that Aramaic influenced the grammar and vocabulary of postexilic Hebrew. Aramaic, on the other hand, was not uniformly applied by the various ethnic and cultural groups that received it. Thus, a number of dialectical forms of the language, commonly referred to as middle Aramaic, evolved: Syriac, Mandean, Samaritan, Jewish Babylonian Aramaic, Galilean Aramaic, and Christian Palestinian Aramaic.

Simultaneously, then, from about the time of the Maccabean revolt until into the third century A.D., the peoples of Palestine coexisted in a state of multilingualism.[15] Native speakers of Hebrew, various dialects of Aramaic, and Koiné Greek lived side by side. It is difficult and somewhat hazardous to draw conclusions about the state of interaction among these various linguistic groups. Horsley observes that

> Greek was apparently the official language of Sepphoris under Herod and Antipas as under the Seleucid and Ptolemaic imperial administrations earlier (and in Tiberias, once it was founded). Yet we cannot conclude, on the basis of their supposed contact with Sepphoris, that most Galileans had become accustomed to speaking Greek by the first century C.E.[16]

We can conclude, he observes, that "language usage in Galilee is heavily interrelated with the fundamental social (political-economic-religious) division between the rulers and the ruled, cities and villages, and the historical changes introduced by the rulers based in cities."[17]

Determining which languages were spoken by Jesus and his Galilean disciples has been the point of considerable debate.[18] Current scholarship tends to support the belief that Jesus may well have spoken at least three languages: Hebrew, Galilean Aramaic, and at least some Greek. Given the pervasive multilingualism of the immediate surroundings, this would seem true. Thus Jesus' fluency in the first two may be assumed;[19] as evidence for Jesus' ability to speak Greek, some salient items may be considered.[20] For Jesus and his adoptive father to have waged a successful business among the inhabitants of Nazareth and Galilee, they would probably have needed to be conversant in Greek.[21] Two notable conversations Jesus held with Gentiles—his first gentile convert, the centurion (Matt. 8:5–13; Luke 7:2–10), and the Syro-Phoenician woman

(Mark 7:25–30), whom Mark observes was a *hellenis,* "Greek"—were possibly conducted in Greek.[22] The disciples mistakenly thought at one point that Jesus himself intended to expand his mission to include the Gentiles (John 7:35), who would probably have had to be taught in Greek. Pilate's interrogation of Christ was most likely conducted in the language of Roman administration in the East, Greek. Pilate can be assumed to have spoken Greek. A Roman magistrate's ability to speak Aramaic or Hebrew would have been worthy of comment, but the writers of the Gospel accounts make none, nor do they mention an interpreter's presence in the New Testament accounts of Jesus' conversations with Roman magistrates. Such evidence suggests strongly that Jesus was able to converse in the region's *lingua franca,* Greek.

Written documents recovered in the Judean desert demonstrate further the pervasiveness of multilingualism around the time of Christ. Beside the familiar hoards of Qumran are the Babatha archive and the scattered literary remains from Masada. Babatha was a Jewish woman who secreted away in a cave a bundle of her personal papers. These papyri constitute a time capsule of enormous historical value.[23] The documents, written in Greek, Nabatean, and Aramaic, provide an uncommonly clear view into the life of an individual and into the administration of Roman imperial affairs in Arabia and Palestine between A.D. 94 and 132.

Languages at Masada

While the literary rubble of Masada pales in comparison to the Babatha material, the bits and scraps that survive—biblical and apocryphal scrolls, ostraca, documentary papyri, *tituli picti* (inscriptions), graffiti, and amphora stamps—also attest the common use of Latin, Greek, Hebrew, and Aramaic.

Wine jars from the period of Herod's residence bear in Latin the name of C. Sentius Saturninus, consul in 19 B.C. and legate of Syria from 9 to 6, whose name was written onto the jars to date their contents. Other similar written fragments—recording the import of Cumean apples, honey, and the renowned fish sauce called *garum* βασιλέως—starkly contrast the extravagance of Herod's residence with that of the zealots. Hebrew letters are chiseled onto the

Fragments of the book of Leviticus. The scroll was apparently mutilated intentionally.

cylinders that made up the columns of the Herodian living quarters, suggesting that the laborers for that complex were Jewish.

The written remains left by the Jewish defenders are more compelling. Numerous ostraca and other tags written in both Aramaic and Hebrew bear individual names or single letters and may have been used in a system of rationing or for tithing. Fragmentary scriptural scrolls of biblical, apocryphal, and sectarian texts are of varied importance.[24]

Other, more mundane scraps of evidence were left by the Roman garrison some time after A.D. 73—documents illuminating the conveyance of hospital supplies, a note regarding the balsam trade, a notice of a soldier's salary, a graffito that quotes Vergil's *Aeneid,* and other odds and ends. In short, the bits and pieces of the literary remains at Masada can help fill out interpretations of Jewish or Roman lifestyles, but none really enlightens single-handedly. As a whole, the multilingual assembly of scraps illuminates a moment when cultures collided in the Judean desert.

Literary remains cannot answer to what degree the population of Masada's fortress was literate. The biblical scrolls were found near the synagogue, which may mean that the texts were used by men who were trained to read biblical Hebrew and who could convey the import of the texts in worship services. The other documents that survive from the period of the Masada siege do not necessarily require extensive literacy on the part of their users, as most of these texts are brief and are restricted to a single name or phrase or alphabetic character. General literacy was probably no higher in Palestine or at Masada than in Hellenized cities of the Roman empire, some of which seem to have achieved 20–30 percent literacy rates.[25] It is impossible to know how completely the documents left behind by Masada's defenders survived the centuries of weather and plundering until the archaeologists uncovered the remnants in the 1960s. The scroll of Leviticus is assumed to have been mutilated intentionally. And there is no telling how many scrolls were removed intact and are now lost or deposited elsewhere. Still, it is intriguing and informative to consider the rock of Masada as a document of the multilingual culture that existed in first-century Judea.

Roger T. Macfarlane is Assistant Professor of Classics at Brigham Young University.

NOTES

[1]John 19:19–20. Of similar nature is the Herodian-period, bilingual—Greek and Latin—inscription posted on the pillars of the temple, prohibiting Gentiles from entering the sacred precinct. Josephus, *Jewish War* 5.193–94. Also see the surviving examples of a similar warning in Greek preserved in the Archaeological Museum at Istanbul and in the Rockefeller Museum at Jerusalem. The text of this inscription is reproduced in *Supplementum Epigraphicum Graecum*, vol. 8, no. 169; the inscription is depicted in Joseph A. Fitzmyer, "Did Jesus Speak Greek?" *Biblical Archaeology Review* 18 (September/October 1992): 61.

[2]Palestinian Talmud, Megillah 4.71b, as translated in Chaim Rabin, "Hebrew and Aramaic in the First Century," in *The Jewish People in the First Century: Historical Geography, Political History, Social, Cultural and Religious Life and Institutions,* ed. Shmuel Safrai and Menahem Stern, Compendia Rerum Iudaicarum ad Novum Testamentum 2 (Assen: Van Gorcum, 1976), 1019 n. 3.

[3]Hannah M. Cotton and Joseph Geiger, "The Latin and Greek Documents," in *Masada II: The Yigael Yadin Excavations 1963–1965, Final Reports,* ed. Joseph Aviram, Gideon Foerster, and Ehud Netzer (Jerusalem: Israel Exploration Society and Hebrew University of Jerusalem, 1989), 35–56, doc. 722.

[4]Compare Alfred R. Leaney, "Greek Manuscripts from the Judean Desert," in *Studies in New Testament Language and Text: Essays in Honour of George D. Kilpatrick on the Occasion of His Sixty-fifth Birthday,* Novum Testamentum Supplement 44 (Leiden: Brill, 1976), 286.

[5]Josephus, *Antiquities* 20.264.

[6]Wisdom of Ben Sira 50:27; 51:30. Alexander A. Di Lella, "Ben Sira and His Times," in *The Wisdom of Ben Sira,* trans. Patrick W. Skehan, comm. A. A. Di Lella (New York: Doubleday, 1987), 8. Di Lella suggests that the Greek translation can be dated to 117 B.C. and that the original composition must have been complete before Antiochus IV's pursuit of utter Hellenization in Judea.

[7]Compare Ben Sira 50:25–26.

[8]In 1896 a substantial portion of the Hebrew text was found in the Cairo Genizah, but bits of the text have also been discovered at Qumran (6:20–31; 51:12–20).

[9]J. T. Townsend, "Education (Greco-Roman)," in *The Anchor Bible Dictionary,* ed. David Noel Freedman, 6 vols. (New York: Doubleday, 1992), 2:317.

[10]Peter van der Horst, "Jewish Funerary Inscriptions," *Biblical Archaeology Review* 18, no. 5 (1992): 46. The frequency of Greek in all Jewish funerary inscriptions is a remarkable 70 percent.

[11]Cotton and Geiger, "Latin and Greek Documents," 85–88, doc. 741.

[12]Cotton and Geiger, "Latin and Greek Documents," 86, further, claim that the fragment is the earliest documentary papyrus from Palestine.

[13]For full documentation and limited discussion of each of these items, see Gerard Mussies, "Greek in Palestine and the Diaspora," in Safrai and Stern, *Jewish People in the First Century,* 1053.

[14]I depend, in this paragraph, on the historical outline of Hebrew and Aramaic of Rabin, "Hebrew and Aramaic," 1012–19. Rabin cites Zellig S. Harris, *Development of the Canaanite Dialects* (New Haven: American Oriental Society, 1939), 22–23, who believes classical Hebrew to be the dialect of Jerusalem.

[15]For Rabin's belief that Mishnaic Hebrew was the spoken language of Judea, see Rabin, "Hebrew and Aramaic," 1015. For distinctions among the terms *bilingualism, lingua franca,* and *diglossia,* see Rabin, "Hebrew and Aramaic," 1007-10.

[16]Richard A. Horsley, *Galilee: History, Politics, People* (Valley Forge, Penn.: Trinity, 1995), 247.

[17]Horsley, *Galilee,* 247.

[18]Rabin, "Hebrew and Aramaic," 1033, wrote that "the language of Jesus has proved to be a problem which has generated much discussion, and can be considered as being still unsolved." Rabin's observation remains true twenty years later.

[19]There are numerous Aramaic expressions in the New Testament; Hebrew is read at Luke 4:16-19.

[20]Joseph A. Fitzmyer, "Did Jesus Speak Greek?" *Biblical Archaeology Review* 18, no. 5 (1992): 58-63, 76-77, reviews the current state of the question; but see also his fuller statement in "The Languages of Palestine in the First Century A.D." in *A Wandering Aramean: Collected Aramaic Essays,* Society of Biblical Literature Monograph Series 25 (Missoula, Mont.: Scholars Press, 1979), 57-84.

[21]Barnabas Lindars, "The Language in Which Jesus Taught," *Theology* 86 (September 1983): 363-64.

[22]Given the multilingual nature of Palestine, one might as easily assume that these Gentiles spoke Aramaic: the Syro-Phoenician woman must have spoken some Semitic language (for example, Phoenician or Aramaic) as her native tongue, and the centurion might have served as an officer in a Roman legion without being necessarily monolingual.

[23]Naphthali Lewis, ed., *Judean Desert Studies: The Documents from the Bar Kokhba Period in the Cave of Letters, Greek Papyri* (Jerusalem: Israel Exploration Society, 1989). Compare Glen W. Bowersock, "The Babatha Papyri, Masada, and Rome," *Journal of Roman Archaeology* 4 (1991): 336-44; and Martin Goodman, "Babatha's Story," *Journal of Roman Studies* 81 (1991): 169-75.

[24]These scrolls are discussed by David Rolph Seely, "The Masada Fragments, the Qumran Scrolls, and the New Testament," in this volume.

[25]William V. Harris, *Ancient Literacy* (Cambridge: Harvard University Press, 1989), 185, 187-88. Martin D. Goodman, "Texts, Scribes and Power in Roman Judea," in *Literacy and Power in the Ancient World,* ed. Alan K. Bowman and Greg Woolf (Cambridge: Cambridge University Press, 1994), 99-108, shows that not reading in itself, but writing, secured real power.

Coins in the New Testament

Nanci DeBloois

The coins found at Masada—Ptolemaic, Seleucid, Herodian, Roman, Jewish, Tyrian, Nabatean, etc.—testify not only of the changing fortunes of Judea, but also of the variety of coins circulating in that and neighboring countries during this time. Such diversity generates some difficulty in identifying the coins mentioned in the New Testament.

Since the beginnings of coinage in the seventh or sixth centuries B.C., Judea had been under the control of the Persians; Alexander the Great and his successors, the Ptolemies of Egypt and the Seleucids of Pergamum; as well as "local" leaders such as the Hasmoneans. Because of internal discord about 37 B.C., Rome became involved in the political and military affairs of the area, with the result that Judea became a Roman province in A.D. 6. Each change of leadership or power meant an accompanying change of coinage, from the gold and silver *Philippi* and *Alexandreis* of Philip II of Macedon and his son Alexander the Great, to the Roman provincial coinage bearing the image of Caesar Augustus and his successor, Tiberius. In addition to the monetary differences resulting from political changes in Judea, Jewish males from throughout the world brought foreign coins with them to pay the "temple tax" when they made their annual pilgrimage to Jerusalem.

For these reasons, among others, it is difficult, if not impossible, to identify with any certainty which coins are meant by the numerous references to them in the New Testament. Seven different types or denominations of coins are mentioned by name: *denarius, drachma, didrachm, stater, assarion, kodrantes,* and *lepton.* In addition, there are general references to money or sums of money, for example to *argurion* and *talenton.*

Probably the most recognizable of all the coins is the one described when Jesus was challenged about paying taxes to Caesar (Matt. 22:15–22; Mark 12:13–17; Luke 20:20–26). According to the accounts, Jesus was asked by the Herodians and the students or followers of the Pharisees, who intended to "entangle him in his talk," if it was legal to pay the *kensos* ("census," poll tax) to Caesar. When he asked them to show him the money to pay the tax, they showed him a denarius, a large silver Roman coin, and identified the image and inscription it bore as belonging to Caesar. Jesus' reply is well known: "Render unto Caesar the things that are Caesar's and to God the things that are God's" (Matt. 22:21; Mark 12:17; Luke 20:25).

The denarius Jesus was shown was stamped with the image of Caesar. But which Caesar? Beginning in 44 B.C. with an issue of silver denarii bearing the image of the wreathed head of Julius Caesar and the legend CAE-SAR.DICT.PERPETVO,[1] each successive Caesar customarily issued

Fig. 1. Silver denarius of Caesar Tiberius. Traditionally, this denarius has been named as the tribute money shown to Christ. However, the Caesar whose image was on the "penny" brought by Christ's detractors could have been Julius or Augustus.

silver (and gold) denarii stamped with his own likeness, or the imperial mints issued such coins in the emperor's honor. A whole series of denarii were struck during the reign of Augustus Caesar (27 B.C.–A.D. 14) with his image on the obverse. Throughout the principate of Tiberius (A.D. 14–37), the imperial mints struck a series of gold and silver coins carrying his image with the legend TI.CAESAR DIVI AVG. F. AVGVSTVS, and on the reverse, a seated woman presumed to be Livia, Tiberius's mother, with the legend PONTIF. MAXIM.[2] (See fig. 1.) The practice of stamping coinage with the emperor's image continued long after Tiberius. It is the silver denarius of Tiberius that has become known as the "tribute penny," although the coin Jesus was shown could also have been a denarius of Julius or Augustus Caesar.

The "census" was instituted in A.D. 6, when Judea was made a Roman province, with the requirement that it be paid in Roman coin. The amount was a denarius, the "standard" silver coin of the Roman Empire. The word is somewhat misleadingly translated "penny" several times in the King James Bible because in Britain *d.* (originally designating a denarius) is the abbreviation for *pence.*[3] Clearly, however, the denarius was worth a good deal more than a penny. Although it is impossible to establish an accurate value for the coin in modern terms, a survey of the value of a denarius in New Testament times can provide some perspective. The accepted salary for a day's work by a common laborer was a denarius, as illustrated in the parable about the man who hired servants to work in his vineyard (Matthew 20:1-16). Each worker received one denarius whether he worked all day or was hired "at the eleventh hour." In the parable of the Good Samaritan (Luke 10:35), the amount paid to the innkeeper for the care and lodging of the injured Jew was two denarii, or two days' wages.

Other references to the denarius occur in the story about the feeding of the five thousand. In Mark's account (6:37), the Apostles ask Jesus if they should buy two hundred denarii worth of bread to feed the crowd, and in John's (6:7), Philip says that two hundred denarii will not buy enough bread for so many people. In Mark 14:5 and John 12:5, which tell similar stories, the value of spikenard ointment is stated to be three hundred denarii (a year's wages for a laborer). In both stories, the ointment is used to anoint Jesus, but others object that a more praiseworthy deed would have been selling it and giving the money to the poor. To teach Simon, the Pharisee, a lesson about service and forgiveness, Jesus uses the example of two debtors, one owing five hundred denarii and the other fifty, both of whom are forgiven their debts (Luke 7:41).

One of the basic silver coins of the Greeks was the drachma, which circulated throughout the Hellenistic eastern Mediterranean in the wake of Alexander the Great and his successors (see fig. 2). The New Testament parable of the lost coin refers to drachmas: "What woman having ten pieces of silver [the King James translation for ten drachmas], if she lose one piece, doth not light a candle, and sweep the house, and seek diligently until she find it?" (Luke 15:8-10). We are also told that the temple tax paid annually

Fig. 2. Obverse and reverse views of a drachma. These silver coins were struck about 130 B.C. in Rhodes. A drachma figures in the parable of the lost coin.

by every Jewish male—even when dispersed throughout the world—was two drachmas, or a didrachm (Matt. 17:24). The amount is established in the Old Testament at half a shekel (Ex. 30:13; 38:26).[4] Some numismatists believe that the drachma was originally about equal in weight and value to a Roman denarius, but by New Testament times, the relationship appears to have been about four drachma to three denarii. A third-century-B.C. source says the drachma was the price of a sheep or one-fifth the price of an ox.[5]

Fig. 3. Gold stater. Struck during the time of Philip III of Macedon (323–316 B.C.).

The most valuable coin mentioned by name in the New Testament is the Greek stater, originally struck in gold but later in silver. The gold stater known as the *Philippus*, first struck by Philip II of Macedon, the father of Alexander the Great, and the one known as the *Alexandreios*, for Alexander, continued to be struck and circulated many years after their deaths. (See fig. 3.) But staters were issued by other Greek cities and states, and the size and value varied from place to place. The silver stater of the New Testament has been estimated to be equal in value to eight denarii or four drachmas (or a tetradrachm or two didrachms). The coin Peter found in the mouth of a fish, with which he was to pay the annual temple tax of a didrachm for both himself and Jesus, was a stater (Matt. 17:27, where the King James Version renders it "a piece of money"). The thirty pieces of silver Judas Iscariot received for betraying Jesus (Matt. 26:15; 27:3, 5–6) may have been staters.[6]

Another Roman coin mentioned in the New Testament, although it is referred to by its Greek diminutive, is the "as," or the assarion. It was a bronze coin originally worth one-tenth of a denarius, but in the mid-second century B.C., it was devalued to one-sixteenth of a denarius to reflect its change of value in the market.[7] At Pergamum and Ephesus, however, the denarius was worth eighteen assaria.[8] The King James Bible translates assarion as "farthing" both at Matthew 10:29, where it is given as the purchase price of two sparrows (presumably for sacrifice), and Luke 12:6, where the price of five sparrows is two assaria (cheaper in bulk, perhaps).

Also translated as "farthing" in the King James Version (Matt. 5:26; Mark 12:42) is *kodrantes,* Greek for the Latin *quadrans,* a coin worth one-fourth an assarion. The context of the citation in Matthew is a lesson on forgiveness and reconciliation with one's opponents, "lest . . . the adversary deliver thee to the judge, and the judge deliver thee to the officer, and thou be cast into prison. Verily I say unto thee, Thou shalt by no means come out thence till thou has paid the uttermost farthing [*kodrantes*]" (Matt. 5:25). The passage in Mark refers to the widow who cast into the treasury "two mites [*lepta*], which make a farthing [kodrantes]."

The last coin mentioned in the New Testament and the smallest both in value and size is the lepton, the widow's "mite." (See fig. 4.) Originally a small, Greek copper coin worth one-seventh of a *chalkos* in Athens,[9] it was the smallest bronze coin used by the Jews and was valued at one-half a quadrans (kodrantes), according to Mark 12:42. The word also appears in Luke's version of the widow's mite story (Luke 21:2) and the "prison" lesson (compare Matt. 5:25): "Thou shalt not depart thence, till thou hast paid the very last mite [lepton]" (Luke 12:59).

Fig. 4. Widow's "mites." Bronze lepta struck during the times of Herod, Herod Agrippa, and Pilate.

One coin not mentioned by name in the New Testament but probably best known to the Jews was the shekel. Like the drachma, the shekel was originally a weight rather than a coin. At the time of the New Testament, a Judean silver shekel was considered to be

Fig. 5. Tyrian shekel, A.D. 54/55. The obverse has the head of Heracles-Melqart, the principal god of Tyre, and the reverse, an eagle standing on a prow and the legend "Tyre the Holy and City of Asylum." Even with the image of a god upon it, this and similar coins had to be accepted by the Jews.

worth four denarii, and a gold shekel was valued at fifteen silver shekels. In the Old Testament, a shekel (weight) of gold was the value of an ox or about two tons of grain; a ram was worth two silver shekels (Lev. 5:15). The average weight of the silver shekels that have survived is 11.4 grams or one-fourth ounce, about the same weight as an American half-dollar.[10] Shekels, along with half- and quarter-shekels, were minted locally at Gaza or Ashkelon as well as at Tyre and Antioch. The thirty pieces of silver (*triakonta arguria*) Judas Iscariot received (Matt. 26:15) are believed by some scholars to have been Tyrian or Antiochan silver shekels (see fig. 5). At the ratio of 4 denarii per shekel, the amount Judas received would be 120 denarii, or about four months' salary for a laborer, a sum considered appropriate compensation or "blood money" when someone was accidentally killed (Ex. 21:32).

Unlike the shekel, the talent is a weight or value that did not become the name of a coin.[11] Two well-known parables in the Gospels use the talent: the parable of the unforgiving servant (Matt. 18:24) and the parable of the talents (Matt. 25:14–30; Luke 19:11–27). The unforgiving servant is excused a debt of ten thousand talents (Matt. 18:23) but refuses in turn to forgive a debt of one hundred pence (18:28). The King James version's "ten thousand talents" is a literal translation of *muriôn talantôn,* although the modifier *muriôn* can also mean "countless," a very large, but indefinite, number. The "hundred pence" is a rendering of *hekaton denaria,* a hundred denarii.

Although the relative value of a talent is even more difficult to pin down than the values of the coins, it represents a great deal of money. The Bible Concordance gives the value at 750 ounces of silver, based on a Roman penny as one-eighth of an ounce. Another source claims that a talent weighed 125 *librae* (Roman pounds of 12 ounces each) or that it was a variable weight between 58 and 80 modern pounds, depending on its composition, whether silver or gold, and place of origin—a Syrian talent, for example, was worth less than one-fourth the value of an Aeginetan or Attic talent.[12] Borowski says it was worth 3,000 shekels or a Babylonian *kikar*.[13] King Solomon's annual income was said to be 666 talents of gold, and the gold mines of Krenides, taken over by Philip II of Macedon, produced 1,000 talents per year.[14] Even making allowances for hyperbole, for a servant to owe 10,000 talents seems very unlikely and to be forgiven of the debt even more unlikely.

The parable of the talents gives amounts that are somewhat more realistic. One servant received five talents, another two, and a third only one talent, "each according to his ability" (Matt. 25:15). The first servant doubled his five talents, as did the one who received two talents, but the third servant, because of his fear, buried the talent and earned no profit on it. He was told by his master, "You should have put my money [*ta arguria,* the silver pieces] to the exchangers [*tois trapezitais*], and then at my coming I should have received mine own with usury [*tokos,* interest]" (Matt. 25:27).

Money changers were necessary to life and commerce in Jerusalem and Judea during the first century A.D. The variety of coins circulating there, plus the Judaic law that required payment of the temple tax in Jewish coin (or coin acceptable to the Jewish law) and the Roman requirement that the tribute be paid in Roman coin, created a need for "professional" money changers. These *kollybistai* had tables (*trapezai*) or booths at the city gates and on the porches of the temple in Jerusalem, where they charged a small commission. However, the money changers were notorious for cheating their customers and were the object of a number of rabbinical rebukes as well as of Jesus' wrath when he drove them from the temple (Matt. 21:12; Mark 11:15; John 2:15).

Because the relative values of the various types of coins were complex and because the intrinsic value of the coins gave rise to the practice of cutting or clipping metal from the edges of coins, especially those made from precious metal, merchants customarily

Table 1. Standard Relative Values of Roman Coins

Coin name	Metal	Weight	Value
Denarius aureus Quinarius aureus	Gold	122.70 grains 61.39 grains	25 silver denarii 12½ silver denarii
Denarius argenteus Quinarius argenteus	Silver	61.39 grains 30.69 grains	16 "asses" 8 "asses"
Sestertius Dupondius	Orichalcum[15]	421.00 grains 210.50 grains	4 "asses" 2 "asses"
"As" Quadrans	Copper	175.40 grains 43.90 grains	1 "as" ¼ "as"

Table 2. Coin Equivalents in Jerusalem

Coin name	Equivalents			
Denarius (gold)	25 silver denarii	8+ shekels		
Tetradrachm	1 stater	1 shekel	3 silver denarii	
Didrachm	½ stater	½ shekel	1½ silver denarii	6 sestertii
Denarius (silver)	4 sestertii	16 "asses"		
Drachma	¾ denarius	¼ shekel	3 sestertii	12 "asses"
Sestertius	⅓ drachma	4 "asses"	8 semisses	16 quadrantes
Dupondius	2 "asses"			
"As"	3 chalcoi	2 semisses	4 quadrantes	
Quadrans	¼ "as"			

weighed coins to be sure they were getting the full amount for their merchandise. The exchange of monies was also based at least partially on weight, although there were apparently certain accepted equivalencies among the various types and denominations of coins.

The Roman system of denominations was based on the silver denarius, or *denarius argenteus.* Table 1 shows the standard relative values of Roman coins that were current in the empire for more than two centuries after the reforms of Augustus.[16] Based on table 1 and equivalencies given in the New Testament and elsewhere , the approximations in table 2 can be formulated (coins are listed in order of decreasing value). The equivalencies are at best tentative; it must be remembered that the system employed in the western part of the empire differed from that of the eastern part, where the basic silver coin was the tetradrachm, with the fractional coinage consisting of *obols* and *chalcoi.* Asia's silver currency was *cistophori,* each equal in value to three denarii. In Syria the silver tetradrachm was probably worth four denarii, while in other areas it was worth only three. Even when "asses" were struck in Asia Minor, they might have been only half the weight of one minted at Rome.[17]

According to the historians Dio Cassius and Tacitus, the yearly salary of a foot soldier in the Roman legions between A.D. 14 and 84 was 900 *sestertii,* paid in three equal *stipendia* on January 1, May 1, and September 1.[18] According to our figures, 900 sestertii equals 225 denarii, which, if the pay is based on a "military year" of 360 days, suggests that the soldier earned only slightly more than half a denarius per day, less than a laborer's wage of one denarius, assuming both the figures are correct.

The conclusions we can draw from these estimates of value are that Judas's price for betraying Jesus was between three and four months' wages, that the amount paid by the Good Samaritan for the care and lodging of the injured Jew was about two days' wages, that the temple tax paid by the Jews was about one and a half days' wages, and that the tribute paid to Rome was about one day's wage. The servant in the parable of the talents who buried his money instead of investing it buried the equivalent of three thousand shekels or about twenty-four years of a laborer's wages.

The value of ten thousand talents, if these figures are accurate, seems beyond comprehension.

The sources of the coins circulating in Judea during New Testament times were as diverse as the coins themselves. In general, the Roman policy regarding the minting of money for Judea was the same as that of earlier governing powers—Persia, Alexander, Egypt, and so on. The imperial mints supplied the gold and silver coins, which were the larger denominations, and local or provincial mints supplied smaller denomination coins made of bronze, brass, or copper.

The earliest Jewish coins—with Hebrew script—are from the fifth century B.C. and are inscribed with the word *beqa*. In the next century, small coins inscribed *yehud,* the name of Israel while a Persian province, were produced. Both coins were minted in Judea "by permission of the Persians."[19] At other later periods, various "Jewish" coins were struck, for example, during the period of Jewish independence under the Hasmoneans, about 134-76 B.C., and a century later during the Jewish revolts against the Romans in A.D. 66-70 and 132-35. The Hasmonean coins bore legends both in Greek and Hebrew while the later "freedom" coins were inscribed only in ancient Hebrew. But both types bore symbols such as a pomegranate, a palm frond, a star, or an anchor, rather than the representations of gods or mortal rulers that were common on Greek and Roman coins. (See fig. 6; compare to fig. 5.)

Fig. 6. *Left:* Silver half-shekel struck in Jerusalem in A.D. 68 during the Jewish war against Rome. Weight 6.94 g. *Right:* Silver shekel struck in Jerusalem in A.D. 69. Weight 14.2 g. The obverse sides of both denominations show a chalice, and the reverse sides, a stem with three pomegranates and the legend "Jerusalem the Holy."

Fig. 7. Silver Greek tetradrachm. Note the Athenian owl (circa 375 B.C.).

Gaza is presumed by most scholars to have been the principal regional mint in the early fourth century B.C. Coins struck there imitated the fifth-century Attic coins, which bore the image of Athena on the obverse and the Athenian owl and Greek abbreviation for Athens on the reverse (see fig. 7). In fact, many consider the copies made at Gaza of these Athenian tetradrachms "among the most beautiful coins of this early period."[20] Alexander the Great established mints at Akko (Acre), Jaffa (Joppa), Ashkelon, and Gaza, as well as at Sycamine (Haifa) in Caesarea and Scythopolis in Samaria.[21] Coins issued by these mints were silver tetradrachms and drachmas and the gold stater known as the Alexandreios because it bore the image of Alexander.

During the Roman period, beginning in 37 B.C., the gold and silver coins for Judea were supplied by the imperial mints at Rome, Alexandria, and Antioch, while the small denominations were minted locally by the Herods under the direction of the high priest or by the Roman procurators (governors). About 15 B.C., Augustus established Lugdunum in Gaul as his great imperial mint, which for the remainder of Augustus's reign and all of Tiberius's was to supply the Empire with gold and silver currency (denarii). The "small change"—coins of orichalcum and copper—were produced for Rome and Italy by the senate, while the provinces had their own supply of lesser-value coins, either in local currency issued with Roman approval or in special provincial issues.[22]

Rome's policies and those of her predecessors regarding coinage are significant in several ways. When the same coins are used by people throughout a vast area, such as that governed by Rome, those common coins serve as "a symbol of cohesion and belonging, affirmed by constant use."[23] On a more pragmatic level, common coinage makes commerce easier for merchants who travel from country to country. The images on the coins—particularly those of the emperors—also provide symbols of the power or authority of the state and of the emperors as representatives of the state: "The affirmation of worldly power through coin portraiture is nicely encapsulated in Christ's words 'of whom is this image and the inscription?' 'give to Caesar the things which are Caesar's' (Matt. 22:17-22; Mark 12:13-17; Luke 20:21-6)."[24] Coinage portraiture may also provide a partial explanation for the persistence of "Jewish" coins; the Jewish people in particular would find the representations of pagan gods and mortal rulers on their coins objectionable. Coins minted by and for the Jews, except for those of Herod, bore images of plants or trees, impressions of the temple at Jerusalem, and other acceptable images.

Just as he used the portrait of Caesar on the Roman denarius to teach a lesson about the differences between temporal and spiritual matters, Christ used money in many other situations to teach the people. In fact, the number of references to specific or indefinite sums of money seems surprising, considering the fact that Jesus repeatedly taught the principle of valuing spiritual matters and denouncing (or keeping in perspective) material things.

Nanci DeBloois is Assistant Professor of Classics at Brigham Young University.

NOTES

[1]"Caesar Dictator uninterruptedly." On the reverse were a caduceus, fasces, axe, globe, and clasped hands. Compare George F. Hill, *Ancient Greek and Roman Coins* (Chicago: Argonaut Publishers, 1964), plate XII.7. The message or "political programme" conveyed by the images on this coin are "Republican office, Felicitas, world rule, Pietas, and Concordia," according to Christopher Howgego, *Ancient History from Coins* (London: Routledge, 1995), 75.

[2]The legends are translated, "Tiberius Caesar Augustus, son of the divine Augustus" and "Pontifex Maximus." Compare Florence A. Banks, *Coins of Bible Days* (New York: Macmillan, 1955), 83; Christopher C. Chamberlain and Fred Reinfeld, *Coin Dictionary and Guide* (New York: Sterling Publishing, 1960), 238; and Carol H. V. Sutherland, *Coinage in Roman Imperial Policy, 31 B.C.- A.D. 68* (New York: Barnes and Noble, 1971), appendix A, 190.

[3]Banks, *Coins of Bible Days,* 78.

[4]Betlyon states that the temple tax at the time Jesus was an adult was a denarius, but after the revolt of 66-70 C.E. it was doubled to a half-shekel. John W. Betlyon, "Coinage," in *The Anchor Bible Dictionary,* ed. David Noel Freedman, 6 vols. (New York: Doubleday, 1992), 1:1082, 1086-87.

[5]Demetr. of Phal. (228 fgm. 22 Jac.), cited by William. F. Arndt and F. Wilbur Gingrich, *A Greek-English Lexicon of the New Testament and Other Early Christian Literature* (Chicago: University of Chicago Press, 1957), s.v. "drachma."

[6]LDS Bible Dictionary, s.v. "money," although others are equally confident they were silver shekels. See Betlyon, "Coinage," 1086; Arndt and Gingrich, *Greek-English Lexicon,* s.v. "*argurion*"; and Oded Borowski, "From Shekels to Talents: Money in the Ancient World," *Biblical Archaeology Review* 19 (September/October 1993): 68–70.

[7]Elio Lo Cascio, "State and Coinage in the Late Republic and Early Empire," *Journal of Roman Studies* 71 (1981): 77.

[8]Lo Cascio, "State and Coinage," 78.

[9]Frederic W. Madden, *History of Jewish Coinage and of Money in the Old and New Testaments* (Chicago: Argonaut Publishers, 1967), 241.

[10]Borowski, "Shekels to Talents," 69.

[11]Arndt and Gingrich claim it was a "unit of coinage," citing Josephus, *Jewish War* 5.571, and others. Arndt and Gingrich, *Greek-English Lexicon,* s.v. "*talanton.*"

[12]Arndt and Gingrich, *Greek-English Lexicon,* s.v. "*talanton*" and "*talantaios.*"

[13]Borowski, "Shekels to Talents," 68.

[14]Chamberlain, *Coin Dictionary and Guide,* 183.

[15]Orichalcum is "a compound of about 4 parts of copper and one of zinc. At the time of its introduction under Augustus, analysis shows that it contained from 78 to 72 p.c. of copper and from 22 to 28 p.c. of zinc. Later on, tin and lead were added to its composition and the proportions of the constituent metals were subject to a good deal of variation." Mattingly and Sydenham, *Roman Imperial Coinage,* 24.

[16]The table is based on that of Mattingly and Sydenham, who say, "*Quinarii* never seem to have been struck in large quantities, and with very few exceptions these small coins rank among the rarities of imperial coins." Harold Mattingly and Edward A. Sydenham, *The Roman Imperial Coinage,* vol. 1, *Augustus to Vitellius* (London: Spink and Son, [1923]), 25.

[17]Andrew Burnett, "Roman Provincial Coins of the Julio-Claudians," in *Essays in Honour of Robert Carson and Kenneth Jenkins,* ed. Martin Price, Andrew Burnett, and Roger Bland (London: Spink, 1993), 149.

[18]Michael A. Speidel, "Roman Army Pay Scales," *Journal of Roman Studies* 82 (1992): 88 n. 6.

[19]Borowski, "Shekels to Talents," 70.

[20]Betlyon, "Coinage," 1082, and plate COI.01.f.

[21]George C. Williamson, *The Money of the Bible* (London: Religious Tract Society, 1894), 31.

[22]Mattingly and Sydenham, *Roman Imperial Coinage,* 3–4.

[23]Howgego, *Ancient History from Coins,* 43.

[24]Howgego, *Ancient History from Coins,* 43.

Woollen fragment bearing a notched, purple, L-shaped gammadia. Three of the cloth fragments found at Masada contain gammadia. The significance of these ancient markings remains obscure.

Gammadia on Early Jewish and Christian Garments

John W. Welch and Claire Foley

Among the textile fragments excavated at Masada were the remains of pieces of fabric with L-shaped cloth markings affixed to them. Dating to before A.D. 73, these are among the very earliest known examples of such marked garments. Scholars refer to these markings as *gammadia,* some of them being shaped like the Greek letter gamma (Γ). Though similar patterns have been found in several locations, the significance of these markings remains unknown to archaeologists and art historians. Because these markings seem to appear artistically in conjunction with some hope for life or glory after death, their presence on the clothing found at Masada may reflect something about the religious hopes and convictions of the Jewish fighters who died there.

Gammadia at Masada

Nearly all cloth found at Masada is "fragmentary, representing only a proportion of each original textile as made and first used."[1] Three of the numerous cloth samples found at Masada contained gammadia, each of which was a purple color, found on both dyed and undyed wool. Of the three, one fragment appears to have been a notched band sewn on wool that had been dyed a salmon-pink color. This marking "is likely to have been part of a 'notched band' or possibly a 'notched gamma.'"[2] The other two fragments, one of which is "almost certainly from a rectangular mantle,"[3] show L-shaped gammas. The ends of one gamma are notched; the other is plain.

Whereas the gammadia from Masada are all quite simple—all appear to be right-angle patterns—in artifacts from other sites, the markings referred to as gammadia could also be of a second design: "a straight bar with two prongs at each end."[4] Goodenough notes that the word *gamma* itself gives some idea of what the basic marking looked like, but there are many variations of it: the word *gamma* has been "used for the mark in any shape," only adding to the perplexity surrounding "the great variety of forms in which the mark could appear."[5]

Other Gammadia Findings

Additional finds show that these markings were widely used as Jewish symbols in the Greco-Roman period. Well-preserved examples of L-shaped gammadia were found at the site of the Bar-Kokhba excavations.[6] Gammadia have also been found in a cache of clothing believed to be *himatia* (shawls) that was discovered in an embankment at Dura-Europos.[7] Goodenough notes that only certain Jewish clothing in Dura-Europos would have had these ornaments or marks on them:

> It seems to me highly unlikely that the ordinary clothing at Dura was either white or ornamented in the way we see it in the paintings or in original textiles. These ornate fragments may well have come from a sacred vestry instead of from a repository of ordinary clothing.[8]

The Dura findings include another variation in the gammadia: "the ornament sometimes takes the form of a stripe ending in an arrow, which also is represented in the synagogue."[9] Interestingly, the Talmud demands that priests execute their most sacred religious duty, that of sacrifice, by applying the blood of the sacrificial animal to the altar in a gamma pattern: "he made the single application in the shape of a Greek Gamma" (Zebaḥim 53b).[10]

Further examples include gamma patterns on a Jewish ossuary from Mt. Scopus dating to the second century A.D.;[11] on several coffins and mummy cases from Egypt, one of which features "a short notched band" that "appears on the left shoulder of a woman";[12] on a sarcophagus lid from Palmyra, Syria;[13] "in a relief on a stone door of a Jewish tomb";[14] on "a banner from Roman Egypt";[15] pieces of art depicting Moses as an infant[16] or Moses as the lawgiver;[17]

other paintings including one of "a priest wearing the Anubis mask";[18] a portrait of Virgil;[19] various wall paintings from Dura-Europos from before A.D. 256;[20] a wall painting in the fourth-century Chapel of the Exodus in western Egypt;[21] and even on textiles from fourth-century-A.D. Egypt, which depict gammas on clothing, drapings, and spreads.[22]

These notched bands and gammas are also seen in many early Christian (fifth century A.D.) mosaics found in Rome, Ravenna, and Naples: "almost all the mantles of biblical figures" have one gamma marking near the knee; occasionally, they are depicted with a notched band.[23] Further evidence indicates that mantles were "still in regular use until about the 6th century; in other words, the depictions of men in white mantles with purple gammas frequently found in Christian art of the fourth and fifth century belong to a period when the garment was still current and familiar."[24] In addition to their appearing on clothing, gammas in Ravenna mosaics are pictured on altar cloths and veils.[25]

What Did These Marks Mean?

The significance of these markings is much disputed. Yadin felt that if these markings did at one time have significance later artists and weavers were no longer aware of it and simply used the markings for design.[26] He recognizes that "if these signs were misunderstood in ancient times, they are even more so in modern literature."[27]

The banner from Roman Egypt mentioned above portrays what could be a figure of Victory, with four right-angled marks with double-pronged ends in the corners of the banner. This has been variously regarded by some as a military banner, a decoration, or a souvenir of war.[28] Others, however, believe it is of religious significance, probably having been carried in a procession of "some group that hoped for immortality."[29]

> Since Victory so commonly appears as a symbol of immortality, and such bars are so artificially emphasized on funerary figures, it seems more likely that the Egyptian banner, which, we assume, came originally from a grave, had had a religious rather than a military use.[30]

Other evidence supports the idea that these markings had religious meaning. Goodenough notes that these markings often appear on significant religious paintings and figures.[31] Admitting that his opinion has not been fully substantiated, he nevertheless believes the importance of the Dura and Palmyra art and textiles in which these markings are depicted substantiates the marks' religious and symbolic significance, calling clothing that contains gammadia "ceremonial garments" with "symbolic force," perhaps from a "ritualistic treasure" of items, the nature of which "neither the paintings nor the textiles, unfortunately, make explicit."[32]

More evidence for a religious significance, according to Goodenough, comes from documentation that the markings are usually in connection with burial and are usually placed in consistent locations on the clothing—they are not just random decorations. As Hugh Nibley adds, they can also be associated with altar cloths and the veil of the temple.[33] Indeed, the markings on the garments found at Dura, Goodenough remarks, may have had sacral or ritualistic significance, for apparently the gamma was worn by those of high authority in the church or of great power in government:

> Near the ends of the himation [shawl] as represented in the synagogue [paintings] usually heavy marks appear, marks that seem always to end in a square prong. . . . This Greek dress of striped chiton [tunic] and marked himation will appear only on characters of especial sanctity—heavenly beings or the very great Patriarchs.[34]

Nevertheless, the meaning of these patterns, whether at Masada or elsewhere, remains obscure. As Nibley has said in summing up the problem of determining just what these symbols meant, "these things do get around. They become lost; they become simply designs; nobody understands what they are. . . . Thus we speculate as we try to reconstruct them."[35]

John W. Welch is the Robert K. Thomas Professor of Law at Brigham Young University. Claire Foley is Research Editor at FARMS.

NOTES

[1]Avigail Sheffer and others, "Textiles from Masada—A Preliminary Selection," in *Masada IV: The Yigael Yadin Excavations 1963–1965, Final Reports,*

ed. Joseph Aviram, Gideon Foerster, and Ehud Netzer (Jerusalem: Israel Exploration Society and Hebrew University of Jerusalem, 1994), 159.

[2]Sheffer and others, "Textiles from Masada," 199.

[3]Sheffer and others, "Textiles from Masada," 200.

[4]Erwin R. Goodenough, *Jewish Symbols in the Greco-Roman Period,* 12 vols. (New York: Bollingen Foundation, 1964), 9:163.

[5]Goodenough, *Jewish Symbols,* 9:164.

[6]Yigael Yadin, *The Finds from the Bar Kokhba Period in the Cave of Letters* (Jerusalem: Central Press, 1963), 227.

[7]Goodenough, *Jewish Symbols,* 9:127.

[8]Goodenough, *Jewish Symbols,* 9:128.

[9]Goodenough, *Jewish Symbols,* 9:127. See the dress of the last person on the lower row of figure 339.

[10]The gamma is also mentioned in the Talmud in association with the boundaries of Jewish towns, houses, and courtyards (Erubin 55a); the repair of clothing (Kelim 7); the layout of wine cellars (Pesahim 8b); and the shape of an addition to the altar in the temple at Jerusalem (Zebaḥim 61b; see also Middoth 3.1).

[11]Yadin, *Finds from the Bar Kokhba Period,* 231 n. 69.

[12]Yadin, *Finds from the Bar Kokhba Period,* 229.

[13]See Goodenough, *Jewish Symbols,* 9:163; 11: figure 145.

[14]Yadin, *Finds from the Bar Kokhba Period,* 230 n. 62.

[15]Goodenough, *Jewish Symbols,* 9:163.

[16]Goodenough, *Jewish Symbols,* 9:163–64.

[17]Hugh W. Nibley, "Sacred Vestments," in *Temple and Cosmos: Beyond this Ignorant Present,* ed. Don Norton, vol. 12 of Collected Works of Hugh Nibley (Salt Lake City: Deseret Book; Provo, Utah: FARMS, 1992), 110.

[18]Nibley, "Sacred Vestments," 110.

[19]From the fifth century at Tamara. Goodenough, *Jewish Symbols,* 9:163; 11: figure 127.

[20]Yadin, *Finds from the Bar Kokhba Period,* 227.

[21]From the fourth century at Kharga Oasis, Libyan Desert. Ahmed Fakhry, *The Necropolis of El-Bagawāt in Kharga Oasis* (Cairo: Government Press, 1951), cited in Yadin, *Finds from the Bar Kokhba Period,* 230 n. 64.

[22]Yadin, *Finds from the Bar Kokhba Period,* 230.

[23]Yadin, *Finds from the Bar Kokhba Period,* 230.

[24]Sheffer and others, "Textiles from Masada," 201.

[25]Nibley, "Sacred Vestments," 109.

[26]Yadin, *Finds from the Bar Kokhba Period,* 231.

[27]Yadin, *Finds from the Bar Kokhba Period,* 230.

[28]Goodenough, *Jewish Symbols,* 9:163.

[29]Goodenough, *Jewish Symbols,* 9:163.

[30]Goodenough, *Jewish Symbols,* 9:163.

[31]Goodenough, *Jewish Symbols,* 9:162.

[32]Goodenough, *Jewish Symbols,* 9:128, 164.

[33]Goodenough recounts the numerous instances of the markings appearing on ancient paintings of garments of important religious figures. See Goodenough, *Jewish Symbols,* 9:126–28. Figures include Abraham, Jonah, Solomon, Moses, Elijah, Samuel, Ezekiel, the twelve heads of the tribes of Israel, and others. But do the marks appear on clothing of less significant people?

[34]Goodenough, *Jewish Symbols,* 9:88–89, see also 164 n. 300:

> The Annunciation and the coming of the Magi: a mosaic at Santa Maria Maggiore, Rome. See the marks on dress at Ravenna in Deichmann, *Früchristliche [sic] Bauten und Mosaiken von Ravenna,* passim, esp. figs. 316–321, and the mosaics in Sant' Apollinare Nuovo. Among these the mosaic representing the kiss of Judas, fig. 187, especially intrigues us, since Christ and the Apostles have the prong-ended angle [garment mark] on the himation [shawl], but Judas does not. We can draw no conclusions, however, because the artist may have not shown it with Judas simply because in turning for the kiss Judas hides the part of the garment where the mark would normally have appeared.

See also Nibley, "Sacred Vestments," 109:

> Another Ravenna mosaic, c. A.D. 520, shows the priest-king Melchizedek in a purple cloak, offering bread and wine at the altar (Genesis 14:18–20). The white altar cloth is decorated with two sets of *gammadia,* as well as the so-called "seal of Melchizedek," two interlocked squares in gold. Abel offers his lamb as Abraham gently pushes Isaac forward. The hand of God reaches down to this sacred meeting through the red veils adorned with golden *gammadia* on either side. The theme is the great sacrifice of Christ, which brings together the righteous prophets from the past as well as the four corners of the present world, thereby uniting all time and space.

[35]Nibley, "Sacred Vestments," 111.

Masada and Religion in
First-Century Judea

The Priestly Tithe in the First Century A.D.

John A. Tvedtnes

The Tithing Vessels

Among the artifacts uncovered during the archaeological excavation at Masada was a terra-cotta pot with these words written on it: *ma'aser kôhēn,* "priestly tithe." It is reminiscent of a Herodian-period stone vessel fragment unearthed near the temple mount in Jerusalem, inscribed with the word *qorban,* "sacrifice."[1] The Herodian vessel fragment also depicts two birds, perhaps indicating that it was used to present doves or pigeons in sacrifice at the temple as specified in Leviticus 12:8.[2] Mishnah Ma'aser Sheni 4.10–11 mentions vessels inscribed with *qorban* or its abbreviation, *q,* and notes that among the other possible abbreviations on such sacred vessels is *m* for *ma'aser,* "tithe"; *d* for *dema',* "mixture";[3] and *t* for *tərûmāh,* the biblical "heave offering"[4] due to the priests.[5] Several vessels marked with a *t* were also found at Masada.[6] The law of Moses sometimes mentions tithes in connection with heave offerings (Num. 18:24–28; Deut. 12:6, 11, 17). The tithing status of mixtures was uncertain. Because of this uncertainty, only priests were allowed to eat food designated as *dema',* so it was treated as tithed.

Dema' vessels are mentioned in the only metallic document found among the Dead Sea Scrolls, the "Copper Scroll,"[7] which is a record purporting to describe where various treasures—possibly from the Jerusalem temple—were hidden. In addition to dema' vessels in general,[8] this scroll also refers to dema' vessels for various types of resin,[9] aloes, and white pine[10] and speaks of dema' vessels of both silver and gold.[11] One passage specifically ties the

"For hallowed things." An inscription that may mean the associated vessel or contents were pure and therefore appropriate for temple service. At Masada, the contents could have been considered clean enough to serve as food for the priest or Levites. Only part of the potsherd is shown.

demaᶜ vessels to the "second tithe."[12] "Vessels of the sanctuary" are also mentioned in the Bible in connection with tithes and offerings of grains, wine, oil, and frankincense (Neh. 10:39; 13:5). Isaiah 66:20 notes that "the children of Israel bring an offering in a clean vessel into the house of the Lord."

It was not the vessels that were important, but their contents. Once an offering had been received by the priest and its contents removed, the vessel could be reused for other purposes,[13] which explains how the tithe vessel came to be at Masada, some miles from the temple in Jerusalem.[14]

What Was the Priestly Tithe?

The first mention of tithes is in Genesis 14:20, where we read that Abraham gave to the high priest Melchizedek a tithe of all the booty he had taken from the invading Mesopotamian army he had defeated.[15] The Hebrew word is *maʿaser,* which means "tenth," which is the way it is translated in Genesis 28:22,[16] where Jacob covenanted to give a tenth of all his increase to the Lord.

Under the law of Moses, the Israelites were required to give a tenth of their produce to the Levites who, unlike the other tribes, had received no land inheritance (Num. 18:21, 24-26; Deut. 12:17-18; 14:27-29; 26:12-13; compare 2 Chr. 31:4-6; and Neh. 10:37-39; 12:44; 13:4-5). A tenth of the Levitic tithe was to be given to the

Potsherd tag inscribed "priest's tithe." The inscription refers to the tithe of the tithe, which was designated for the priest's use. This tag was found in the synagogue at Masada.

priests, descendants of Aaron (Num. 18:26–28). In effect, then, the priestly tithe was a hundredth of the donations given by the Israelites. This was in addition to the heave offering (*tərûmāh*), which, in the Second Temple period, consisted of the first 2 percent of the harvest.

The Storehouse

Some passages indicate that the tithes of the third year were also to be used to help "the stranger, and the fatherless, and the widow" (Deut. 14:28–29; 26:12–13). This use of tithes is reflected in the Joseph Smith Translation of the account of Abraham's payment of tithes to Melchizedek:

> And this Melchizedek, having thus established righteousness, was called the king of heaven by his people, or, in other words, the King of peace. And he lifted up his voice, and he blessed Abram, being the high priest, and the keeper of the storehouse of God; Him whom God had appointed to receive tithes for the poor. Wherefore, Abram paid unto him tithes of all that he had, of all the riches which he possessed, which God had given him more than that which he had need. (JST, Gen. 14:36–39)

This storehouse of the Lord is also mentioned in several Bible passages. King Hezekiah ordered the construction of "chambers in the house of the Lord" for storage of "the tithes and the dedicated things" and appointed Levites to oversee the donations (2 Chr. 31:11-12). When the temple was rebuilt after its destruction by the Babylonians, "chambers for the treasures, for the offerings, for the firstfruits, and for the tithes" were again constructed in the temple, and priests and Levites were placed over these treasuries (Neh. 10:34-39; 12:44; 13:4-5, 12-13). Of the treasuries of this second temple, Malachi wrote, "Bring ye all the tithes into the storehouse, that there may be meat in mine house" (Mal. 3:10). One of the Dead Sea Scrolls, known as the Temple Scroll, also mentions places for storage of firstfruits and tithes.[17]

By the time of Christ, the rabbis made a distinction between "first tithe" and a "second tithe." The second tithe comprised one-tenth of what remained of the harvest after donation of the first fruits and the regular tithes to the priests and Levites.[18] This tithe was taken to Jerusalem, where the peasant family had to eat it or sell it. This procedure was followed in the first, second, fourth and fifth years of the seven-year agricultural cycle.[19] In the third and sixth years, instead of bringing the second tithe to Jerusalem, it was set aside for the poor as the *ma'aser ani,* "tithe of the poor."[20] The Bible refers only to the tithe of the third year being given to "the Levite . . . and the stranger, and the fatherless, and the widow" (Deut. 14:28-29; 26:12-13).[21]

What Was Tithed?

In Leviticus 27:30-33, the Lord instructed Moses that the Israelites should give a "tithe of the land, whether of the seed of the land, or of the fruit of the tree" and a "tithe of the herd, or of the flock." Elsewhere, the tithe was considered to consist of "the corn [grain][22] of the threshingfloor," the product "of the winepress" (Num. 18:26-28), and "the firstlings of your herds and of your flocks" (Deut. 12:5-6; 14:22-23). In 2 Chronicles 31:4-6, we read that the Israelites gave tithes of "corn, wine, and oil, and honey, and of all the increase of the field . . . tithe of oxen and sheep, and the tithe of holy things which were consecrated unto the Lord their God." Nehemiah 10:37-39 speaks of "the firstfruits of our dough . . . the fruit of all manner of trees, of wine and of oil . . . and the tithes of our ground . . . the offering of the corn, of the new wine, and the oil."[23] Corn, wine, and oil are also listed as tithes in Deuteronomy 12:17 and 14:22-23 and in Nehemiah 13:5, 12.

From these passages, it is clear that the Israelites were required to tithe the increase of the field, the orchard, the vineyard, and the flocks and herds.[24] If an individual lived too far from the temple to bring his produce and animals in, he was allowed to sell them for money and bring his money with him to purchase food-stuffs to present at the temple (Deut. 14:22-27).[25] It was also allowable to "redeem" one's tithe (for example, retain a prize bull calf for one's own use) by paying a surcharge of one-fifth of the tithe's value (Lev. 27:13). In such an event, one's "tithe" would actually be 12 percent.

Originally, tithes were required only of animals and produce raised by man. Mishnah Ma'aseroth 1.1 outlines the "general rule . . . about Tithes: whatsoever is used for food and is kept watch over and grows from the soil is liable to Tithes."[26] The law seems to have excluded animals killed in the hunt and plants that grew in the wild. By Jesus' time, these also were being tithed, and he chided the scribes and Pharisees for requiring "tithe of mint and anise[27] and cummin"—all of which grew in the wild—while ignoring more important parts of the law (Matt. 23:23-24; Luke 11:42). The Temple Scroll, in addition to the normal tithe of grains, wine, oil, and booty taken in war,[28] also imposes a levy on animals and honey collected in the wild. But the tithe of things found in the wild was not 10 percent. The scroll requires a payment of 1 percent of the wild birds, animals, and fish thus obtained and one fiftieth of the pigeons and honey, with 1 percent of the pigeons going to the priests.[29]

Chosen Vessels of the Lord

Offering vessels provide a comparison with human beings throughout the scriptures. Just as an offering vessel can be sacred when presented at the temple and profane when reused for common produce, humans can be sanctified or polluted. In both the Old and New Testament, God is likened to a potter and human beings to the clay from which he makes pots (Isa. 64:8; Jer. 18:6; Lam. 4:2; Rom. 9:20-21; Rev. 2:27).[30] Paul compared humans to "vessels of wrath fitted to destruction" and "vessels of mercy," depending on their obedience to God (Rom. 9:22–23; compare D&C 76:33).[31] Elsewhere, the righteous are called "chosen vessels of the Lord" (Moro. 7:31; Acts 9:15). Alma spoke of Mary, the mother of Christ, as "a virgin, a precious and chosen vessel" (Alma 7:10). Similarly, Paul, speaking of chastity, counseled the Thessalonians "that every one of you should know how to possess his vessel in sanctification and honour" (1 Thes. 4:3–5). He told Timothy that he who purges himself from sin becomes "a vessel unto honor, sanctified, and meet for the master's use" (2 Tim. 2:20–21). The "sanctified" vessel is a clear reference to vessels dedicated to the Lord in the ancient temple. Elsewhere, Paul compares the human body to the temple of God itself, saying that God will inhabit that temple only as long as it remains chaste (1 Cor. 6:18–19). The idea gives meaning to a frequently quoted passage: "Be ye clean, that bear the vessels of the Lord" (Isa. 52:11; 3 Ne. 20:41; D&C 38:42; 133:5).

John A. Tvedtnes is Senior Project Manager at FARMS.

NOTES

[1]For a photo and description, see *Inscriptions Reveal: Documents from the Time of the Bible, the Mishna, and the Talmud,* 2d ed. (Jerusalem: Israel Museum Catalogue No. 100, winter 1973), no. 167. The term *qorban* (spelled *Corban* in the King James Bible) appears in Mark 7:11 in reference to an offering authorized by the rabbis in place of the original requirement of the law of Moses that one who curses a parent should die.

[2]One is tempted to see, in this vessel, the one referred to in Leviticus 14:5, 50, in which birds offered in sacrifice were to be killed. But the text specifies that this should be an "earthen vessel," whereas the one found in Jerusalem is made of stone.

[3]During the period of the second temple, it was permitted to mix tərûmāh with common foods, though the rabbis imposed rules on such mixtures (Mishnah Terumoth 4.7–13; 5.2–9; 7.5–6; 9.4). It is this mixture that the Jews termed *demaʿ*, a word originally referring to liquid produce (usually wine or olive oil).

[4]Exodus 29:27–28; Leviticus 7:14, 32, 34; 10:14–15; Numbers 6:20; 15:19–21; 18:8, 11, 19, 24, 26–29; 31:29, 41; Deuteronomy 12:6, 11, 17. The Mishnaic tractate Terumoth details how the "heave offering" was regulated during the Second Temple period. For an English translation, see Herbert Danby, *The Mishnah* (London: Oxford University Press, 1933 and 1974).

[5]These abbreviations are also explained in Tosefta Maᶜaser Sheni 5.1. For vessels used for the heave offering, see also Mishnah Terumoth 11.7-8; and Jerusalem Talmud, Ḥagigah 3.4.

[6]The offering and tithe vessels are mentioned in Yigael Yadin, *Masada: Herod's Fortress and the Zealots' Last Stand* (New York: Random House, 1966), 96.

[7]3Q15.

[8]III.2-3; V.6-7; VIII.3; XI.1.

[9]XI.4, 10.

[10]XI.4.

[11]XII.6-7.

[12]I.9-11. For a description of the "second tithe," see section on the storehouse.

[13]Mishnah Terumoth 11.6-8.

[14]It is important to make a distinction between offering vessels used by the people to bring tithes and other offerings to the temple and the metal vessels made specially for the tabernacle or temple and used only in that setting (Ex. 27:3; 30:27-28; 35:13, 16; 37:16; 38:3, 30; 39:36-37, 39-40; 40:9-10; Lev. 6:28; 8:11; 11:32-34; Num. 4:14; 7:1, 84-85; Josh. 6:19, 24; 1 Kgs. 7:45, 50; 2 Kgs. 12:13; 25:14; 1 Chr. 9:28; 2 Chr. 24:14; 29:18-19; Ezra 6:5; Neh. 13:5, 9; Jer. 52:18-19; Dan. 5:1-4, 23). Note that the Hebrew word rendered "vessel" can refer to any instrument and is therefore not always a dish.

[15]The Temple Scroll from Qumran requires that a tenth of the booty from war be given to the king, a thousandth to the priests, a hundredth to the Levites, with half of the remainder going to those who fought in battle and the other half to those who remained behind in the cities (11Q19 58.12-15).

[16]Abraham's payment of a tithe to Melchizedek is also mentioned in Hebrews 7:2-10 and Alma 13:15.

[17]11Q19 37.10; 11Q20 fragment 12.

[18]Detailed instructions for observance of the second tithe are contained in Mishnah Maᶜaser Sheni.

[19]Every seventh year is a year of rest for the land, in which no crops may be planted or harvested (Ex. 23:10-11; Lev. 25:3-7, 20-22).

[20]See the discussion in Abraham Chill, *The Mitzvot: The Commandments and Their Rationale* (Jerusalem: Keter, 1974), 90-91, 315.

[21]A literal reading of these passages could lead one to conclude that, originally, tithes were given only on the third year. This seems to be implied in Amos 4:4. But since a tithe on all produce was required and some produce could not be kept for three years, we can rule this conclusion out.

[22]Americans have come to use *corn* to denote a specific grain—maize. But the word really refers to cereal grains in general and, in the Bible, usually means wheat and barley.

[23]Detailed regulations concerning tithing of crops were developed during the Second Temple period. The Mishnaic tractate Maᶜaseroth (1.2-8) details at precisely what point in the maturing process various crops were liable to be tithed, describing the physical appearance of each.

[24]One of the Dead Sea Scrolls, known as 4QMMT, as reconstructed from two copies (4Q394, 4Q396), requires that a tithe of fruit trees, cattle, and flocks go to the priests.

[25]This necessity to purchase foodstuffs explains the presence of money-changers and sellers of doves in the temple in Jesus' day. Christ did not condemn what they did, only that they were doing it inside the temple compound rather than in the marketplace (Matt. 21:12-13).

[26]Danby, *Mishnah,* 66.

[27]Other translations read "dill" instead of "anise."

[28]When Genesis 14:20 says that Abraham "gave him [Melchizedek] tithes of all," it is generally presumed that he gave him a tenth of the spoils of war referred to in verses 16 and 21. This is how the author of the epistle to the Hebrews read it, "Abraham gave the tenth *of the spoils*" (Heb. 7:4; italics added). But Alma 13:15 says that "Abraham paid tithes of one-tenth part *of all he possessed,*" while the Joseph Smith Translation, Genesis 14:39, cited earlier, says "Abram paid unto him tithes *of all that he had, of all the riches which he possessed,* which God had given him more than that which he had need" (italics added).

[29]11Q19 60.4-10.

[30]King James Version, Revelation 2:27, says of the wicked that "as the vessels of a potter shall they be broken to shivers." But the Joseph Smith Translation reads, "They shall be in his hands as the vessels of clay in the hands of a potter."

[31]Christ, speaking of the Judgment, compared people to fish gathered in a net, which the fishermen sort, placing "the good into vessels, but cast[ing] the bad away" (Matt. 13:47-49).

The Masada Synagogue and Its Relationship to Jewish Worship during the Second Temple Period

E. Jan Wilson

The Discovery of the Synagogue at Masada

During the first season of excavations at Masada in 1963, Yigael Yadin and his crew discovered a strange structure adjoining the northwestern wall. The building was not like any other they had thus far excavated in the casemate wall. It contained clay-plastered benches along all the walls and two rows of pillars in the center of the main room. The inside dimensions were twenty-seven by thirty-six Roman feet (one Roman foot equals 0.2957 meters). A second, smaller room was on the western side and immediately adjacent to the casemate wall. On the floor were coins of the period of the revolt.

Because the entrance faced east and the building as a whole was oriented toward Jerusalem and because one ostracon found on the floor was inscribed "priestly tithe" and another "Hezekiah," Yadin decided that this structure must have been a synagogue.[1] Although the original structure apparently had been modified somewhat by the Zealots, it was quite likely built as a synagogue and used as such even by Herod or his entourage. This find was especially significant, because until that time, no synagogue earlier than the end of the second century A.D. had been discovered in Israel—certainly none from the Second Temple period.[2] This, in spite of the fact that the New Testament and Josephus's works contain numerous literary attestations of the presence of synagogues during that period.

If any doubts remained that this structure represented a synagogue, those doubts were removed during the second season when Yadin's team discovered a *genizah* (a place where orthodox Jews buried old or unuseable scriptures, since they could not destroy them) under the floor of the rear cell. Two scrolls were recovered from that area. The first was a portion of the book of Deuteronomy, and the second was a portion of the book of Ezekiel—parts of chapter thirty-seven to be precise (the chapter with the vision of the dry bones and the sticks of Judah and Joseph). Since these scrolls were obviously buried there before the destruction of Masada by the Romans, they must be dated no later than A.D. 73.

Synagogue at Masada. Lining the walls of the main room are clay-plastered benches.

The Masada Synagogue in Context:
The Origin and Development of Synagogue Worship

To appreciate the significance of the synagogue at Masada, one must consider the broader context of Jewish religious practices that led to the development of synagogues as an institution.

Scholars generally assume that the institution of the synagogue arose after the destruction of Jerusalem and the First Temple in 586 B.C. because of a need to find a substitute form of worship when temple worship was no longer possible. There can be no doubt that the Jewish exiles in Babylonia faced a crisis in religious worship, and some scholars assume that Ezekiel may have played a role in establishing synagogue worship. This assumption is based on Ezekiel 11:16, where the Lord states that although he has removed his people to distant places and scattered them in various lands, he will nevertheless be to them as a "small temple" (*miqdāš mě'aṭ*). The "small temple" is interpreted as the synagogue.[3]

Some see a possible reference to the origin of synagogues in Jeremiah 39:8, which mentions the destruction of the palace and also of a structure called the *beth ha'am* in Jerusalem at the time of the Babylonian exile.[4] If the *beth ha'am* really represents a synagogue (or at least the forerunner to synagogues), that would mean that the institution was already in place *before* the destruction of the First Temple. Such an idea is not really farfetched. The temple and the synagogue, after all, had separate functions. The latter was not really a substitute for the former: the main activity at the temple was sacrificial worship, and such was never attempted in synagogues.

There are scholars who assume (based on later pronouncements that followed the destruction of the Second Temple) that, after the destruction of the temple, prayer was an acceptable substitute for animal sacrifice and therefore the synagogue was really a replacement for the temple. But this assumption ignores the fact that prayer and study always went hand in hand in Judaism, and there had to be facilities for such activities even when the temple was still functioning. It therefore makes a great deal of sense to assume that even during the time when the temple in Jerusalem was fully operational there would have been other institutions for religious education and the *beth ha'am* may have been just such an institution. Indeed, the mention of this building in the same context as the palace suggests that it was a meeting place for the general populace and hence quite possibly a center for religious discussion and education.

Additional evidence for the existence of a synagogue type of worship during the First Temple period may perhaps be found in the pericope of the Shunammite woman in 2 Kings 4. In verse twenty-three, her husband says, "Why would you go after him? Today is neither a new moon, nor a sabbath!" Louis Finkelstein sees this locution as an indication that there was already some institution of religious instruction given on a regular basis during the First Temple period.[5] He goes even further and interprets Solomon's dedicatory prayer in 1 Kings 8 as also substantiating that supposition, because in that prayer there is mention of people praying at the temple but no mention of sacrifices. He therefore thinks that exclusion indicates that prayer was an alternative form (perhaps we should say "supplemental form") of worship to sacrifice even during the time of Solomon.[6]

The term *synagogue* (Gr. *synagōgē*) had two meanings. Initially it referred to an assembly of people, without regard to any building. Only later did the term come to be applied primarily to the building where such an assembly took place. That history is significant, because the early "synagogues" were actually assemblies of townsfolk meeting for secular purposes as well as for religious purposes. These meetings usually took place in the town square or near the gate.[7] Eventually, these assemblies became increasingly associated with a particular building.

In the Diaspora, synagogue buildings were used for various types of religious activities, but in Palestine, while the temple was still functioning (particularly during the Second Temple period, for which we have the most information), the synagogue was a place for reading the law but not for much else of a religious nature. The presence of the temple presumably satisfied all other religious needs. Thus the synagogues were used for banking, political meetings, hostels for strangers, and sites where money for charity could be collected.[8] Functions such as marriages, circumcisions, and funerals took place in private homes.

One fact that may be very significant concerning the role of the Masada synagogue in contributing to our understanding of the development of synagogue worship is the lack of any Torah shrine. In later periods—from at least the third century A.D. onward—one of the walls of a synagogue would always have a niche that contained the ark and the Torah.[9] Such a niche is lacking, however, from all known structures from the Second Temple period (namely,

Masada, Herodium, Gamla, and Delos). These synagogues also lacked the platform (*bema*) that was characteristically present in later synagogues. These facts support the assumption that the synagogues of the Second Temple period were not just religious structures, but rather general purpose communal buildings where religious functions *also* took place on specified days.[10]

According to Solomon Zeitlin, the transition of the synagogue from a mainly secular establishment to a mainly religious establishment may have taken place when the Pharisees converted the continual daily sacrifice from a sacrifice made by the wealthy to a sacrifice offered of and for all of Israel.[11] In order to bring this change about, they divided Israel into twenty-four *ma'amadot*, and at least a few people from each *ma'amad* were expected to go to Jerusalem to participate in the prescribed sacrifices at the specified times. Those who stayed home in their villages were then expected to gather together in their local meeting places at precisely the time that sacrifices were being offered in Jerusalem and to read the portions of the Torah dealing with sacrifices. These meetings made the establishment of permanent gathering places more important than ever, but also converted the synagogue from a mainly secular to a mainly religious institution.

Synagogues thus eventually developed into the mainly religious institutions known from later Pharisaic Judaism. It is important to note in that regard, however, that initially the synagogues were not under Pharisaic control. That fact is especially true during the Second Temple period, but also for the first few centuries A.D. Indeed, they may not have come fully under rabbinic control until the seventh century.[12]

Summarizing the above discussion, we may conveniently divide the development of synagogues into three phases: (1) The assembly phase. During this first phase, the "synagogue" was an assembly of townspeople and was not associated with a special building because the meetings took place outside—at the city gates or in the town square. The transition from this phase to the next phase was very gradual, but for sake of discussion, we may arbitrarily set the boundary for that transition during the Hellenistic period (perhaps with the earliest mention of synagogues as buildings in the Diaspora in Egypt during the third century B.C.).

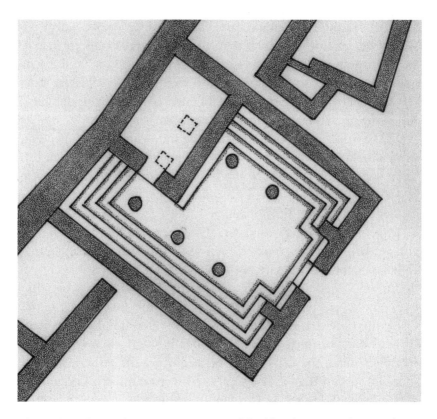

Floor plan of Masada synagogue. As modified by the Sicarii, bases of two of the original columns were under the floor of the rear cell. A genizah, a storage place for worn-out or unusable scriptures, was also discovered under the floor of that room.

(2) The secular edifice phase. During this period (especially in Israel), the temple was still functioning in Jerusalem. This phase would therefore extend from approximately the middle of the third century B.C. to the appearance of the first synagogues with Torah shrines as part of their architecture (third century A.D.). (3) The sacred edifice phase. Characterized by the inclusion of the niche for the Torah (approximately third century A.D. to present).[13]

The Significance of the Genizah in the Masada Synagogue

Documents and utensils of a sacred nature could not simply be destroyed; they were therefore deposited in compartments in walls or hidden under floors of synagogues or even in nearby caves (in the case of the Qumran writings). The genizah at Masada is important because the only other such find from the Second Temple period is that of the Dead Sea Scrolls from Qumran. Fragments of sixteen scrolls were found at Masada. Two of these fragmented scrolls, both from the book of Ezekiel, were found in the genizah. The Ezekiel text was very significant to the Zealots because of the apocalyptic nature of the vision of the dry bones and because of the zealots understanding that the message contained in that text was one of eventual political redemption for Israel.

E. Jan Wilson is Hebrew and Cognate Languages Specialist at FARMS.

NOTES

[1]Yigael Yadin, *Masada: Herod's Fortress and the Zealots' Last Stand* (New York: Random House, 1966), 184.

[2]Actually, some of the synagogues formerly thought to date from the end of the second century A.D. may have been built later than that. An example is the synagogue at Capernaum, which was originally thought to date from the end of the second century but has since been shown to date no earlier than the end of the fourth or beginning of the fifth century A.D. See also Doron Chen, "The Design of the Ancient Synagogues in Judea: Masada and Herodium," *Bulletin of the American Schools of Oriental Research* 239 (summer 1980): 37–40.

[3]One scholar who points to this passage in Ezekiel as indicating the origin of the synagogue is Azriel Eisenberg, *The Synagogue through the Ages* (New York: Bloch, 1974), 30. Eric Meyers, "Synagogue," in *The Anchor Bible Dictionary*, ed. David Noel Freedman, 6 vols. (New York: Doubleday, 1994), 6:252, on the other hand, questions any such involvement of Ezekiel in establishing an alternative to Jerusalem temple worship in view of the fact that he was a priest who supported the temple cult and eagerly anticipated the prospect of a restored temple. One must keep in mind, however, that the synagogue was not really a substitute for temple worship, because the two had differing roles, and Ezekiel's support of the one does not necessarily mean that he did not support the other.

[4]For example, Leopold Loew, *Gesammelte Schriften,* 4 vols. (Szegedin: Alexander Baba, 1875), 4:5–7.

[5]Louis Finkelstein, "The Origin of the Synagogue," in *The Synagogue: Studies in Origins, Archaeology, and Architecture,* ed. Joseph Gutmann (New York: Ktav, 1975), 4.

[6]Finkelstein, "Origin of the Synagogue," 4.

[7]See Lee I. Levine, "The Second Temple Synagogue: The Formative Years," in *The Synagogue in Late Antiquity,* ed. Lee I. Levine (Philadelphia: American

Schools of Oriental Research, 1987), 9; or Richard A. Horsley, *Galilee: History, Politics, People* (Valley Forge, Penn.: Trinity Press International, 1995), 226.

[8]Attestations of these activities in the early literature is listed by Levine, "Second Temple Synagogue," 14.

[9]For a list of ancient synagogues with such niches, see Rachel Hachlili, "The Niche and the Ark in Ancient Synagogues," *Bulletin of the American Schools of Oriental Research* 223 (October 1976): 43-53.

[10]See Levine, "Second Temple Synagogue," 12-13.

[11]Solomon Zeitlin, "The Origin of the Synagogue," in Gutmann, *Synagogue,* 14-26, especially 21-23.

[12]Horsley, *Galilee,* 234.

[13]The sacred character of the later synagogues is indicated by references in the Babylonian Talmud (for example, Berachot 6a and 6b) to the divine presence in the synagogue, a phenomenon formerly thought to occur only in temples.

Miqvaot: Ritual Immersion Baths in Second Temple (Intertestamental) Jewish History

Stephen D. Ricks

One of the most intriguing developments in the archaeology of the Second Temple (intertestamental) period of Judaism occurred during excavations supervised by Yigael Yadin and other archaeologists at Masada, the residence built for King Herod the Great. While excavating the south casemate wall at Masada, these archaeologists came upon three structures that looked like a Jewish ritual bath complex—a small pool, a medium-sized pool, and a large pool. During a routine press conference, it was announced that a possible Jewish ritual bath—a *miqveh*—had been uncovered. News of this discovery spread quickly throughout Israel, particularly in the very orthodox Hasidic community.

Yadin received word that Rabbi David Muntzberg, an expert on Jewish miqvaot and author of a study on the subject,[1] and Rabbi Eliezer Alter, another expert on miqvaot, wished to examine the miqveh installation at Masada. Yadin replied that he would be happy to receive them. One intensely hot day, Rabbi Muntzberg and Rabbi Alter arrived at the base of Masada. Without stopping to rest, the rabbis and their entourage slowly labored up the steep snake path on the western side of Masada in the torrid heat in their heavy Hasidic garb. When Rabbis Muntzberg and Alter arrived at the summit, they asked to be led directly to the miqveh installations. Armed with a tape measure, Rabbi Muntzberg went directly into one of the pools in order to determine if it conformed with the requirements of the rabbis. The furrowed brow and grave, unsmiling expression of Rabbi Muntzberg placed the outcome in doubt, and Yadin and his associates were worried that the result would be negative. Finally Rabbi Muntzberg's expression relaxed, and he said with satisfaction that this Jewish ritual bath was "among the finest of the finest, seven times seven," a parade example of Jewish miqvaot.[2]

Masada miqveh, used for ritual immersion

Jewish Ritual Baths

How was a miqveh, such as the one unearthed at Masada, constructed? To understand the answer to this question, we must, first of all, grasp two essential features of Israelite and Jewish religion: the need for ritual purity and the requirement of ablutions in "living" (that is, flowing) water.[3]

In Israelite and Jewish religious traditions, ritual purity must be achieved and maintained. Impurity results from nocturnal emissions (Deut. 23:10-11), sexual relations (Lev. 15:16-18), flows of blood from menstruation or childbirth (Lev. 12:2; 15:19), or contact with a corpse (Num. 5:2-3). Achieving ritual purity required lustrations in flowing water; failing that, "smitten" (salty or warm) water was permissible, and, if that was unavailable, well water or "any quantity of water not less than forty seahs"[4] was also acceptable. However, rivers and streams in Palestine are rare, and during several months of the year—from late May to early October—there is little or no rain in this east Mediterranean land. As a result, structures such as miqvaot (into which water flowed) had to be built that would permit lustrations.

The miqveh complex included a conduit for rainfall; the pool itself, connected by a pipe to the reserve pool; and a small pool for washing one's hands and feet before immersion in the miqveh (see plan of miqvaot at Masada, p. 280).

Many other miqvaot dating from the Second Temple period have also been unearthed—all told about three hundred.[5] Besides the miqveh complex examined by Rabbi Muntzberg, another was discovered at the northern end of Masada in the court of the administration building.[6] In addition, miqvaot were discovered at a number of other sites, including the Herodium in the Judean wilderness,[7] Herod's winter palace at Jericho,[8] and in Samaria.[9] The late Professor Benjamin Mazar of the Hebrew University, excavating the area south of Herod's temple, uncovered approximately forty miqvaot near the monumental staircases that led to the Temple Mount.[10] These ritual baths served Jews who visited Jerusalem during the pilgrimage festivals—Passover (Pesach), Weeks or Pentecost (Shavuot), and Tabernacles (Sukkot).[11]

Professor Nahman Avigad, also of the Hebrew University, uncovered some sixty miqvaot in the homes of wealthy and priestly families in the Second Temple Upper City of Jerusalem, west of the Temple Mount across the Tyropoean Valley. At least one miqveh, and sometimes more than one, was found in each of the homes, cut from the rock and lined with gray plaster.[12] One particularly elegant miqveh installation excavated by Professor Avigad also had an *otzar,* or reserve pool, for collecting rainwater connected to the miqveh proper, the only such installation discovered in Jerusalem. A pipe, which could be stopped up with a bung, connected the otzar to the miqveh itself, allowing additional water to flow into the miqveh, which received its usual supply of water from a cistern. Beside the otzar and miqveh was another room with a bathtub designed for normal, not ritual, bathing.[13]

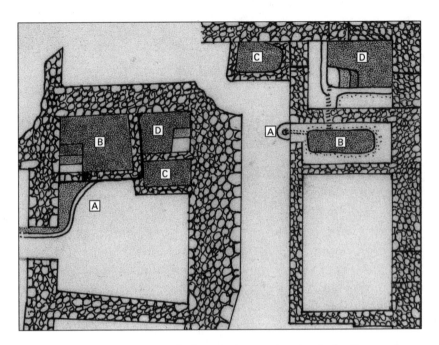

Plans of Masada miqvaot. *Left:* the southern miqveh. *Right:* the northern miqveh in the court of the administration building. Each structure had a method of capturing rainwater, either a cesspool or a conduit (A); a pool (B) for collecting the water from A; a small pool (C) for washing hands and feet before entering D; and an immersion pool, the miqveh itself (D).

In the early seventies, just outside of the wall of Jerusalem's Old City by the Dung Gate, Israeli archaeologist Meir Ben-Dov uncovered several miqvaot in the homes of wealthy families. Many of these immersion fonts contain stairways separated by a low plaster wall. These stairs were probably used by individuals to enter and exit the miqveh. According to Hershel Shanks, "Especially palatial *mikvaot* . . . have two sets of stairs divided by a low wall or pillars. Presumably one set of steps was used to enter (while the bather was in an impure state); the other sets of steps was used to leave the purifying bath, uncontaminated by any contact with the impurities of the entrance steps."[14]

The water installations at Qumran have recently been persuasively shown to be miqvaot. Earlier researchers of the site, including its excavator, Father Roland de Vaux of the École Biblique et

Archéologique (Biblical and Archaeological School) in Jerusalem,[15] Frank Moore Cross,[16] and even Yadin, either failed to recognize the water installations at Qumran as miqvaot or have rejected them as such.

Bryant Wood, of the University of Toronto, in his study of the water installations at Qumran, gives reasons for arguing that they are miqvaot: (1) In the view of Wood, who estimated the average population at Qumran and calculated their daily water requirements and the available water supply, the residents of Qumran had twice as much water as they needed to maintain themselves; the excess water was used for ritual baths.[17] (2) Wood observes that there are two types of water installations: those with stairs running the length of the water installations, and those without. Those with stairs Wood identifies as miqvaot, since "this design required more care in shaping and was, in fact, a very inefficient design for a water storage tank . . . necessitating an increase in the other dimensions to obtain the required volume."[18] Those installations without steps Wood views as cisterns for culinary and drinking water. (3) Wood believes that the water installations were too elegant to

Miqveh at Qumran

be merely pools for bathing: "Such a well-appointed bathing facility [is] totally out of keeping with the austere life of a religious sect living in an arid region. A simple tub is sufficient for most people, even those of us privileged to live in an affluent society where water is abundant."[19]

Jewish Ritual Baths and Christian Baptism

What are the Jewish antecedents of Christian baptism? How are *miqvaot* connected to John the Baptist? Like Jesus, John the Baptist was of Jewish parentage. John's father, Zechariah, was a member of the priestly course of Abijah, who served by lot in the Jerusalem temple (Luke 1:5, 9). While John was preaching in the wilderness, a delegation of Pharisees asked him if he were Elijah or "the prophet we await" (John 1:19–28, esp. 21). John the Baptist was sent to preach repentance to his fellow Jews, saying that "the kingdom of heaven is at hand" (Matt. 3:2). Given the value placed by the Jews on observing and maintaining tradition, it is likely that John's mission of preaching repentance and performing baptism reflected traditional Jewish forms of ritual immersion.[20]

As we noted above, miqveh ritual immersions took place in "living water." This Jewish tradition was maintained in John's practice of baptizing in the Jordan River (Matt. 3:6; Luke 3:3). John 3:23 notes that John baptized "in Aenon near to Salim, because there was much water there." The actual location of Salim is unknown, but, as suggested by Eusebius and Jerome, it may have been Salumias, near the modern Beth-Shean, where there are numerous springs close by sufficient to satisfy the requirement of "living water."

In the Didache, a very early writing reflecting deep Jewish-Christian influence, directions are given for baptism in "running water."[21] This practice of baptizing in the Jewish fashion also reveals that baptism took place by immersion and not by affusion (sprinkling or pouring). Didache 7:3, however, moves away from the Jewish practice of baptism by immersion by allowing for affusion—pouring water "on the head thrice in the name of Father and Son and Holy Spirit."[22]

The baptism practiced by John and the Apostles and spoken of by Jesus was not only "purificatory" (for remission of sins) but also "initiatory" (for entrance into the kingdom of God). This also appears to follow the precedent of Jewish proselyte baptism, which the majority of twentieth-century investigators of this subject regard as pre-Christian in origin.[23] While Emil Schürer observes that Jewish proselyte baptism is dated to the first century A.D. "because of the silence of Philo and Josephus," he notes that "the *argumentum e silentio* from Philo and Josephus would be valid only if it could be shown that reference to proselyte baptism is absent from passages where it should have appeared."[24]

Three things were required of proselytes to Judaism as an indication that they had accepted the Torah (Law): circumcision, the offering of a sacrifice, and complete immersion in a miqveh. Whereas the requirement of sacrifice was eliminated after the destruction of the Temple of Herod in A.D. 70, and circumcision was abrogated as the early church attempted to reach out to the Gentiles, baptism (by immersion) was retained and became a fundamental teaching and practice of the church.

At Qumran, too, there must have been a sort of "proselyte baptism" for those entering the community. The *Community Rule* approaches the subject negatively, stating that those "not reckoned in His Covenant . . . shall not enter the water to partake of the pure Meal of the men of holiness."[25] Interestingly, John the Baptist lived in the Judean wilderness at no great distance from the home of the Qumran covenanters, and, though he may never have been a member of the Qumran community, his proximity to Qumran surely heightened his appreciation for the vitality of baptist traditions within the movements of Judaism.

In the Talmud, a convert to Judaism is compared to a newborn child.[26] Jesus also compared baptism to new life when he said that "except a man be born again, he cannot see the kingdom of God" (John 3:3). He explains his meaning by tying being "born again" directly to baptism: "Except a man be born of water and of the spirit, he cannot enter into the kingdom of God" (John 3:5). Paul, in his epistle to the Romans, extends the metaphor to death and rebirth (Rom. 6:3–4).[27]

The birth of Christianity occurred in the matrix of Judaism, and for nearly a century the large majority of Christians were Jews either by birth or by conversion. The practices of earliest Christianity were profoundly affected by preexisting Jewish rites, including rites and beliefs surrounding the miqveh, ritual immersion, and proselyte baptism. Learning about the impact of these Jewish practices upon Christianity will help us better to appreciate the nature of that influence and the underlying richness of the unfolding Christian tradition.

Stephen D. Ricks is Professor of Hebrew and Semitic Languages at Brigham Young University.

NOTES

[1]David Muntzberg (Mintsberg), *Mivneh Miqva'ot ve-Hekhšeram: al halakhot u-minhagim be-hakhsharat mikva'ot* (Jerusalem: Merkaz ha-artsi le-ma^{c}an tāharat ha-mishpahāh, 1985/86).

[2]Yigael Yadin, *Masada: Herod's Fortress and the Zealots' Last Stand,* trans. Moshe Pearlman (Jerusalem: Steimatzky's Agency, 1966), 164, 166.

[3]Jacob Milgrom, *Leviticus 1-16,* Anchor Bible, ed. William Foxwell Albright and David Noel Freedman (New York: Doubleday, 1991), 923, renders the Hebrew *bəmayim ḥayyîm* ("living water") in Leviticus 15:13 as "in spring water," noting that "the water is found in an artesian well (Gen. 26:29; Cant. 4:15) and in running water. . . . Thus spring water either above the ground . . . or below . . . is what is meant, but stored water ([Hebrew] *bôr,* "cistern") or drawn water . . . is excluded."

[4]Harold H. Rowley, "Jewish Proselyte Baptism and the Baptism of John," *Hebrew Union College Annual* 15 (1940): 325-26; reprinted in Harold H. Rowley, *From Moses to Qumran: Studies in the Old Testament* (New York: Association, 1963), 224-25. The list of bodies of water that are suitable/unsuitable for lustrations is found in the Mishnaic tractate Mikwa'oth 1.1-8.

[5]Ronny Reich, "The Great Mikveh Debate," *Biblical Archaeology Review* 19 (March 1993): 52.

[6]Yadin, *Masada,* 167.

[7]Georg Foerster, "Herodium," *Revue Biblique* 77, no. 3 (1970): 400-1, esp. pl. XXIb. Compare V. Corbo, "L'Herodian di Gabal Fureidis: Relazione preliminare della terza e quarta campagna di scavi archeologici," *Liber Annuus* 17 (1967): 65-121, esp. figs. 7, 18, 19.

[8]Suzanne F. Singer, "The Winter Palaces of Jericho," *Biblical Archaeology Review* 3 (June 1977): 1, 6-17, esp. figures on p. 11; Ehud Netzer, "The Winter Palaces of the Judean Kings at Jericho at the End of the Second Temple Period," *Bulletin of the American Schools of Oriental Research,* no. 228 (December 1977): 1-13, esp. figs. 3, 6, 7; compare Ehud Netzer, "*Mikvaot* (Ritual Baths) of the Second Temple Period at Jericho" (in Hebrew), *Qadmoniot* 11 (1978): 54-59.

[9]J. W. Crowfoot, Kathleen M. Kenyon, and E. L. Sukenik, *The Buildings at Samaria* (London: Palestine Exploration, 1942), 134, pl. LXXII, 2; LXXIII, 1.

[10]Benjamin Mazar, *The Mountain of the Lord* (Garden City, N.Y.: Doubleday, 1975), 146, 210-12; William S. La Sor, "Jerusalem," in *International Standard Bible Encyclopedia,* ed. Geoffrey W. Bromiley, 4 vols. (Grand Rapids, Mich.: Eerdmans, 1982), 2:1025.

[11]Shmuel Safrai, *Die Wahlfahrt im Zeitalter des Zweiten Tempels,* trans. Dafna Mach (Neukirchen-Vluyn: Neukirchener Verlag, 1981), 18, 85, 163-73, 179, 217-18, discusses the requirements and ceremonies for achieving and maintaining purity at these pilgrimage festivals.

[12]Nahman Avigad, *Discovering Jerusalem* (Nashville: Thomas Nelson, 1983), 139-42.

[13]In a reply to Walter Zanger, Ronny Reich, "Great Mikveh Debate," 52-53, argues persuasively that a miqveh even without a otzar is still a miqveh.

[14]Hershel Shanks, "Report from Jerusalem," *Biblical Archaeology Review* 3 (December 1977): 21. Ronny Reich has provided a thorough treatment of miqvaot with double entrances in "Mishnah, *Sheqalim* 8:2 and the Archaeological Evidence" (in Hebrew), in *Jerusalem in the Second Temple Period,* ed. A. Oppenheimer, V. Rappaport, and Menahem Stern (Jerusalem: Magnes, 1980), 225-56.

[15]Roland de Vaux, *Archaeology and the Dead Sea Scrolls* (London: Oxford University Press, 1973), 131-32; Roland de Vaux, "Qumran, Khirbet-'Ein Feshkha," in *Encyclopedia of Archaeological Excavations in the Holy Land,* ed. Michael Avi-Yonah and Ephraim Stern, 4 vols. (Englewood Cliffs, N.J.: Prentice-Hall, 1958), 983-86.

[16]Frank Moore Cross, *The Ancient Library of Qumran and Modern Biblical Studies* (Garden City, N.Y.: Doubleday, 1958), 50.

[17]Bryant G. Wood, "To Dip or Sprinkle? The Qumran Cisterns in Perspective," *Bulletin of the American Schools of Oriental Research,* no. 256 (fall 1984): 53-58.

[18]Wood, "To Dip," 47.

[19]Wood, "To Dip," 51.

[20]William Sanford La Sor, "Discovering What Jewish *Miqva'ot* Can Tell Us about Christian Baptism," *Biblical Archaeology Review* 13 (January/February 1987): 57.

[21]Didache 7:1.

[22]See also Nathan Mitchell, "Baptism in the *Didache,*" in *The* Didache *in Context: Essays on Its Text, History, and Transmission,* ed. Clayton N. Jefford (Leiden: Brill, 1995), 252.

[23]Wilhelm Brandt, *Die jüdischen Baptismen* (Gießen: Töpelmann, 1910), 57-62 (with some caution); Joachim Jeremias, "Der Ursprung der Johannestaufe," *Zeitschrift fur die Neutestamentliche Wissenschaft* 28 (1929): 312-20; Nahum Levison, "The Proselyte in Biblical and Early Post-Biblical Times," *Scottish Journal of Theology* 10 (1957): 45-56; Thomas F. Torrance, "The Origins of Baptism," *Scottish Journal of Theology* 11 (1958): 158-71; Emil Schürer, *The History of the Jewish People in the Time of Jesus Christ,* ed. Fergus Millar and others, 3 vols. (Edinburgh: Clark, 1986), 3:174; Lawrence H. Schiffman, *Who Was a Jew? Rabbinic and Halakhic Perspectives on the Jewish Christian Schism* (Hoboken, N.J.: Ktav, 1985), 26; compare Thomas W. Manson, "Baptism in the Early Church,"

Scottish Journal of Theology 2 (1949): 392 n. 7. Nineteenth-century investigators of the antiquity of Jewish proselyte baptism took the view that Jewish proselyte baptism was instituted after (rather than before) the introduction of Christian baptism; compare Ernst Gottlieb Bengel, *Über das Alter der jüdischen Proselytentaufe: eine historische Untersuchung* (Tübingen: C. F. Ostlander, 1814); and Matthias Schneckenburger, *Ueber das Alter der jüdischen Proselytentaufe und deren Zusammenhang mit dem johanneischen und christlichen Ritus: nebst einer Beilage über die irrlehrer zu Colossa* (Berlin: Dümmler, 1828).

[24]Schürer, *Jewish People,* 3:174 n. 89.

[25]*The Community Rule* (1QS) 5:11, 14, in Geza Vermes, *The Dead Sea Scrolls in English* (London: Penguin Books, 1995), 76; compare Otto Betz, "Die Proselytentaufe Taufe in der Qumransekte und die Taufe im Neuen Testament," *Revue de Qumran* 1, no. 2 (1958-59): 213-34.

[26]Babylonian Talmud, Yebamot 48b; on this see Hermann L. Strack and Paul Billerbeck, *Kommentar zum Neuen Testament aus Talmud und Midrasch: Das Evangelium nach Markus, Lukas und Johannes und die Apostelgeschichte,* 4 vols. (Munich: Beck, 1924), 2:421-23.

[27]La Sor, "Discovering," 59.

The Masada Fragments,
the Qumran Scrolls,
and the New Testament

David Rolph Seely

Discovery and Inventory

During the last fifty years, the Judean Desert on the western shore of the Dead Sea has yielded a wealth of textual material from many locations, evidence that has illuminated our understanding of the history of Israel and Judaism in the two centuries preceding and the two centuries following Christ.[1] All of these manuscripts are properly referred to as the Dead Sea Scrolls.[2]

In the years 1947–56, eleven caves in the vicinity of the ruins at Qumran produced over eight hundred documents. Yigael Yadin, who would eventually excavate Masada, was closely connected with the discovery of the Qumran Scrolls. His father, Elazar Sukenik, was the Israeli scholar who secured three of the seven scrolls from Cave 1. Yadin himself was instrumental in obtaining the other four scrolls after seeing them advertised for sale in the *Wall Street Journal*.[3] And later, in 1967, it was Yadin who secured and eventually published the Temple Scroll.[4]

Following the dramatic finds at Qumran, Israeli scholars organized in 1960 a systematic search in the caves to the south of Qumran, looking for any further manuscripts. The team led by Yadin excavated the caves in Nahal Hever, where they discovered the Cave of Letters, which contained letters written by Simon Bar-Kokhba, fragments of a Psalms scroll, and an entire archive of legal documents of a woman named Babata.[5] We can imagine Yadin's anticipation as he prepared in 1962 to excavate the site of Masada. Yadin wrote:

> Before starting the excavations at Masada, we dreamed of the possibility of finding scrolls there. I say "dreamed" because the hope that we would could not be very bright. Hitherto, all the scrolls which had been found in the vicinity of the Dead Sea had been discovered only in caves, where they had been hidden intentionally, and where the only damage they suffered—comparatively slight—had been damage by nature, such as mild dampness, or by the nibbling of small animals. Now, as we approached Masada, we asked ourselves: "Had the Zealots hidden their writings before committing suicide? And if they had, would any of them still be preserved? And would we find them?"[6]

Fortunately, Yadin did discover written material at Masada. Most important of his discoveries are fragments of sixteen parchment Hebrew scrolls,[7] of which six were biblical scrolls and the rest were categorized as apocryphal and pseudepigraphical texts or fragments too small to identify. These manuscripts, together with the hundreds of other texts found near the Dead Sea, give us vivid and detailed evidence of the history of Judaism in the period just before and after the ministry of Christ. While none of the documents mention Jesus or allude to Christianity, they help us to better understand and appreciate a myriad of contemporary religious beliefs and practices reflected in the various books of the New Testament. In this short study, we will describe the written evidence found at Masada, compare it with the texts found at Qumran, and identify and discuss some of the interesting issues relevant to the New Testament.

The scrolls were found in various locations at Masada. For example, in a small room constructed in the casemate wall (room 1039),[8] under six feet of debris, excavators found fragments from the book of Psalms, the book of Leviticus, and a text known at Qumran as Songs of the Sabbath Sacrifice. In addition, they found small fragments of a text tentatively identified as an apocryphal book of Joshua, a fragment of a text written in paleo-Hebrew, and a text in Aramaic—both too fragmentary to identify or classify. Most of the fragments found at Masada appear to have been cut and torn intentionally, a fact that led Yadin to speculate they were deliberately destroyed by Romans soldiers garrisoned at Masada after its fall.[9]

In another casemate wall near the gate leading to the "Snake Path," excavators found another fragment of white leather containing the last chapter of the book of Psalms, Psalm 150. In casemate room 1109, they found a fragment of the apocryphal text called Ben Sira, and in a wall tower west of the Western Palace, under almost nine feet of debris, excavators found a small fragment of a text many scholars believe to be the book of Jubilees, a book widely attested in Jewish and Christian traditions. In a heap of debris outside the walls, they found another copy of Leviticus. And in a building Yadin designated as a synagogue, in a pit dug beneath the floor, the excavators found parchment fragments of Ezekiel and Deuteronomy.

Most scholars believe the place of discovery of these two scrolls was an ancient *genizah*—a special burial place for worn-out scrolls written in the holy language of Hebrew and containing the sacred name of God. In antiquity, scrolls were buried in a genizah because they were damaged or worn out or because they contained mistakes.

In addition to the scrolls, the catalogues list 951 items (excluding coins) that preserve written evidence.[10] These items include remains of writing on parchment, papyri, pottery, and wood. Items numbered 1–720 consist of *ostraca* (inscribed fragments of pottery) containing, in Hebrew and Aramaic writing, single letters or names that identify the owners of the pottery vessels, designations of type or amount of the contents of the vessels, some short letters, lists of names, inscriptions designating priestly shares, and a series of twelve pieces of pottery with names written on them identified by Yadin as "lots."

Items numbered 721–951 are papyrus documents and ostraca written in Latin and Greek. These include papyrus fragments of a passage from Virgil's *Aeneid*, legionary pay records, letters and military documents in Latin, one piece of a Greek wooden writing tablet, ostraca written in Greek and Latin, graffiti, and amphora stamps in Latin.

The written remains from Qumran and Masada are significant for many reasons. Even from very fragmentary texts and ostraca containing only single letters, names, or words, scholars can learn much about ancient writing methods and materials. Most of the writing from the ancient world was done by trained scribes, and it is clear that writing conventions—in particular the shapes and forms of the letters—changed and developed in a relatively orderly manner through the centuries. Scholars have established typologies of letter forms by which they have been able to date documents to within fifty years of composition or copying.

The dates assigned to these texts were originally determined from a few documents that bear internal dates and have been confirmed by various forms of scientific testing such as carbon-14 dating. The texts from Masada are of particular significance because we know the date of the destruction of Masada; thus we can be certain that all of the Hebrew and Aramaic writing found there can be dated before A.D. 73. Therefore they can be used to verify and alter the paleographic typologies.

The sixteen parchment texts found at Masada represent the same three categories of texts found at Qumran: biblical, apocryphal and pseudepigraphical, and sectarian[11] (composed by the sect at Qumran believed by most to be the Essenes). We will utilize these categories in discussing the texts.

Biblical Texts

Partial copies on parchment of Leviticus, Deuteronomy, Psalms, and Ezekiel were found at Masada. Some of these books are the same as the most frequently attested books at Qumran, where Psalms is represented with the most copies (36), followed by Deuteronomy (29) and Isaiah (21). It is not surprising that these books are the three Old Testament books quoted most frequently in the New Testament.[12]

Before the discovery of the scrolls at Qumran in 1947, scholars were not sure what an ancient biblical manuscript would look like. The earliest Old Testament manuscripts containing more than a fragment of text were the medieval Masoretic manuscripts from the tenth century A.D. Many ancient translations of biblical books into Aramaic, Greek, Latin, Syriac, and other languages preserved manuscript traditions that were significantly different from the Masoretic tradition. Scholars had long debated whether these differences were caused by the translation process or whether they represented ancient variants in earlier Hebrew manuscripts. In addition, scholars had no ancient texts to verify the accuracy of the transmission of the manuscripts of the Masoretic tradition.

The discoveries at Qumran changed everything. On the one hand, biblical texts were found that demonstrated many significant textual variants in the ancient Hebrew manuscripts, including significant additions to and deletions from individual books. Some of these textual variants were apparently the source of many of the variations found in the ancient translations. On the other hand, texts were found that closely match the Masoretic text—the text type that has become standard from the ninth century A.D. onward—which, along with the Septuagint, was the basis for the King James Version of the Bible. Such texts are called Proto-Masoretic since they antedate the work of the Masoretes and yet represent essentially the same textual tradition.

The texts found at Masada closely match the Masoretic text. Apart from very small details, they are virtually identical. The only differences are to be found in some of the spelling practices, such as whether a scribe wrote vowel letters to render vowel sounds or left them out. In terms of spelling, the Masada texts are distinct from those at Qumran. Many Qumran works are noted for their *plene,* or full spellings (using the vowel letters for vowels), while the scrolls at Masada are much more defective (without the vowel letters). Many scholars argue that the general uniformity of these texts, as opposed to the diversity found at Qumran, is evidence of the standardization of the Proto-Masoretic text that occurred in this period.

The Psalms scrolls are of particular interest. The fragment designated Ps[a] (1039–160) contains Psalms 81:6–85:6. The text is written in two columns and divided into poetic lines. The order of the psalms, the division of the chapters, and the headings appearing before each psalm are identical to the Masoretic text. Likewise Ps[b] (1103–1742), which contains Psalm 150:1–6, is also divided into poetic lines and is identical with the Masoretic text.

One of the texts found in the genizah of the synagogue consisted of the fragments of Ezekiel (1043–2220) preserving the passage at the beginning of chapter 37 recounting Ezekiel's vision of bringing the dry bones to life. The passage is a prophecy that the house of Israel will be revived and restored to their land. Latter-day Saints usually understand this passage as also an allusion to resurrection. This piece raises a very important issue from the time of the New Testament. How would the different groups of Jews in the first century have read and understood this passage in light of the doctrine of resurrection? While there is no evidence from Masada how those who buried this manuscript would have understood this doctrine, a review of the ancient evidence will give us some insight into the world at the time it was buried.

The references to the Resurrection in the Old Testament were variously understood by the different sects of Judaism at the time of the New Testament. Josephus recounts that the Pharisees believed in resurrection of the just (as do Jews today), the Sadducees did not, and the Essenes believed in the immortality of the soul, though Josephus states that they did not believe in the resurrection of the body.[13] However, texts recently published from Qumran suggest that the Essenes did believe in resurrection from the dead.[14] The gospels record that the dispute over resurrection was ongoing between the Pharisees and the Sadducees. Of course, Jesus taught and demonstrated the literal resurrection of the body.

Apocryphal and Pseudepigraphical Texts

Fragments of several apocryphal and pseudepigraphical books were found at Masada, among them Ben Sira (a book of the Apocrypha), the pseudepigraphical book of Jubilees, and several small fragments of texts that are variously described as apocryphal or pseudepigraphical writings similar to Jubilees, Joshua, and Esther. While the terms "apocryphal" and "pseudepigraphical" are often used interchangeably, more precisely there is a difference between the Apocrypha and the pseudepigrapha. The Apocrypha are a specific collection of books, many of which have Jewish origins, that formed part of the Christian, but not the Jewish, canon.

In the Protestant Reformation, Martin Luther designated these books as "deuterocanonical," and eventually they dropped out of the Protestant canon. The Apocrypha were bound into the King James Bible that Joseph Smith used for the Joseph Smith Translation. While he was working on the JST, Joseph Smith asked the Lord whether the books of the Apocrypha should be included. The Lord's response is found in Doctrine and Covenants 91, where he revealed that there are many things contained in the Apocrypha that are true and many things that are not true; therefore the Apocrypha should not be translated but should be read and understood through the Spirit.

Pseudepigraphical works include a host of other books from antiquity, many of them written under the pseudonym of a biblical figure, hence the designation pseudepigrapha—a book written under the name of another. There were probably hundreds of such books in antiquity. One modern collection of pseudepigrapha contains sixty-three texts.[15]

Copies of four texts from the Apocrypha were found at Qumran: Ben Sira, Tobit, the Letter of Jeremiah, and Psalm 151. Fragments of only three texts previously known as pseudepigrapha were found at Qumran: Jubilees, Enoch, and the Testament of the Twelve Patriarchs. However, fragments were found of numerous texts that had not been previously attested from antiquity. Most famous of these is the Genesis Apocryphon, an Aramaic retelling of the stories in Genesis. Many other texts would fit into this category, works that have survived only in small fragments—writings about Noah, Jacob, Joseph, Moses, Joshua, Samuel, David, Jeremiah, Ezekiel, Daniel, and Esther.[16]

We will discuss the only two identifiable nonbiblical texts found at Masada: Ben Sira (1109-1357), a book from the Apocrypha, and Jubilees (1039-317), a pseudepigraphical work.

The Wisdom of Ben Sira, also called Sirach or Ecclesiasticus, is a poetic book of wisdom similar to the book of Proverbs, teaching one how to live a good life and how to find success through proper speech and behavior, honesty, diligence, and patience. Unlike the writers of the biblical books, the author of this work signed his name—"Jesus, son of Eleazar son of Sirach of Jerusalem" (50:27). The book was written by Ben Sira before 180 B.C. in Hebrew and later translated by his grandson into Greek.

While the Greek translation of this work survived first in the Septuagint (the Greek translation of the Old Testament) and then in the Christian canon, the Hebrew text of this work was lost to the western world from A.D. 400 to 1900. For many years, scholars had debated whether the text was originally written in Hebrew or Greek. At the end of the nineteenth century and the beginning of the twentieth century, various Hebrew fragments of the text were discovered in the famous Cairo Genizah. Since then fragments of this text in Hebrew have been found at Qumran and Masada that are virtually identical to the medieval copies from Cairo. These fragments have confirmed that the text was originally composed in Hebrew.

Ben Sira was a widely read book in antiquity and was a work incorporated into the Septuagint (often abbreviated as LXX), which formed the basis of the early Christian canon. Although the book Ben Sira was known in early Jewish communities and discussed in rabbinic writings, it never became part of the Jewish canon, probably because it was not written by a prophet. Fragments of at least two Ben Sira manuscripts were found at Qumran, but it is not quoted or alluded to by any of the sectarian works from Qumran.

Many passages of Ben Sira are similar to those found in the New Testament, leading some scholars to believe that the authors of the New Testament were familiar with the text. For instance, many theological concepts are phrased in language similar to that of the New Testament. Further, some of the teachings of Jesus reflect the same principles taught in Ben Sira. In the Sermon on the Mount, Jesus warned about vain repetitions in prayer: "But when ye pray, use not vain repetitions" (Matt. 6:7). Ben Sira has the same advice: "Do not babble in the assembly of the elders, and do not repeat yourself when you pray" (Ben Sira 7:14). Jesus' teaching "It is more blessed to give than to receive" (Acts 20:35) is paralleled by "Do not let your hand be stretched out to receive and closed when it is time to give" (Ben Sira 4:31).

The parable of the rich man has a very interesting parallel. Luke records this parable of a man who had more wealth in his crops than his barns would hold so he planned to build more barns and to say to himself, "Soul, thou hast much goods laid up for many years; take thine ease, eat, drink, and be merry. But God said unto him, Thou fool, this night thy soul shall be required of thee: then whose shall these things be, which thou hast provided? So is he that layeth up treasure for himself, and is not rich toward God" (Luke 12:16-21). One finds a similar sentiment in Ben Sira: "One becomes rich through diligence and self-denial, and the reward allotted to him is this: when he says, 'I have found rest, and now I shall feast on my goods!' he does not know how long it will be until he leaves them to others and dies" (Ben Sira 11:18-19).

Paul taught that one of the obligation of Christians is to "rejoice with them that do rejoice, and weep with them that weep" (Rom. 12:15), while Ben Sira taught, "Do not avoid those who weep, but mourn with those who mourn. Do not hesitate to visit the sick, because for such deeds you will be loved" (Ben Sira 7:34-35). Both of these passages resonate with a passage from the Book of Mormon explaining the covenant made at baptism: "Yea, and are willing to mourn with those that mourn; yea, and comfort those that stand in need of comfort" (Mosiah 18:9). Perhaps Ben Sira has preserved here an ancient phrase, "mourn with those who mourn," that was known already by the Book of Mormon peoples before they left Jerusalem.

Whether there is a direct connection between Ben Sira and the New Testament text or not, the teachings of Ben Sira show us that much that is taught in the New Testament was already known in Judaism.

For many years, scholars have shown the book of Jubilees (1039-317) to be among the fragments found at Masada and have identified another fragment as a work similar to Jubilees (1276-1786). Some have recently argued that the fragment 1039-317 is a not from Jubilees after all but is a fragment of a Genesis scroll.[17] In either case, a discussion of Jubilees can give a sense of the nature of the pseudepigraphical traditions read by those who lived at Qumran and Masada.

Jubilees purports to be an account of the revelation given to Moses on Sinai, recounting the history of the world from Genesis 1 through Exodus 20. Most scholars believe the text was written by a priest since it expresses interest in priests and priestly things.[18]

Jubilees is a form of pseudepigrapha called by scholars "rewritten Bible" in that the text follows the biblical narrative, occasionally adding nonbiblical episodes and details and occasionally deleting portions of the biblical narrative. On its part, Jubilees divides the history of the world from Adam to Moses into fifty units of forty-nine years, each following the biblical injunction to celebrate jubilees after every forty-ninth year.

The book of Jubilees was a widely read book in ancient Judaism and Christianity and yet was never included in the canon. It circulated anciently in Greek, Syriac, Latin, and Ethiopic translations, but like Ben Sira, the original Hebrew texts as well as the Greek translations were lost anciently. The only complete copy of the text survived in Ethiopic in the Abyssinian church, in which it is considered canonical. The copies of this text found at Qumran confirm that the original was written in Hebrew.[19]

Jubilees is one of the most important of the pseudepigraphical texts found at Qumran. It is attested in fifteen or sixteen different manuscripts, making it the fifth most attested book after Psalms, Deuteronomy, Isaiah, and Genesis. On several points, Jubilees reflects Essene theology known at Qumran. For example, the Qumran calendar and the calendar in Jubilees both calculate their festivals according to a solar calendar of 364 days—a number of days divisible by seven—allowing for each festival mandated by the Bible to fall on the same day of the week each year. This was a very different calendar than the solar-lunar calendar used by the other sects of Judaism at the time.[20]

It is clear that some of these books were considered authoritative since they are attested in multiple copies and are quoted as authoritative by other books. The various rule books of the Qumran community such as the Damascus Document, the Rule of the Community, and the War Rule were certainly viewed as having a status tantamount to scripture. They identify themselves as revelations from the Lord that were binding on the community. These works quote extensively from biblical books, and in addition, they quote extensively from the books of Jubilees and the books of Enoch. For example, in the Damascus Document, the members of the community were advised "to return to the Torah of Moses, for in it everything is specified. And the explication of their times, when Israel was blind to all these; behold, it is specified in the Book of the Divisions of the Times in their Jubilees and in their Weeks" (Damascus Document 16.1–4). If the people of Qumran accepted books in addition to the biblical books as authoritative, Jubilees was likely one of them.

Like Ben Sira, Jubilees offers us a valuable look at the theology as well as the formulations of religious ideas found in the world of the New Testament. One of the most prominent of the editors of the Ethiopic texts, R. H. Charles, wrote a commentary on Jubilees in which he pointed out the influence that this text had on other works. Of the influence of Jubilees on the New Testament, he wrote, "It appeals to the New Testament scholar, as furnishing the first literary embodiment of beliefs which subsequently obtained an entrance into the New Testament, and as having in all probability formed part of the library of some of the apostolic writers."[21] Some of the similarities with New Testament passages are quite interesting. Whether they bear a direct relationship or they derive from a common source we may never know, but let us consider the following.

Several examples demonstrate the close relationship between concepts and phraseology in the New Testament and concepts and phraseology in the book of Jubilees. The first occurrence of the term "son of perdition" in the Bible is found in 2 Thessalonians 2:3, but the phrase is already found in Jubilees 10:3. The first biblical text to note that "one day is with the Lord as a thousand years" is found in 2 Peter 3:8, but it is already attested in Jubilees 4:30: "For one thousand years are as one day in the testimony of the heavens and therefore was it written concerning the tree of knowledge: 'On the day that ye eat thereof ye shall die.'"[22]

Some of the additions and changes are of interest for Latter-day Saints. Jubilees, for example, shows a developed theology of Satan, called Mastema, and his demons, which were cast out of heaven and which led many of the children of men astray. In the Exodus story, Mastema assists the Egyptian sorcerers in the contest against Moses and Aaron, and it is Mastema, rather than the Lord, who hardens the hearts of Pharaoh and the Egyptians (Jubilees 48:12, 16–17).

Sectarian Texts

The most surprising text discovered at Masada was a fragment of Songs of the Sabbath Sacrifice (1039-200)—a text that is known from eight fragmentary copies at Qumran.[23] Whether the text originated with the Qumran Essenes or not is unclear, but the Songs of the Sabbath Sacrifice reflects distinctive sectarian beliefs and appears to have influenced other sectarian texts found at Qumran. In addition, several other small fragments found at Masada preserve distinctive vocabulary, phrases, and spelling of other Qumran texts, leading Talmon, who has been assigned to edit them, to suggest the possibility that they were, along with Songs of the Sabbath, also imported to Masada from Qumran.[24]

The question is how these sectarian texts came to Masada. Although Josephus named John the Essene as a general in the revolt against Rome,[25] there was no evidence that the Qumran community participated with the Jewish rebels in the revolt. Yadin hypothesized the presence of these texts at Masada to be evidence that Essenes had joined with the rebels in the revolt against Rome at Masada.[26] Most scholars simply conclude that some of the Essenes fled from the Roman destruction of Qumran in 68 and came to Masada for refuge, bringing some of their texts with them. Other scholars believe the presence of sectarian texts at Qumran illustrates that the texts were not unique to Qumran but were circulated widely in Palestine.[27]

The Songs of the Sabbath Sacrifice originally contained a cycle of thirteen songs—one for each of the first thirteen Sabbaths of the year (the first quarter of a solar year). These songs contain descriptions of the seven archangels and their angelic praises, the heavenly temple, and the heavenly throne.[28] The imagery is reminiscent of Ezekiel's vision of the chariot throne (Ezek. 1, 10) and his vision of the future temple (Ezek. 40-48).

There are several points which remind us of the New Testament. The concept of the kingdom of heaven, so prevalent in the Gospels, is found in the Qumran texts only in Songs of the Sabbath Sacrifice: "And they will recount the splendour of his kingdom, according to their knowledge, and they will extol [his glory in all] the heavens of his kingdom" (Frag. 2:3-4).[29] The descriptions of the heavenly temple are similar to those found in the book of Revelation.

Summary

The written documents found at Masada, mirroring the imagery of Ezekiel 37, breathe life into the dry bones of the archaeological remains at Masada. The Hebrew and Aramaic ostraca give us the names of those who lived on the solitary rock and bring to life the transactions of storing and drawing on the supplies of food and drink stored in pottery vessels in that remote place. They attest to the observance of the priestly tithe and perhaps to the final human drama of drawing the lots of death described by Josephus. The Latin texts attest to the presence of the Roman military garrison that burned the fortress and stayed at Masada, where they drew their military pay, attended to their military matters, and were entertained by a text of Virgil in this place far away from home. The Greek texts remind us of the Byzantine monks who occupied the ruined site centuries later.

Biblical scrolls witness to the devotion to the law of those who lived at Masada and worshipped at the synagogue, purified themselves in the ritual baths, and finally perished there. In addition, the uniformity of these texts suggests the developing supremacy of the Masoretic text as compared to the textual diversity at Qumran. Apocryphal and pseudepigraphical books remind us of the richness of literary traditions surrounding the Bible, some of which have been preserved in the Apocrypha and in the extant pseudepigraphical works, but most of which have disappeared forever. The sectarian scrolls were likely brought to Masada by a group of Essenes fleeing from Qumran, seeking refuge and deliverance from the Romans, anticipating the final battle between the sons of light and the sons of darkness and awaiting the divine intervention which would deliver them from their enemies. They instead witnessed the victory of the sons of darkness and died beside the defenders of Masada.

David Rolph Seely is Associate Professor of Ancient Scripture at Brigham Young University.

NOTES

[1]Two excellent introductions to the Dead Sea Scrolls have recently been published: James C. VanderKam, *The Dead Sea Scrolls Today* (Grand Rapids, Mich.: Eerdmans, 1994); and Lawrence H. Schiffman, *Reclaiming the Dead Sea Scrolls* (Philadelphia: Jewish Publication Society, 1994).

[2]Fragments of texts have been found in many locations in this area. Sites of manuscript discoveries from north to south are Qumran, Wadi Murabbaᶜat, Nahal Hever, Nahal Mishmar, Nahal Seᶜelim, and Masada. In addition, a very important collection of Samaritan documents from the fourth century B.C. were found in a cave in Wadi ed-Daliyeh, north of Jericho.

[3]Yadin documented his involvement in the attainment of the scrolls in Yigael Yadin, *The Message of the Scrolls,* ed. James Charlesworth (New York: Simon and Schuster, 1957).

[4]Yigael Yadin, *The Temple Scroll: The Hidden Law of the Dead Sea Sect* (New York: Random House, 1985).

[5]Yigael Yadin, *Bar-Kokhba: The Rediscovery of the Legendary Hero of the Second Jewish Revolt against Rome* (New York: Random House, 1971).

[6]Yigael Yadin, *Masada: Herod's Fortress and the Zealots' Last Stand* (Jerusalem: Steimatzky's Agency, 1966), 168.

[7]The account of the discovery of the texts at Masada is dramatically recounted in Yadin, *Masada,* 168–91.

[8]A casemate wall at Masada is a wall consisting of two walls running parallel to each other. Often the space between is filled with rocks and other rubble creating a very wide wall; in other situations, the space is used for living or storage. At Masada the space between the two walls was used as living quarters by Masada's defenders.

[9]Yadin, *Masada,* 172–73.

[10]Bibliographical information on the publication of the scrolls, the Hebrew, Aramaic, Greek, and Latin ostraca can be found in Stephen A. Reed, *The Dead Sea Scrolls Catalogue,* rev. and ed. Marilyn J. Lundberg, SBL Resources for Biblical Study, vol. 32 (Atlanta: Scholars, 1994).

[11]The term "sect" should be defined here. In terms of religious history, a sect is a small religious group (if it was a large and dominant group it would be considered a religion) that claims to have the only "true" doctrine.

[12]These figures come from VanderKam, *Dead Sea Scrolls Today,* 30–32.

[13]Josephus, *Jewish War* 2.154–65.

[14]For a succinct discussion of this issue see VanderKam, *Dead Sea Scrolls Today,* 78–81. VanderKam quotes a fragmentary text from Cave Four, 4Q521, line 12, where it is said of the Messiah that "then he will heal the slain, and the dead he will cause to live."

[15]James Charlesworth, *The Old Testament Pseudepigrapha,* 2 vols. (Garden City, N.Y.: Doubleday, 1985).

[16]VanderKam, *Dead Sea Scrolls Today,* 42–43.

[17]James C. VanderKam, "Book of Jubilees," in *The Anchor Bible Dictionary,* ed. David Noel Freedman, 6 vols. (New York: Doubleday, 1992), 3:1030–32; Shemariyahu Talmon, "Hebrew Scroll Fragments from Masada," in *The Story of*

Masada: Discoveries from the Excavations, ed. Gila Hurvitz (Provo: BYU Studies, 1997), 101.

[18]VanderKam, "Book of Jubilees," 3:1031.

[19]VanderKam, "Book of Jubilees," 3:1030.

[20]VanderKam, *Dead Sea Scrolls Today,* 39–40. Because Latter-day Saints accept several sacred nonbiblical books as part of their standard works, a common question asked when confronted with the many different religious works at Qumran is whether the community accepted books as scripture besides those found in the Bible. The answer to this question is not a simple one since nowhere do we find in the Dead Sea Scrolls a list of "canonical" books.

[21]R. H. Charles, *The Book of Jubilees or the Little Genesis* (1902; reprint, Jerusalem: Makor, 1972), viii.

[22]Latter-day Saints understand this same concept from Abraham 3:4, where Abraham learned in a vision that, according to the reckoning of time in Kolob, "one revolution was a day unto the Lord, after his manner of reckoning, it being one thousand years according to the time appointed unto that whereon thou standest." Stephen, in his speech in Acts 7:23, says that Moses was "full forty years old" when he smote the Egyptian and that he spent forty years in Midian (Acts 7:29–30). The Old Testament never specifies how old Moses was at each of these times in his life, yet Jubilees says he was forty-two years old when he killed the Egyptian (Jubilees 47:10–12) and that he spent thirty-eight years in Midian (Jubilees 48:1).

[23]A preliminary edition of this text has been published by Carol A. Newsom, *Songs of the Sabbath Sacrifice: A Critical Edition,* Harvard Semitic Studies, vol. 27 (Atlanta: Scholars, 1985). The fragments from Qumran have also been published by Carol A. Newsom and Yigael Yadin, "The Masada Fragment of the Qumran Songs of the Sabbath Sacrifice," *Israel Exploration Journal* 34, no. 2–3 (1984), 77–88.

[24]See Talmon, "Hebrew Scroll Fragments."

[25]Josephus, *Jewish War* 2.567; 3.11.

[26]Yadin, *Masada,* 173–74.

[27]Shiffman, *Reclaiming the Dead Sea Scrolls,* 355.

[28]Latter-day Saints are familiar with the "eternal councils" mentioned throughout this text (Ps. 82:1; Abr. 4:26; D&C 121:32).

[29]Florentino García Martínez and Julio Trebolle Barrera, *The People of the Dead Sea Scrolls: Their Writings, Beliefs, and Practices,* trans. Wilfred G. E. Watson (Leiden: Brill, 1995), 220.

Sacred Books:
The Canon of the Hebrew Bible
at the End of the First Century

Robert L. Maxwell

Introduction

A number of fragmentary manuscripts in Hebrew and Aramaic have been found at Masada, including seven from the Hebrew Bible. These are Mas1a (Lev. 4:3-9), Mas1b (Lev. 8:31-11:40), Mas1c (Deut. 33:17-21, 34:2-6), Mas1d (Ezek. 31:11-37:15), Mas1e (Ps. 81:6-85:6), Mas1f (Ps. 150:1-6), and Mas1g (Ps. 18:26-29). Aside from minor orthographic differences, these are, in all cases, the same as the Masoretic text (MT) of the Hebrew Bible we have today. There are, in addition, a number of extrabiblical fragments, including a fragment of Ben Sira (Ecclesiasticus) (Mas1h) and a fragment apparently of the book of Jubilees (Mas1i).[1]

The presence of biblical and "apocryphal" texts at Masada demonstrates that these texts were valued by the various groups that occupied the site before the Roman conquest, but it also brings up the question of canon. Which if any of these texts had been "canonized" or considered sacred and binding scripture by their readers? Their presence at the site alone says nothing of their canonicity, for many writings of a clearly noncanonical nature were also found at Masada. While it is impossible to know the exact opinion of the inhabitants of Masada on these writings, there is some evidence for the development of a Hebrew Bible canon in the larger Jewish community, and interestingly enough, certain defining events for the Hebrew canon were probably occurring almost at the same time as the fall of Masada in 73 C.E.

Definition of the Hebrew Canon

Jerome. While we lack evidence for most of the details of this defining process, we can set some terminating dates after which the canon was clearly fixed. Because of conflicting Latin versions of the Bible in the late fourth century, Jerome was commissioned by Pope Damasus in A.D. 382 or 383 to produce a new, authoritative Latin translation. Jerome departed from the former tradition of translating the Hebrew Bible from the Greek Septuagint version and instead embarked on an intensive study of Hebrew in the Holy Land.[2]

Jerome's study apparently also included research into the canon as it existed among the Jews of his time, for in the preface to the first biblical book he translated from Hebrew (Samuel/Kings, published about 390[3]), he outlines what he has learned: "Just as there are twenty-two letters (*elementa*) with which we write everything we say in Hebrew . . . so there are a total of twenty-two books (*volumina*) [in the Hebrew scriptures]." Having explained that as there are five "double" letters in Hebrew, so there are also five "double" books in the Hebrew Bible, he goes on to list the books.

First come Genesis, Exodus, Leviticus, Numbers, and Deuteronomy. "These are the five books of Moses, which they call the 'Torath,' or 'The Law.'" "Second is the order of the Prophets," which are Joshua, Judges/Ruth, Samuel, Kings, Isaiah, Jeremiah, Ezekiel, and the twelve minor prophets, eight books in Jerome's count. "The third order comprises the Hagiographa": the nine books of Job, Psalms, Proverbs, Ecclesiastes, Song of Songs, Daniel, Chronicles, Ezra (in two books, namely, Ezra and Nehemiah), and Esther—for a grand total of twenty-two. Because of the significance of the correspondence of the number of the letters in the Hebrew alphabet with this number of books in the Bible, Jerome felt he had arrived at a sure method of determining which books were canonical and which were excluded, and in this preface, he names some of the more important noncanonical ("non . . . in canone") books.[4]

If we can assume that Jerome includes Lamentations with Jeremiah (as one of the "double" books),[5] the canon of Jerome's Hebrew Bible is the same as that of the Masoretic text; in other words, it had reached its final state—at least in Palestine—at the latest by the end of the fourth century C.E.

Origen. The content of the Hebrew canon was discussed in the third century by the Greek Christian Origen (circa 185–255 C.E.). According to the historian Eusebius, who was born during the generation following Origen's death, Origen cataloged the books of the Hebrew Bible as follows: "It ought to be known that the conventional [ἐνδιαθήκους, in other words, canonical] books which the Hebrews have handed down number twenty-two, the same number as letters in their alphabet."[6]

Origen, working from the Greek tradition, did not divide the Hebrew Bible into three parts as Jerome did, but instead simply listed the books: Genesis, Exodus, Leviticus, Numbers, Deuteronomy, Joshua, Judges, Ruth, Kingdoms 1–2 (in other words, Samuel), Kingdoms 3–4 (Kings), Chronicles, Ezra (probably Ezra/Nehemiah), Psalms, Proverbs, Ecclesiastes, Song of Songs, Isaiah, Jeremiah/Lamentations/Letter of Jeremiah, Daniel, Ezekiel, Job, and Esther. "Outside [of] these" (ἔξω δὲ τούτων) falls Maccabees.[7] Origen's twenty-two include several "double" books and one "triple" book, Jeremiah/Lamentations together with the Letter of Jeremiah, which is now included in the Apocrypha. Strangely, his list omits the twelve minor prophets.

Melito. Eusebius also quoted Melito, Bishop of Sardis, on the question of the canon. Melito lived during the reign of Marcus Aurelius (161–80 C.E.) and was active just before the birth of Origen. In the section of Melito's writings quoted by Eusebius, the bishop listed the "recognized writings" (ὁμολογουμένων γραφῶν) of the Old Testament. The list was made on behalf of a church member, Onesimus, who had inquired of Melito which books were authoritative, in order to make a compilation of passages about the Lord from "the Law and the Prophets" (ἔκ τὲ τοῦ νόμου καὶ τῶν προφητῶν). It appears that Melito did not know the answer to this question when asked, for he made a special trip to the Holy Land (εἰς τὴν ἀνατολὴν), where he could learn the facts more accurately.

Melito does not inform us from whom he learned which writings were "recognized," but it seems likely at that period and in that place that it might have been an official of the Jewish Christian church, or possibly even one of the authoritative teachers of the Palestinian rabbinic schools. His list is as follows: Genesis, Exodus, Numbers, Leviticus, Deuteronomy, Jesus the son of Nun (Joshua), Judges, Ruth, 1-4 Kings, 1-2 Chronicles, the Psalms of David, Solomon's Proverbs and Wisdom (Σολομῶνος Παροιμίαι ἡ καὶ Σοφία), Ecclesiastes, Song of Songs, Job, Isaiah, Jeremiah, the twelve prophets, Daniel, Ezekiel, and Ezra.[8]

Missing from this list (assuming the same doubling of certain books as Jerome and Origen assumed) is Esther, which, as we shall see below, was in fact one of the last books to be recognized as authoritative.[9] It is clear that at the end of the second century the canon of the Hebrew Bible was not fixed in the same form it would later assume. Indeed, it was so nebulous that average church members, and even ecclesiastical officials, did not know which books were authoritative without doing quite a bit of research.

Josephus. A final post-Masada witness to the state of the canon is the Jewish witness, Josephus (born circa 37-38 C.E.). In one of his last works, *Against Apion,*[10] Josephus used the consistency of the scriptures as a proof of the truth of the Israelite faith. He claims that because only prophets were allowed to write the records there is no disagreement (διαφωνίας) within them. These prophets were able to write accurate history because they learned the facts through inspiration from God (τὴν ἐπίπνοιαν τὴν ἀπὸ τοῦ θεοῦ). Thus (in a not-so-subtle criticism of the state of the Greek religious writings), the Jews do not have thousands (μυριάδες) of conflicting books but instead have only twenty-two consistent texts.

Josephus does not list the books but does note the tripartate division of the scriptures, informing us that there are five books of Moses, then thirteen books written by prophets subsequent to Moses, and finally four books of "hymns and counsel."[11] Josephus also claimed that nothing authoritative was written after the thirteen prophetic books because prophecy and the succession of prophets (τὴν τῶν προφητῶν ἀκριβῆ διαδοχήν) had ceased from the time of Artaxerxes (465-424 B.C.E.; Josephus probably saw Ezra as the last of the prophets). Histories of the later period had indeed been written, but they were not thought worthy of faith equal (πίστεως δ᾽ οὐχ ὁμοίας ἠξίωται) to those of the earlier period.[12] This detail is presumably missing from the Christian witnesses because for them prophecy had again revived, at least for a time, in the ministry of Jesus and with the writings of the New Testament.

A comparison of the witnesses of Jerome, Origen, Melito, and Josephus reveals that the closer we get to the first century, the less clear the Hebrew canon becomes. If these four may be taken as representative of the thought of their own ages, then it is evident that the canon becomes less fixed the farther back we go.

Development of the Canon

It was not until quite late—about Jerome's time—that the books of the Bible began to be copied physically into a single book and then only in the Greek or Latin translations. Unlike these translations, which were copied onto sheets (paper, papyrus, or parchment) and bound into books (codices), Hebrew biblical manuscripts were always copied onto leather scrolls. Jerome's use of the word *volumina* for the books of the Bible shows that he was using scrolls in his translation: the Latin *volumen* (from which we get our "volume") usually refers to a book in scroll form.

The scroll format mandated the physical separation of individual sections of the whole into manageable parts. Many readers may own a copy of the Bible on audio tape. Suppose that, instead of a few dozen separate tapes, the entire production was recorded on a single tape. Not only would the resulting tape be enormous, but access to particular parts would be nearly impossible. The disadvantages of such an arrangement are obvious.

The same disadvantages exist for a work written onto a scroll. In the ancient world, lengthy works were typically divided into smaller segments for this very reason: so that they could be copied onto more than one scroll. This is the reason for the division of the *Iliad* and the *Odyssey,* for example, into twenty-four books each. The Bible is different from these classical examples in that it did not begin as a single book. It started out as separate books, each of which was about the right size to fit onto a single scroll (the twelve minor prophets were usually grouped together, their total extent being the right length for a scroll, and were thus considered, in the minds of most ancient witnesses, one book). It was only gradually that the individual books began to be associated with each other and recognized as authoritative and canonical.[13]

Records of Evolving Canon. This "evolving canon" began at different times, apparently, for different parts of the Bible. One of the earliest signs of consciousness of a canon occurs in the biblical record itself, in the seventh century B.C. Second Kings 22–23 and 2 Chronicles 34 relate the story of how, after many years of incompetent and irreligious rulers, the pious King Josiah came to power in Israel. His reign may be summarized as an attempt to steer Israel back toward God, and Josiah spent much of his time suppressing false forms of worship in his kingdom.

During Josiah's administration (circa 640–609 B.C.E.) the "book of the law"[14] was discovered in the temple, which was being renovated in order to accommodate Josiah's reforms.[15] Upon its discovery, the book is given to the king (2 Kgs. 22:10; 2 Chron. 34:18). When it is read to him, he rends his clothing as a sign of mourning or penitence. It is clear from the whole narrative that this book is entirely new to the king and indeed everyone else. The king, who has after all been trying to do the right thing, has now discovered from the book that Israel has apparently been cursed for the actions of his predecessors. He orders his servants to inquire of the Lord about the book. They dutifully approach the prophetess Huldah, who declares that the prophecies in the book will be fulfilled, but that because Josiah has humbled himself, disaster will strike only after his lifetime (2 Kgs. 22:14–20; 2 Chron. 34:22–28). At this point, Josiah puts himself and all of Israel under covenant to obey and keep the commandments of the book (2 Kgs. 23:1–3; 2 Chron. 34:30–33). This is clearly a formal act of canonization, if canonization is understood in its usual sense as causing a set of writings to be made authoritative and binding upon a group.

Josiah's reforms were short-lived, and within his children's lifetime, the Babylonian captivity began. Apparently during that period of captivity most of Israel was again without its scriptures (the destruction of Jerusalem did not bode well for much being saved). Consequently, when the Israelites were later allowed to return to Jerusalem, Ezra, who himself had studied and observed "the law of the Lord"[16] (Ezra 7:10), had to formally initiate a covenant between Israel and the Lord to obey the law, thus recanonizing these writings (see especially Neh. 9–10).

The book of Nehemiah records that Ezra brings the book of the law of Moses out to show the people and reads it to them; he then has the priests explain it to them (probably because the law itself is written in Hebrew, while by that time the people speak Aramaic). The people weep to hear the law; they study it thoroughly and as a result reinstitute the Festival of the Booths, which, though prescribed in the scriptures, has not been practiced since the time of Joshua (Neh. 8:1–17)! All this implies that before Ezra's action there was little or no knowledge of the law among the general Israelite populace and that there had not been for a very long time.

To receive the law, the Lord commands Ezra to take five scribes and go to a secluded place for forty days, during which time the scriptures will be revealed to him (2 Esdras 14:23–26). Having gathered his scribes, Ezra begins to speak and continues without stopping for the entire time. The five scribes take turns writing Ezra's words down, and, after forty days, ninety-four books have been written. God tells Ezra to make the first twenty-four public, "'to be read by the good and bad alike.'" But the remaining seventy are to be "kept back, and given to none but the wise among your people. They contain a stream of understanding, a fountain of wisdom, a flood of knowledge" (2 Esdras 14:41–48).

The number twenty-four is an alternative ancient calculation for the number of books in the Hebrew Bible (Jerome notes in his preface to Samuel/Kings that, in addition to his calculation of twenty-two, others count the same books as twenty-four). These numbers, as we have seen, were calculated by combining or not combining various books such as Judges and Ruth and were probably chosen for symbolic reasons. Second Esdras, probably written around 100 C.E., attributes the entire canon as the author knew it to Ezra. What the twenty-four books are he does not explain. Whatever they were, the author of Esdras clearly makes a distinction between these canonized books and other apocryphal or pseudepigraphical books. He asserts that these books were also revealed to Ezra, along with the canonized books, thus explaining their existence and claims to inspiration.

Division of the Canon. Israel's rededication under Ezra, as under Josiah, was temporary, and the people appear to have lapsed into unrighteousness more than once during the intertestamental period. The history recorded in 1 Maccabees notes three times when a prophet would have been useful, but none was to be found (1 Macc. 4:46; 9:27; 14:41). However, attitudes toward the canon appear to have been evolving. It is probable that during this period the familiar tripartite division of the Hebrew Bible into the Law, the Prophets, and the Writings began to become standard. Second Maccabees 2:13 (written around 124 B.C.E.) has Nehemiah collecting "the chronicles of the kings, the writings of the prophets, the works of David, and royal letters," and a few years earlier (132 B.C.E.), the prologue to Ben Sira refers to the "legacy of great value [that] has come to us through the law, the prophets, and the writers who followed in their steps."[17] The author is not very specific about the third division, the Writings: referring to the scriptures three times in the prologue, he simply calls the Writings "the others" or "the rest" (τῶν ἄλλων, τὰ λοιπὰ).

Evidence in the New Testament shows that by the time of Christ it had become usual to refer to the scriptures as "the Law and the Prophets" (Matt. 5:17; 7:12; 22:37–40; Luke 16:16, 29, 31; see also Rom. 3:21), demonstrating that at least those portions of the Hebrew Bible had become fairly standardized by that age. Jesus also refers to the scriptures once as including at least part of the Writings, when, giving his final words to the disciples, he says that all things "which were written in the law of Moses, and in the prophets, and in the psalms" concerning him have been fulfilled (Luke 24:44).

The tripartite division is important to the question of canon because it appears that the canon was established more or less in three stages. The law of Moses had been accepted by Israel, at least in theory if not in practice, since ancient times and was formally canonized from the time of Ezra (fifth century B.C.E.), as already discussed.[18] The section that came to be known as the Prophets was accepted as authoritative later, probably in postexilic times.

As pointed out by Anderson, the words of the prophets had been clearly proven true by the captivity and exile, thus substantiating their claim to divine inspiration and authority. "So long as prophecy was still a living force, the various collections of prophetic teaching continued to be preserved and enlarged [that is, in an "open" canon]. . . . This involved not only the addition of new material but also the adaptation and interpretation of older prophecies . . . to apply them to new situations. . . . But prophecy did not continue as a living force."[19] That this was recognized by Israel is evidenced by Josephus's statement that prophecy had ceased around the time of Ezra.[20] Possibly this cessation, with its accompanying cessation of additions to and modifications of the prophetic writings, was the impetus for collecting them together into an authoritative, canonized, and closed unit.

Anderson believes that this section, the Prophets, was established by 200 B.C.E. Part of his evidence is that the book of Daniel, which was written down around 165 B.C.E., is not a part of this section, but it undoubtedly would have been if the canon had not already been established previous to that date.[21] On the other hand, the canonicity of the book of Ezekiel, which *is* included in this section, was under discussion as late as the years immediately preceding the destruction of Jerusalem and the events at Masada.[22]

The final form of the third section, the Writings or Hagiographa, seems to have coalesced during the first two centuries C.E. A Talmudic discussion recording a tradition dating to this period states that "our rabbis taught . . . the order of the Prophets is, Joshua, Judges, Samuel, Kings, Jeremiah, Ezekiel, Isaiah, and the Twelve Minor Prophets. . . . The order of the Hagiographa is Ruth, the Book of Psalms, Job, Proverbs, Ecclesiastes, Song of Songs, Lamentations, Daniel and the Scroll of Esther, Ezra and Chronicles" (Baba Bathra 14b). These books correspond exactly to the later tradition as canonized in the Masoretic text. But this authoritative listing did not emerge without lively discussion. In addition to questions about the canonicity of Ezekiel (mentioned above), the books of Esther, Ecclesiastes, Song of Songs, and the Aramaic portions of Daniel and Ezra came under scrutiny at this time (Megillah 7a; Shabbath 30b; Mishnah Yadaim 4.5; Tosefta Yadaim 2.14). Ben Sira also was discussed and apparently considered for inclusion though eventually rejected (Tosefta Yadaim 2.13).

Some of these first- and second-century discussions on the Hebrew canon took place at the great rabbinic school of Jabneh (sometimes called by its Greek name Jamnia). According to rabbinic sources, just before the fall of Jerusalem the rabbi Johanan ben Zakkai manages to escape the doomed city, enter the Roman

Fragment of Ben Sira. This fragment is one of the incomplete extra-canonical texts found at Masada. Ben Sira was considered for inclusion in the biblical canon but was eventually rejected.

camp, and receive an audience with Vespasian. When he greets
Vespasian as "imperator" (general/emperor), Vespasian objects that
the greeting is treasonous since he is *not* the emperor. Johanan
predicts that Vespasian will in fact be king, and he is proved correct three days later when Vespasian learns the news that he has
indeed been acclaimed emperor. Impressed, Vespasian grants
Johanan any wish. When Johanan asks him to lift the siege and
leave the city, Vespasian naturally refuses, but he does grant
Johanan's second wish, to allow certain scholars to leave the city
and establish a rabbinic school at the town of Jabneh.[23]

After the fall of Jerusalem, Jabneh became the center of
Israelite religion. Johanan became the head of the group of Jewish
scholars who gathered there, and he was followed by Gamaliel II.
Under Gamaliel (about 80–117 c.e.), a number of discussions appear
to have occurred at the school concerning what should be
included in the Hebrew Bible, although in contradiction to scholarly consensus of the first part of this century, the sources do not
record any official debate or final decision at Jabneh on the canon.[24]
What the sources do record is continuing discussion, particularly
about the status of the Writings. That the content of the Writings
was becoming set is evidenced by the fact that the ancient sources
begin to speak of them as a group: the Law, the Prophets, and the
Writings, which from then on meant "the Bible." Gamaliel II was
the first to use this terminology; when asked where in the scriptures the doctrine of the Resurrection was found, he replied:
"From the Torah [Law], in the Prophets, and the Hagiographa
[Writings]" (מן התורה ומן הנביאים ומן הכתובים) (Sanhedrin 90b).

Conclusion

Anderson's article on canon in the *Cambridge History of the
Bible* gives three reasons why it was urgent for Jews that the issue
of canon be settled at this time (the first century c.e.) namely,
(1) the dispersion, and particularly the destruction of the temple,
meant that the only source of guidance in practice and belief was
the written word; (2) the existence of numerous apocalyptic writings, claiming to be written by earlier prophets, required some
sort of authoritative decision on their authenticity; and (3) the

appearance of Christian scripture also required some official exclusion of those books from the canon.[25] This argument makes sense, but only after the fact; while Talmudic discussions of heretical Christian writings determined that they "do not make the hands unclean" (in other words, are not in the canon),[26] no evidence exists for formal exclusion of apocalyptic works, at least not at Jabneh,[27] and certainly no evidence for a "council" or "synod" held there. The most the sources offer is the later listing of books in the Prophets and the Writings, already discussed (Baba Bathra 14b).

Thus evidence documenting the formation of the Hebrew canon is inconclusive. Yet it is clear from the Talmudic list that by the third century at the latest the canon had been set for the Jews; Christians began to formalize their canon a bit later (see Jerome's list, above).[28] Unlike the Christians, who eventually ratified their canonical lists in formal councils, there is no evidence of such an event for the Jewish faith. It appears that their canon, which did in fact become closed and fixed, developed organically, by consensus and tradition.

What, then, of the canon at Masada? If the Jewish groups that took refuge there were traditional in their belief about the canonicity of the Hebrew Bible, they would likely have included the Law and Prophets portions largely as we have them now. As seen above, three of the Masada fragments come from the Law (Leviticus and Deuteronomy), one from the Prophets (Ezekiel), and three from Psalms; there are no fragments from other portions of the Writings.[29] It may be fair, then, to say from this scant evidence and our general knowledge of the state of the Hebrew Bible at the time that the canon at Masada was similar to that embodied in Jesus' statement a generation earlier: that "which [is] written in the law of Moses, and in the prophets, and in the psalms" (Luke 24:44).

Robert L. Maxwell is Special Collections Librarian at Brigham Young University.

NOTES

[1]For additional information, see Stephen A. Reed, comp., *The Dead Sea Scrolls Catalogue: Documents, Photographs, and Museum Inventory Numbers,*

ed. M. J. Lundberg and M. B. Phelps (Atlanta: Scholars, 1994), 185–86; She-mariyahu Talmon, "Hebrew Scroll Fragments from Masada," in *The Story of Masada,* ed. Gila Hurvitz (Provo, Utah: BYU Studies, 1997), 101–7; and David Rolph Seely, "The Masada Fragments, the Qumran Scrolls, and the New Testa-ment," in this volume.

[2]See H. F. D. Sparks, "Jerome as Biblical Scholar," in *The Cambridge His-tory of the Bible,* 3 vols. (Cambridge: Cambridge University Press, 1970), 1:518, 521; and D. C. Parker, "Vulgate," in *The Anchor Bible Dictionary,* ed. David Noel Freedman, 6 vols. (New York: Doubleday, 1992), 6:860.

[3]Parker, "Vulgate," 6:860.

[4]Jerome's preface may be found in *Biblia Sacra Iuxta Vulgatam Ver-sionem,* 2d ed., 2 vols. (Stuttgart: Württembergische Bibelanstalt, 1975), 1:364–66. Translations are the author's.

[5]This count is problematic, since although Jerome claims to be counting five "double" books in his total of twenty-two, there are in fact six if Jeremiah/Lamentations is counted as one: Judges/Ruth, Samuel, Kings, Jeremiah/Lamenta-tions, Chronicles, and Ezra/Nehemiah.

[6]Eusebius, *Ecclesiastical History* 6.25.1. The Greek text of Eusebius is most conveniently accessible in the 1926–32 Loeb edition of Kirsopp Lake and J. E. L. Oulton. Translations by the author.

[7]Eusebius, *History* 6.25.2.

[8]Eusebius, *History* 4.26.12–14.

[9]In addition, Melito's peculiar phrase "Solomon's Proverbs and Wisdom" makes one wonder if he is including the now apocryphal book Wisdom of Solomon (which, however, was originally written in Greek, not Hebrew).

[10]Written after 93–94 c.e., the publication date of his *Jewish Antiquities.*

[11]Josephus, *Against Apion* 1.37–40. The Greek text of *Against Apion* may be found in the first volume of the Loeb edition of Josephus (1926). Translations are by the author.

[12]Josephus, *Against Apion* 1.41.

[13]For a good discussion of the problem of the physical format of ancient books in relation to the books of the Bible, see Nahum M. Sarna, *Ancient Libraries and the Ordering of the Biblical Books: A Lecture Presented at the Library of Congress, March 6, 1989* (Washington, D.C.: Library of Congress, 1989).

[14]It is not entirely clear what the neglected "book of the law" that was discovered in the temple included. Some suppose it included only the central portion of Deuteronomy (chs. 5–28). See G. W. Anderson, "Canonical and Non-Canonical [in the Hebrew Bible]," in *Cambridge History of the Bible,* 1:120. The fact that the entire book is read aloud twice in the episode (2 Kgs. 22:10–11; 23:2; 2 Chron. 34:18–19; 34:30; see also the footnote to 2 Kings 23:1–3 in the New English Bible [NEB]) does appear to be evidence for a shorter work than the entire Pentateuch. On the other hand, the book is referred to as "sefer ha-Torah" (ספר התורה) every time it is mentioned. This later became the normal way of refer-ring to the Pentateuch. Further, Josiah seems particularly worried about certain dire prophecies directed against Israel, which presumably come from prophets later than Moses. Perhaps the text included selections of the Pentateuch, as well as parts of later prophecies. The important points for this discussion are that

the text was unknown to Israel before its discovery under Josiah, that it included portions of what is now the Hebrew Bible, and that it was formally canonized under the king's direction.

[15]The chronology of Josiah's reforms differs significantly between the two sources, Chronicles recording that they began in the eighth year of his reign, about 632 (2 Chr. 34:3), and Kings claiming they began in the eighteenth year, 622-21 (2 Kgs. 22:3). Chronicles records that the discovery of the book of the law occurred in the eighteenth year of Josiah's reign (2 Chr. 34:8).

[16]As with Josiah's book of the law, it is not clear precisely what is contained in Ezra's—certainly at least the Pentateuch. Anderson, "Canonical and Non-Canonical," 1:123. The account found in 2 Esdras (4 Ezra) claims it was the entire Hebrew Bible and gives an interesting story of how Ezra obtained the scriptures: Ezra was disturbed that Israel was sinking into wickedness, and, speaking to the Lord in vision, blamed it on the fact that the law was burned in the destruction of Jerusalem, "so no one can know about the deeds you have done or intend to do." He asked to have the scriptures revealed to him: "the whole story of the world from the very beginning, everything that is contained in your law," so that the people would at least have the chance to choose to do right (NEB, 2 Esdras 14:21-22).

[17]Samuel Sandmel, M. Jack Suggs, and Arnold J. Tkacik, eds., *The New English Bible with the Apocrypha* (New York: Oxford University Press, 1976), 115.

[18]James A. Sanders, "Canon," in *Anchor Bible Dictionary,* "Hebrew Bible" section, 1:840, dates the sequence Genesis-2 Kings, both as to content and as to order, to the sixth century B.C.E.

[19]Anderson, "Canonical and Non-Canonical," 1:127.

[20]Josephus, *Against Apion* 1.41.

[21]Anderson, "Canonical and Non-Canonical," 1:129.

[22]Hananiah reconciled Ezekiel with the Torah at least four years before the destruction of the temple. "In truth, that man, Hananiah son of Hezekiah by name, is to be remembered for blessing: but for him, the book of Ezekiel would have been hidden [a technical term for excluded from the canon], for its words contradicted the Torah." I. Epstein, ed., *Hebrew-English Edition of the Babylonian Talmud Translated into English* (London: Soncino, 1960-90), Shabbath 13b and footnote a(1). All direct English quotations are from this edition. There are actually two Talmuds, one compiled in Babylonian rabbinic centers (the Babylonian Talmud) and one compiled in Palestine (the Jerusalem Talmud). Both consist of extended commentary on the Mishnah (a summation of oral traditions about the law of Moses, competed in 200 C.E.), and both were written down between the early third and the fifth centuries C.E. They include, however, numerous traditions about much earlier rabbis, such as the one preserved in this quotation. The Talmud and Mishnah are divided into subject sections called "tractates," by which reference is made. Within each tractate of the Babylonian Talmud, references are to the page number of the *editio princeps,* that of Daniel Bomberg (Venice, 1520-23). As is customary, in this article tractates in the Babylonian Talmud will be referred to by tractate alone, with no notice that reference is to the Babylonian (vs. the Jerusalem) Talmud. References to the Mishnah are to section and verse within the tractate and are preceded by the word "Mishnah."

A second supplement to the Mishnah, the Tosefta, came into existence at the end of the fourth century c.e. References to the Tosefta are cited "Tosefta [tractate] [chapter.verse]."

[23]The story is found in Gittin 56a–b and Lamentations Rabbah 1.5.

[24]See Jack P. Lewis, "What Do We Mean by Jabneh?" *Journal of Bible and Religion* 32, no. 2 (1964): 125–32, esp. 126; see also Sanders, "Canon," 1:841.

[25]Anderson, "Canonical and Non-Canonical," 132–33; see also Sanders, "Canon," 1:843; and Albert C. Sundberg, *The Old Testament of the Early Church*, Harvard Theological Studies, vol. 20 (Cambridge: Harvard University Press, 1964), 116–17.

[26]Mishnah Yadaim 4.6; Tosefta Yadaim 2.13; see also Tosefta Shabbath 13.5; and Tosefta Sanhedrin 13.4–5. The use of the expression "makes the hands unclean" as a technical term for "canonical" originates, according to the Talmud, with the very early practice of keeping the Torah next to the food offerings in the temple. It was found that the rodents that came and ate the food also enjoyed chewing on the scrolls, so to guarantee that the two would no longer be stored together (thus ensuring the protection of the scrolls), the rabbis imposed uncleanness on the scriptures (Shabbath 14a). This designation meant that one was required to purify oneself after using the scriptures. This ruling probably also protected the scriptures from indiscriminate handling. See also Mishnah Yadaim 4.6; and Tosefta Yadaim 2.10.

[27]Lewis, "Jabneh?" 131.

[28]Harry Y. Gamble, "Canon: New Testament," in *Anchor Bible Dictionary*, 1:853.

[29]However there is a fragment of Ben Sira, whose canonicity we have seen (as well as Ezekiel's) was in fact under discussion at the very time and would have been included with the Writings had it been accepted into the canon.

The Romans in Judea

The Roman Province of Judea: A Historical Overview

John F. Hall

The Coming of Rome to Judea

Rome's acquisition of Judea and subsequent involvement in the affairs of that long-troubled area came about in largely indirect fashion. For centuries Judea had been under the control of the Hellenistic Greek monarchy centered in Syria and known as the Seleucid empire, one of the successor states to the far greater empire of Alexander the Great, who conquered the vast reaches of the Persian empire toward the end of the fourth century B.C. As the decaying Seleucid monarchy disintegrated, Rome was compelled to take control of the eastern littoral of the Mediterranean and its hinterland in order to prevent ambitious petty kings in the region—and more importantly a renascent Parthian empire—from filling the vacuum left with the fall of the Seleucids and so posing a threat to Rome's Mediterranean empire. As a part of this larger region and as a place once ruled by the Seleucids, Judea became a subject area of Rome.

Rome was not interested in Judea per se and for too long did not understand the problems unique to Judea which should have prevented the Romans from dealing with the Jews in the same way they did the other subject peoples in the eastern reaches of the empire. Similarly, the Jews made no effort to become acquainted with their Roman rulers, to whom they regrettably attributed the characteristics of their previous Greek masters, whose efforts to encourage Hellenization entailed a lack of religious toleration which threatened Jewish worship. By contrast, Rome was actually quite tolerant of the religions of all its subject peoples. This mutual misunderstanding of the nature of Judea by the Romans and of

Rome by the Jews clearly made more difficult the administration of Judea. However, by itself it cannot account for the tragic events in Judea, which derived less from any relation to Rome than from the vehement struggle among rival Jewish factions whose ambitions for power harmed their countrymen and ultimately brought an end to Judea as an entity.

In 63 B.C., the territory of Judea for the first time came under the direct administration of Rome. While Rome had been for nearly a century an important determinant in the affairs of this region, increased Roman supervision was the natural result of administrative inefficiency on the part of local dynasts and minor chieftains who governed portions of the Roman Near East as client kings. Local rivalries and ambitions among native rulers sometimes led to outright armed conflict among themselves and occasionally even with their Roman overlords. In the mid–first century B.C., such problems, both in Judea as well as throughout the eastern Mediterranean in general, occasioned a Roman reordering of the entire region.

When a challenge to Roman rule was made by Mithridates of Pontus, who sought to assert control over the whole of Asia minor, murdering Romans, Greeks, and many other local inhabitants in his path, Pompey the Great concluded the conflict with the expected Roman victory.[1] Afterward Pompey turned his attention to reorganizing administratively Rome's eastern holdings. In 63 B.C., Rome attached the territory of Judea to the newly created Roman province of Syria, where a high-ranking Roman governor of proconsular status would exercise ultimate authority over Judea along with Syria and other areas in the vicinity. The action was taken as part of Pompey's general settlement of the eastern Mediterranean and in response to specific disruptive conditions in Judea occasioned by the rivalries of Jewish noble families claiming the high priestly office and with it local rule.[2] Though not yet organized as a separate province, Roman Judea takes its beginning in these events.

Roman Administration in Judea

Roman interest and involvement in the administrative affairs of Judea actually predates Pompey's arrival. Rome had on several occasions, upon the repeated requests of Jewish rulers, intervened diplomatically to prevent the Seleucid monarchs of Syria from reasserting their previous authority over Judea and had thereby preserved Judean independence under the rule of the high priest and Sanhedrin.[3] Had it not been for rivalry among Jewish noble families vying with one another for the power to rule, Jewish independence may perhaps have continued. However, the chaotic conditions produced by such internal conflict threatened the peace of surrounding territories and mandated Roman intervention to maintain law and order not only in Judea, but throughout the immediate region.

Despite the administrative redistricting of Judea, little change, in fact, transpired as regards the actual day-to-day administration of Judea. In accordance with Roman policy for provincial administration, in Judea as in other provinces the continued influence of local leaders was maintained and as much local governance as possible was placed in their hands. The high priest and nobles continued to direct the internal affairs of Judea, no longer with independent authority, but subject to the oversight of a Roman proconsul in Antioch. However, Antioch was far distant, and as long as problems did not surface, direct Roman concern with the area would have been extremely minimal. Roman policy had long adhered to the perspective that local governance was the most convenient provided the status quo be maintained, including the preservation of law and order, the collection of assessed revenues, and the support of Roman foreign policy with the supply of troops when required.

Rome's major concerns for the provinces were to maintain a peace in which Roman trade and commerce could be conducted and Romans could come and go in safety. Taxes were collected to support the framework of government, including the army as guardians of internal security and providers of protection from the threats of foreign powers or barbaric enemies without the empire. Rome's attitude toward the administration of Judea differed not at all from that of Rome in regard to all its holdings.

Intervention in the domestic affairs of Judea was unavoidable for Pompey. Rivalry among Jewish factions interrupted order and prevented commerce. Moreover, the Jewish conflict threatened to spill over into neighboring areas also under Rome's control. Judea's latest internecine conflict was a struggle for succession between the two sons of Alexander Jannaeus. The rightful heir, Hyrcanus, had been displaced by his brother Aristobulus, but, with the aid of the Idumean chieftain Antipater, Hyrcanus sought to reassert his rights militarily. Both claimants appealed to Rome for support in much the same way in which rival Jewish factions had appealed for centuries for aid or intervention, military and otherwise, from the Hellenistic monarchs of Seleucid Syria, Judea's ostensible enemies since the time of the Maccabees. In their eagerness for the support of their enemies, Jewish leaders had been willing to concede much. Such willingness extended to making whatever concessions were necessary for Roman support as well. The formal organization of Judea as a Roman territory, while a natural consequence of Rome's acquisition of Seleucid territories and organization of the province of Syria, was also a direct result of internal conflict between Jewish factions. Nevertheless, in establishing Hyrcanus as high priest to continue local administration subject to the direction of the Roman proconsular governor of Syria, standard Roman practice of preferring local government where possible was followed despite the factional rivalry within Judea. Rome obviously did not wish to become too directly involved in Judea.[4]

Hyrcanus did not rule as king, but as ethnarch, a far less important position and as high priest. Antipater continued to cultivate Rome and Roman involvement in the region, receiving in return the ruling power in his native Idumea. Antipater's position as a chief advisor to Hyrcanus and his other involvements in Judean affairs laid the foundation for ruling positions later granted by Roman overlords to himself and his sons Herod and Phasael, chief administrators for Galilee and Jerusalem respectively, so establishing Idumean rulers over Judea.[5]

Roman Affairs around Judea

While Pompey's settlement of Jewish affairs was in the main necessitated by internal happenings in Judea, subsequent Roman actions toward Judea were occasioned by larger events external to Judea. Invasions of Roman territory, including Judea, by a new Parthian kingdom in what had been the Mesopotamian reaches of the Seleucid empire and civil conflicts between Roman factions effected frequent change in the administration of Judea over the next four decades.[6] Ultimately Herod was established as client king of Rome in charge of an expanded Judea. The Hasmonean dynasty of the Maccabees, and with it a modicum of self-government by Judeans, was brought to an end with Herod's accession. Continued internal conflict among branches of the Hasmonean family and the intrigue with and appeal to Parthia for aid by the sons of Aristobulus was responsible for yet another Roman intervention and the fall of the Hasmonean dynasty.

The first of these interventions was directed by a lieutenant and supporter of Pompey, Aulus Gabinius, who succeeded Scaurus as governor of Syria. In 55 B.C., Gabinius was forced to intervene militarily to restore order in Judea, where Alexander, son of Aristobulus, had raised his supporters in revolt against the ethnarch Hyrcanus and his Idumean supporters, Antipater and his sons. Aristobulus himself escaped from Rome and joined his son's insurrection. Not only did Rome need to deal with the consequent civil disorder and interruption of commerce, but in this instance, the Roman response to the insurrection had to be especially swift and effective since Rome supported the established government of Hyrcanus. In addition, the rival faction sought to end that support through overthrowing Roman rule entirely by soliciting the military intervention of Parthia against Rome. Because such an act was considered treasonable and violated the most important Roman dictum for provincial noninvolvement in foreign affairs, direct and massive Roman military intervention was dictated. Gabinius and his lieutenant Marc Antony led Roman troops into Judea, defeated the revolutionaries, restored Hyrcanus to power, and increased the authority of Antipater and Herod, who had proven themselves as supporters of Rome. From this time on, Rome's interest in Judea increased and closer attention was paid to the area which bordered the important province of Syria, which was organized as a military province of the first rank and was the key to Roman control over the empire's entire eastern frontier. Thus, Judea comes to have a strategic if not an economic importance for Rome.[7]

The powerful Marcus Licinius Crassus, partner in Rome's "First Triumvirate" with Pompey and Julius Caesar, succeeded Gabinius as governor of Syria in 54 B.C. Eager to equal the military exploits of Pompey in the East and those of Caesar in Gaul, Crassus used the excuse of Parthian intrigue in areas of the Roman eastern frontier, including Judea, as reason to initiate hostilities against the Parthians. Crassus suffered one of the greatest defeats of Roman arms at Carrhae in 53 B.C.[8] With this Parthian victory, Roman concern increased over the affairs of her eastern territories, held in large part by only semiloyal client kings. Questions were raised in Rome over the wisdom of its policy regarding the involvement of provincial leaders in governing the provinces. No doubt, the disloyalty and intrigue of Jewish factions contributed to reassessment of the policy. However, Roman action against Parthia and reconsideration of its eastern provincial arrangements were delayed by the great civil war between Pompey and Caesar.

Caesar defeated Pompey at Pharsalus in 48 B.C., essentially ending the civil war, although with a small legionary force Caesar followed the fleeing Pompey to Ptolemaic Alexandria. Upon his arrival, Caesar was presented with Pompey's head by the teenage monarch Ptolemy XII, who was comonarch with his sister Cleopatra. Ptolemy had waged civil war against Cleopatra and driven her from Alexandria. Highly displeased that a leading Roman would be executed at the hand of Alexandrians, Caesar took Alexandria with his small force. He supported the returned Cleopatra, who became his mistress, and ultimately he placed her alone on Egypt's throne. Besieged by Ptolemy's army, Caesar required immediate aid in the form of troops from Rome's client rulers in surrounding territories. Hyrcanus and Antipater were fast to respond and accompanied Roman legions from Syria to effect the relief of Caesar at Alexandria. Their loyalty was well rewarded by Caesar, who increased the territory under Hyrcanus's control, confirmed Antipater as chief minister of Judea, and extended to him and his sons both Roman citizenship and the lucrative tax collection franchise for Judea. Moreover, as undisputed master of Rome, Caesar promulgated laws to protect the religious freedom of Jews throughout the empire, extending to the Jews an unprecedented grant of special privileges.[9]

The support of the Idumean royal family for Caesar not only laid the foundation for their own rule over Judea and other surrounding areas, but also had the added consequence of securing for the Jews as a group the grant of special privilege which protected Jews from Greek anti-Semitism. The privilege also secured for the Jews special rights of religious worship even beyond those extended to all subject peoples of the empire as part of Rome's general tolerance of religion. Furthermore, Caesar's actions in effect restored the full authority of rule to Hyrcanus. If any necessity of reporting to Syria's governor lingered, it was surely ended in the events following Caesar's assassination with the establishment of Herod as Judean monarch.

Herod's Alliance with Rome

In the struggle for power after Caesar's death, Caesar's lieutenant Marc Antony and Caesar's nephew and adopted son, Octavian Caesar (the future Augustus), emerged as the two primary claimants of power in the Roman world. Antony, who had also served as Gabinius's lieutenant in the East and during his 55 B.C. expedition to Judea, made the eastern provinces his base of operations for the struggle with Octavian. Antony's liaison with Cleopatra is, of course, well known. However, for Judea, Antony's importance cannot be overestimated. For it was Antony who made Judea an independent client kingdom of Rome, ruled over by a king, Antipater's son Herod.

In 42 B.C., when Antony disposed of eastern problems and reassigned territories in the eastern part of the empire, delegations of Jews approached him, demanding the removal of Antipater's sons Herod and Phasael from power. The Idumean brothers reminded Antony of their family's services to Caesar and donated a substantial sum to Antony's war chest. In return they became the de facto regents for the aged Hyrcanus, showing respect to the old ethnarch, but, in fact, ruling with the titles of tetrarch.[10]

The occasion for Antony's reorganization of Judea entailed another attempt by yet another of Aristobulus's sons, Antigonus, to depose Hyrcanus and with him, the real powers in Judea, the Idumean tetrarchs. Antigonus was aided in his cause by an invading Parthian army which briefly seized control of Judea and areas of Syria before Antony's lieutenants drove the Parthians out of Roman territory. Herod escaped death at the hands of the Aristobulus faction and the Parthians by taking refuge in Idumea in his family's specially prepared stronghold on the heights of Masada.

He subsequently fled to Rome in 40 B.C., where Antony and Octavian agreed to bestow upon Herod the long-vacant title of king of Judea. It is surprising that that direct Roman rule in Judea was not opted for after so direct a challenge to Roman rule in Judea by a Jewish faction seeking their advancement over the faction in power—a challenge which even entailed a Parthian incursion. The fact that Roman control was instead actually loosened with the creation of a full-fledged semiautonomous client kingdom demonstrates Antony's adherence to the principle of local administration for provinces, as well as a definite lack of interest in Judea by comparison with more important areas. Antony's legate Sosius and Herod were entrusted with the responsibility of driving Parthians out of Judea and deposing Antigonus. By 37 B.C., the task was accomplished and Herod's long rule over Judea commenced.[11]

Judea as a Client Kingdom of Rome

From 37 to Herod's death in 4 B.C. and into the brief reign of Herod's son Archelaus, which came to an end in A.D. 6, Judea was technically not a province of Rome, but rather a dependent client kingdom of Rome administered by Herod and Archelaus as client kings. The dependent kingdom was not unique to Judea but was a standard form of administration for areas under Roman control, particularly in the eastern reaches of the empire. Under this type of administration, Herod would have been subject not to a proconsul in Syria, but directly to the triumvirs Antony and Octavian and, after the establishment of the principate, directly to Augustus.[12]

During the early years of Herod's rule, civil war decided the contest for power between Antony and Octavian. Antony, in control of the eastern parts of Roman territory, enlisted the aid of the many client kings of the East in his struggle against Octavian. Herod chose to support Antony and contributed money and troops to Antony's cause. When Octavian defeated Antony and Cleopatra in 31 B.C. at Actium and later saw to their deaths in Egypt, Herod, as a loyal supporter of Antony, found himself in an uncomfortable position vis-à-vis the triumphant Octavian, soon to be elevated Augustus Caesar. Herod protested to Octavian that the loyalty he had shown was far from criminal, but rather a quality to be sought in a client king. He persuaded Octavian that he would show him as ruler the same loyalty he had demonstrated toward Antony. Herod not only persuaded Octavian to permit him to retain his rule of Judea, but Octavian also added many surrounding territories to Herod's Judean realm, including those which in 63 B.C., Pompey had attached to Syria and other administrative units in the region. For the next twenty-seven years until his death, Herod remained a faithful client to Octavian, now Augustus Caesar, sending his grandson Herod Agrippa, named for Augustus's son-in-law and Herod's friend, Marcus Vipsanius Agrippa, to be raised in Augustus's own household. In Judea, Herod built the Samaritan city Sebaste (the Greek form of Augustus's name) in honor of the emperor, constructed a Roman amphitheater in Jerusalem dedicated to Augustus, and required all Jews to swear an oath of allegiance to Augustus, the implementation of which violated Jewish religious law. Moreover, Herod was in private, if not in public, a devotee of the emperor's cult.[13] Needless to say, Herod worried about the ever-increasing antagonism many Jews harbored for him. To protect himself from the occasional anger of his Jewish subjects, the family fortress at Masada was strengthened and improved. In this manner, Herod kept the peace in Judea and served his Roman masters faithfully. Judea was a peaceful, if a poor and insignificant corner of the great empire. Its strategic importance declined as Parthian designs on Rome's eastern reaches retreated before the might of the well-governed realm of Augustus Caesar.[14]

Restabilizing Judea after Herod's Death

The stability of Judea as a Roman holding was disrupted at the death of Herod. The problems of factionalism, now not only among Jewish nobles, but also among religious sects and other Jewish ideological factions, reemerged as a source of conflict. Initially Augustus recognized as successors to Herod's fiefdom his declared heirs—his three surviving sons: Archelaus, ethnarch of Judea, Samaria, and Idumea; Antipas, tetrarch of Galilee and Perea; and Philip, tetrarch of Iturea. None succeeded to the office of king, but occupied lesser posts. The now-divided regions of Herod's once significant holdings again were officially subject to the Roman governor of Syria, as they had been before Herod. Archelaus maintained power in face of Jewish resistance only with the help of Augustus's legate in Syria, Publius Quintilius Varus. Finally, faced with chaotic conditions in Judea, as well as revolt and clamor from the Jews at Jerusalem, who preferred direct Roman government to rule by Archelaus, the unfortunate and ineffective ethnarch was stripped of his titles and exiled to Gaul. Archelaus's holdings were annexed as a province under the administrative oversight of the larger province of Syria in A.D. 6. This act constituted the formal organization of Judea as a Roman province. The new governor of Syria, the Augustan legate Publius Sulpicius Quirinius, sent as his local administrator for Judea one Coponius, who first occupied the office of Judean prefect.

Quirinus himself traveled south with the Roman legions of Syria to restore order in Judea and assure the position of Coponius. The level of Roman interest in Judea had not changed, but the civil disorder created by increased factionalism and Archelaus's inability to govern necessitated a response to the request of leading Jews for the order they rightly believed would accompany direct Roman administration. The establishment of orderly government in Judea was resisted at this time by Sicarii, who for the first time are noted as disruptors of order. They failed to offer a challenge to the disciplined troops of Rome, however, and Coponius's authority was established. The Jews at Jerusalem had the Roman government they had petitioned for.[15]

Roman Governors of Judea

The so-called office of Roman governor of Judea was very limited in authority by comparison to the Augustan legates. The legates were governors of major provinces, commanding a large legionary compliment, by contrast to the individual cohorts or auxiliary troops which constituted the smaller and less professional military contingent for a place like Judea. The governor of Judea is identified inaccurately by some sources such as Josephus as the minor governor known as the procurator. In fact, his office was even less significant. Inscriptional evidence leaves no doubt whatever that Pilate and other Judean governors held the position of *praefectus Iudaeae.* While the Roman administrator at Jerusalem was apparently in some fashion subject to the much-higher-ranking governor of Syria, within Judea he nevertheless exercised full civil and criminal jurisdictional powers. The permanent residence of the Roman prefect seems to have been at Caesarea on the coast, rather than at Jerusalem. His authority throughout the province was enforced by Roman troops—not a full legion, but several cohorts of Roman regulars, as well as non-Roman auxiliary troops in Rome's service. In Jerusalem a Roman cohort of six hundred men occupied the Fortress of Antonia, built by Herod adjacent to his temple and named in honor of Marc Antony. Herod's palace and citadel complex in the upper city was also held by a Roman garrison. The prefect's authority, prestige, and power base was sufficient for what Rome considered a small and insignificant province like Judea, at least until the time of the Jewish rebellion. It is important to recognize that Judea was not considered an important province; it had a governor of rather low rank and status. The governor's office would not be filled by the most capable or important Romans; and the lack of prestige or ability on the part of its governors may have ultimately affected adversely the administration of the province.[16]

Roman sources, both literary and epigraphic, as well as the writings of Josephus provide us with a good record of the Roman rulers over Judea. Fourteen prefects of Judea served between A.D. 6 and the outbreak of the Jewish War in the year 66. They were not men otherwise known for accomplishments at Rome. Three are mentioned in the account of the New Testament: Pilate, who served as governor from 26 to 36; Felix, who served from 52 to 59; and Festus, who governed from 60 to 62. Of the province's Roman administrators, Valerius (15–26) and Pilate served for far longer terms than other governors who could expect a tenure of only a few years. The longer tenure in office of Valerius and Pilate probably had less to do with the quality of their service and more to do with their service transpiring during the period when Tiberius was emperor. It was a general practice of Tiberius to leave governors in office for long periods of time throughout all the provinces of the empire. The tenure of Roman governors in Judea was briefly interrupted from 41 to 44, when the emperor Claudius rewarded his boyhood friend, Herod's grandson Herod Agrippa, with the restoration of Herod's kingdom, including not only Judea, Samaria, and surrounding areas once ruled by Herod, but also adding to it additional new lands. The very act of ending the existence of a Roman province, which at that time Judea had been for thirty-five years, and reverting its territory into a client kingdom was extraordinary, but to take additional lands from other Roman holdings to add to the restored client kingdom speaks to both the confidence and affection which Claudius possessed for Herod Agrippa.[17]

Benefits of Roman Rule

Once direct Roman government had been established in Judea in A.D. 6, the province benefited not only in terms of freedom from the internal civil conflict and dissatisfactions which had marked its history for centuries, but also came to enjoy a new prosperity which strengthened the allegiance to Rome of at least those who most reaped the wealth deriving from the improved economy.[18] There were no popular revolts of the sort which had threatened the reign of Herod and brought to an end the rule of Archelaus. Roman demands on Judea were not particularly heavy, certainly no heavier than those placed on other provinces. Little change would have occurred in the day-to-day life of people in Judea from the time of Herod's rule to the time of the Roman governors. Most matters relating to Jews would have been administered by local Jewish leaders. The fact that Jesus was subjected to the jurisdiction of high priest and Sanhedrin before that of Pilate highlights Jewish leaders' involvement in provincial administration alongside the Roman governor. Discontent among some segment of society, especially groups like zealots, Sicarii, and others who sought for political power and control, was overshadowed by the relative peacefulness of the general population.

In such a setting, unfolded the events of the ministry of Christ and the acts of the apostles after the Savior's death. Christians, who were themselves the frequent target of zealots and Sicarii, followed Christ's injunction to render unto Caesar. Accordingly, among Christians there is no record of the opposition to Rome which is found among other Judean groups. Roman overlordship guaranteed the peace and made it possible for Judea to become more completely a full, participating partner in the Roman ecumene, with the increased economic prosperity which derived therefrom. Many Jews eager for the opportunities of personal advancement left Judea, migrating to other parts of the Roman world. Just as the Hellenistic ecumene had proved an attraction for opportunity which resulted in the establishment of the Jewish Diaspora, so too a second Diaspora was established as Jews settled throughout not only the eastern, but also in the western parts of Rome's empire. Similarly, the *pax Romana* provided opportunity for Christians to travel throughout a vast empire to proselyte.[19]

Mounting Tensions with Rome

With the inception of the reign of Gaius (Caligula) in A.D. 37, an increased level of tension developed in Judea stemming from two sources. First, as a result of Gaius's policy to increase the scope and function of the client kings administering Rome's holdings in various parts of the eastern segment of the empire, various branches of the Herodian house began to compete with each other for increased authority and power. This climate of heightened political conflict no doubt served in turn to encourage political discontent among various groups within Judea. Second, gentile inhabitants of Judea along with some Jews, as a result of increased emphasis throughout the empire on the maintenance of the cult of the emperor, attempted to erect altars to Gaius. The reaction of other Jews was one of extreme opposition. Gaius, by then beginning to show symptoms of the mental disorder which brutalized Rome and eventually caused most leading Romans to encourage his murder at the hands the Praetorian Guard, acted in a way counter to the usual Roman tolerance for local religious customs by ordering a statue of himself to be erected in the Holy of Holies of Herod's temple. The imperial legate of Syria, Petronius, was ordered to advance into Judea with the legions under his command to assure that Gaius's order was effected. Petronius, aware of the protests and deteriorating civil order in Judea which the order provoked, appealed to the emperor to revoke these instructions, for which wise request Petronius was instructed to commit suicide. Before this could occur, all was ended by Gaius's death in 41.[20]

Much of the harm Gaius had caused in all areas of the governance of the empire was set aright by the responsible and concerned reign of Claudius. Discontent in Judea was decreased when Claudius restored his boyhood companion and still close friend, Herod Agrippa, as king of the realm his grandfather Herod had once ruled. Regrettably for Roman aims in Judea, Herod Agrippa died after ruling only three years. Upon Herod's death, Claudius intended to bestow the kingdom of Judea and Samaria on the king's son, also called Herod Agrippa, who was being raised in Claudius's household. Since the younger Herod was only sixteen, however, Claudius's advisors dissuaded the emperor from his intention on grounds that so young a man could never effectively handle the dynastic rivalries raised by his ambitious relatives, nor the political discontents and ambitions of various Jewish factions, nor the everyday administration of an area which was becoming more difficult to rule. Consequently, Judea reverted to its former status as a Roman province. A Roman governor, now for the first time with the title of procurator, assumed the administration of Judea. The stage was set for the two rebellions which would occur as several Jewish factions, each for different reasons, sought to overthrow Roman rule.

The Jewish War against Rome

The circumstances which led to the Jewish War are thoroughly explicated in Josephus's history of the same name. It is important to remember that not all Jews, nor even a majority of the Jews in Judea, participated in the rebellion. Indeed, many Jews and certainly the Christians who fled Judea in large numbers to avoid the atrocities of the zealots directed toward them were as much the target of the insurrectionists as were the Roman and Greek inhabitants of Judea. One of the most important consequences of the Jewish rebellion is that Judea ceased to be the center of the Christian movement. Christians forced from Judea by zealous Jews spread throughout the empire where their proselyting engendered the growth of Christianity.

The war was successfully prosecuted by Rome in two stages: first, the siege and conquest of Jerusalem by the future emperor, Flavius Vespasianus, and following the civil war which brought about Vespasian's accession, by Vespasian's son and heir, Titus; and second, after the rest of the country was pacified, the siege of Masada by Flavius Silva. The detailed events of the rebellion are beyond the scope of this study. Suffice it to say that Rome dealt with Judea as it would any subject province where a small segment of the population had fomented a rebellion, violently seizing power. Moreover, the indiscriminate deaths of many Jews at the hands of the zealots, Sicarii, and other insurrectionists made the rebellion in the eyes of Rome less a political rebellion than a riot where all law and order of any kind disappeared. From the Roman perspective, her opponents in Judea were neither patriots nor simply armed political opponents, but merely criminals engaged as much in pillage and rapine against their own people as attacks upon Romans and Greeks in the area. Rome pursued only those members of Jewish factions in rebellion. Other Jews in Judea were unaffected, as were the many Jews living throughout the empire. As Rome prosecuted the Jewish war, it not only had to root out the hidden strongholds of the rebellious factions, but also secure the protection of the general Jewish population from raids of the zealots. The war in both its stages lasted from 66 to 74. The time no doubt would have been considerably shortened if the Roman legions in Judea under Vespasian had not become involved in the Roman civil war from A.D. 68 to 70, which was resolved with the elevation of Vespasian as emperor.

The result of the war is more important for a consideration of the province of Judea than the events of the conflict. Millar's summary remarks about the effects of the war on Judea are instructive:

> It would be impossible to exaggerate the significance, from many different points of view, of the great revolt which broke out in Judea in A.D. 66 and did not end until the suicide of the defenders of Masada in 74. Within the Jewish community it was marked by internal conflicts of unparalleled ferocity, and led to the destruction of the Temple, the disappearance of sacrifice as a central element of Jewish religious practice and the ending of the long line of High Priests.[21]

Not only did the nature of the Jewish entity within Judea change as a result of the war, but Judea as a place of strictly Jewish identity also disappeared. Strong Roman garrisons thereafter permanently occupied the province; new settlers were introduced to the area from throughout surrounding regions of the eastern part of the empire. The province of Judea, in both a cultural and juridical sense, came to an end. Once more, Millar's remarks are instructive in aptly summarizing the final result of the Jewish rebellion:

> After the second of those rebellions, the province would be given a new name, "Syria Palaestina," from which all reference to the Jewish character of its population was lacking; it would have a garrison of two Roman legions and be the location of two Roman *coloniae*, Caesarea and Aelia Capitolina (Jerusalem). The long hesitation of Roman rule was over.[22]

Conclusion

The brief history of the Roman province of Judea reveals a fundamental lack of understanding on the part of the Romans about the passions of the Jewish people. The Jews were in part motivated by religion, but certainly were also motivated by personal ambitions for power, material gain, or individual prestige, at least in the case of the Jewish factions whose struggles against one another not only harmed their own people, but also were instrumental in destroying Judea. Rome dealt with Jewish factionalism for over a century by resorting back and forth to rule by local dynasts or to direct Roman administration, often in response to demands from leading Jews for a Roman presence. Rome, or individual Romans, may have regretted that they had any connection with Judea, a small and poor province, hardly worth its cost in time and material expended on it by Rome. However, once Rome held Judea, a consequence of filling the vacuum left in the region when the Hellenistic monarchies decayed, it had to maintain Judea. What worked so successfully for Rome in the administration of myriad peoples throughout its huge empire did not work in Judea. Accordingly, Rome was compelled to resort to arms to insure the peace when all else failed. Rebellions in the provinces were extremely rare; there simply was not the need to use Roman legions against provincials instead of using them in their assigned role of protecting the frontiers from the barbarians without. However, the Jewish rebellion clearly demonstrates the effectiveness of the legions if they had to be called upon to perform a peacekeeping role. Unfortunately, the efficiency of Roman arms was disastrous for all the many factions of Jews in Judea and even more regrettably for the innocent inhabitants of the province, who were as often the victims of injustice at the hands of their countrymen as at the hands of the Romans.

John F. Hall is Professor of Classics and Ancient History at Brigham Young University.

NOTES

[1]For Pompey's succession in command to Lucullus and his prosecution of the final stages of the Mithridatic war, see Erich S. Gruen, *The Last Generation of the Roman Republic* (Berkeley and Los Angeles: University of California Press, 1974), 63-66, 83-86; see also John Leach, *Pompey the Great* (London: Croom Helm, 1978), 74-92.

[2]Pompey's settlement of the eastern empire is discussed in detail by Leach, *Pompey the Great,* 93-101; specific reasons for and actions precipitating the annexation of Judea to Pompey's newly formed standing Roman province in Syria are given in F. E. Peters, *The Harvest of Hellenism: A History of the Near East from Alexander the Great to the Triumph of Christianity* (New York: Simon and Schuster, 1970), 320-24, 336-38.

[3]Judas Maccabeus in 160 B.C. entered into a protective treaty with Rome when it was particularly interested in limiting the power of Seleucid Syria in the region. Twenty years later the treaty was renewed. On several occasions Rome warned the Seleucid kings from making incursions into Judean territory. The independence of Maccabean Judea was largely a result of Rome's protection. See Michael Grant, *The History of Ancient Israel* (New York: Charles Scribner's Sons, 1984), 212-13; and Peters, *Harvest of Hellenism,* 268-70.

[4]Pompey's intervention overturned the previous act of Pompey's chief legate, the newly appointed governor of Syria, Marcus Aemilius Scaurus, who had accepted a huge bribe from Aristobulus to confirm his rule. It may be presumed that Hyrcanus was able to reward Pompey in similar monetary fashion for his support. See Peters, *Harvest of Hellenism,* 321-24.

[5]For discussion of the advance of the Idumean royal family, see Grant, *History of Ancient Israel,* 225-26. Sixty years previous John Hyrcanus, son of Simon Maccabee, had asserted Jewish authority over Idumea requiring the conversion of the area and the forced circumcision of its male inhabitants. Therefore, while they were technically Jewish, the Idumeans were held by devout Jews to be false believers at best. Much of the opposition to Herod's monarchy derives form the

anti-Idumean attitude of not only Jewish nobles but the populace in general. See Peters, *Harvest of Hellenism,* 286–88.

[6]Parthians derived in part from the Scythian Parni who migrated in the third century B.C. from southeastern European steppes to the western territories of the Persian empire settling in Parthava, joining with the local remnants of Persians and laying the political and linguistic foundations of Iran. See Peters, *Harvest of Hellenism,* 343–45.

[7]The events are discussed in detail in Peters, *Harvest of Hellenism,* 336–38. Also see Eva Matthews Sanford, "The Career of Aulus Gabinius," *Transactions of the American Philological Association* 70 (1939): 64-92.

[8]Peters, *Harvest of Hellenism,* 341–49; see also T. J. Cadoux, "Marcus Crassus: A Reevaluation," *Greece and Rome,* 2d ser., 3 (1956): 153–61.

[9]Peters, *Harvest of Hellenism,* 380–82; Grant, *History of Ancient Israel,* 225-27; also see Matthias Gelzer, *Caesar: Politician and Statesman,* trans. Peter Needham (Oxford: Basil Blackwell, 1968), 239–52. Of course, Caesar's own *Bellum Alexandrinum* provides an account of the Alexandrian campaign.

[10]Antony's role in these events is analyzed in detail by Eleanor Goltz Huzar, *Mark Antony* (London: Croom Helm, 1978), 161–62.

[11]Peters, *Harvest of Hellenism,* 384–87; Grant, *History of Ancient Israel,* 228; Huzar, *Mark Antony,* 162–66.

[12]For a thorough discussion of the institution as well as the entire Roman system of *clientelae,* see Ernst Badian, *Foreign Clientelae (264-70 B.C.)* (Oxford: Oxford University Press, 1958).

[13]Ronald Syme, *The Roman Revolution* (Oxford: Oxford University Press, 1939), 474.

[14]Grant, *History of Ancient Israel,* 229–32; Peters, *Harvest of Hellenism,* 387–94; A. H. M. Jones, *Augustus* (New York, Norton, 1970), 50, 57, 63–64; Fergus Millar, *The Roman Near East, 31 B.C.-A.D. 337* (Cambridge: Harvard University Press, 1993), 27–31, 38–39.

[15]Jones, *Augustus,* 70–72; Peters, *Harvest of Hellenism,* 393–94; Millar, *Roman Near East,* 39–49; Steve Mason, *Josephus and the New Testament* (Peabody, Mass.: Hendrickson, 1992), 100-103. For the office of *legatus Augusti pro praetore* and the administration of Syria under the Augustan principate, see Millar, *Roman Near East,* 31-36.

[16]Millar, *Roman Near East,* 45; John F. Hall, "Procurator," in *The Anchor Bible Dictionary,* ed. David Noel Freedman, 6 vols. (New York, Doubleday, 1992), 5:473–74; John F. Hall, "Antonia, Tower of," *Anchor Bible Dictionary,* 1:274.

[17]Mason, *Josephus,* 100-117, offers a good summary of the role and activities of the Roman governors of Judea, particularly as they are portrayed in the pages of Josephus's historical record. A more comprehensive discussion of the office and activities of the prefects of Judea is found in Millar, *Roman Near East,* 44-63.

[18]Zeev Safrai, *The Economy of Roman Palestine* (London: Routledge, 1994), offers an excellent presentation of the economic aspects of Roman Judea.

[19]Millar, *Roman Near East,* 44–63; Peters, *Harvest of Hellenism,* 508–14.

[20]Millar, *Roman Near East,* 56–59.

[21]Millar, *Roman Near East,* 70.

[22]Millar, *Roman Near East,* 61.

The Roman Army in the First Century

William J. Hamblin

At the time of Jesus, the Roman army was at the height of its power and prestige. In the preceding four centuries, Roman legions had raised Rome from a small regional city-state to master of the entire Mediterranean world. Barring a few notable defeats—such as during the war against Hannibal or the battle of the Teutoberg Forest—Roman arms had proved victorious against Gauls, Germans, Iberians, Britons, Mauritanians, Numidians, Cartheginians, Libyans, Egyptians, Illyrians, Macedonians, Greeks, Thracians, Capadocians, Armenians, Persians, Syrians, Arabs, and Judeans, creating one of the greatest military empires of world history.[1] The overwhelming military power of Rome was the most important political reality in Judea at the time of Christ.

Organization and Numbers

The fundamental organizational unit of the Roman army during the early empire (31 B.C. to A.D. 193) was the legion (*legio*).[2] In theory the legion consisted of ten cohorts (*cohors*) of 600 men, each composed of six centuries (*centuria*, "hundred") of 100 men, giving a theoretical total of 6,000 infantry in a legion.[3] To this was added a small cavalry detachment (*ala*)[4] of 120 men for scouting and communications. In practice, cohorts were independent administrative units that could be detached from legions. Furthermore, units would have had losses from illness or casualties. Many legions would therefore have been under strength, giving the ten cohorts an average of approximately 480 men each,[5] with 80 men per century.[6] However, the first cohort was sometimes a double-strength unit of perhaps 960 men, giving a practical total of about

5,280 infantry in a legion. Each legion was usually designated by both a number and name, such as the "Second Augustan" or the "Tenth Fretensis" (which participated in the siege of Masada and later garrisoned Jerusalem).

Legions were commanded by a legate (*legatus*), usually a member of the Roman senate or aristocracy, who was under the command of the governor of the province in which the legion was stationed. Six tribunes—roughly equivalent of modern colonels—were assigned to each legion as staff officers. They may or may not have been attached to specific cohorts, but could be given *ad hoc* assignments by the legate. In actual combat, the most important officer was the centurion, who commanded the century. Other important officers included the senior centurion, known as *Primus Pilus* (First Spear); the *Praefectus castrorum* (Camp Prefect or commander), who was in charge of logistics and organizing formal camps; and the *Aquilifer* (Eagle Bearer), who bore the sacred legionary eagle standard.

During the first centuries of the empire, the number of legions varied between twenty-five and thirty. According to Tacitus, in A.D. 23 there were twenty-five legions in the provincial Roman army, giving a total of about 125,000 regular legionaries.[7] In addition there were 10,000 men forming the garrison, police force, and imperial bodyguard at Rome, and another 40,000 in the navy.[8]

Except for the cavalry used for reconnaissance duty, Roman legionaries were exclusively heavy infantry, armed with javelins and swords (see below). At the time of Jesus, the approximately 125,000 regular infantry legionaries were assisted by an equal or greater number of auxiliary troops (*auxilia*), recruited from allied and conquered peoples, bringing the total standing army to at least 250,000 men.[9] Auxiliaries began as non-Roman allied troops who served with Roman legions during the wars of conquest under the Republic. The auxiliaries included a wide range of specialized troop types. The most important was cavalry, in which traditional Roman legions were notably deficient. A strong auxiliary force of cavalry was especially important when facing the armies of North Africa or Parthia. Other auxiliaries included light infantry, archers, and slingers. Most infantry auxiliaries were organized into cohorts—roughly the equivalent of legionary cohorts—but various other types of units based on local military traditions from which the auxiliaries were recruited were also known. They sometimes had specific ethnic identities, such as German infantry, slingers from the Baleric islands, Cretan archers, or light cavalry from Mauritania or Numidia in North Africa. Although originally *ad hoc* units raised for specific purposes or campaigns, these auxiliaries became increasingly regularized and permanent as time progressed. At the time of Christ, there were several auxiliary cohorts stationed in Judea (see below).[10]

Arms and Armor

The arms and armor of the imperial Roman army have been reconstructed in some detail, using archaeological, artistic, and philological and historical evidence.[11] The first-century imperial legionary was a heavy infantryman with fairly standardized equipment. An iron helmet with large neck and cheek guards protected the head. Legionary body armor was in a state of transition in the first century. Late Republican armor consisted of a coat of mail (*lorica hamata*), perhaps ultimately derived from Celtic models.[12] Beginning around A.D. 20, however, the mail coat was increasingly replaced by the so-called *lorica segmentata*—segmented plate armor covering the shoulders and torso, with, occasionally, a knee-length apron or kilt of eight leather straps strengthened by metal studs, protecting the waist and upper thighs. Scale armor—small, roughly two-inch rectangular plates sewn in overlapping fashion on leather coats—also continued in use among both cavalry and infantry.[13]

The protection provided by the armor was supplemented by a large, curved, rectangular, leather-covered wooden shield (*scutum*), reinforced by iron bosses.[14] The two major legionary weapons were the javelin (*pilum*) and double-edged short sword designed for stabbing (*gladius*—see p.341). The javelin was generally thrown at the enemy just before contact, after which the sword was drawn for close combat. The military tunic was generally white or reddish brown.

As noted above, the standard Roman legions often had insufficient missile and cavalry troops. These deficiencies were

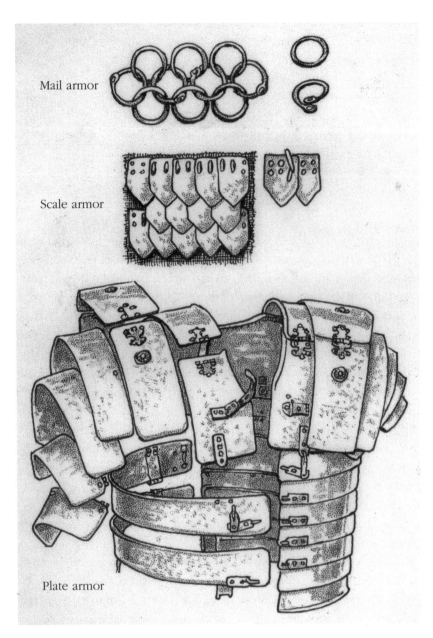

Mail armor

Scale armor

Plate armor

Roman legionary armor. Starting A.D. 20, the Roman army replaced mail armor with plate armor. Scale armor was also in use about the time of Masada.

Facing page:

Armed Roman legionary. Wearing plate armor, the legionary is also protected by his shield (*scutum*). In his hand is his javelin (*pilum*), and at his waist is his *gladius,* a double-edged short sword.

remedied by the use of non-Roman auxiliary troops, who were equipped with a wide array of arms and armor, ranging from unarmored light infantry and missile troops to heavily armored cavalry. Heavy cavalry could be equipped with heavy scale or mail armor, a long (about 30 inches) cutting sword, and a lance.

As cavalry became increasingly important to the Romans, formal cavalry regiments (*ala quingenaria*) of about five hundred men were organized, equipped with mail or scale armor, shields, lances, and long cutting swords. To some extent, the equipment of early imperial auxiliary infantry cohorts was standardized, with a mail jacket, a large, oval shield, several six- to seven-foot-long broad-headed spears that could be used for throwing or thrusting, and a short sword.[15] As a general rule, the equipment of the auxiliaries during the early empire was inferior to that of the legionaries. During the later empire (third and fourth centuries), distinctions between legionary and auxiliary infantry in both equipment and functions tended to blur.

Thus, although Roman legions were quite regular in uniforms and equipment, the presence of auxiliaries would make the composition and appearance of each specific Roman army unique. Auxiliaries could be recruited and armed according to the military practices of their ethnic group and region. Mounted archers were used along the Parthian frontier, camel-mounted troops were found on desert borders, and Gallic troops assisted in the Roman conquest of their British cousins. Furthermore, auxiliaries and mercenaries from any ethnic group or military type could be found serving in different parts of the empire at one time or another. For example, Herod the Great had a bodyguard of four hundred Gauls, while North African light cavalry campaigned with Trajan in Dacia (Romania).

Legions also often included various forms of mechanical artillery, ranging from small bolt- or stone-throwing ballistae and catapults to larger siege engines. Some of the smaller machines could be mounted on carts and moved about on the battlefield. Larger machines were used only for sieges.[16] Roman legions excelled in military engineering and almost always included skilled military engineers to build roads and bridges, to construct camps and field fortifications, and to create siegecraft.

Swords. The sword is the most frequently mentioned weapon in the New Testament. The English word *sword* translates two Greek terms: *machaira,* meaning "large knife, short sword, or dagger,"[17] and *romphaia,* meaning "large, broad sword."[18] In the Vulgate—often followed by the King James translators—both romphaia and machaira are almost always translated as *gladius,* "sword."[19]

The meaning of *machaira* can range from a knife or dagger to a short sword.[20] It often translates the Latin *gladius,* meaning sword in a broad sense, but often refers more technically to the short sword of Roman legionaries. The sword of the legionaries of the late Republic was the *gladius Hispaniensis* (Spanish sword), adopted from the Iberian steel-cutting sword in the third century B.C. and measuring about thirty inches long and two inches wide.[21] By the early Principate, however, this weapon was replaced by a shorter gladius, a steel, double-edged weapon ranging from sixteen to twenty-two inches long, and from two to three inches wide, designed for either cutting or thrusting.[22] This was the standard Roman legionary sword at the time of Christ. Cavalry swords averaged around thirty inches.

However, swords manufactured from many different sources—Judean, Nabatean, Syrian, Greek, or Parthian—were undoubtedly available in Palestine in the first century and manifested a variety of shapes and functions. Furthermore, swords used by Roman auxiliaries could be less standardized. Nonetheless, it is likely that the machaira mentioned in the New Testament generally refers to weapons broadly similar to the Roman short sword, double-edged and pointed, ranging from about one and one-half to two feet long and two to three inches wide.

The romphaia refers to a longer cutting weapon than the standard legionary gladius, with somewhat exotic or barbarian overtones; it is said to have originated in Thrace. In the New Testament, the romphaia is generally used to designate the swords carried by angels or other celestial beings.[23] The sword of Christ's mouth is a romphaia (Rev. 1:16; 2:12, 16; 19:15, 21). The sword carried by the apocalyptic horseman of war is a machaira in Revelation 6:4, but a romphaia in Revelation 6:8. Since the horsemen of the apocalypse are probably supernatural beings or metaphors, the romphaia, as an angelic weapon, is perhaps appropriate. The saints, on the other hand, are slain by a machaira of the beast (Rev. 13:10, 14). Thus it seems that for New Testament writers, the word romphaia is reserved almost exclusively as the celestial weapon of angels and God, while the machaira is an earthly weapon of mortals.

Spears. The word *logchē,* meaning "lance, spear, or javelin," occurs only once in the New Testament, referring to the spear which pierced the side of Christ.[24] The standard spear of the Roman legionary was the pilum, "a short-range, armour-piercing, shock weapon, thrown shortly before physical contact was made between the Roman line and its foe."[25] The pilum was characterized by a wooden staff around four feet long, onto which was bolted a thin iron head, one and one-half to two feet long, with a small, arrowlike pointed tip. The thin iron shaft was meant to penetrate an enemy's shield and then bend on impact, making the shield more cumbersome to use and preventing the enemy from throwing the pilum back at the Romans. If the soldier who thrust the spear into Christ's side was a Roman standard legionary, the weapon used was probably the pilum.

On the other hand, it is quite possible, if not likely, that the soldiers who executed Christ were not legionaries, but auxiliary infantry. The Roman garrison of Judea at the time of Christ consisted of five cohorts of infantry and one ala of cavalry. Some of these units were auxiliary, comprised of Samaritan and Greek troops (see below). The Roman administrative capital was Caesarea, not Jerusalem, and the cohort which garrisoned Jerusalem could have been a regular legionary unit or an auxiliary unit. The

Facing page:

Silva's camp. To besiege Masada, the Romans established several camps outside the wall they built around the base of Masada. This photo shows the remains of camp F, which housed Silva, the Roman commander. The camp was more than thirty meters away from the siege wall and had its own stone walls with a gate in the middle of each. The small camp at the top left was built after Silva left.

Roman siege ramp *(agger).* Because of the cliffs protecting Masada on all sides, the Romans had to build a ramp to attack the fortress walls. The ramp was about 175 meters long with a slope of about 1:3. The ramp was constructed from dirt and wooden beams, which shored it up.

presence of Pilate at Jerusalem, however, may indicate that he had brought regular legionary troops with him as a guard.

Recruitment

In theory, all citizens in the Roman Republic owed military service as part of their duties of citizenship. Although the original Roman army was composed of citizen-soldiers serving as needed for a particular campaign before returning to other careers in private life, by the time of Jesus, service in the Roman army had become professional, with soldiers serving from sixteen to twenty-five years before being discharged with a pension and other grants.

Service in the legions was limited, theoretically, to Roman citizens, with non-citizens serving only in the auxiliaries. In practice, however, citizenship could be granted to non-Roman volunteers who entered legionary service. Thus, as time progressed, Roman legions garrisoning the provinces became increasingly composed, not of Roman citizens from Italy, but of provincials who had been granted citizenship. At the time of Jesus, the legions in Judea would probably have been still partly composed of Italian Romans, but the number of provincials serving in the legions would perhaps have been on the rise. Auxiliaries were enrolled under various terms of service and for different periods of time, sometimes for a single campaign, but increasingly on a more permanent basis.[26]

The Roman Army in Judea at the Time of Christ

Throughout the first century, Judea was ruled either by client kings or princes or as a Roman province under either Roman prefects or procurators appointed by the emperor. In either case, as a frontier province at risk from Arab desert raiders, Parthian invasion, and internal revolt, Judea generally had a Roman military presence. In the greater Roman province of Syria, which included Judea, there were three legions during the reign of Augustus[27] and four under Tiberius,[28] though more could have been transferred there in times of war.

> There is general agreement that from the reign of Herod the Great to the destruction of the Jerusalem temple in A.D. 70 the garrison of Judea comprised one cavalry regiment of Sebasteni (*ala I Sebastenorum*)

[referring to its original recruitment under Herod at Sebastia, the Hellenistic name for Samaria] and five cohorts of infantry, among them at least one cohort of Sebasteni (*cohors I Sebastenorum*).[29]

Roman military power in Judea was not based solely on Roman legionaries. Gentile, Samaritan, and Jewish mercenaries were recruited from Caesarea, Sebastia, and other Hellenistic and Jewish towns. These troops might be recruited as full-time auxiliaries, hired for a single campaign, or made to serve in the provincial armies of Jewish client rulers such as Herod and Agrippa I.[30]

William J. Hamblin is Associate Professor of History at Brigham Young University.

NOTES

[1]On the rise of Rome from city-state to empire, see Frank W. Walbank, ed. *Cambridge Ancient History,* vol. 7/2, *The Rise of Rome to 220 B.C.,* 2d ed. (Cambridge: Cambridge University Press, 1989); A. E. Aston, ed., *Cambridge Ancient History,* vol. 8, *Rome and the Mediterranean to 133 B.C.,* 2d ed. (Cambridge: Cambridge University Press, 1989); and J. A. Crook, ed. *Cambridge Ancient History,* vol. 9, *The Last Age of the Roman Republic, 146–43 B.C.,* 2d ed. (Cambridge: Cambridge University Press, 1994).

[2]P. G. W. Glare, *Oxford Latin Dictionary* (Oxford: Clarendon, 1982), 1013c (hereafter cited as *OLD*). The term *legion* is related to *lego,* "to gather, select, pick or choose." *OLD,* 1014b. The men of the legion are those gathered or chosen for warfare. For detailed studies with full bibliographies and sources on the organization of the early imperial Roman army, see Yann le Bohec, *The Imperial Roman Army* (New York: Hippocrene, 1994); Lawrence Keppie, *The Making of the Roman Army* (London: Batsford, 1984); and Graham Webster, *The Roman Imperial Army* (London: A. and C. Black, 1979). A brief survey is provided by Brian Dobson, "The Empire," in *Warfare in the Ancient World,* ed. John Hackett (New York: Facts on File, 1989), 192–221. More popular sources with excellent artistic reconstructions of Roman military equipment are Peter Connolly, *Greece and Rome at War* (London: Macdonald, 1981); and John Warry, *Warfare in the Classical World* (New York: St. Martin's, 1980).

[3]*Oxford Classical Dictionary,* 2d ed., s.v. "legion."

[4]*Ala* literally means "wing" (*OLD,* 92a), reflecting the usual position of the cavalry on the flanks or wings of an army.

[5]*OLD,* 348b; the Greek term for a Roman cohort, used in the New Testament, is *speirai,* originally a Ptolemaic tactical unit. Henry George Liddell and Robert Scott, *A Greek-English Lexicon* (Oxford: Clarendon, 1968), 1625b (hereafter cited as *GEL*).

[6]*OLD*, 299c. Although originally of one hundred men as its name implies, the century at the time of early empire had been reduced to eighty men.

[7]Tacitus, *Annals* 4.5.

[8]For details on legionary organization see Bohec, *Imperial Roman Army*, 19–35; and Webster, *Roman Imperial Army*, 107–42; these figures are all estimates.

[9]According to one estimate, in the mid-second century the Roman army included about 157,000 legionaries and 227,000 auxiliaries, for a total of 384,000 men, of whom about 70,000 were cavalry (cited by Dobson, "The Empire," 198).

[10]For details, sources, and bibliography on the *auxilia*, see Bohec, *Imperial Roman Army*, 25-29, 30-32; Webster, *Roman Imperial Army*, 142-55; and Dobson, "The Empire," 196-201.

[11]The archaeological evidence has been collected and summarized by M. C. Bishop and J. C. N. Coulston, *Roman Military Equipment: From the Punic Wars to the Fall of Rome* (London: B. T. Batsford, 1993). The two most important representational sources for the early imperial Roman army are Trajan's Column (Ian A. Richmond, *Trajan's Army on Trajan's Column* [London: British School at Rome, 1982]) and Trajan's *Tropaeum Traiani* or "Adamklissi," a military monument in modern Romania (Florea B. Florescu, *Das Siegesdenkmal von Adamklissi*, 3d ed. [Bucharest: Verlag der Akademie der Romanischen Volksrepublik, 1965]). For a full survey of the representational sources on Roman military equipment, see Bishop and Coulston, *Military Equipment*, 19-32. Modern artistic reconstructions of Roman military equipment can be found in Connolly, *Greece and Rome at War*, and Warry, *Warfare in the Classical World*.

[12]On Roman mail, see Bishop and Coulston, *Military Equipment*, 59-60.

[13]On first century legionary armor, see Bishop and Coulston, *Military Equipment*, 81-101.

[14]Bishop and Coulston, *Military Equipment*, 81-96.

[15]Bishop and Coulston, *Military Equipment*, 206-9.

[16]Eric William Marsden, *Greek and Roman Artillery*, 2 vols. (Oxford: Oxford University Press, 1969-71).

[17]*GEL*, 1085a. *Machaira* occurs twenty-seven times in the New Testament: Matthew 10:34; 26:47-55; Mark 14:43-48; Luke 21:24; 22:36-52; John 18:10-11; Romans 8:35; 13:4; Ephesians 6:17; Hebrews 4:12; 11:34, 37; and Revelation 6:4; 13:10; 13:14. *Machaira* is probably cognate with the Greek *machomai*, "to fight," and related terms. *GEL*, 1085b. There is no unique word used in the New Testament for knife or dagger. See also Gerhard Kittel, ed., *Theological Dictionary of the New Testament*, trans. and ed. Geoffrey W. Bromiley, 10 vols. (Grand Rapids, Mich.: Eerdmans, 1964-76), 4:524-27 (hereafter cited as *TDNT*).

[18] *GEL*, 1574b. *Rompbaia* appears seven times in the New Testament: Luke 2:35; and Revelation 1:16; 2:12,16; 6:8; 19:15, 21; see also *TDNT*, 6:993-98.

[19]The exception is Luke 2:35, which transliterates the Greek *rompbaia* as *rompheam*. In all other cases, *rompbaia* is translated as *gladius*. On *gladius*, see *OLD*, 765c.

[20]*TDNT*, 4:525. *Machaira* is used in the Septuagint to refer to knives on several occasions (Josh. 5:2; Gen. 22:6) and refers to a sacrificial knife in Homer.

[21]Bishop and Coulston, *Military Equipment*, 53-54.

[22]Bishop and Coulston, *Military Equipment*, 69-74.

[23]*TDNT,* 6:995-98. In the Septuagint, the sword of the *cherubim* (Gen. 3:24)—*hereb* in Hebrew—is translated by the Greek *romphaia,* which may be the origin of the tradition of the *romphaia* as an angelic weapon. On the other hand, *romphaia* is a standard Septuagint translation of *hereb.*

[24]John 19:34. On the meaning of *logchē,* see *GEL,* 1059b. The term is translated in the Vulgate as *militum lancea.* Spearmen (*dexiolabos*) are mentioned in Acts 23:23, translated in the Vulgate as *lancearios.* Hebrew terms translated as "spear" or "javelin" in the KJV Old Testament include *chanith* and *romach.*

[25]Bishop and Coulston, *Military Equipment,* 208. The pilum is also described as a "throwing-spear or javelin." *OLD,* 1380a. For a survey of the archaeological evidence, see Bishop and Coulston, *Military Equipment,* 48-53, 65-69.

[26]On recruitment in the Roman armies, see Bohec, *Imperial Roman Army,* 68-102.

[27]Josephus, *Antiquities* 17.286.

[28]Tacitus, *Annales* 4.5.

[29]Michael Speidel, "The Roman Army in Judea under the Procurators," in *Roman Army Studies,* ed. M. P. Speidel, 2 vols. (Stuttgart: Franz Steiner, 1992), 2:224. A dated but still useful survey is Thomas Robert Shannon Broughton, "Note XXXIII. The Roman Army," in *The Beginnings of Christianity, Part I: The Acts of the Apostles,* ed. Fredrick John Foakes Jackson and Kirsopp Lake, 5 vols. (London: Macmillan, 1933), 5:427-45. Also see E. Mary Smallwood, *The Jews under Roman Rule* (Leiden: Brill, 1976), 146-47.

[30]Fergus Millar, *The Roman Near East: 31 B.C.-A.D. 337* (Cambridge: Harvard University Press, 1993), 356.

Artist's reproduction of siege tower. Faced with the seemingly impregnable cliffs and walls of Masada, the Romans built a ramp on the western side of Masada. They also built a moveable tower tall enough to stand above Masada's walls and rolled it to the top of the ramp. Covered with iron plates for fireproofing, the tower contained a battering ram and sheltered the Roman artillery. Many of the specialized materials were transported to Masada from the legion's home base.

Casting Stones:
Ballista, Stones as Weapons,
and Death by Stoning

James V. Garrison

Stones at Masada

Josephus reports that once the Romans had completed their great siege ramp on the west side of Masada, they brought up an enormous tower on wheels, over one hundred feet high (based on a twenty-inch cubit) and entirely encased in iron. From this tower, Roman artillery opened fire on those defending the walls, sending showers of stones and other missiles down on them and forcing them to retreat into the fortress. With this objective accomplished, a great battering ram began the assault on the walls, and the fall of Masada became imminent.

Nineteen hundred years later, the excavation team led by Yigael Yadin found strewn all about Masada the remains of this episode: hundreds of rounded stones of the sort fired from Roman artillery. The excavation reports indicate that these stones were found in most areas of the fortress. Many were piled in the rooms along the casemate wall[1] and were "of the size of oranges and grapefruits."[2]

These stones are typical of projectiles thrown by various Roman *ballistae,* catapults, and "artillery machines."[3] Indeed, Josephus speaks of "numerous quick-firers and ballistae."[4] "Quick-firers" refers to the *scorpio,* or the *manuballista,* a small, quick-firing catapult that shot thin arrows and could be loaded and fired by just one man. The stones found at Masada belonged to the ballista, a very versatile and powerful artillery piece that resembled a large crossbow rather than the conventional one-armed catapult. The versatility came from its ability to fire a wide range of stones and to be aimed with great precision even at high angles, such as those required to bombard fortress walls. This capability, coupled with the powerful force with which it fired stones, made the ballista a dreaded machine.[5]

The Romans were quite selective as to the stones they chose for the ballista. Vegetius claimed that river stones were optimal; they were round, smooth, and dense.[6] The ballista stones found at Masada were chiseled to be as round as possible.

A number of large round stones, "very roughly dressed, of about half a metre's diameter," were also discovered at Masada. "Their size, weight and the way they [were] worked suggest that these were not thrown at Masada from ballistae but were prepared inside the fortress to be rolled down on the assailants."[7] This defense against attacking siege engines could inflict serious damage. Other Jewish tactics were to throw stones by hand (Ex. 21:18; Num. 35:17, 22–23; 2 Sam. 16:6, 13) and by sling.[8] They were also familiar with the catapult. Around 800 B.C., King Uzziah "made in Jerusalem engines, invented by cunning men, to be on the towers and upon the bulwarks, to shoot arrows and great stones withal" (2 Chr. 26:15).

Stoning in the Old Testament

Another significant use of stones in ancient Judaism was largely unfamiliar to the Romans—execution by stoning. Modern opinions of stoning are often tainted with images of mob frenzy and lynchings. In reality, stoning under the law of Moses was an orderly and rational procedure, carried out with the purpose of leaving a strong impression on the minds of the participants and conducted as a court-ordered form of capital punishment. Under the law of Moses, death by stoning was specifically prescribed for nine capital offenses: idolatry (Lev. 20:2–5), sorcery (Lev. 20:27), blasphemy (Lev. 24:14–16), profanation of the Sabbath (Num. 15:31–36), incitation of others to apostasy (Deut. 13:6–10), worship of false gods (Deut. 17:2–7), rebellion against parents (Deut. 21:18–21), unchastity by an unwed girl (Deut. 22:20–21), and sexual relations with a betrothed woman (Deut. 22:23–24). In addition, in the case

Roman ballista. The ballista was used to bombard high walls. It could be constructed in a wide variety of sizes to handle different diameters of stone and was powered by twisted skeins of rope and horsehair.

of a goring ox, the ox itself is stoned (Ex. 21:28–32). Stoning was the preferred method of execution in Israel and was probably used in capital cases for which no other method of execution was specified.

A typical trial[9] was conducted at the city gate before the elders of the city, with at least two witnesses[10] to the crime. In difficult cases, the elders might refer the matter to a higher court; otherwise, they would deliver a verdict based on the testimonies. When the sentence was death, the execution would follow immediately.

The condemned party was usually led outside the city to be stoned.[11] The area away from the city provided open space and plenty of stones; stray stones would not harm property; and the

Defense stones. Stones like these were likely rolled down on the Roman assailants. At about twenty inches in diameter, they were too large to throw or to serve as ballistae ammunition.

town would not risk corpse pollution within its walls. But a bride guilty of entering marriage under false pretenses of virginity was stoned at the door of her father's house, inside the city (Deut. 22:21).

The witnesses came forward and laid their hands on the head of the condemned party (Lev. 24:14; compare Susanna 34), after which they were charged to cast the first stone (Deut. 13:9; 17:7). This directive "had the effect of placing the witnesses in a very sobering position,"[12] for "it made them specifically liable for a wrongful execution."[13] Under the law of Moses, the outcome of the trial was largely determined by the accuracy of oral testimony, so such safeguards were necessary to deter false or irresponsible witnesses.[14] After the witnesses had each cast a stone, all the people were to join in until the condemned person was dead. Following execution, the body could be hung on a tree until sundown.[15]

This form of capital punishment allowed Israel as a whole community to "put away the evil" from among them, as they had been commanded. Failure to fulfill this duty subjected the entire community to divine justice. Consequently, all the people were responsible to see that capital crimes were properly punished. Stoning had the advantage of community participation in fulfilling this obligation. Moreover, public stoning created a strong deterrent to crime as a moving reminder of the significance of covenants and the consequences of breaking those covenants (Deut. 13:11; 17:13; 19:20).

We can illustrate the mechanisms of judicial stoning through four cases from Old Testament times. In the cases of the blasphemer (Lev. 24:10-14) and the Sabbath woodgatherer (Num. 15:32-36),[16] the accused were brought before Moses to be tried, but Moses sought the will of the Lord concerning the matters. In each case, the Lord told Moses to proceed with the punishment. In regard to the blasphemer, the Lord answered: "Bring forth him that hath cursed without the camp; and let all that heard him lay their hands upon his head, and let all the congregation stone him" (Lev. 24:14). In the third case, Naboth had refused to sell his vineyard to king Ahab. Falsely accused of blasphemy, he was immediately taken, stoned, and his property confiscated: "They carried him forth out of the city, and stoned him with stones, that he died" (1 Kgs. 21:1-13). Finally, in the story of Susanna,[17] a virtuous woman was accused of adultery. Two corrupt elders falsely accused her, placed their hands on her head, and presented their testimonies. When the court condemned Susanna to die, she was immediately seized and led out toward the place of execution. Suddenly a young Daniel stopped the proceedings and insisted on cross-examining each witness alone. In so doing, he exposed them as false witnesses. Susanna was set free, and the two elders were given the punishment Susanna would have received—death by stoning.[18]

Stoning in New Testament Times

Not every stoning was legal. Nonjudicial stonings also occurred. According to Philo, lynching was a legitimate extralegal mode of punishing gross religious offenses.[19] In New Testament times, many stonings may have been lynchings, especially because the Roman government seems to have reserved to itself the power to approve all capital punishments (John 18:31). And even if the Romans were to grant the Jews permission to conduct an execution, they may not have allowed stoning to be the method. Accordingly, scholars generally agree that all New Testament stonings were extralegal, although not necessarily frenzied or disorderly. For example, the stoning of James by the Sanhedrin was an orderly affair, even if illegal.[20] Thus the issue is not whether the stonings in the New Testament were legal, but whether any formal procedure was followed in those cases.

By New Testament times, biblical law had evolved in several respects.[21] Several Jewish sects interpreted the ancient law differently. The Sadducees accepted only the written law, while the Pharisees accepted oral traditions as law. Beginning in the second century A.D., the oral law was codified as the Mishnah. Therefore, the Mishnah may indicate to some extent the state of Jewish law during New Testament times.

The Mishnah's procedures on stoning are found mainly in the tractate Sanhedrin. It states that stonings were to take place as soon as the case was decided, at an established place of stoning quite a distance outside the court area.[22] When the execution party was within ten cubits of the stoning place, the condemned person was to confess, "because any one who confesses has a share in the World to Come."[23] When the party was four cubits from the stoning place, the condemned was stripped if a man but not if a woman.[24] The party then arrived at the stoning place, which had some sort of precipice "elevated twice the height of a man." The condemned was taken to the top of this precipice. The first witness seized the condemned by the hips and pushed him or her off the precipice. "If he dies from this, it is sufficient; if not, the second witness takes the stone and throws it upon his chest. If he dies from this, it is sufficient; if not, his stoning is by all of Israel."[25] Finally, the corpse was hung until sundown.

The major motive behind these rabbinic provisions was to make stoning as merciful as possible. "Precipitation" (pushing or throwing down from a high place, or precipice) would have hastened the culprit's death. The practice may have originated with the Romans, who at times used precipitation as a form of execution.[26]

Another change from Old Testament procedures involved the witnesses. Instead of casting the first stone, the witnesses pushed the condemned from a height and dropped a stone if necessary.[27]

Deuteronomy 17:7 required that "the hands of the witnesses shall be first upon him to put him to death" (see also Lev. 24:14), an injunction which the rabbis understood to mean that the witnesses must literally place their hands upon the accused to put him or her to death. Precipitation was thought to satisfy this requirement because it forced the witness to touch the condemned as death was inflicted.

Oddly, the rabbinic form of stoning lacked one of the main elements of the Old Testament procedure: community participation. As Blinzler has said, "Only [community participation] really merits the designation 'stoning.'"[28] But the rabbis minimized the role of community participation in their rules about stoning.

Although the Mishnah is very clear on its procedures, it is uncertain whether these specific rules were followed during the New Testament period. Most of the New Testament stoning cases supply little information. For example, we know only that Paul was stoned within the city (Acts 14:5, 19; 2 Cor. 11:25). Still, the information these cases do provide is occasionally enough to give a dim idea of what procedure was followed.

Twice in the temple, Christ made statements that invoked rage from the Jews, who, perceiving the words as blasphemy, immediately took up "stones to cast at him" (John 8:58–59; 10:30–39). This casting of stones is simply a case of stoning by pelting. More interestingly, when Christ was rejected in Nazareth, the Jews became riled up and seized him "and thrust him out of the city, and led him unto the brow of the hill whereon their city was built, that they might cast him down headlong" (Luke 4:29). Some scholars see here an example of precipitation.[29] Their view may well be justified. Christ was led out of the city to what seems to be a predetermined spot, just as the Mishnah called for a predetermined "place of stoning." And from this point they intended to "cast him down," also following the Mishnaic procedure.

In the case of the woman taken in adultery,[30] her accusers were not coming from nor going to a formal trial.[31] Yet they had it clearly in mind to stone the woman (John 8:5). This all points to an intended lynching. When pressed on his view of the matter, Christ responded, "He that is without sin among you, let him first cast a

stone at her"[32] (John 8:7), clearly assuming the older stoning procedures of the law of Moses, where stones were cast first by the
witnesses and then by the people. This stance is consistent with
Christ's general unwillingness to acknowledge the oral laws of
the Pharisees. By Christ's response, one should not assume that the
Scribes and Pharisees contemplated the same type of stoning. In
fact, they may well have been leading the woman out to stone her
by precipitation, as their oral laws probably required. Obviously,
lack of detail leaves this point open.

In the case of Stephen, an actual trial culminates in his stoning (Acts 6:8–7:60). Stephen was brought before the Sanhedrin
and accused of blasphemy. At first glance, the trial has an official
appearance, but the jurisdiction of the Sanhedrin was questionable,
and they failed to render a formal verdict.[33] The fury and hurry of
this case draws doubt about the legitimacy of this trial. After Stephen
declared that he beheld "the Son of man standing on the right
hand of God," a statement that amounts to blasphemy to Jewish
ears,[34] these Jews cast him out of the city and stoned him. Based on
the account in Acts, it is unknown what method of stoning the
Jews used. Scholars generally assume the method was precipitation,[35] which is perhaps the best conclusion. Some of the evidence,
such as the stoning taking place outside the city and the witnesses
initiating the stoning (Acts 7:58), could fall either way. Yet other
evidence points to Pharisaic procedures. Paul, who was a Pharisee
(Acts 22:3), played an official role in the stoning by keeping the
witnesses' clothes and consenting in the death (Acts 7:58; 8:1). His
role seems to indicate that the Pharisees controlled this stoning.

Conclusion

If these procedures in New Testament times seem confused
and unpredictable, this is fitting—for those were chaotic times.
And who would know that better than the defenders of Masada?
We sense their despair in the speeches attributed to Eleazar and in
their impression that God had condemned the rebels to die.[36] This
being so, might not the ballistae of the Romans have had some special significance to those Jews? As we have seen, stoning was an
integral part of the law of Moses and of Jewish society. Conceivably,

many of those holed up at Masada had participated in stonings. So what would it have meant to them to have the Romans shower them with artillery stones? Perhaps the words ascribed to Eleazar are revelatory: "All this betokens wrath at the many wrongs which we madly dared to inflict upon our countrymen. The penalty for those crimes let us pay not to our bitterest foes, the Romans, but to God through the act of our own hands."[37] The occupants of Masada were known as Sicarii, or "dagger-men." They had for years terrorized Jerusalem and its outlying towns, raping and pillaging their own people. So, according to Josephus, in their own eyes, it may have been fitting that God should condemn them to death—a long-deserved punishment for their many crimes. Whether that death came by stoning, by Roman sword, or by their own hand, they might have felt it was merited.

James V. Garrison is a law student at Brigham Young University.

NOTES

[1]Yigael Yadin, "The Excavation of Masada—Preliminary Report," *Israel Exploration Journal* 15, nos. 1-2 (1965): 45, 76, 80. The main outer wall of the fortress had rooms built into it on the inside, much like American frontier forts.

[2]Yadin, "Excavation," 76.

[3]For more information, see two books by E. W. Marsden, *Greek and Roman Artillery: Historical Development* (Oxford: Clarendon, 1969) and *Greek and Roman Artillery: Technical Treatises* (Oxford: Clarendon, 1971), continue to be the definitive works in the field. Both present the original writings of the ancient authors side by side with an English translation, followed by extensive notes, analyses and technical commentary. Also recommended is Dietwulf Baatz, "Recent Finds of Ancient Artillery," *Britannia* 9 (1978): 1-17. Surprisingly, very few ancient catapults have been excavated, the first in 1912. Baatz gives an interesting summary of the excavations, along with details of the reconstructions.

[4]Josephus, *Jewish War* 7.309.

[5]The ballista could be constructed in a variety of calibers, ancient authors giving detailed formulas for computing the size of ballista required for a given diameter of stone. Vitruvius, 10.11. At the siege of Jerusalem, the Romans used a ballista that could fire a one-talent stone two furlongs or more. Josephus, *Jewish War* 5.270. For a gruesome account of the power of the ballista, see Josephus, *Jewish War* 3.243 and following.

[6]Vegetius, *Epitome of Military Science* 4.8.

[7]Yadin, "Excavation," 80, see also 86, 97.

[8]As when David downed Goliath (1 Sam. 17:40, 49-50). Reportedly, some soldiers "could sling stones at an hair breadth, and not miss" (Judg. 20:16). Other references to casting a stone by sling: 1 Chronicles 12:2; 2 Chronicles 26:14; and Proverbs 26:8. We should not mistakenly assume that the Israelites grabbed any stone in reach. Rather, the account of David and Goliath, in which David carefully selects his stones from a brook, may indicate that the Israelites, like the Romans, were selective when choosing their stones. Compare Vegetius, *Epitome of Military Science* 4.8.

[9]For more information, see Donald A. McKenzie, "Judicial Procedure at the Town Gate," *Vetus Testamentum* 14, no. 1 (1964): 100-104. McKenzie goes through a mock trial to demonstrate the typical trial under the law of Moses.

[10]See Numbers 35:30; Deuteronomy 17:6; 19:15; and 1 Kings 21:13; compare Susanna 28-29, 34 and following. See also Deuteronomy 21:19.

[11]See Leviticus 24:14, 23; Numbers 15:36; and 1 Kings 21:13; compare Susanna 44-45. The stoning could also take place right at the gates of the city. See Deuteronomy 17:5; 21:19; 22:24.

[12]James E. Priest, *Governmental and Judicial Ethics in the Bible and Rabbinic Literature* (New York: Ktav, 1980), 124.

[13]Anthony Phillips, *Ancient Israel's Criminal Law: A New Approach to the Decalogue* (New York: Schocken, 1970), 24; see also Josef Blinzler, "The Jewish Punishment of Stoning in the New Testament Period," in *The Trial of Jesus,* ed. Ernst Bammel (London: SCM, 1970), 150.

[14]Another safeguard was the rule that a false witness must receive the punishment the accused party would have received (Deut. 19:16-19). Thus a false witness in a capital case would be put to death. Just such an example, the case of Susanna, follows.

[15]See Deuteronomy 21:22-23. The reason for hanging is not certain. It was probably not for a deterrent to crime, since the whole community had already participated in the execution, an act which would be an even stronger deterrent. Phillips, *Israel's Criminal Law,* 25. Possibly the hanging of the corpse was for ignominy (Hyman E. Goldin, *Hebrew Criminal Law and Procedure* [New York: Twayne, 1952], 33-34), since there is some evidence for this in the Old Testament (Josh. 8:29; 10:26-27). There is no evidence that hanging the corpse was mandatory in any way. Goldin, *Hebrew Criminal Law,* 32-34.

[16]Leviticus 24:10-14; Numbers 15:32-36. See also Philo's accounts of these trials in *On the Life of Moses* 2.193-203, 213-19. For more information, see J. Weingreen, "The Case of the Blasphemer," *Vetus Testamentum* 22, no. 1 (1972): 118-23; and J. Weingreen, "The Case of the Woodgatherer," *Vetus Testamentum* 16, no. 3 (1966): 361-64.

[17]The story of Susanna comes from the Old Testament Apocrypha. It is normally found in the thirteenth chapter of the book of Daniel (although some versions of the Apocrypha place it ahead of the first chapter of Daniel). The story of Susanna exists in two different Greek versions: the old Septuagint version and the more dramatic Theodotion version. While the two versions are identical in their main points, only the Septuagint version indicates the witnesses were executed by stoning.

[18]Apparently, the elders were not actually "stoned" in the sense of pelting them with stones but rather were pushed down from a height onto stones (Sus. 62). This method is similar to the stoning procedures established later by the Pharisees, as we will see below.

[19]"And it is well that a charge should be given to all those who have any admiration for virtue to inflict all such punishment out of hand without any delay, not bringing them before either any judgment seat, or any council, or any bench of magistrates, but giving vent to their own disposition which hates evil and loves God." Philo, *The Special Laws* 1.55.

[20]See Josephus, *Antiquities* 20.199-203. The trial, illegal though it was, may well have followed proper procedure for the times. The illegality of the trial came because the Sanhedrin had assembled without the permission of Albinus, Roman procurator of Judea. Josephus, *Antiquities* 20.202.

[21]For more information, see Blinzler, "Jewish Punishment of Stoning," 147-61.

[22]Mishnah Sanhedrin 6.1. Apparently the distance was such that a man on horse was able to stay between the execution party and the city, keeping both in sight. This was to allow every possible opportunity for late evidence and hopefully acquittal. If late evidence arrived, the man on horseback could be signaled from the courthouse to ride out to the execution party and stop the execution.

[23]Mishnah Sanhedrin 6.2. If the condemned did not know how to confess, they would give the words to say: "Say: Let my death be an atonement for all my sins." There are a few examples of confessions in the Old Testament, but none seem to be part of a legal procedure. The best example is the stoning of Achan, who took spoils from Jericho against an explicit commandment (Josh. 7:19-26). "And Joshua said unto Achan, My son, give, I pray thee, glory to the Lord God of Israel, and make confession unto him" (Josh. 7:19).

[24]Mishnah Sanhedrin 6.3. The purpose of stripping the condemned was to make the death as quick as possible. For a woman, her embarrassment was an overriding concern.

[25]Mishnah Sanhedrin 6.4. The height of two persons was just high enough to kill the condemned if he or she should fall just right but not high enough to mutilate the body.

[26]See *The Twelve Tables* 8.14, 23.

[27]Maimonides thought precipitation still satisfied the requirement that the person be stoned with stones, because throwing the condemned down on stones was really no different than throwing stones at the condemned. Maimonides Sanhedrin 6.4.

[28]Blinzler, "Jewish Punishment of Stoning," 152.

[29]See Fred B. Craddock, *Luke* (Louisville: John Knox, 1990), 63-64; John Nolland, *Word Biblical Commentary,* 51 vols. (Dallas: Word, 1982), 35A:201; I. Howard Marshall, *The Gospel of Luke: A Commentary on the Greek Text* (Exeter: Paternoster, 1978), 190; and Ray Summers, *Commentary on Luke* (Waco: Word, 1972), 58.

[30]John 8:3-11. For more information, see J. Duncan M. Derrett, "Law in the New Testament: The Story of the Woman Taken in Adultery," *New Testament Studies* 10, no. 1 (1964): 1-26, reprinted in *Law in the New Testament* (London: Darton, Longman, and Todd, 1970), 156-88.

[31]See Derrett, *Law in the New Testament,* 166-67.

[32]As we have already seen, the witnesses, in casting the first stone, took upon themselves the responsibility for the execution. If these turned out to be false witnesses, they would likewise be stoned. Derrett points out that a false witness could be either a witness who gives "factually false evidence" or a witness who gives accurate evidence yet who is "a disqualified, incompetent witness," where freedom from sin was one of the requirements for competence. So we can see that Jesus' statement not only pierces their consciences, but also threatens them with a charge of false witness. See J. Duncan M. Derrett, "The Woman Taken in Adultery: Its Legal Aspects," *Studia Evangelica,* no. 2 (1964): 173.

[33]Moreover, there is a possibility that in a capital case the Sanhedrin had to reconvene a second time to pronounce the verdict. See Mishnah Sanhedrin 5.5. If this is the case, the Sanhedrin failed to follow procedure here.

[34]Stephen's statement is a declaration that Christ, whom the Jews had rejected and crucified, obtained a place at the right hand of God—a statement so blasphemous to the Jews that they "cried out with a loud voice, and stopped their ears" (Acts 7:57) to avoid hearing the words.

[35]See M.-É Boismard, "Stephen," in *The Anchor Bible Dictionary,* ed. David Noel Freedman, 6 vols. (New York: Doubleday, 1992), 6:209; and F. F. Bruce, *The Book of Acts* (Grand Rapids, Mich.: Eerdmans, 1988), 159-60.

[36]Josephus, *Jewish War* 7.328-29, 331-33.

[37]Josephus, *Jewish War* 7.332-33.

The End of Masada

And They Cast Lots:
Divination, Democracy, and Josephus

Eric D. Huntsman

κλήρῳ δ᾽ ἐξ αὐτῶν ἑλόμενοι δέκα τοὺς ἁπάντων σφαγεῖς ἐσομένους, καὶ γυναικί τις αὐτὸν καὶ παισὶ κειμένοις παραστρώσας καὶ τὰς χεῖρας περιβαλών, παρεῖχον ἑτοίμους τὰς σφαγάς.

After the men had chosen by lot ten of their number who would be their butchers, and when they had laid down beside and thrown their arms around their wives and children who lay waiting, they offered themselves up for the slaughter. —Josephus, Jewish War 7.395 *(author's translation)*

A gruesome scene confronted the Roman soldiers after they took the fortress of Masada. According to Josephus, they found that all but seven of the defenders had taken their own lives rather than submit to Roman slavery. The Romans, if we can believe Josephus, might have admired the resolve and courage of their foes, but the modern reader, even though separated from the event by nearly two millennia, is often troubled by it. While wondering at the resolution of those who allowed themselves to be killed, we must also try to comprehend those who were able to provide this deadly service. These men did not volunteer; rather they were chosen by lot, each one running an equal risk either to kill or be killed.

The sortition that first chose ten men for the general slaughter and then chose one of the ten to dispatch the others before killing himself appears to have been a random method of selecting men for an unwanted task. The idea of making choices by lot, however, had a long history in the ancient world, and it was a procedure that did not have ethnic or chronological limits. To understand the use of the lot in this instance of group suicide, we must first survey the religious use of lots as a method of divination. By then examining the role of lotteries at the time of Josephus, we will be better able to evaluate his treatment of the final events of Masada.

Divination in the Ancient World

Divination consists either of obtaining information by supernatural means or of securing answers to questions that are beyond human understanding. In the ancient world, many methods were developed to discern the will of the gods and to receive guidance, with or without elements of religious ceremony. Often this was done through observing and interpreting signs in the natural world, such as the flight of birds, the frequency of thunder, the movement and pattern of astronomical bodies, or the arrangement of organs in a sacrificial animal. Divination was sometimes practiced by performing a seemingly random act and allowing divine intervention to determine its outcome. The casting or drawing of lots falls into this latter category, and divination of this sort is known either as *psephomancy* (drawing of different pebbles) or *cleromancy* (drawing or casting of any type of lot).

Divination, especially the use of lots, was a common practice among the different peoples who surrounded the ancient Israelites. Many examples are found in ancient Near Eastern texts, in which a god or the gods were believed to effect the outcome of the action. Throughout Mesopotamia diviners would frequently cast two dice; one die represented a desirable result and the other an undesirable answer. The Sumerians in the south of Mesopotamia appear to have used sticks as lots, while the Assyrians in the north frequently used specially made clay dice.[1] The Canaanites, who preceded the Israelites in Palestine, are known to have used either marked pebbles or specially selected twigs as lots.[2] The Hittites in Anatolia employed oracles that might have been based upon lots, although their most common forms of divination seem to have been discerning signs in nature and in the viscera of sacrificial animals.[3] In northern Arabia, the practice was to draw from a number of headless arrows (*belomancy*), each of which indicated a different answer from the gods.[4]

Elsewhere in the Mediterranean lands and in Europe, the casting of lots was likewise used to indicate the will of the gods. In

Greek oracular centers where prophecy, soothsaying, and other kinds of divination regularly occurred, the casting of lots was rare although not unknown.[5] Before the battle at Leuctra in 371 B.C., for instance, the Spartans inquired at the oracle of Zeus at Dodonna, where a monkey turned over an urn filled with lots.[6] *Klērōsis,* or the choice of an official by lot, was also used for the appointment of some priests and other temple officials, leaving the choice to the gods.[7]

Much of Roman religion, including the arts of divination, was borrowed from the Etruscans, who practiced elaborate methods of *augury* (discerning signs in nature, especially from the flight of birds) or of *haruspicy* (interpretation of various kinds of portents, especially from the size and shape of the internal organs of sacrificial animals, a practice earlier performed by the Hittites).[8] Nevertheless, at several sites the use of *sortes* or lots was a feature of Italic divination. The primary center of this type of divination in classical times was the famous lottery of Fortuna at Praeneste, where an innocent child randomly drew a wooden lot to obtain an answer to a specifically posed question.[9] In northern Europe, the Germans also used lots. One method was to mark and throw strips of branches—the first one that a priest picked up indicated the will of the gods.[10] Women often played a prominent role in the consultation of lots, as seen in the trial of Caesar's aide C. Valerius Proculus during the Gallic Wars.[11]

Divination in Ancient Israel

Despite the prevalence of lot-casting in the ancient world, the ancient Israelites rejected many methods of divination of neighboring cultures around them because they were associated with pagan, magical practices.[12] The primary injunction against such "magical" practices appears in Deuteronomy 18:10–12, which prohibits divination, "observers of times," enchanters, witches, and necromancy. Nevertheless, Israelite practice accepted that Yahweh, as the one true God, was able to produce signs or influence the outcome of events just as the surrounding people believed that their gods did. Some forms of divination besides direct prophecy received sanction, namely the expression of God's will through the ephod, the Urim and Thummim, and the casting of certain kinds of lots.

The way the ephod, a part of the priestly regalia, was used in divination is unclear. Its use was lost before the translation of the Hebrew scriptures into the Greek Septuagint in the mid–third century B.C., but it probably had a revelatory function because, in the case of the high priest at least, the ephod held the breastplate that contained the Urim and Thummim.[13] These latter devices were the most direct, mechanical means available to the Israelites for discerning God's will.

Although the Urim and Thummim are attested seven or possibly eight times in the Old Testament,[14] there is little agreement in the academic world as to their exact nature and function. At some time before the Babylonian captivity, they must have been lost, stolen, or moved, for it is generally agreed that no postexilic Jew had seen them or knew exactly how they were used.[15] In fact, the very meaning of the terms is uncertain, although some Hebrew roots for Urim and Thummim have been proposed based upon the Septuagint translation of them as *dēlōsis* (revelation or manifestation) and either *alētheia* (truth) or *teleōsis* (perfection). The underlying Hebrew plurals are commonly postulated to mean something like "lights" and "perfections."[16]

A prevalent theory today is that the Urim and Thummim were actually lots that, like the Mesopotamian version of the same, were cast in order to obtain either a yes or no answer from Yahweh. This view is based largely on the Septuagint version of 1 Samuel 14:41, which reads, "Then Saul said, 'O Lord, God of Israel, why have you have not answered your servant this day? If the guilt is in me or in Jonathan my son, O Lord, God of Israel, give Urim; and if you indicate that it is in the people of Israel, give Thummim.' And Jonathan and Saul were taken, but the people escaped."[17] Such a practice could account for two otherwise unspecified forms of divination in which a single person was identified by successively narrowing the congregation by choosing first a tribe out of Israel, then a clan from that tribe, then a family from that clan, and finally a single individual out of that family.[18]

Later in Israelite history when the Urim and Thummim were either lost or their use forgotten, the most common form of divination was the use of *gôrālōt* or conventional lots. Attested seventy-eight times in the Old Testament, this kind of lot was one of the most frequently used Israelite tools, and references to its use with sacrifices and in the temple indicate that it functioned under divine auspices.[19] For example, on the Day of Atonement, Aaron cast lots over two goats to determine which would be sacrificed to the Lord and which would be driven out into the wilderness, carrying away Israel's iniquities (Lev. 16:8–10). Lots continued to be used throughout the intertestamental period, and their use to reveal God's will appears in the New Testament in Acts 1:26 when Matthias, the apostolic successor to Judas, was selected by lot.[20]

Divination in Hellenistic and Roman Times

By the time of Josephus, such lotteries were no longer used only as a means of divination. Among the Greeks and Romans, for example, sortition, or the selection of officials and public duties according to lot, had become standard practice. Although this form of selection may have originally indicated that the gods were making their choice known,[21] in fifth-century Athens the use of the lot was seen by Aristotle as a prime feature of democracy.[22] As Athenian democracy developed, direct elections seemed to favor aristocrats since they had the money and name recognition necessary to garner votes, whereas selection by lot from a pool of candidates (*klērōsis ek prokritōn*) seemed to guarantee that any citizen had a chance for high office.[23]

Even the Romans, whose balanced political system under the so-called republic tried to limit the excesses of democracy and afford public positions to the qualified, used the lot in the distribution of tribes in voting, the selection of legates and *interreges,* the empaneling of juries, and in the assignment of *provincia* or "spheres of action" to elected magistrates.[24] The lot device most frequently used by the Romans was the *sitella,* an urn with a narrow mouth that was filled with water and small balls marked with either a name or a province.[25] The mouth was so narrow that only one lot could float to the surface to be drawn first.

Although the Greeks and Romans continued to speak of the role of *Tyche* or *Fortuna* (Greek and Latin respectively for "fortune" or "chance") in the decisions reached by lots, apparently the use of lots had begun to be seen as a method of making some decisions more random or more fair. In accordance with Greek political thinking, lots were democratic in that they gave each participant, regardless of station, an equal chance.

Casting lots as a fair means of making a difficult choice might have been the rationale employed following the unsuccessful defense of the Galilean fortress of Jotapata during the early stages of the Jewish War. Josephus and forty others managed to hide from the Romans in a cave but, after some discussion, resolved that the only way out for them was through mutual suicide.[26] They decided to draw lots in order to determine the order of their deaths: the drawer of the first lot was to be killed by the drawer of the second, who was to be killed by the holder of the next lot. The use of lots made the process fair, random, and, if we can use the Greek meaning of the term here, democratic. Josephus managed to draw the final lot, and when he and the second to the last participant were left, they decided not to follow through with the suicide pact, and both turned themselves over to the Romans rather than die at their own hands. This result, of course, leads to the suspicion that Josephus had somehow "fixed" the lots, a practice that apparently has been common as long as lots and other devices of chance have been used.[27]

Lots at Masada

At last we have arrived at the point in our discussion at which we can consider the use of lots in the mass suicide at Masada.[28] There is no indication in the text that the defenders of Masada necessarily felt that Yahweh himself determined the death order, although the most religious of them might have believed that this was the case since God was sovereign over all. Instead, the ten men were selected randomly by lot, thereby distributing the responsibility fairly among them all. Physical proof of this lottery may actually exist. During the extensive excavations of Masada by Yigael Yadin, twelve *ostraca* or pottery sherds were found in room 113, a long, narrow chamber running north and south. Each of these ostraca had a different name written on it, and among these was one sherd that bore the name of the leader of the Sicarii, Eleazar ben Yair.[29] One of these sherds can be discarded as incomplete, but could the remaining eleven ostraca not be the actual lots used in that final, desperate selection?

Several problems, however, arise regarding the suicide at Masada. The first difficulty centers on these very ostraca. The number of surviving sherds itself causes suspicion.[30] According to Josephus, the first sortition selected ten men out of the entire number of adult males on Masada. Thus there should have been numerous inscribed sherds. Admittedly many of them might not have survived, but pottery pieces once broken are virtually indestructible and since all eleven were found together, at least some others should have survived. There was a second sortition that chose one man out of the ten who was to dispatch his nine companions after the first round of slaughter was completed. In that case, there should have only been ten sherds, not eleven. On the other hand, these ostraca could have been used to elect leaders or, if they were used as lots, might as easily have been used for distributing stores.

Another problem stems from Josephus's account of the suicide. According to our historian, everyone was killed prior to the Roman taking of Masada except for two women and five children who had hidden themselves in a cistern. Strangely, few remains of the 960 corpses that were said to greet the Romans were found in the fortress itself. The Romans, of course, could have cremated (which would have left some traces) or moved the bodies.

Strangely, some of the only skeletal remains which Yadin found in his excavations were *not* in the confines of Masada itself. Three skeletons were found on the lower terrace of the Northern Palace, and 25 others were found in a cave part way down the southern slope. Yadin supposed that the Romans had tossed the bodies there in order to dispose of them.[31] This view has come under attack: one cannot easily get the bodies to the cave from the fortress above, and the question remains as to why only 25 of 960 bodies were placed there. A more plausible explanation is that these 25 Jewish defenders tried to flee from the Romans and hid in the cave where they were later found and killed.[32] The fact that not all of the Sicarii killed themselves, together with the fact that numerous small fires were set in different places in Masada, such as the courtyard, rather than the one large fire that Josephus claims that the defenders had set to destroy their goods, undermines the credibility of our historian's account of Masada's final hours.

A third problem revolves around the very issue of suicide. First, was suicide against Jewish law at the time? It was not explicitly, although it was certainly against the spirit of the law as demonstrated by Josephus himself in his speech against suicide at Jotapata.[33] Perhaps the defenders of Masada could be exonerated according to *Hillul Hashem,* where their suicide can be compared to the example of Phineas in the Torah.[34] Second, did the mass suicide really occur as Josephus presented it? Suicide, particularly under circumstances such as these, was accepted in much of the rest of the ancient world.[35] Regardless of the legality or acceptance of suicide, we are not certain that all 960 really died at their own hands. One imaginative argument maintains that the suicide did not happen at all; the Romans murdered everyone, and Josephus concocted the Masada suicide to compensate for the fall of Jotapata and his own escape from the suicide pact there.[36] One strong argument against this view and for the veracity of Josephus's account is that it must have happened because there were too many witnesses; both the Roman soldiers and the prisoners of war who had served them would have seen or heard about the carnage atop Masada.[37]

One of the most important of these witnesses would have been the Roman general Flavius Silva. He was serving as *consul ordinarius* in Rome in A.D. 81, just as Josephus was finishing his *Jewish War.* One assumes that he would have contradicted Josephus if the latter had blatantly fabricated the account. Nevertheless, as an educated Roman familiar with the standards of the rhetorical historiography of the time,[38] Silva could have accepted an exaggerated account as long as it had some basis.[39] Ancient writers of history regularly exaggerated and embellished their accounts for effect, and the image of besieged citizens preferring death to capture was a common historiographic trope.[40]

Another factor in favor of some historical license on the part of Josephus is the excessively close parallel with the situation at Jotapata. The respective speeches given by Josephus and Eleazar are similar in form even though they come to different conclusions.

At Jotapata, Josephus created a speech for himself that condemned suicide; at Masada he wrote a speech for Eleazar[41] that praised suicide and publicly confessed that the Sicarii had started the war and that they were being punished for their sins.[42] The message here is subtle but clear. Josephus submitted but lived; the Sicarii refused to submit but died to the last man, woman, and child.

This negative picture of the defenders of Masada is supported by Josephus's overall depiction of them. They were, after all, *lēistēs*, or bandits, just like the Zealots in Jerusalem had been.[43] They had victimized Jewish noncombatants as well as Roman soldiers. In fact, contrary to the Hollywood glamorization of the defenders of Masada, Josephus's account of the siege of Masada ignores their supposed bravery or military skill.[44] If their suicide can be compared to anything, it is to the fruitless suicide of the stoic philosophers in Rome who were opposed to the Flavian emperors,[45] a comparison that works nicely for these Jewish opponents of the same regime.

What actually happened? It is probable that some of the defenders on Masada chose suicide over capture; others tried to escape or died fighting. Nevertheless, there was neither opportunity nor unanimity for the kind of mass action described by Josephus.[46] When the Romans entered Masada, they found many bodies of those who had killed themselves, and they might also have found some lots lying about. Those who did take their own lives and those of their wives and children might have employed ostraca, either potsherds specially prepared for this purpose or existing ones that had been used for distribution and other routine decisions, to determine the order of their death. Josephus took this information and embellished it, borrowing from classical historiography the motif of city defenders taking their own lives.

Since the use of a lottery in a suicide scene is not found in any of the Greek or Roman authors available to Josephus, it was enough of an innovation that the involvement of lots does not seem to have been a literary invention. Lots were probably used either at Jotapata or by some at Masada. It is doubtful that divine determination, whether in the minds of the Sicarii or in actuality, had anything to do with the use of the lot here. Instead the drawing of lots injects an element of chance or randomness, which reveals a democratic equality in the death of both those who submitted to death and those who inflicted it. The key to Josephus's rendering of the Masada suicide scene is then found by contrasting it with the suicide pact at Jotapata. Josephus was not glamorizing the action of the Sicarii; rather he expanded the suicide of a few of the defenders of Masada to include almost all of them in order to illustrate that the entire effort of the Sicarii was vain, bound for failure, and led all of them equally to death.

Eric D. Huntsman is Instructor/Lecturer of Classics and Ancient History at Brigham Young University.

NOTES

[1]O. R. Gurney, "The Babylonians and Hittites," in *Divination and Oracles,* ed. Michael Loewe and Carmen Blacker (London and Boston: George Allen and Unwin, 1981), 165; Cornelis Van Dam, *The Urim and Thummim: A Study of an Old Testament Means of Revelation* (Kampen: Uitgeverij van den Berg, 1986), 170.

[2]Van Dam, *Urim and Thummim,* 170.

[3]Gurney, "Babylonians and Hittites," 142-57; Van Dam, *Urim and Thummim,* 170.

[4]Van Dam, *Urim and Thummim,* 170-71; see also the arrow lottery used to distribute tribal meals among the Arabs, in Hugh Nibley, *The Ancient State: The Rulers and the Ruled,* ed. Stephen D. Ricks and Donald W. Parry, vol. 10 of *Collected Works of Hugh Nibley* (Salt Lake City: Deseret Book and FARMS, 1991), 9.

[5]J. S. Morrison, "The Classical World," in Loewe and Blacker, *Divination and Oracles,* 98; *Oxford Classical Dictionary,* 3d ed. (New York: Oxford University Press, 1996), s.v. "Divination." See also Franz Heinevetter, *Würfel- und Buchstabenorakel in Griechenland und Kleinasien* (Breslau: Koebner, 1912); and W. R. Halliday, *Greek Divination* (Chicago: Argonaut, 1967).

[6]Callisthenes, *Die Fragmente der griechischen Historiker* 124 F22a and b; Cicero, *De Divinatione* 1.34, 76; 2.32, 69.

[7]C. Hignett, *A History of the Athenian Constitution to the End of the Fifth Century B.C.* (Oxford: Clarendon Press, 1962), 228.

[8]William Warde Fowler, *The Religious Experience of the Roman People: From the Earliest Times to the Age of Augustus* (London: Macmillan, 1911), 292-304. For a survey of the two major types of divination, see *Oxford Classical Dictionary,* s.v. "Augures" and "Haruspices."

[9]Otto, "Fortuna," in *Real-Encyclopädie der classischen Altertumswissenschaft,* vol. 7 (Stuttgart: J. B. Metzler, 1912), cols. 23-27 (hereafter cited as *RE*); R. Hans, "Praenestine Sores," *Mitteilungen des deutschen archäologischen Instituts (röm. Abt.)* (1987): 131-62, especially 137-39. See also Nibley, *Ancient State,* 161.

[10]The main primary source for German practice is Tacitus, *Germania* 10. See also H. E. Davidson, "The Germanic World," in Loewe and Blacker, *Divination and Oracles,* 116-22.

[11]Caesar, *Gallic Wars* 1.47.

[12]Frederick H. Cryer, *Divination in Ancient Israel and Its Near Eastern Environment* (Sheffield, UK: JSOT, 1994), 233.

[13]Cryer, *Divination,* 277-82; Van Dam, *Urim and Thummim,* 58-61. Eric J. Olson maintains that there were different types of ephods and that the idol, the vestment, and the divinatory device were each different from the others. Eric J. Olson, "Divination in Ancient Israel" (master's thesis, Harvard University, 1969), 11-15.

[14]Exodus 28:30; Leviticus 8:8; Numbers 27:21; Deuteronomy 33:8; 1 Samuel 28:6; Ezra 2:63; Nehemiah 7:65. Depending upon the rendering of the verb in 1 Samuel 14:41, there may be an eighth attestation. In actuality, not all of these references refer to the Urim and Thummim as a pair: sometimes either appears separately, or the order is reversed.

[15]Cryer, *Divination,* 275. Both Ezra 2:63 and Nehemiah 7:65 seem to indicate that the Urim and Thummim were no longer present but that their restoration was awaited.

Van Dam holds that the process of using the Urim and Thummim consisted of the high priest first receiving revelation, which revelation was spoken to the congregation and then confirmed by a physical manifestation of the Urim and Thummim. Under his argument, the problem after the exile was not so much the loss of the Urim and Thummim but rather the lack of an inspired high priest who could use them. Van Dam, *Urim and Thummim,* 126-32.

Urim and Thummim, although not necessarily the same Urim and Thummim held by the Old World high priest, represent within an LDS context one mechanical form of revelation. See Omni 1:20-21; Mosiah 8:13-19; 21:26-28; 28:11-20; Ether 3:21-28; 4:1-7; Doctrine and Covenants 10:1; 17:1; Abraham 3:1-4; and JS-H 1:35, 42, 52, 59, 62. See also Joseph Fielding Smith, *Doctrines of Salvation: Sermons and Writings of Joseph Fielding Smith,* comp. Bruce R. McConkie, 3 vols. (Salt Lake City: Bookcraft, 1971), 3:222-26.

[16]Van Dam, *Urim and Thummim,* 4, 76-79. Josephus never uses the Greek expression *dēlōsis kai alētheia,* although in several passages in *Antiquities* (for example, 3.163, 166, 185, 216-17; and 4.421) he seems to refer to them as part of the high priest's breastplate, especially when their flashing was seen as a sign that God was present with the Israelites.

[17]See Olson, "Divination in Ancient Israel," 15-17. Van Dam vigorously rejects this so-called lot theory for the Urim and Thummim. Van Dam, *Urim and Thummim,* 38-39.

[18]Cryer, *Divination,* 277. For Achan's guilt, see Joshua 7:16-26; and for Saul's selection as king, see 1 Samuel 10:17-24.

[19]Cryer, *Divination,* 276-77; Olson, "Divination in Ancient Israel," 17; Van Dam, *Urim and Thummim,* 118-22.

[20]Johannes Munk, apparently trying to dismiss the use of a lottery among the early Christians, argues that this verse "can be understood as voting by ballot rather than drawing lots." Johannes Munk, *Acts of the Apostles* (New York: Doubleday, 1967), 9. See also Bruce R. McConkie, *Doctrinal New Testament Commentary,* 3 vols. (Salt Lake City: Bookcraft, 1973), 2:32-33. The Greek texts

can be understood variously. Following Walter Bauer, *A Greek-English Lexicon of the New Testament and Other Early Christian Literature,* 2d ed. (Chicago: University of Chicago Press, 1979), s.v. "κλῆρος," 435, the phrase ἔδωκαν κλήρους αὐτοῖς means "they gave them (namely the candidates) lots," and the lot of the candidate that was chosen identified the new Apostle. Alternatively, other Greek manuscripts of Acts 1:26 read ἔδωκαν κλήρους αὐτῶν, meaning "they gave, or cast, their lots." Obviously, it is unclear from the New Testament what kind of procedure the Apostles followed.

[21]V. Ehrenberg, "Losung (κλήωσις, sortitio)," in *RE,* 13.2 (1927), cols. 1451-67.

[22]Aristotle, *Politics* 1317b18-1318a3.

[23]Pseudo-Aristotle, *Athenean Politics* 22.5; Ehrenberg, "Losung," cols. 1467-90; Hignett, *History of the Athenian Constitution,* 226-32.

[24]Ehrenberg, "Losung," cols. 1493-97.

[25]For examples of the *sitella,* see Cicero, *Natura Deorum* 1.38.106; Livy, *Ab Urbe Condita* 25.3.16; and *Auctor ad Herenniun* 1.12.21.

[26]Josephus, *Jewish War* 3.340-91.

[27]Ehrenberg, "Losung," cols. 1493-97, for Roman abuses of the lot. Josephus's alleged arrangement of the death order at Jotapata has led to a famous mathematical problem that seeks to explain how the historian did it. For "Flavius Josephus' Permutation," see W. Ahrens, *Mathematiche Unterhaltungen und Spiele,* 2d ed. (Leipzig: Teubner, 1910), chapter 15.

[28]Josephus, *Jewish War* 7.395.

[29]Yigael Yadin and Joseph Naveh, "The Aramaic and Hebrew Ostraca and Jar Inscriptions," in *Masada I: The Yigael Yadin Excavations 1963-1965, Final Reports,* ed. Joseph Aviram, Gideon Foerster, and Ehud Netzer (Jerusalem: Israel Exploration Society and Hebrew University of Jerusalem, 1989), 28-31. For a review of these findings, see Ehud Netzer, "The Last Days and Hours at Masada," *Biblical Archaeology Review* 17, no. 6 (1991): 22-23, 28.

[30]Shaye J. D. Cohen, "Masada: Literary Tradition, Archaeological Remains, and the Credibility of Josephus," *Journal of Jewish Studies* 33, nos. 1-2 (1982): 398 n. 42.

[31]Yigael Yadin, *Masada: Herod's Fortress and the Zealots' Last Stand* (New York: Random House, 1966), 197.

[32]Cohen, "Masada: Literary Tradition," 394-95.

[33]Josephus, *Jewish War* 3.361-82. See the discussion of suicide by Daniel K. Judd, "Suicide at Masada and in the World of the New Testament," in this volume.

[34]Shubert Spero, "In Defense of the Defenders of Masada," *Tradition* 11, no. 1 (1970): 31-43.

[35]See Yolande Grise, "De la fréquence du suicide chez les Romains," *Latomus* 39, no. 1 (1980): 17-46; and Anton van Hoof, *From Autothanasia to Suicide: Self-killing in Classical Antiquity* (New York: Routledge, 1990).

[36]Trude Wiess-Rosmarin, "Masada Revisited," *Jewish Spectator* 34 (1962): 29-32.

[37]Louis H. Feldman, "Masada: A Critique of Recent Scholarship," in *Christianity, Judaism, and Other Greco-Roman Cults,* ed. Jacob Neusner, 4 vols. (Leiden: Brill, 1975), 3:218-48.

[38]See Eric D. Huntsman, "The Reliability of Josephus: Can He Be Trusted?" in this volume.

[39]Cohen, "Masada: Literary Tradition," 400. See also Cohen's comment, "If any ancient historian loved exaggerations and embellishments, it was Josephus; we may therefore suppose that his Masada narrative is not an unalloyed version of the truth." Cohen, "Masada: Literary Tradition," 393.

[40]Cohen documents sixteen examples from Greco-Roman literature in which desperate defenders destroy their property and kill their women and children before capture. Cohen, "Masada: Literary Tradition," 386–90.

[41]For Eleazar's speech as a literary creation, see Huntsman, "Reliability of Josephus."

[42]David J. Ladouceur, "Masada: A Consideration of the Literary Evidence," *Greek, Roman, and Byzantine Studies* 21, no. 3 (1980): 247–52. For an analysis of the *logos/antilogos* arrangement of the two speeches, see Cohen, "Masada: Literary Tradition," 396–97.

[43]For the difference between the two groups, see Solomon Zeitlin, "Masada and the Sicarii," *Jewish Quarterly Review* 55 (April 1965): 305; and Kent P. Jackson, "Revolutionaries in the First Century," in this volume. For the censure that Josephus places upon Jewish extremists as the cause of the war, see Huntsman, "Reliability of Josephus."

[44]Cohen, "Masada: Literary Tradition," 400.

[45]Ladouceur compares Eleazar's speech to those of the Stoic opposition. It is clearly not the type of speech that a Jewish extremist would compose. Ladouceur, "Masada: A Consideration," 253–57.

[46]Cohen, "Masada: Literary Tradition," 397.

Suicide at Masada and in the World of the New Testament

Daniel K. Judd

One of the most problematic issues surrounding the story of Masada is the reported mass suicide of 960 men, women, and children. Assuming that the suicides actually occurred, were they expressions of courage, selfish acts of cowardice, or blind obedience to authoritarian rule? Were the inhabitants of Masada faithful and devout Jews defending their homeland and families, or were they terrorists using political and religious justifications for their selfish deeds? Because the writings of the Jewish historian Josephus are the only primary sources of information concerning the events at Masada, definite answers to these questions are impossible to ascertain. Thus, the intent of this paper is only to provide religious and philosophical background information suggesting possible motives and explanations relevant to the morality of the reported suicides.

Historical and Religious Contexts

Late in the autumn of 63 B.C., the Roman army conquered Jerusalem, ending a nearly one-hundred-year period of Jewish independence.[1] At the beginning of their occupation of Jerusalem, the Romans were "content to rule" through local appointees. However, in A.D. 6, Rome responded to Jewish requests to bring an end to the chaos of Archelaus's rule and appointed a Roman governor. This more "direct rule," combined with an increased emphasis on taxation, "led to the first Jewish revolt against Rome."[2] A glimpse of these tumultuous times is given in the New Testament writings of Luke concerning an early Jewish tax protestor, Judas of Galilee: "Judas of Galilee in the days of the taxing . . . drew away much people after him: he also perished; and all, even as many as obeyed him, were dispersed" (Acts 5:37). Judas the Galilean is identified by Josephus as the founder of a Jewish revolutionary movement that came to be known in later generations as the Sicarii.[3] Judas has also been identified as being an ancestor of Eleazar ben Yair, the leader of the people of Masada at the time of their demise.[4]

Understanding the relationships between Judas of Galilee, Eleazar ben Yair, and the Sicarii is essential to understanding the events and suicides at Masada. While some modern scholars and writers have labeled the Sicarii as "patriots" and "freedom fighters,"[5] Josephus clearly viewed them as robbers and assassins:

> It happened that Judea was afflicted by the *robbers,* while all the *villages were set on fire, and plundred* by them. And then it was that the *Sicarii,* as they were called, who were robbers, grew numerous. They made use of small swords . . . but somewhat crooked, and like the Romans *sicæ* [or sickles], as they were called: and from these weapons these robbers got their denomination, and with those weapons they slew a great many.[6]

In addition to being the name used to identify this specific group of revolutionaries, the word *sicarii* also portrays their modus operandi. Sicarii comes from the Latin, *sica,* which means "small dagger."[7]

In the initial period of their existence, the Sicarii may have been motivated by a zealous desire to live the law of Moses by promoting social equality; however, it is apparent from the historical accounts that the Sicarii adopted terrorist tactics of assassination and arson and in the end resorted to suicide in carrying out their fanatical agenda.[8] Not only did the Sicarii engage in acts of violence against the Romans, but they also terrorized fellow Jews who willingly submitted to Roman rule. While the Sicarii claimed to be justified in these acts of aggression toward those whom they saw as guilty of treason, Josephus asserted that their accusations were only a cover for their evil deeds: "Now, this [claims of treason against fellow Jews] was in reality no better than a pretence, and a cloak for the barbarity which was made use of by them, and to colour over their own avarice."[9]

At the beginning of the Jewish War, the Sicarii under the leadership of Menahem (son of Judas of Galilee) seized Masada from a small post of Roman guards and took over their arsenal of weapons.[10] With these weapons, the Sicarii were able to take over the leadership of the revolutionary forces in Jerusalem. But Menahem was soon killed, and his followers fled back to Masada, where they were then led by Eleazar ben Yair. Josephus records that after the Sicarii fled from Jerusalem to Masada they had little to do with the other Jewish revolutionary factions and did not participate in the defense of Jerusalem. Josephus also wrote that the Sicarii attacked the Jewish settlement of En Gedi (a settlement near Masada) and killed hundreds of people, including women and children.[11] These facts support the argument that the Sicarii were more oriented to their own extreme political agenda than toward defending the freedom of the Jewish people as a whole, and to this extent, their suicides should be seen primarily as an act of political desperation rather than a deed motivated by religious principles or objectives.

The Fall of Masada and the Suicide Narrative

Soon after the fall of Jerusalem to the Romans in A.D. 70, Masada became the last stronghold of Jewish resistance. In the winter of A.D. 72, Flavius Silva ordered the Roman Tenth Legion to gain control of Masada. One source estimates the Roman forces to be six thousand in number.[12] After a siege of several months, the Romans finally entered the fortress to find 960 of the 967 inhabitants of Masada dead.[13] Josephus reports that, as the Romans entered the inner confines of Masada,

> [they] saw nobody as an enemy, but a terrible solitude on every side, with a fire within the palace, as well as a perfect silence. . . . They [the Romans] came within the palace, and so met with the multitude of the slain, but could take no pleasure in the fact, though it were done to their enemies.[14]

As with much of the story of Masada, the accuracy of the information concerning the events surrounding the mass suicide are dependent on the contested, but assumed, reliability of the writings of Josephus.[15] Josephus reports that when Eleazar ben Yair came to the realization that Masada was going to fall to the Romans, he called his most loyal companions around him to propose a plan.[16] An analysis of the first speech attributed to Eleazar reveals that his initial argument was threefold: (1) Eleazar reasoned that since he and his followers had promised to serve God and not the Romans, God had now given them the right to die in freedom; (2) he asserted that death at their own hands would be a better choice than death or captivity at the hands of the Romans; and (3) he also insisted that killing themselves would be fulfilling God's will as punishment for their sins:

> Wherefore, consider how God hath convinced us that our hopes were in vain, by bringing such distress upon us in the desperate state we are now in . . . we are openly deprived by God himself of all hope for deliverance. . . . This was the effect of God's anger against us for our manifold sins, which we have been guilty of in a most insolent and extravagant manner with regard to our own countrymen; the punishments of which let us not receive from the Romans, but from God himself as executed by our own hands.[17]

When Eleazar saw that most, but not all, of his followers were swayed by his first speech, he made a second attempt using a different logic. This time his reasoning began with a philosophical perspective that was more consistent with Greek philosophy than Jewish belief:

> It is life that is a calamity to men, and not death; for this last affords our souls their liberty, and sends them by a removal into their own place of purity, where they are to be insensible to all sorts of misery; for while souls are tied down to a mortal body, they are partakers of its miseries . . . for the union of what is divine to what is mortal, is unsuitable. . . . Souls, when the body does not distract them, have the sweetest rest.[18]

Josephus's account of Eleazar's second speech ends by his returning to the Hebrew "persuasion" that their deaths were necessary because of God's judgments upon them and that death at their own hands was better than death, torture, or slavery at the hands of the Romans:

> But put the case that we had been brought up under another persuasion, and taught that life is the greatest good which men are capable of, and that death is a calamity: however, the circumstances we are now in ought to be inducement to us to bear such calamity courageously, since it is by the will of God, and by necessity, that we are to die; for it now appears that God hath made such a decree against the whole Jewish nation. . . . Let us make haste to die bravely. Let us pity ourselves, our children, and our wives, while it is in our own

power to shew pity to them; for we are born to die, as well as those were whom we have begotten. . . . But for abuses, and slavery, and the sight of our wives led away after an ignominious manner, with their children, these are not such evils as are natural and necessary among men.[19]

Eleazar also detailed some of the torture his followers could expect at the hands of the Romans:

Some of them have been put upon the rack, and tortured with fire and whippings, and so died. Some have been half devoured by wild beasts, and yet have been reserved alive to be devoured by them a second time, in order to afford laughter and sport to our enemies; and such of those as are alive still, are to be looked on as the most miserable, who being so desirous of death, could not come at it.[20]

Josephus then reports that toward the end of the final speech "they all cut him [Eleazar] off short, and made haste to do the work."[21] Josephus describes the executions of the women and children:

While yet everyone of them still retained the natural passion of love to themselves and their families, because the reasoning they went upon appeared to them to be very just, that they were doing what was best to those that were dearest to them; for the husbands tenderly embraced their wives, and took their children into their arms, and gave the longest parting kisses to them, with tears in their eyes. Yet at the same time did they complete what they had resolved on, as if they had been executed by the hands of strangers. . . . Nor was there at length anyone of these men found that scrupled to act his part in this terrible execution, but everyone of them dispatched his dearest relations. Miserable men indeed were they! whose distress forced them to slay their own wives and children with their own hands.[22]

After burning all of their personal possessions, those who yet survived selected ten men to carry out the final execution:

They then chose ten men by lot out of them, to slay all the rest; every one of whom laid himself down by his wife and children on the ground, and threw his arms about them, and they offered their necks to the stroke of those who by lot executed that melancholy office.[23]

The ten executioners then cast lots to select the final individual who would in turn slay them. Josephus records:

The nine offered their necks to the executioner, and he who was the last of all took a view of all the other bodies, lest perchance some or

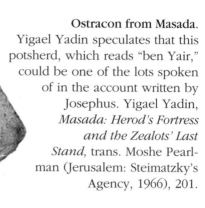

Ostracon from Masada. Yigael Yadin speculates that this potsherd, which reads "ben Yair," could be one of the lots spoken of in the account written by Josephus. Yigael Yadin, *Masada: Herod's Fortress and the Zealots' Last Stand,* trans. Moshe Pearlman (Jerusalem: Steimatzky's Agency, 1966), 201.

other among so many that were slain should want his assistance to be quite dispatched, and when he perceived that they were all slain, he set fire to the palace, and with the great force of his hand ran his sword entirely through himself, and fell down dead near to his own relations.[24]

The Logic of Suicide

Josephus's report of Eleazar's arguments for the deaths of himself and his followers are manifold and sometimes contradictory. While this internal tension has led some to question the authenticity of Josephus's description,[25] Eleazar's use of contradictory Hebrew and Greek thought may be evidence of his desperate willingness to use any argument that would justify his own position and persuade his followers to submit to his desires and die willingly.

Greco-Roman Perspectives. Eleazar may have been aware of several precedents from Greek philosophy and history that would have justified or supported his decision to lead his group to commit suicide. "Greek literature as early as Homer" contains accounts of suicide.[26] Some Greek philosophers accepted suicide, but their justifications differed. Zeno believed that suicide was appropriate, but "a person must not kill himself until god sends some necessity upon him"; however, such a "necessity" could be as minor as a bro-ken finger (a toe in some accounts) that was a sign from god that one's work was complete.[27] On the other hand, Seneca empha-sized the "right to die" as evidence that a man is free and cannot be held against his will:

> In any slavery the way lies open to freedom. . . . Wheresoever you cast your eyes there lies an end to affliction. Look at that precipice— down it runs the way to freedom. Look at the sea there, the river, the well—at its bottom lies freedom. . . . Are you asking for the road to freedom? Take any vein you like in your body![28]

Greco-Roman philosophy has had a profound influence on both Hebrew and Christian theology. One scholar has suggested that the Hellenization of Hebrew and Christian culture brought with it a fascination (if not preoccupation) with suicide.[29] How much direct influence these philosophies had on the inhabitants of Masada is unclear, but distinct ideas found in Eleazar's speeches such as the reported enmity between body and spirit, the freedom gained through death, and the justification of suicide through "necessity" are consistent with Greco-Roman perspectives. While Eleazar's arguments may have been influenced by Greco-Roman thought, another possibility is that Josephus, in his attempt to recreate the final words of Eleazar, used both Hebrew and Greek arguments in an attempt to appeal to both Jewish and Greco-Roman audiences.

More likely, Eleazar was familiar with numerous instances in the Hellenistic world when men, facing certain defeat and horrible torture, enslavement, or death, voluntarily killed their women and children and either committed suicide or charged hopelessly into certain death in battle. One historian has identified sixteen separate examples of groups under siege (540–35 B.C.) who were reported to have preferred death to surrender or enslavement. In eleven of the sixteen cases, men took their own lives as well as the lives of their wives and children. In the other five cases, the men killed the women and children and then died in battle with the enemy.[30]

Hebrew Perspectives. Another often-discussed problem in Eleazar's arguments for suicide is the fact that the taking of one's life was strongly condemned in Jewish literature.[31] It is not clear, however, when Jewish thought began to take a strong stand against suicide in cases such as those faced by the defeated warriors at Masada.

The Hebrew Bible (Old Testament) does not contain a specific prohibition against suicide but makes the intent of personal accountability for one's own life clear. The book of Genesis states, "And for your lifeblood I will surely demand an accounting" (NIV, Gen. 9:5). The sixth commandment reads, "Thou shalt not kill" (Ex. 20:13). In addition to the sanctity of life, the Hebrew scriptures also portray a reverence for the body: "Ye are the children of the Lord your God: ye shall not cut yourselves" (Deut. 14:1).

Hebrew scripture contains six recorded incidences of suicide: Abimelech (Judg. 9:54), Samson (Judg. 16:29-30), King Saul and his armor-bearer (1 Sam. 31:4-5; compare 1 Chr. 10:4-5), Ahithophel (2 Sam. 17:23), and Zimri (1 Kgs. 16:18). While the people at Masada might have considered these scriptural incidents of suicide as honorable precedents that might make suicide acceptable under extreme conditions, it is important to note that the majority of the individuals described in these accounts were not faithful to the covenants they had made with God. Abimelech's death was described as God's punishment for his "wickedness" (Judg. 9:56). Samson, while having periods of faithfulness and devotion, was also guilty of serious sins (see Judg. 14:19; 16:1). King Saul, chosen by God to institute the monarchy, was later found guilty of disobedience and lost his divine sanction (1 Sam. 15:22-23). Ahithophel, once King David's respected counselor, eventually rebelled and sought the king's life (2 Sam. 15:12; 17). Zimri became king after murdering his predecessor (1 Kgs. 16:10), and his suicide is described in scripture as punishment for "doing evil in the sight of the Lord" (1 Kgs. 16:18-19). Of the six recorded incidences of suicide in the Hebrew scriptures, five of the accounts provide ample evidence that the individuals described have been guilty of serious sins (there is no evidence either way concerning Saul's armorbearer). While Samson, Saul, and Ahithophel demonstrated periods of faithfulness, it appears that each of them died outside their covenants with God. The scriptural evidence suggests that none of these individuals was worthy of emulation—in life or in death.

In the ensuing years, orthodox rabbinic writers took a strong stand against suicide, as is represented in the statement, "One who destroys oneself wittingly has no share in the world to come."[32] The only exceptions were in cases of *kiddush hashen* (to sanctify God's name). According to the Talmud, one may accept death when faced with the alternative of being forced to commit idolatry, incest, or murder.[33] Some scholars have asserted this was the case for the inhabitants of Masada, as they were willing to die rather than be forced to live under Roman rule, which they considered to be an act of idolatry.[34]

Josephus records an incident from his own life that may be more representative of the Hebrew attitude toward suicide in the first century. During the early stages of the Roman-Jewish war, Josephus was the commander of Jewish forces in the town of Jotapata in Galilee. Josephus reports that he saw little hope in continuing to fight against the Roman troops led by Vespasian and thought it best that they surrender. His troops refused, Jotapata eventually fell, and Josephus escaped to a cave where forty of his soldiers were already hiding. By Josephus's report, the Jewish soldiers favored a mass suicide, but he strongly argued against it:[35]

> O my friends, why are we so earnest to kill ourselves? And why do we set our soul and body, which are such dear companions, at such variance?[36] . . . It is a brave thing to die in war; but so that it be according the law of war, by the hand of conquerors. . . . Now, self-murder is a crime most remote from the common nature of all animals, and an instance of impiety against God our Creator. . . . And do you not think that God is very angry when a man does insults what he hath bestowed on him? For from him it is that we have received our being, and we ought to leave it to his disposal to take that being away from us. . . . The souls of those who have acted madly against themselves, are received by the darkest place in Hades.[37]

The soldiers ignored the counsel of Josephus, cast lots, and executed one another. Only Josephus and one other soldier were left alive. The two of them chose to remain alive as long as possible by delivering themselves up to the Romans.[38]

The contrast between Josephus and the majority of his soldiers at Jotapata are representative of the differences between most other Jews (such as the Pharisees) and the Sicarii. Josephus did not believe that he had the right to take his own life; in all likelihood, neither did the majority of Jews believe that one had the right to take one's own life but believed that the right to give and take life was in the hands of God. Josephus did not regard the acceptance of Roman sovereignty as a sin to be avoided even at the cost of one's life—the Sicarii obviously did.

A New Testament Perspective. While the writings in the New Testament do not have a direct connection to the events of Masada, they represent a contemporary perspective. With respect to suicide, the New Testament contains only one specific incidence—the death of Judas Iscariot:

> Then Judas, who had betrayed him [Jesus Christ], when he saw that he was condemned, repented himself, and brought again the thirty pieces of silver to the chief priests and elders, saying, I have sinned in that I have betrayed innocent blood. And they said unto him, What is that to us? See thou to it; thy sins be upon thee. And he cast down the pieces of silver in the temple, and departed, and went, and hanged himself on a tree. And straightway he fell down, and his bowels gushed out, and he died. (JST, Matt. 27:3-6).[39]

In addition to Luke's account of the Apostle Paul preventing the "keeper of the prison" from committing suicide (see Acts 16:26-31), the New Testament also contains a poignant account of Paul's own thoughts of death:

> *For I am in a strait betwixt two, having a desire to depart, and to be with Christ; which is far better: Nevertheless to abide in the flesh is more needful for you.* And having this confidence, I know that I shall abide and continue with you all for your furtherance and joy of faith; That your rejoicing may be more abundant in Jesus Christ for me by my coming to you again. (Philip. 1:23-26; italics added)

Paul's words show that he was willing to submit his own will to the needs of others and ultimately to the will of God. He was willing to live for God and neighbor as opposed to die for self. Early Christian theology was compatible with its Hebrew counterpart but was in direct conflict with much of Greek philosophy and popular morality in the Roman empire.

Concluding Thoughts

One modern philosopher has written, "There is but one truly serious philosophical problem, and that is suicide."[40] Not only is this comment representative of the present philosophical debate over suicide, but it is also indicative of the ideological conflicts concerning the events of Masada.[41]

The evidence suggests that although the Sicarii at Masada were faithful and devout Jews[42] they may have taken their devotion beyond what God had commanded. In the words of the Book of Mormon prophet Jacob, the Jews as a people were guilty of "looking beyond the mark" (Jacob 4:14). Perhaps the intentions of the Jews of Masada to live a life faithful to God may have become distorted into a fanatical desire for death. The story of the inhabitants of Masada may be, if the historical sources are accurate, an important commentary on the consequences of rejecting God. The following biblical prophecy of Moses speaks about the consequences of such a rejection:

> The Lord shall bring a nation against thee from far, from the end of the earth, as swift as the eagle flieth; a nation whose tongue thou shalt not understand; A nation of fierce countenance, which shall not regard the person of the old, nor shew favour to the young. . . . And he shall besiege thee in all thy gates, until thy high and fenced walls come down, wherein thou trustedst, throughout all thy land: and he shall besiege thee in all thy gates throughout all thy land, which the Lord thy God hath given thee. . . . And ye shall be left few in number, whereas ye were as the stars of heaven for multitude; because thou wouldest not obey the voice of the Lord thy God. (Deut. 28:49–50, 52, 62)

Latter-day Saint literature also provides insight into what may have been the early LDS perspective on the events at Masada. The July 15, 1841, edition of the official Latter-day Saint publication *Times and Seasons* included an article concerning the events of Masada. Editors Don Carlos Smith (Joseph Smith's brother) and Robert B. Thompson wrote the following note preceding the article:

> The following thrilling account of the self devotedness of the Jews, scarcely has its equal on the pages of history. *Although such a course must be condemned,* it shows their attachment to their ancient religion, the God of their fathers, and also their abhorrence of the Romans.[43]

While acknowledging the drama of Masada, the editors condemn the actions of Eleazar and his followers. In the body of the article, the editors also describe Eleazar as possessing "most stubborn fanaticism."[44]

While the evidence suggests that the suicide at Masada was unjust and possibly the consequence of fanatical religious zeal, there are no definite answers concerning the morality of the motives of the individual men, women, and children who died. For some, their deaths may have been acts of selfishness, for others, their dying may have been a type of martyrdom—only an omniscient God can judge. The Prophet Joseph Smith taught:

> While one portion of the human race is judging and condemning the other without mercy, the Great Parent of the universe looks upon the whole of the human family with a fatherly care and paternal regard. . . . He is a wise Lawgiver, and will judge all men, not according to the narrow, contracted notions of men, but, 'according to the deeds done in the body whether they be good or evil,' or whether these deeds were done in England, America, Spain, Turkey, or India. . . . We need not doubt the wisdom and intelligence of the Great Jehovah; He will award judgment or mercy to all nations according to their several deserts, their means of obtaining intelligence, the laws by which they are governed, the facilities afforded them of obtaining correct information, and His inscrutable designs in relation to the human family; and when the designs of God shall be made manifest, and the curtain of futurity be withdrawn, we shall all of us eventually have to confess that the Judge of all the earth has done right.[45]

Daniel K. Judd is Assistant Professor of Ancient Scripture at Brigham Young University.

NOTES

[1]Peter Schäfer, "The Hellenistic and Maccabean Periods," in *Israelite and Judaean History,* ed. John H. Hayes and J. Maxwell Miller (Philadelphia: Westminster, 1977), 604.

[2]David L. Barr, *New Testament Story: An Introduction,* 2d ed. (Belmont, Calif.: Wadsworth, 1995), 281.

[3]Josephus, *Wars of the Jews,* in *The Complete Works of Josephus,* trans. William Whiston (Grand Rapids: Kregel, 1995), 7.7.1.

[4]Arthur J. Droge and James D. Tabor, *A Noble Death: Suicide and Martyrdom among Christians and Jews in Antiquity* (San Francisco: HarperSanFrancisco, 1992), 92.

[5]Nachman Ben-Yehuda, *The Masada Myth: Collective Memory and Mythmaking in Israel* (Madison: University of Wisconsin Press, 1995), 180.

[6]Josephus, *Antiquities,* in *The Complete Works of Josephus,* trans. William Whiston (Grand Rapids: Kregel, 1995), 20.8.10; italics added.

[7]Ben-Yehuda, *Masada Myth,* 35.

[8]David Rhoads, "Zealots," in *The Anchor Bible Dictionary,* ed. David Noel Freedman, 6 vols. (New York: Doubleday, 1992), 6:1048.

[9]Josephus, *Wars of the Jews* 8.1.

[10]Josephus, *The Jewish War,* trans. Geoffrey Arthur Williamson, rev. E. Mary Smallwood (New York: Penguin, 1981), 2.408, 433–34.

[11]Josephus, *Wars of the Jews* 4.7.2.

[12]Christopher Hawkes, "The Roman Siege of Masada," *Antiquity* 3, no. 10 (1929): 195–213.

[13]Josephus recorded that there were two women and five children who had concealed themselves in underground caverns during the events of Masada. These survivors were reported to be the source of information concerning the events that transpired. See Josephus, *Wars of the Jews* 7.9.1.

[14]Josephus, *Wars of the Jews* 7.9.2 .

[15]Shaye J. D. Cohen, "Masada: Literary Tradition, Archaeological Remains, and the Credibility of Josephus," *Journal of Jewish Studies* 33, no. 1-2 (1982): 385–405.

[16]Josephus, *Wars of the Jews* 7.8.6.

[17]Josephus, *Wars of the Jews* 7.8.6.

[18]Josephus, *Wars of the Jews* 7.8.7.

[19]Josephus, *Wars of the Jews* 7.8.7.

[20]Josephus, *Wars of the Jews* 7.8.7.

[21]Josephus, *Wars of the Jews* 7.9.1.

[22]Josephus, *Wars of the Jews* 7.9.1.

[23]Josephus, *Wars of the Jews* 7.9.1.

[24]Josephus, *Wars of the Jews* 7.9.1.

[25]Cohen, "Masada," 396–97.

[26]Arthur J. Droge, "Suicide," in *Anchor Bible Dictionary,* 6:226.

[27]Droge and Tabor, *Noble Death,* 31.

[28]Lucius Seneca, "On Anger," in *Seneca/Moral and Political Essays,* ed. and trans. John M. Cooper and J. F. Procopé (Cambridge: Cambridge University Press, 1995), 3.15.3–4.

[29]Arthur Darby Nock, *Conversion: The Old and the New in Religion from Alexander the Great to Augustine of Hippo* (Oxford: Clarendon, 1933), 197–98.

[30]Cohen, "Masada," 386–88.

[31]Leon D. Hankoff, "Judaic Origins of the Suicide Prohibition," in *Suicide: Theory and Clinical Aspects,* ed. Leon D. Hankoff (Littleton, Mass.: PSG Publishing, 1979), 3–20.

[32]Reuven P. Bulka, "Rabbinic Attitudes towards Suicide," *Midstream: A Monthly Jewish Review* 25, no. 8 (1979): 44.

[33]Matthew Schwartz and Kalman J. Kaplan, "Judaism, Masada, and Suicide: A Critical Analysis," *Omega* 25, no. 2 (1992): 127–32.

[34]I. Jacobs, "Eleazar Ben Yair's Sanction for Martyrdom," *Journal for the Study of Judaism: In the Persian, Hellenistic, and Roman Period* 13, nos. 1-2 (1982): 183–86.

[35]Josephus, *Wars of the Jews* 3.8.1, 4.

[36]Notice the distinctly Hebrew theology of the compatibility of the body and the spirit.

[37]Josephus, *Wars of the Jews* 3:8:5.

[38]Josephus, *Wars of the Jews* 3.8.6-7.

[39]One scholar asserts that the Greek word *Iscariot* becomes *sicarius* in Latin. See Neil Elliot, review of *Judas Iscariot and the Myth of Jewish Evil,* by Hyam Maccoby, *Bible Review,* 10 (February 1994): 14-15.

[40]Albert Camus, *The Myth of Sisyphus and Other Essays,* trans. Justin O'Brien (New York: Random House, 1955), 3, quoted in Droge and Tabor, *Noble Death,* 17.

[41]Droge and Tabor, *Noble Death,* 17.

[42]Yadin, *Masada,* 164-67.

[43]"Fall of Herodio [*sic*]—Machaerus—Masada—Fate of Josephus—Agrippa—Bernice," *Times and Seasons* 2 (July 15, 1841): 476; italics added.

[44]"Fall of Herodio," 477.

[45]Joseph Fielding Smith, comp., *Teachings of the Prophet Joseph Smith* (Salt Lake City: Deseret Book, 1972), 218.

The Reliability of Josephus: Can He Be Trusted?

Eric D. Huntsman

The author Joseph ben Matthias ha-Cohen, like most members of the Judean upper class, lived in several worlds at once. Born in A.D. 37 to an aristocratic family of priestly lineage, Josephus was ostensibly connected with the Hasmonean family that had ruled Judea between 165 B.C. and 38 B.C.[1] His native language was Aramaic, although he was well versed in Hebrew, which by his time was largely a liturgical language. He was an observant Jew whose religious interests led him to affiliate with the three major schools of Judaism—the Sadducees, Essenes, and the Pharisees.

Nevertheless, Josephus was educated in Greek literature and was comfortable with the Hellenistic culture that then dominated the eastern Mediterranean. He was also familiar with Roman civilization, not only from the Romanizing efforts of the Herodians and the subsequent direct Roman occupation, but also from his own visits to the imperial capital. When he finally wrote the works that immortalized him, he had, by some surprising turns of events, become a Roman citizen and had taken the name Flavius Josephus.[2]

An awareness of Josephus's multicultural background is essential in order to understand his extant writings: *Jewish War, Jewish Antiquities, Against Apion,* and his *Vita* or "Life."[3] All of these works, in their final form at least, were published in Greek rather than in Aramaic or Hebrew.[4] In addition to writing in Greek, Josephus also closely followed the Greek historiographic tradition, adopting many elements of its style and outlook and employing Greek historical methods.[5]

Josephus was also uniquely equipped to be a writer of Jewish history; he had the correct religious foundation, knowledge, and background.[6] Furthermore, he had access to the necessary sources and was an eyewitness for many of the later events, especially those recorded in *Jewish War.* Such firsthand knowledge was a qualification that Thucydides, the first "scientific" Greek historian, thought was absolutely necessary for writing any contemporary history.[7] For all these reasons, Josephus had such success as a historical author that Jerome once called him "the Greek Livy," comparing him to one of the great Latin authors of Roman history.[8]

Josephus, however, was sometimes inaccurate, somewhat evasive, prone to tangents, and even sloppy in his writing.[9] The difficulty of working in a second language and the author's own personality might explain some of these failings. Even other acknowledged ancient historians, such as Herodotus, who is the earliest Greek historian whose works are fully extant, were also known for their digressions. Nevertheless, when elements of Josephus's works are contradictory, inaccurate, obviously fabricated, or simply wrong, the modern reader may begin to question Josephus's reliability. To understand how an author like Josephus could be both a great writer and, at the same time, a questionable historian, we must understand the difference between history and historiography.

First we must realize that our current view of history is quite a modern concept. Not until the late nineteenth century did historians begin to believe that the "facts" of past events were recoverable if all the surviving pieces of evidence could be gathered and weighed.[10] Students of ancient history during this period readily adopted this approach, particularly in Germany, where encyclopedias and vast collections of evidence were amassed and detailed histories of the ancient world were written. This, however, was not the ancient approach to history. In antiquity historiography was "writing about history" and was a literary genre of its own.

To the sophisticated reading audiences of Greece and Rome, rhetoric was as important as accuracy. It was a truism that "history was nothing but rhetoric"—meaning that the authors tried to persuade their audiences that what the authors thought happened or even what they thought *should* have happened actually occurred. Therefore, Greek and Roman writers of history omitted, expanded, or compressed historical material to suit their own needs, freely appropriated whole passages from other writers, and readily invented detail while adorning their narrative to make it more persuasive and aesthetically pleasing.

How clearly Josephus falls into the classical historiographic tradition is clear from the direct influence exerted on him by previous Greek authors. His prologue to the *Jewish War* is immediately reminiscent of Thucydides' history of the Peloponnesian War; both authors began by asserting that their works would cover "the greatest of all wars."[11] Josephus also appears to have deliberately modeled himself on Thucydides, both in his use of alternating direct and indirect discourse and in the use of other compositional techniques, such as using the first book to establish the background and to identify the causes of the upcoming war. More striking are the reflections of Thucydides' plague-stricken Athens that one finds in Josephus's depiction of Jerusalem as famine settled in during its long siege.[12] Another model for Josephus was Polybius, a Greek author who lived in the second century before Christ. Like Josephus, Polybius had watched his homeland, the Greek city-states of the Achaean League, fall before the onslaught of Rome. Both authors sought to explain to their countrymen Rome's apparently invincible power, and they both identified their captors as the divinely appointed masters of the world.[13] From Polybius, Josephus adopted some Greek terms commonly used in Hellenistic period—such as, *to theion* (godly power or being), *to daimōn* (divinity), or *hē tychē* (fortune)—and regularly used these expressions where one would expect him to make a traditional reference to God.[14] Finally, Josephus, Thucydides, and Polybius all shared similar experiences: each was successively an aristocrat, a politician, a general, and finally an exile from his homeland.[15]

Josephus's other major work, *Jewish Antiquities,* while still part of the classical tradition of historiography, seems to have been based on slightly different models. It is not a history of contemporary events like the *Jewish War* or Thucydides' history of the Peloponnesian War. Instead it is a survey of the history of the Jewish people from the time of creation. Although the influence of Polybius is still present in this work, Josephus seems to have adopted from Dionysius of Halicarnassus the same scheme that Dionysius had employed in his work on Roman Antiquities.[16] Remembering Josephus's multicultural background, however, we are not surprised to find that this work in particular reflects some Near Eastern elements in both its style and purpose.

Gregory Sterling has identified a subgenre of history writing that he calls apologetic historiography.[17] He sees this as a type of writing, particularly in the Hellenized Near East, in which a local content (the history of a particular people) is recounted in a nonnative form adapted from a superimposed, dominant culture. The earliest examples of this kind of historical writing are Berossos and Mantheon, a Hellenized Babylonian and Egyptian respectively, who wrote their national histories in Greek according to the outward form of classical historiography.[18] Josephus engaged in this kind of apologetic writing when he tried to redefine Judaism within the context of a Greco-Roman world. By doing so, he hoped to inform others about his people, while defending them and their traditions from growing anti-Semitism among the Greeks.[19]

The importance of rhetoric is apparent in the regular use of set speeches by the ancient historians. Direct speeches in Greek literature developed out of the epic tradition, and Herodotus subsequently introduced speeches into prose writing.[20] Thucydides further developed the speech by using it to convey the intentions of historical characters and to illustrate other factors that narrative alone could not. Although Thucydides claimed that he tried to keep close to the sense of what was actually said in such situations, he admitted that he had his speakers say what *seemed* to be appropriate for a given situation.[21] Thucydides' rhetorical speeches, written by the historian, but placed in the mouths of his characters, later became a standard feature of classical historiography. These speeches often became set or stock pieces for a given situation and never claimed to be a verbatim reproduction of what a real historical figure actually said.

Hence, in a famous episode prior to the fall of Masada to the Romans, Josephus composed an elaborate, philosophical treatise for the rebel leader, Eleazar. Josephus was not present to hear what speech, if any, Eleazar actually gave; neither were the Roman troops, nor, for that matter, were the Masada survivors, who by this time had safely hidden themselves in a cistern.[22] The speech, like others in Josephus's works, is a literary creation, and while it contains views that Eleazar might have shared, it nonetheless belongs to Josephus.

Chronological inconsistency is another frequent factor in the historiographic genre; although Thucydides made an effort to maintain a regular chronology, most ancient authors followed the example of another writer named Ephorus, who arranged his material thematically. The latter approach was favored for its clarity even if it meant that the narrative lost some chronological accuracy.

Classical historiography also privileged political and military history and often failed to provide the kinds of material that many modern historians feel is necessary. Consequently, one must supplement the literary sources with material such as archaeological evidence, inscriptions, and numismatics in order to produce social, economic, or cultural history for the period. Accordingly, Josephus's *Jewish War* underestimates the widespread apocalyptic beliefs of his contemporaries and practically omits social and economic factors that contributed to the outbreak of the war.[23]

Since ancient history was intended to be didactic, its writers fashioned their narratives for their own purposes, subordinating events that they recounted to their theme, while at the same time creating a new literary work.[24] The purpose of the history affected authors' selection of material, determining what they would include and what they would omit. Ancient writers were thus subjectively selective: if an event did not support their point, they were free to ignore or modify it.

Writers of this period were also heavily dependent upon their own sources. For the modern student of ancient history, therefore, source criticism becomes particularly important as we try to identify an ancient author's sources and to assess the reliability of those sources. As mentioned above, Josephus was an eyewitness to many of the events in *Jewish War,* in which case he was often his own source. His captivity after the fall of Jotapata in A.D. 67 afforded him time to take notes on what was transpiring and to reflect upon the course of the war,[25] but as his own ideas regarding the causes of the war and its final outcome developed, his recollections could have been affected.

Many other witnesses to the events of the war on both sides would have been available to Josephus, and they could both provide information and verify his account.[26] Because of his later association with the Flavian emperors, Josephus would also have had ready access to the *commentarii* or field reports of Vespasian, Titus, and succeeding commanders, as well as to other Jewish and Roman archives.[27]

Some of Josephus's sources were in as much a position to approve or even censure his account as they were to provide information for it. Josephus tried to bolster the veracity of his history by soliciting the endorsement of Herod Agrippa II and the Flavians, particularly Titus. Josephus reminded his readers that the *Jewish War* had received the approval of Titus and revealed that during the composition of the history he had regularly provided Agrippa II with installments of the work for his review. The king wrote Josephus sixty-two letters confirming Josephus's accuracy and commending him for his efforts.[28] Nevertheless, it is apparent that these political figures were able to influence and even direct his history, insomuch that it has been suggested that *Jewish War* was a work commissioned by the imperial government.[29] Josephus's account indeed did take the Roman point of view, since to the Jews the "Jewish War" was actually the "Roman War."

The need to please his patrons provided Josephus with an external bias that imposed limits on what he could and could not include in his work. He regularly praised the roles of both Vespasian and Titus and worked to legitimize the new Flavian dynasty. Accordingly, Josephus emphasized his belief that Vespasian was chosen by God to rule the world, noting his own role in prophesying Vespasian's accession before it occurred.[30] Even when Josephus included questionable actions of the Flavians, such as the Roman burning of the temple, he modified them. Thus Josephus portrayed Titus as anxious to spare the holy edifice and attributed its destruction to common Roman soldiers and Jews alike.[31]

It was Josephus's *internal* bias, however, that had the greatest affect on his selection and use of evidence. Sometimes this bias was purely personal, such as when he exaggerated his own achievements and skills or tried to justify his surrender at Jotapata.[32] More importantly, Josephus's subject presented him with two seemingly conflicting loyalties: he was at the same time pro-Roman and pro-Jewish. Josephus's solution to this dilemma was to blame the war on neither the Romans nor the aristocratic Jewish leaders, whom he regularly portrayed as desiring peace and working for accommodation. Instead he held responsible the Jewish extremists whom, whether they were the zealots in Jerusalem or the Sicarii who seized control of Masada,[33] he called *lēstēs* or "bandits."

This shifting of blame, however, is probably only the proximate purpose of *Jewish War;* Josephus's ultimate intent seems to lie far deeper.[34] His later works, especially *Antiquities* and *Against Apion,* were written largely to defend the history and current rights of the Jews. Outwardly the *Jewish War,* by shifting the responsibility of the war away from the body of the Jewish people, achieved this same purpose. Inwardly, however, Josephus's *Jewish War* served to promote within the Jewish community greater openness and more cooperation with Rome.[35] The Roman Empire, with divine sanction, had conquered the Jewish homeland; it was necessary, therefore, for the remnants of the Jewish people to submit to God's will and work within the Roman system to preserve their way of life.

The reliability of the works of Josephus suffered even more after the texts actually left his hands. As with any ancient text, those of Josephus experienced the usual problems of copying and transmission. Unlike the Bible, for which the textual tradition is surprisingly and fortunately strong, the survival of the works of Josephus is similar to that of other Greco-Roman literature. Except for a single fragment of *Jewish War,* which dates to the third century A.D., the oldest manuscripts date between the ninth and eleventh centuries, at least eight hundred years after Josephus first began to write.[36] During that time, copying errors were made, marginal notes were accidentally included, and interpolations were willfully injected into the text.

This last type of change is particularly significant because of the popularity that Josephus gained among early Christian writers. Josephus provided a link between the Old and New Testaments that furnished the young religious community with a connection to the more ancient Jewish tradition. For the Christians, the destruction of Jerusalem was a clear fulfillment of the prophecies of Jesus (Matt. 24:1–2). Later when the Jewish and Christian communities had clearly split and begun to grow hostile to each other, the destruction of the Jewish state and the further dispersion of its populace seemed to the Christians to be fitting punishments for the death of Christ.[37]

Most importantly, Josephus's *Antiquities* occasionally provided corroborating evidence for events in the Gospels and the book of Acts. The census of Quirinius (Luke 2:2), the reported general cruelty of Herod, the activity of John the Baptist (Matt. 3:5), the death of Herod Agrippa I (Acts 12:20–23), and the existence of James the brother of Jesus are all attested by Josephus.[38] In each of these instances, there are some discrepancies between the biblical and Josephan accounts,[39] but these may actually strengthen the Josephan references' claim to legitimacy, since Christian copyists or editors would have been likely to harmonize the accounts completely.

Many scholars feel, however, that the mention of James the Lord's brother, the material about John the Baptist, and any direct references to Jesus are deliberate interpolations.[40] The most suspect of these is the so-called *Testimonium Flavianum* in *Antiquities* 18.63–64, which gives an account "of a wise man, if one really should say that he is a man" who "was Christ." It then speaks of the Lord's trial, crucifixion, and resurrection and concludes by stating that the Christians "have not disappeared to this day."

Although the historical aim of Josephus was to recount the truth about his people, he also endeavored to write beautifully and dramatically as an heir to the classical rhetorical tradition.[41] Thus, when using Josephus's writings to reconstruct a certain period, we must remember the traditions in which he worked and be aware of the historical (we might occasionally call them "ahistorical") methods that were accepted in his own time. As with any other literary source of the period, the evidence he presents must be evaluated critically and used carefully, especially when he provides the only literary account for a particular event.

While Josephus's writings may not always be completely reliable, his works can nonetheless be trusted to recreate a dramatic image of a people and the critical events in their history that have been important for Jews, Christians, and other students of the ancient classical world.

Eric D. Huntsman is Lecturer in Classics at Brigham Young University.

NOTES

[1]Josephus, *Jewish War* 1.3; Josephus, *Antiquities* 16.187; Josephus, *Life* 1-2, 7. See Mireille Hadas-Lebel, *Flavius Josephus: Eyewitness to Rome's First-Century Conquest of Judea,* trans. Richard Miller (New York: Macmillan, 1993), 7-11. Opinions are divided as to the veracity of Josephus's claim of Hasmonean descent: *for,* Max Radin, "The Pedigree of Josephus," *Classical Philology* 24 (1929): 193-94; *against,* Hölscher, "Josephus," in *Real-Encyclopädie der klassischen Altertumswissenschaft* 9 (Stuttgart: J. B. Metzler, 1916), col. 1935; and Shaye J. D. Cohen, *Josephus in Galilee and Rome: His Vita and Development as a Historian* (Leiden: Brill, 1979), 107-8 n. 33.

[2]Per Bilde, *Flavius Josephus between Jerusalem and Rome: His Life, His Works, and Their Importance,* Journal for the Study of the Pseudepigrapha, Supplement Series 2 (Sheffield, Eng.: Sheffield Academic Press, 1988), 27-32; Gregory E. Sterling, *Historiography and Self-Definition: Josephus, Luke–Acts, and Apologetic Historiography* (New York: Brill, 1992), 229-35.

[3]The usual dating of these documents is *Jewish War* circa A.D. 78, *Antiquities* circa A.D. 94, *Life* shortly after A.D. 94 as a supplement to *Antiquities,* and *Against Apion* in A.D. 95. See Steve Mason, *Josephus and the New Testament* (Peabody, Mass.: Hendrickson, 1992), 58-81; and Michael Grant, *Readings in the Classical Historians* (New York: Charles Scribner's Sons, 1992), 367-68. Hadas-Lebel places the publishing of the Greek version of *Jewish War* during the reign of Titus A.D. 70-81. Hadas-Lebel, *Josephus,* 213.

[4]Although Josephus read and spoke Greek with relative ease (Josephus, *Antiquities* 1.7-8, 20.263), writing the language well still caused him some difficulty. Accordingly, he often composed in Aramaic, his native tongue, and then reworked the material into suitable Greek with the help of secretaries who helped him with his style. See Bilde, *Josephus between Jerusalem and Rome,* 62; Mason, *Josephus and the New Testament,* 58-59; and Hadas-Lebel, *Josephus,* 209.

[5]Bilde, *Josephus between Jerusalem and Rome,* 203-4; Cohen, *Josephus in Galilee and Rome,* 28-29.

[6]Josephus, *Jewish War* 3.352; Josephus, *Antiquities* 20.262-63; Josephus, *Against Apion* 1.54. See also Bilde, *Josephus between Jerusalem and Rome,* 62.

[7]Josephus, *Jewish War* 1.3; Josephus, *Antiquities* 1.4; Josephus, *Against Apion* 1.48-49, 53, 55. For the methodology of Thucydides, see Thucydides, *Peloponnesian War* 1.20-23.

[8]Jerome, *Epistles* 22.35. Admittedly Jerome, like many early Christian writers, was favorably disposed towards Josephus because he saw him as a link between the Old and New Testaments and as a witness of the apocalyptic punishments of the Jews.

[9]Mason, *Josephus and the New Testament,* 29.

[10]H. E. Barnes, *A History of Historical Writing* (New York: Dover, 1963), 266-75.

[11]Mason, *Josephus and the New Testament,* 59; Sterling, *Historiography,* 241; Cohen, *Josephus in Galilee and Rome,* 91.

[12]Hadas-Lebel, *Josephus,* 211.

[13]Hadas-Lebel, *Josephus,* 211-12.

[14]Bilde, *Josephus between Jerusalem and Rome*, 200–201. Contrast Hadas-Lebel, who maintains that Josephus did not see God as Nemesis or Fortune, but rather as a judge and father. Hadas-Lebel, *Josephus*, 212.

[15]Bilde, *Josephus between Jerusalem and Rome*, 202. Thucydides was an upper-class Athenian who was active in politics and was later elected general. After the loss of Amphipolis during the Peloponnesian War, he was exiled from his home. Likewise Polybius was elected a general of the Achaean League but was later deported to Italy by the Romans. For the different stages of Josephus's life, see notes 1 and 2 above.

[16]Emilio Gabba, "Literature," in *Sources for Ancient History*, ed. Michael Crawford (Cambridge: Cambridge University Press, 1983), 18–19; Cohen, *Josephus in Galilee and Rome*, 25–26.

[17]"Apologetic historiography is the story of a subgroup of people in an extended prose narrative written by a member of the group who follows the group's own traditions but Hellenizes them in an effort to establish the identity of the group within the setting of the larger world." Sterling, *Historiography*, 17.

[18]Sterling, *Historiography*, 104–36.

[19]Hadas-Lebel, *Josephus*, 215–18.

[20]C. W. Fornara, *The Nature of History in Ancient Greece and Rome* (Berkeley and Los Angeles: University of California Press, 1983), 142–68; Michael Grant, *Greek and Roman Historians: Information and Misinformation* (New York: Routledge, 1995), 44–47.

[21]What Thucydides actually meant in *Peloponnesian War* 1.22 has been the subject of much discussion. See A. W. Gomme, *A Historical Commentary on Thucydides*, 5 vols. (Oxford: Oxford University Press, 1945–70), 1:140–48; and J. S. Rusten, *Thucydides: The Peloponnesian War Book 2* (Cambridge: Cambridge University Press, 1989), 7–17.

[22]Solomon Zeitlin, "Masada and the *Sicarii*," *Jewish Quarterly Review* 55 (April 1965): 305.

[23]Cohen, *Josephus in Galilee and Rome*, 188–91.

[24]Cohen, *Josephus in Galilee and Rome*, 30–31.

[25]Josephus, *Against Apion* 1.49. Hadas-Lebel suggests that the Jotapata account reads as if it were "new information," suggesting that Josephus wrote an early draft of the siege shortly after the city fell. Hadas-Lebel, *Josephus*, 122.

[26]Bilde, *Josephus between Jerusalem and Rome*, 62–63, noting Josephus, *Against Apion* 1.150–51 and *Life* 361–64. For the frequent collusion of witnesses with the artistic license taken by ancient historians, see the discussion of Josephus and Flavius Silva in Eric D. Huntsman, "And They Cast Lots: Divination, Democracy, and Josephus" in this volume.

[27]Josephus, *Antiquities* 14.185–89, 265–67; 16.161, 164–78; Josephus, *Against Apion* 1.56; Josephus, *Life* 342, 358. For a discussion, see Bilde, *Josephus between Jerusalem and Rome*, 62.

[28]Josephus, *Life* 363. Josephus even goes to the extent of quoting two of Agrippa's letters, an unusual expedient in ancient history writing. See Hadas-Lebel, *Josephus*, 213–14.

[29]Hadas-Lebel, *Josephus*, 207–8.

[30]Opinions differ on Josephus's "prophecy" to Vespasian, who was proclaimed emperor in A.D. 69 by his legions while still campaigning in Judea. See

Mason, *Josephus and the New Testament,* 45–49; and Hadas-Lebel, *Josephus,* 104–6. One possibility is that Josephus conspired with Vespasian after the fact for propaganda purposes, saving his own life in the process. Another possibility is that he was reinterpreting existing oracles that claimed that a future prince would arise in Judea and rule the world. Josephus apparently came to believe that, although the promised ruler was to come from Judea, he did not need to be Jewish. Josephus, *Jewish War* 6.313. There remains the possibility that Josephus had a revelatory experience of some kind, especially since he seems to have been a mystic who viewed himself as a "chosen" messenger to his people. Cohen notes that his self-perception as a latter-day Jeremiah helped him justify his surrender at Jotapata. Cohen, *Josephus in Galilee and Rome,* 98.

[31]Josephus, *Jewish War* 1.28; 6.250–80.

[32]Cohen, *Josephus in Galilee and Rome,* 94–97.

[33]Mason, *Josephus and the New Testament,* 60–61; Cohen, *Josephus in Galilee and Rome,* 97. For the difference between the Zealot party and the *Sicarii* ("dagger men") who recognized no human lordship of man over man, see Zeitlin, "Masada and the *Sicarii,*" 310, 314–17. See also S. Kent Jackson, "Revolutionaries in the First Century," in this volume.

[34]Compare Thucydides, *Peloponnesian War* 1.23, and his discussion of the pretexts as opposed to the actual causes of the Peloponnesian War.

[35]Bilde, *Josephus between Jerusalem and Rome,* 121–22. The first, Aramaic version of *Jewish War* seems to have been directed towards the Jews in the eastern Diaspora as a warning for them not to challenge Rome. The later Greek edition, however, targeted the largely Greek-speaking Jewish population within the Roman Empire.

[36]*Papyrus Graecus, Vindobensis* 29810 contains *Jewish War* 2.576–79 and 582–84. See Bilde, *Josephus between Jerusalem and Rome,* 63, for a discussion of the earliest manuscripts and their transmission.

[37]Hadas-Lebel, *Josephus,* 223–29.

[38]Josephus, *Antiquities* 18.26–28 (census and its aftermath); 18.116–19 (John the Baptist); 19.343–52 (death of Herod Agrippa); 20.200 (James).

[39]See Hadas-Lebel, *Josephus,* 259 nn. 9–12. The New Testament account in Luke places the census (translated as a "tax" in the King James Version) *before* the slaughter of the innocents. Josephus does not mention the slaying of the children of Bethlehem in his list of Herod's atrocities, but it must have occurred before Herod's death, which Josephus places in 4 B.C. The census, however, took place when P. Sulpicius Quirinius (translated as "Cyrenius" in the King James Version) was governor of Syria, and his governorship was in A.D. 6. See *The Oxford Classical Dictionary,* 3d ed., s.v. "Sulpicius Quirinius, Publius." Josephus also does not draw a connection between John the Baptist and Jesus, and Herod Antipas executes the former only because he fears that John will raise a revolt.

[40]Bilde, *Josephus between Jerusalem and Rome,* 88, 126–28; Hadas-Lebel, *Josephus,* 225–27. Lengthy interpolations and other additions are found in the late Slavonic versions of Josephus. In addition to longer treatments of Christ and John the Baptist, the Slavonic Josephus is more readily anti-Roman and anti-Herodian than existing Greek versions.

[41]Bilde, *Josephus between Jerusalem and Rome,* 191–92.

Book Review

History and Fable, Heroism and Fanaticism: Nachman Ben-Yehuda's *The Masada Myth*

Arnold H. Green

Nachman Ben-Yehuda, *The Masada Myth: Collective Memory and Mythmaking in Israel*. Madison: University of Wisconsin Press, 1995. xxi; 401 pp. Illustrations, tables, appendix, bibliography, index. $22.95.

This evaluation of Nachman Ben-Yehuda's *The Masada Myth: Collective Memory and Mythmaking in Israel* will summarize the book's main thrust, examine its conceptual framework, offer criticisms of the author's argument and method, then discuss two implications of Masada for LDS culture.

Summary

Perhaps to cushion the shock inflicted on fellow Israelis by his debunking of the "Masada myth," Nachman Ben-Yehuda prefaces his analysis with a confession of the trauma he personally experienced in 1987 when his own faith was shaken. Involved in a group studying political assassinations by Jews, he read a paper by David Rapoport[1] portraying the Sicarii on ancient Masada as Jewish terrorists. Since that portrayal conflicted with what he had learned in his Israeli schooling and military service, Ben-Yehuda rushed to check the main extant source: Josephus's *The Jewish War*. To his temporary angst, he says, he discovered "that Rapoport was right and I was wrong." Moreover, he recounts,

> I felt cheated and manipulated. I tried to reconstruct in my own mind how, during my formative years, going through the Israeli socialization process, I acquired "knowledge" about Masada that was not only wrong but also very biased. . . . What was I supposed to do when it turned out that such a major element of my identity was based on falsehood, on a deviant belief? (5)

To this "personal angle" of his investigation into the Masada myth, Ben-Yehuda joins a "professional angle." A sociology professor at the Hebrew University of Jerusalem, he has published extensively in the fields of deviance and of social psychology.[2] The book's cover and introduction imply that such training and experience qualify him to explain why and how a "deviant belief" entered the memories of many Israelis of his generation.

As to the story of Masada, Ben-Yehuda defines a "deviant" narrative, in large part, as a retelling that digresses from the only surviving literary source: Josephus's *The Jewish War.* He summarizes (27–43) that text as follows. In the context of the Jews' increasing resentment at Roman rule, two distinct groups arose. The Zealots, extreme Pharisees willing to take up arms against Rome in the cause of Jewish independence, emerged about A.D. 6 over issues of worship and taxation. A half-century later, there materialized a more indiscriminately violent faction called the Sicarii (from Latin *sica:* dagger), who specialized in assassinating (and robbing) Jewish collaborators as well as Romans. In A.D. 66, under a leader named Menachem, the Sicarii captured Herod's fortress on Masada, a mesa overlooking the Dead Sea. They went from there to Jerusalem, participated in the seizure of the Upper City, and assassinated the High Priest, Hanania. Hanania's followers retaliated by killing Menachem, whose party, now led by Eleazar ben Yair, fled back to Masada—all this before the end of A.D. 66. Josephus says that ben Yair "acted the part of a tyrant at Masada afterwards" (36). During the next six years, the Sicarii conducted raids for supplies and booty against nearby Jewish villages. They made a particularly brutal attack on En Gedi, killing several hundred women and children. Meanwhile, the Roman army secured Galilee in A.D. 67, capturing Josephus at Jotapata, then besieged and destroyed Jerusalem in A.D. 70. Roman "mop up" operations ensued against fortresses like Herodium and Macherus, which the Zealots defended fiercely.

It was not until late in A.D. 72 that the Romans moved against the Sicarii on Masada, which they took early in A.D. 73. So, although Josephus does not specify the siege's length, his text implies that it lasted about six months and possibly only four. Nor does Josephus mention any military forays by the Sicarii against the Roman troops; it is possible that conflict occurred only when the Roman siege ramp reached Masada's wall. Then, rather than resisting until overwhelmed as did the Zealots at Jerusalem, Herodium, and Macherus, ben Yair urged the option of suicide upon his followers, who probably balked at the suggestion, for the "tyrant" had to make two impassioned speeches to convince them. Ben-Yehuda assumes that the decision was "made by men from the dominant social category on Masada (the Sicarii) and that the men killed everyone, including the women and children. The Sicarii on Masada left no choice for anyone who may have been reluctant" (37). The Sicarii then cast lots to select those who would kill first their colleagues and then themselves. By hiding in a cavern, two "reluctant" women and five children survived the massacre. Josephus comments on the feelings of the Roman troops, encountering an eerie silence after breaching the wall: "nor could they do other than wonder at the courage of their [the Sicarii] resolution." Yet Josephus expresses disgust at the mass murder-suicide: "Miserable men indeed they were!" (41).

In that regard, Ben-Yehuda points out (228–32) that Orthodox Judaism essentially repressed the memory of Masada, which is mentioned neither in the Talmud (codified oral law) nor in the Midrash (commentaries). He speculates that the rabbis omitted it for two reasons. First, the incident entails Jews choosing death over life, whereas the opposite priority is enshrined in Jewish law, which forbids suicide as well as murder. Second, Masada signifies unyielding fanaticism to the point of communal extinction. Yet Yohanan ben Zakkai and other moderate Pharisaic rabbis preserved Judaism after the Great Revolt by compromising with Roman officials, who allowed a Sanhedrin to function at Yavneh/Jamnia,[3] where the Haggadah (ceremonial text) for Passover was prepared and the compilation of the Mishnah (oldest part of Talmud) begun. So the rabbis preferred Jamnia over Masada as a symbol for postbiblical Judaism.

In the twentieth century, however, Josephus's account of the episode at Masada was rediscovered by Jews,[4] some of whom engaged in selective omission and outright fabrication to create a largely different story—what Ben-Yehuda calls "the Masada mythical narrative." He itemizes (299–301) the omissions, including: distinctions between Zealots and Sicarii, the latter's attacks on fellow Jews (especially at En Gedi), their apparent unwillingness to fight the Romans, ben Yair's *two* speeches, the existence of survivors—suggesting that others would have opted to live had they been given the choice, and so the involvement of murder as well as suicide in the mass death. He cites (300–303), as examples of fabrication, these ideas: that Masada was populated mainly by Zealot veterans from Jerusalem who fled there to continue their resistance after the city's fall, that the Roman siege lasted up to three years, that the "freedom fighters" on Masada frequently attacked the besieging Roman forces, and that the whole episode represents a "heroic stand" deserving to function as a prominent symbol for Judaism and Israel.

"In essence," concludes Ben-Yehuda,

> [the Masada mythical narrative] assumes the following [typical, composite] form: The leaders of the Great Revolt belonged to a group of Jews referred to as Zealots. The Roman imperial army crushed the revolt and conquered and destroyed Jerusalem together with the Second Temple. The Zealots who survived the siege and destruction of the city escaped to the fortress of Masada, a difficult-to-reach stronghold on top of a mountain near the Dead Sea. The Romans reached Masada too. They surrounded the fortress and put it under siege. After three years of a heroic battle by the few Zealots against the huge Roman army, the Zealots on top of Masada realized that there was no more hope. They faced a grim future: either be killed by the Romans or become slaves. They thus decided to kill themselves, a heroic death, rather than become slaves. When the Roman soldiers entered Masada, they found there only silence and dead bodies. (13–14; compare another composite version on 302–3)

Conceptual Framework

Ben-Yehuda acknowledges that he is by no means the first to recognize mythical elements in the tourist-media-schoolbook version of Masada. He cites Bernard Lewis's *History: Remembered, Recovered, Invented* (1975) as identifying the popular narrative as

an example of "invented history" then discusses (14–16) several
other scholarly critics whose work preceded his.[5] He therefore jus-
tifies his own extensive research and full volume on two other
grounds. First, he sets his explanation within a conceptual framework. Second, he explains "*how* that mythical narrative was created,
in maximum detail"[6] (19). So an evaluation of his contribution ought
to focus on these two related claims.

Ben-Yehuda identifies three components in his conceptual
framework: constructionism (in this case, why and how a society
constructs a myth), the Allport and Postman model of rumor circulation, and Barry Schwartz's reconciliation of continuity and
discontinuity in collective memory. By far his most important theoretical referent is constructionism, which, in his article on "Moral
Panics" (1994), he contrasts with "objectivism." In this juxtaposi-
tion, those familiar with social science debates will recognize the
spilling over into sociology of a controversy originating in history.
The objectivist disciples of Leopold von Ranke (1795–1886) asserted
that careful research based on contemporaneous documents could
yield—about the reality of past events—as objective an understanding as that produced about matter or nature by physical or life scientists. Benedetto Croce (1866–1952) and other "subjectivists"
countered that past events cannot be repeated as experiments—
much less under controlled conditions—and that historical "evidence" is typically fragmentary and biased. They also referred to
the distinction made by Immanuel Kant (1724–1804) between
objectively "unknowable reality" and conditioned human perceptions of it. So they argued that historians can at best offer plausible,
but subjective, explanations that indulge the changing interests of
successive generations. Within sociology, the likes of Max Weber
(1864–1920) embraced objectivism, while Florian Znaniecki (1882–
1958) and others espoused subjectivism or "constructivism." Ben-
Yehuda's intellectual pedigree can be traced through Howard Saul
Becker (1928–) back to Znaniecki.[7]

History's objectivism-subjectivism controversy was transposed
in sociology to the field of "social problems." In his 1994 article,
Ben-Yehuda explains that a social problem (for example, drug craze,
witchcraft) is viewed by objectivists as "an objective, concretely real,
damaging or threatening condition." However, he continues, "To

the constructionist, social problems do not exist objectively; they are constructed by the human mind. . . . Definitions of social problems derive from or are produced by specific sociocultural circumstances."[8] So the constructionist investigates, not an objectively real problem, but rather the circumstances, moods, and needs of a society some of whose members subjectively perceive a problem. Ben-Yehuda used constructionism first in his doctoral dissertation (1977) to explain twentieth-century America's "myth of the Junkie" and then in a 1980 article to explain late medieval Europe's construction of a panic over witchcraft.[9] He now draws upon the same concept to explain twentieth-century Zionism's construction of the "Masada myth."

He does so by exploring the circumstances, moods, and needs of the Zionist movement and modern Israel. In brief, modern (secular) Zionism, which urged the Jews' return to *Eretz Yisrael,* deemphasized the inglorious Jewish past in the Diaspora. Rather, it sought to bond the immigrants to their ancestors' homeland while overcoming the Diaspora image of passive Jews in order "to create a new type of hard-working and determined Jews. This new Jew *had* to seek personal freedom and national liberty and, above all, to be connected to his or her land, ready to fight for it and—if necessary—to die for it" (75–76).

Also, maintains Ben-Yehuda, for secular nationalists (Zionists, for example) their patriotism becomes a "civil religion,"[10] in which political leaders function as priests, while national symbols acquire sacred dimensions. Moreover, he points out (98–100, 131–36), this was occurring in a context of danger to the emerging Jewish nation. Associating Zionism with European imperialism, Arabs were beginning to use violence against Jewish settlers. In 1932— culminating decades of increasing anti-Semitism throughout Europe—the newly empowered Nazis launched "legal" then physical attacks on European Jews.

In 1941, when Germany's Afrika Korps threatened to invade Palestine from Egypt, Zionist strategists formulated what they called "the Masada Plan" to coordinate a "last stand" in their "last refuge" of *Eretz Yisrael.* In other words, the early twentieth-century Holy Land represented for Zionist immigrants a circumstance of nation-building and a mood of determination to stand fast against nation-threatening perils. So there existed an urgent need for a visual symbol of national heroism as well as of Jewish claims to the land of Palestine, a symbol that could accordingly function as a pilgrimage shrine for the "civil religion." The Masada myth was socially constructed in such a context, explains Ben-Yehuda (232–39), to satisfy that need.

He also uses constructionism to explain how and by whom the myth was constructed, identifying (287–92) several "moral entrepreneurs." After the Hebrew translation of Josephus's *The Jewish War* appeared in 1923, Yitzhak Lamdan (1899–1954) wrote a poem, "Masada" (1927), which contains the famous lines: "Ascend, chain of the dance / Never again shall Masada fall." Ben-Yehuda notes that this book-length poem went through twelve editions and, by the 1930s, was required reading in Zionist (later, Israeli) schools. Lamdan's use of Masada as a heroic emblem received academic legitimacy when Hebrew University historian Joseph Klausner wrote, among other works, "Masada and Its Heroes" (1937). Ben-Yehuda also quotes several passages from a booklet by Bar-Droma from the same year, including: "We will recall the memory of the heroes of Masada—the last of a war of freedom, of a nation that is rooted in its land" (192). In turn, "historical" accounts by Klausner and Bar-Droma inspired Yoseph Braslawski to compose historical novels, like *When Masada Fell* (1941) and *Masada* (1944), along with guidebooks, such as *Do You Know the Land?* (1950).[11]

Ben-Yehuda pins the label of most active "moral entrepreneur" on Shmaria Guttman, an amateur archaeologist who first climbed Masada in 1933. Thereafter, Guttman devoted himself energetically to promoting the site as a national shrine of heroism. He encouraged youth clubs, school groups, and paramilitary units of Zionist political factions to make Masada the destination of their pilgrimage outings. For these occasions—as well as for the media and tourism—he prepared handouts and guidebooks. Ben-Yehuda gives some credit to Guttman for the decision, in the mid-1950s, by armored units of the Israeli Defense Forces (IDF) to hold their swearing-in ceremonies for new recruits atop Masada. While taking their oaths, the new soldiers recited: "Because of the bravery of the Masada fighters, we stand here today."[12] Upon learning that the heroic account disseminated by the IDF in these dramatic ceremonies disagreed with the lone historical source, one officer recalled: "I got it from Shmaria Guttman. . . . We did not read Josephus Flavius in the original" (154–55).

If Guttman was the most active promoter of Masada, then perhaps the most influential was Yigael Yadin (1917–84). Initially reluctant to excavate Masada, Yadin was persuaded to do so—according to Ben-Yehuda—by Guttman. Once Israel's most famous archaeologist (and natural showman) joined the enterprise, he endowed the myth with its ultimate degree of credibility. Ben-Yehuda makes two sets of observations about Yadin's contribution to the Masada myth. The first set treats possible light shed by archaeology on what happened, which Ben-Yehuda describes as minimal. "The excavations did not confirm or refute many of the important aspects of Josephus Flavius's narrative," he concludes,

> except for the facts that there was a fortress called Masada built by Herod, that the Romans put a siege around it, that they built a siege ramp, and that they were effective in winning. The questions regarding the Sicarii, the suicide, Elazar Ben-Yair's speeches, the massacre at Ein Gedi, and the length of the siege, as well as a few others, still remain unanswered to this day. (57)

In his other set of observations, Ben-Yehuda detects a pattern. Mythical assertions, he says, exist mainly in Yadin's later, popular writings—for example, *The Story of Masada by Yigael Yadin, Retold for Young Readers by Gerald Gottlieb* (1969). The archaeologist's earlier, professional publications contain more guarded language. Ben-Yehuda illustrates this pattern by discussing Yadin's comments, on separate occasions, about the discovery on Masada of three skeletons (a man, a young woman, and a child). First, Yadin's field notes reveal merely an inconclusive discussion with colleagues about the possible genders, ages, and relationships of the skeletons. Second, in a popular book, *Masada: Herod's Fortress and the Zealots' Last Stand* (1966), he asked (editorially), "Could it be that we had discovered the bones of . . . [the last] fighter [on Masada] and of his family?" Finally, in a 1971 encyclopedia entry, he asserted, "The skeletons undoubtedly represent the remains of an important commander of Masada and his family" (68).[13] With Yadin's archaeology, it seems, as with war stories and sporting tales, certitude and magnitude tend to increase in proportion to distance from the facts.

To explain precisely that phenomenon, Ben-Yehuda uses, as his second theoretical referent, a model on the dissemination of rumors.[14] Allport and Postman identify three related subprocesses—leveling, sharpening, and assimilation—in the tendency of rumors to change while spreading. "Leveling refers to the fact that much of the detail in the original message gets lost." Sharpening "explains how certain themes in a (rumor) message tend to become sharper, crisper, and more salient" (263). Finally, the assimilation subprocess molds the message to the transmitter's values and agenda. Ben-Yehuda then shows how, as the Masada myth grew, it was leveled (omissions), sharpened (emphases), and assimilated to the agenda of secular Zionism. This sociological explanation does make a certain amount of sense.

Criticisms

However, exploiting the immense theoretical literature on how myths interact with historical accounts—a process discussed at length in the earliest critique of the Masada myth cited by Ben-Yehuda (Lewis's *History: Remembered, Recovered, Invented*)—would make at least as much sense, if not more, than Ben-Yehuda's approach.

In that regard, I acknowledge that there are risks in having a historian such as myself evaluate a book from a field which its author calls "historical sociology." Among them is that the reviewer may not resist the temptation to quibble about issues persisting between sociology and modern history, which are twentieth-century branches from the same eighteenth-century trunk—including an issue like appropriate kinds and amounts of theorizing.[15] Many historians still view theory as Puritans viewed art—the simpler the better— whereas some sociologists indulge their tastes for conceptualization to a level of baroque splendor. Ben-Yehuda's third theoretical referent—Schwartz's reconciliation of continuity and discontinuity in collective memory—exceeds my puritanical tolerance for theorizing and triggers my quibble reflex.

In the first place, as applied by Ben-Yehuda, this reconciliation theory rests on a misunderstanding of the historiographical issues. Briefly, he restates the controversy between past-oriented objectivism and present-oriented subjectivism within a sociological field called collective memory—"how human societies remember their past" (272)—a very old sphere of inquiry known to nonsociologists as historiography. Objectivism, he says, assumes "continuity" between past and present, whereas subjectivism assumes "discontinuity." "[Schwartz] claimed that these approaches are not contradictory and that one may integrate them both into a coherent interpretation that emphasizes both continuity and discontinuity," states Ben-Yehuda at the outset. "It is my intention to test Barry Schwartz's integrative hypothesis, directly, explicitly, and meticulously, in this study" (22–23). Toward the book's end, he pronounces the theory confirmed because, besides mythical elements representing discontinuity, "the *basic* historical facts appear in the mythical narrative most of the time" (297), thus representing continuity.

But these "*basic* facts" derive from Josephus—not from some direct pipeline to objective reality, which subjectivists-constructionists like Croce, Znaniecki, and Ben-Yehuda have branded unknowable. If popular versions of Masada contain "facts" from Josephus along with mythical elements, this combination demonstrates fidelity blended with fabrication in exploiting available source materials—not teamwork between objectivism and subjectivism.

The status of Josephus as the *only* surviving literary account does not render it an *objective* account. Ben-Yehuda acknowledges (27–31) the debate about problematic issues concerning Josephus. For example, *The Jewish War* constitutes a self-justification for Josephus's defection to the Roman side; he was unlikely an eyewitness of Masada's siege and fall, and—in the Greek tradition exemplified by Thucydides—he very probably fabricated the speeches that he put into the mouth of Eleazar ben Yair. Yet Ben-Yehuda insists that

> For my purposes, Josephus Flavius's credibility and reliability are a side issue. . . . The many arguments about the validity and accuracy of Josephus's narrative are simply irrelevant to this work. . . . The analytical puzzle of this work is [rather] . . . how some modern Israeli interpreters . . . changed and molded Josephus's original narrative. (21, 29)

So, in the second place, the theoretical discussion of continuity-discontinuity is also—with respect to the purpose stated—an irrelevant side issue; it does more to confuse than to advance the main argument of the Masada myth's social construction.

Yet, in another sense, that discussion helps to reveal Ben-Yehuda's tactic, for—although asserting that "A historical explanation . . . is always an exercise in constructionism" (276)—he resorts to objectivism when it suits his purposes. That is, he assumes the pose of an objectivist when summarizing Josephus (see his chapter 2: "The *Historical* Events of Masada" (italics added). He then employs his own "objective" summary as a baseline when, now switching to the stance of a subjectivist-constructionist, he explains why and how mythical components arose in the twentieth century. A mischievous reader or reviewer might insist that Ben-Yehuda approach Josephus from the same theoretical posture from which he approaches Klausner, Braslawski, and Yadin. Besides taking seriously the problems with Josephus's account, this would entail acknowledging viability in readings of Josephus that differ from his own.

Or, if indeed every historical explanation is subjective, then we may look for subjective emphases in Ben-Yehuda's summary of Josephus. A careful reading of *The Jewish War,* whose author was justifying his defection and flattering his new patrons, might yield the following thesis: the Great Revolt occurred because hotheaded Jewish "terrorists"[16] overreacted to the unwise acts of irresponsible Roman procurators in Judea. Ben-Yehuda, creating a foil as well as a baseline for the Zionist-Israeli heroic myth, wants to expose the Sicarii in particular as having been worse than terrorists; he wants them to have been *cowardly* terrorists. So his summary teases Josephus's data in that direction. Because *The Jewish War* mentions no attacks by the Sicarii on besieging Roman troops, Ben-Yehuda concludes that the Sicarii "avoided opportunities to fight" and lacked "fighting spirit" (42–43). Although the text indicates that the Sicarii captured Masada in A.D. 66, it doesn't say explicitly that they seized it from the Roman soldiers stationed there since Herod's death (4 B.C.). Therefore, speculates Ben-Yehuda, another Jewish faction may have first fought and displaced the Romans from the fortress, of which the Sicarii later gained control "by treachery" (328 n. 12). Ben-Yehuda complains that "Yadin systematically ignores Josephus's insistence that the rebels on Masada were the Sicarii. Yadin uses the term *defenders,* but much more frequently, *Zealots*" (58–59). Yet, in his chronology of events,

Ben-Yehuda's entry under A.D. 66 reads, "The Jewish Great Revolt begins. A group of Jewish rebels takes the fortress from the Roman Garrison" (xix). By deciding that "rebels" (not necessarily Sicarii) took Masada in A.D. 66, he subjectively underscores the Sicarii's probable cowardice.

It is perhaps to avoid tarnishing his foil that Ben-Yehuda minimizes the contributions of archaeology in piecing together the ancient story. He consequently does not mention that thousands of iron arrow- and spearheads were found throughout the area, and that many of these weapons can be traced to a pair of forges the rebels, presumably the Sicarii, created atop Masada.[17] In other words, an alternate interpretation of the Sicarii, based on Josephus and on archaeology, is that they were tolerably *brave* terrorists. But it suits Ben-Yehuda's purposes to "level," "sharpen," and "assimilate" Josephus's account in the direction of cowardice.

A fuller understanding of his motives for doing so can be acquired by examining Ben-Yehuda's explanation of the Masada myth's decline, which is disappointingly superficial. He points out that Israel's devotion to Masada peaked in the 1960s; by the 1970s, "pilgrimages" to the site by Israeli youth and military groups were sharply down and critics were beginning to challenge the myth. Later, the IDF's armored units shifted their swearing-in ceremonies to Latrun, the site of a crucial battle in the 1948 war. By the late 1980s, Masada seemed to function less as a national shrine of heroism and more as just another tourist attraction.

Ben-Yehuda accounts for this phenomenon with growth metaphors. "Some very major and basic cultural changes were taking place in Jewish Israeli society during the 1970s," he observes. So "Israeli society and culture, particularly its intellectual elite, are beginning to look at themselves (and the society in which they live) in a more mature and independent way" (257, 287). The myth was needed during Zionism's youthful nation-building phase, in other words; but Israel outgrew the need, so the myth started to wane.

In expounding this maturation thesis, Ben-Yehuda fails to apply his constructionist theory as well as he might. If a myth is socially constructed in response to a society's circumstances, moods, and needs, stating that "things changed" constitutes an inadequate explanation of the myth's deconstruction. A more satisfactory

explanation would spell out how the changes comprised fresh circumstances, moods, and needs that increasingly provoked identifiable categories of the society to attack the myth on behalf of their
new concerns. Ben-Yehuda does offer some hints in this direction:
"The Masada mythical narrative became an ideological burden and
could no longer be viewed as a completely positive, problem-free
symbol" (291). He also quotes Baila Shargel: "by the middle of the
1970s, Masada has become, for many, a symbol of what Israel did
not want to become" (256). But, unlike Kedar and Shargal, Ben-
Yehuda devotes very little discussion to the transformation of Masada into a negative image "for many" and none at all to the "many"
critics' political circumstances, moods, and needs.

Such a discussion might be summarized as follows. The June
1967 war resulted in Israel's acquiring control of territories, including the Sinai, the Golan Heights, the West Bank, and the Gaza Strip—
the latter two containing large Palestinian Arab populations. Over the
issue of these territories' future, Israeli political culture soon polar-
ized into two general factions. The right called for Israel's permanent control over the territories on two grounds: (1) history (the
main Old Testament sites are in the West Bank), and (2) what
might be called "outpost-maintenance security," because the West
Bank and the Golan Heights provide "strategic depth" on the East.
The left countered by drawing attention to "the demographic problem": owing to their much higher birthrate, the Palestinians may
within a generation constitute the majority within "Greater Israel"
(the pre-1967 state, plus the territories). That development would
put Jewish Israeli society into a situation dangerously resembling
that of the white minority regime in pre-1990 South Africa. The
left consequently formulated a plan that may be called "quagmire-
exiting security." That is, it advocated giving up the territories in
exchange for a negotiated peace. Such an exchange occurred in the
Camp David Agreement (1979); Israel returned the Sinai to Egypt,
which signed a peace treaty with Israel. Leftists called for the
extension of the lands-for-peace formula to other neighboring Arab
states and to the Palestinians.

Israel's right and left have not just expressed conflicting pro-
posals for the territories' future; they have implemented opposing
policies when in power. Winning the 1977 elections, the right-wing

Likud bloc subsidized Jewish settlements in the West Bank, Golan Heights, and Gaza Strip. The left-leaning Labour alliance, returning to office after the 1992 elections, acted on its concerns by signing first the land-for-peace Oslo Agreement (1993) with Yasser Arafat's Palestine Liberation Organization (PLO) and then a peace agreement with Jordan (1994). But, arguing that Israel needs resoluteness rather than concession-making, the Likud bloc won (barely) the 1996 elections, following which it greatly slowed the "peace process" with the PLO and spoke of expanding the Jewish West Bank settlements. So, while the Israeli right has not ceased emphasizing the need to "stand fast" against military threats to the nation, the left has stressed the need for compromise and has criticized the right's inflexibility as one of the main problems facing Israel.

Thus, Masada persists as a useful, positive emblem for the right wing of Israel's political culture.[18] Indeed, Ben-Yehuda mentions that, the myth having now come under attack, even the *religious* right has begun to espouse it (287). For the left wing, however, in these new circumstances Masada has come to symbolize unyielding fanaticism to the point of willingness to risk national calamity. Quoting Henry Kissinger, General Y. Harkabi, Israel's ex-chief of intelligence, stated in 1981, "A wrong strategic doctrine can lead to disaster." Harkabi also said, "The proponents of the 'resoluteness' doctrine do not seem to be aware of this." He then cited the example of Hitler's convincing Germans that their nation could not exist without *Lebensraum* (additional territory for "living space"), a policy which led to World War II and to catastrophe for Germany. "The price of a Greater Land of Israel," novelist Amos Oz told a rightist settler group in 1983, is "that people will go to the battlefield with the feeling that they were being dragged into giving up their lives for an issue on which at least half of this nation sees, unlike you, a possibility of compromise."[19] Thus, to the Israeli left, Masada has come to be, not a shrine of heroism, but a "complex" functioning as the myth's *verso* side. "An Israeli leader who sees himself standing on the heights of Masada is surely liable to lose his capacity of seeing reality as it is," warned Hebrew University historian Benjamin Kedar in 1982.

There is yet another danger. It is unavoidable that behavior influenced by identification with Masada will indeed resuscitate it. If 'the entire world is against us', then one begins to behave as if 'we are against the entire world', and such behavior is bound to lead to ever-increasing isolation, which in several important aspects will really resemble that of Ben-Yair and his companions. . . .

Nineteen hundred years after the fall of Masada we would do well to detach ourselves from the myth and to uproot the complex. An ancient people like ourselves has not a single past to draw symbols from. . . . Let us choose the Book of Isaiah rather than the Book of Joshua.[20]

"Kedar," explains Baila Shargel, summarizing the historian's earlier (1973) article in Hebrew, "found in Ben-Yair's famous motto ['to live free or to die'] not the transcendent value of liberty but an eagerness to court death."[21]

In short, Israel's post-1967 circumstances engendered among leftists a mood of strategic compromise over the future of the territories occupied in June 1967. So that political culture's intellectuals—including Y. Harkabi, A. Oz, B. Kedar, and (lately) N. Ben-Yehuda—have acted on their perception of this current need by assailing the Masada mythical narrative, now associated by them with the paranoid "complex" of their rightist opponents. Perhaps Ben-Yehuda glossed over such circumstances, moods, and needs because he is one of the "moral entrepreneurs" pursuing the Masada myth's deconstruction.

LDS Contexts

The Israeli discussion, concerning the promotion of steadfastness while avoiding suicidal extremism, is one of the two contexts in which Masada's symbolism has diffused into LDS culture. Latter-day Saints have experienced and can learn from several of the same tendencies as the Israelis that influence the social and ideological presentation of historical accounts.

In 1841, about two years after the Mormons' forced eviction from Missouri, *Times and Seasons* (Nauvoo) reprinted an unnamed historian's account—containing some heroic overtones—of Masada's fall. The editors (Don Carlos Smith and R. B. Thompson) affixed a preface mixing admiration with censure:

The following thrilling account of the self devotedness of the Jews, scarcely has its equal on the pages of history.—Although such a course must be condemned, it shows their attachment to their ancient religion, the God of their fathers, and also their abhorrence of the Romans.[22]

More than a century later, Neal A. Maxwell explored the same borderland between steadfastness and zealotry. He asserted that "There should be no Mormon Massadas, but, in addition to Carthage, there were Haun's Mill and many other times and places forebearers gave everything they had." A footnote—containing mythical ingredients—explains the reference to Masada:

> Masada (or Massada) was a fortified town on the south end of the Dead Sea where the Jews, after the fall of Jerusalem, made their last stand for three years against 10,000 Romans, ending around 72 A.D. The Zealots killed their wives and children and committed suicide rather than surrender to the Romans, who were greeted by a solemn stillness and an awful silence as they finally entered the fortress.[23]

The editors of the Infobases "LDS Collectors Library" on CD-ROM cross-referenced that footnote to James E. Talmage's account of Jesus' calling Simon Zelotes ("the Zealot") to be one of the twelve Apostles. So, ironically, a footnote describing the Zealots on Masada in semiheroic terms finds itself juxtaposed to Talmage's own observation: "Doubtless Simon had learned moderation and toleration from the teachings of Christ; otherwise he would scarcely have been suited to the apostolic ministry."[24]

The second LDS context in which the Masada account appears also somewhat parallels the Jewish-Israeli experience. It sets the scholarly ideal of dealing honestly with source materials against the temptation to embellish for greater impact—perhaps toward some larger purpose. In the Jewish experience, the overriding need for a national shrine of heroism justified Klausner, Guttman, Yadin, and others in exaggerating or misrepresenting Josephus's account of Masada. A similar "larger purpose" has justified some LDS scholars in assimilating the Masada mythical narrative to their own agenda. For example, Jerald Johansen's "Masada, Citadel of Freedom's Cry" (May 1972 *Ensign*), even while citing Josephus as its source of information, describes the event largely in heroic terms:

> After Herod's death, Masada was commandeered by a Roman garrison until Jewish Zealots captured it. The dramatic and courageous defense of Masada by those 960 men, women, and children against

> Flavius Silva's besieging Roman Tenth Legion has won the admiration and respect of everyone who has read of their valiant effort. . . .
>
> May this provide fresh inspiration for liberty-loving people everywhere. For death is sweeter than loss of liberty. And freedom is still worth dying for today.

Perhaps, in this case, the larger, misrepresentation-justifying purpose was to reinforce a tendency among some Latter-day Saints to equate the modern (secular) nation-state of Israel with scriptural "spiritual Israel."[25] Johansen and others of this trend have thus pursued for Mormonism an objective which the rabbis rejected for Judaism: transforming Masada into a religious emblem.

Nevertheless, various perceptions of the events at Masada are found in LDS literature. For example, LaMar C. Berrett's *Discovering the World of the Bible*—which has been used by thousands of LDS tourists who have visited the Holy Land—provides a largely mythical account of Masada. The version in the 1973 edition of Berrett's guidebook is preserved in the 1996 edition, which lists D. Kelly Ogden as coauthor. Yet for another recent book, *Jerusalem: The Eternal City*, Kelly Ogden composed the section on Masada (204–23), which scrupulously follows Josephus's account and avoids mythical assertions.[26]

Conclusion

In summary, Nachman Ben-Yehuda formulates a credible, detailed, concept-based explanation of why and how the Masada myth entered the memory of secular Zionists and modern Israelis. It is an explanation, however, which is "irritatingly repetitive," overloaded with theory, devious in overtly rejecting objectivism while employing it *sub rosa,* and superficial in accounting for the myth's decline. If all historical explanations are social constructions, then so is this one by Ben-Yehuda. His "objective" summary of Josephus includes subjective emphases. And his *Masada Myth* may be seen in part as springing from Israeli leftists' perception of a need to deconstruct Masada's "resoluteness" associations in the post-1967 circumstances of peacemaking.

Masada teaches lessons beyond the site's immediate geographical and cultural settings. Two of these are especially instructive for

Mormons as well as for Jews and Israelis. First, in cultivating stead-fastness, a religious or national community needs to avoid all-or-nothing fanaticism. Second, in recounting episodes about the human past, Latter-day Saints, as well as all good historians, ought to avoid the extremes of exaggeration as well as debunking and to apply the affirmation that "We believe in being honest" (A of F 13) to their assertions based on historical texts as well as to their dealings with fellow beings.[27]

Arnold H. Green is Professor of History at Brigham Young University.

NOTES

[1]David Rapoport, "Fear and Trembling: Terrorism in Three Religious Traditions," *American Political Science Review* 78, no. 30 (1984): 658–77.

[2]Ben-Yehuda's earlier publications include "The European Witch Craze of the Fourteenth to Seventeenth Centuries: A Sociologist's Perspective," *American Journal of Sociology* 86 (July 1980): 1–31; "History, Selection, and Randomness—Towards an Analysis of Social Historical Explanations," *Quality and Quantity* 17 (1983): 347–67; *Deviance and Moral Boundaries: Witchcraft, the Occult, Science Fiction, Deviant Sciences and Scientists* (Chicago: University of Chicago, 1985); *The Politics and Morality of Deviance* (Albany: SUNY Press, 1990); *Political Assassinations by Jews: A Rhetorical Device for Justice* (Albany: SUNY Press, 1993); and with Erich Goode, "Moral Panics: Culture, Politics, and Social Construction," *Annual Review of Sociology* 20 (1994): 149–71.

[3]While including no references to Masada, the Talmud contains five separate versions of Rabbi Yohanan ben Zakkai's defection to the Romans, who permitted him to establish the first *yeshiva* (rabbinical seminary) at Jamnia.

[4]Y. N. Simchoni's Hebrew translation of Josphus's *Jewish War* was published in 1923.

[5]Bernard Lewis, *History: Remembered, Recovered, Invented* (Princeton: Princeton University Press, 1975); Baila R. Shargel, "The Evolution of the Masada Myth," *Judaism* 28, no. 3 (1979): 357–71; Yael Zerubavel, "The Last Stand: On the Transformation of Symbols in Modern Israeli Culture" (Ph.D. diss., University of Pennsylvania, 1980); Benjamin Kedar, "Masada: The Myth and the Complex," *Jerusalem Quarterly*, no. 24 (summer 1982): 57–63; Benjamin Kedar, "The Masada Complex" (in Hebrew), *Ha-Aretz* 22 (April 1973): 16; Pierre Vidal-Naquet, "Josephus Flavius and Masada" (in Hebrew), *Zemanim* 13 (1983): 67–75; Pierre Vidal-Naquet, *The Murderers of Memory* (in Hebrew) (Tel Aviv: Am Oved, 1991). This article is an adaptation of Vidal-Naquet's introduction to his 1976 French translation of Josephus's *Jewish War*. The book was originally written in French as *Les assassins de la mémoire: Un Eichmann de papier et autres*

essais sur le révisionnisme (Paris: Editions La Décou+rerte, 1987). Ben-Yehuda does not cite Vidal-Naquet's *The Jews: History, Memory, and the Present* (New York: Columbia University Press, 1996), also first published in French (1991). See Bernard Knox's essay on Vidal-Naquet's writings in "Victims and Executioners," *New York Review of Books* 43, no. 17 (October 31, 1996): 18-21. Edward M. Bruner and Phyllis Gorfain, "Dialogic Narration and the Paradoxes of Masada," in *Text, Play, and Story: The Construction and Reconstruction of Self and Society,* ed. Stuart Plattner and Edward M. Bruner (Washington: American Ethnological Society, 1984), 56-75; Barry Schwartz, Yael Zerubavel, and Bernice M. Barnett, "The Recovery of Masada: A Study in Collective Memory," *Sociological Quarterly* 27, no. 2 (1986): 147-64; Dan Bitan, "Masada—The Symbol and the Myth" (in Hebrew), in *The Dead Sea and the Judean Desert, 1900-1967,* ed. Mordechai Naor, Idaw Series, vol. 13 (Jerusalem: Yad Yitzhak Ben-Tzvi, 1990), 221-35; Robert Paine, "Masada between History and Memory" (paper presented at the Canadian Historical Association, Memorial University of Newfoundland, June 1991); Robert Paine, "Masada: A History of a Memory," *History and Anthropology* 6, no. 4 (1994): 371-409; Anita Shapira, *Land and Power (The Sword of the Dove)* (in Hebrew) (Tel Aviv: Am Oved, 1992).

[6]With reference to the "maximum detail" part of Ben-Yehuda's objective, one reviewer describes *The Masada Myth* as "irritatingly repetitive." B. Kraut (University of Cincinnati) in *Choice* 33 (July-August 1996): 1834.

[7]Leopold von Ranke, "On the Character of Historical Science" (1830s), translated and published in Leopold von Ranke, *The Theory and Practice of History,* ed. Georg G. Iggers and Konrad von Moltke, trans. Wilma A. Iggers and Konrad von Moltke (Indianapolis: Bobbs-Merrill, 1973), 33-46; J. B. Bury, "History as a Science," in *The Varieties of History,* ed. Fritz Stern (New York: Vintage Books, 1973), 209-23; Benedetto Croce, "L'attitude subjective et l'attitude objective dans la composition historique," *Revue de Synthèse Historique* 6 (June 1903): 261-65; Benedetto Croce, *History: Its Theory and Practice* (1916; reprint, New York: Russell and Russell, 1960); Max Weber, "Objective Possibility and Adequate Causation in Historical Explanation," in *Zur Soziologie und Sozialpolitik* (1924)/*On the Methodology of the Social Sciences* (1938; reprint, New York: Free Press, 1969): 164-88; Florian Znaniecki, *Cultural Reality* (Chicago: University of Chicago Press, 1919); Nachman Ben-Yehuda and others, "Howard S. Becker: A Portrait of an Intellectual's Sociological Imagination," *Sociological Inquiry* 59 (fall 1989): 467-89; Howard S. Becker, ed., *Social Problems: A Modern Approach* (New York: John Wiley and Sons, 1966).

[8]Ben-Yehuda and Goode, "Moral Panics," 151.

[9]Nachman Ben-Yehuda, "The Myth of the Junkie—Towards a Natural Typology of Drug Addicts" (Ph.D. diss., University of Chicago, 1977); Ben-Yehuda, "European Witch Craze ," 1-31.

[10]The concept of civil religion was pioneered by Robert N. Bellah, "Civil Religion in America," *Daedalus* 96 (winter 1967): 1-21; and John A. Coleman, "Civil Religion," *Sociological Analysis* 31 (summer 1970): 67-77. Ben-Yehuda cites Charles S. Liebman and Eliezer Don-Yehiya, *Civil Religion in Israel* (Los Angeles: University of California Press, 1983).

[11]Joseph Klausner, *Masada and Its Heroes* (in Hebrew), Lanoar Library of Eretz Israel, booklet no. 62 (Tel Aviv: Omanut, 1937), 3-33; Yoseph Braslawski,

When Masada Fell (in Hebrew) (Tel Aviv: Am Oved, 1941); Yoseph Braslawski, *Masada* (in Hebrew) (Tel Aviv: Hakibbutz Hameuchad, 1944); Yoseph Braslawski, "Did You Know the Land?" in *The Dead Sea, Around and Around* (in Hebrew) (Tel Aviv: Kibbutz Hameuchads, 1955), 297–448.

[12]Shargel, "Evolution of the Masada Myth," 363.

[13]Yigael Yadin, *Masada: First Season of Excavations, 1963–1964: Preliminary Report* (in Hebrew; Jerusalem: Israel Exploration Society, 1965); Yigael Yadin, *Masada: Herod's Fortress and the Zealots' Last Stand*, trans. Moshe Pearlman (New York: Random House, 1966); Yigael Yadin, *The Story of Masada by Yigael Yadin, Retold for Young Readers by Gerald Gottlieb* (New York: Random House, 1969); *Encyclopedia Judaica* (Jerusalem: Keter, 1971), s.v. "Masada," 11:1078–91.

[14]Gordon W. Allport and Leo J. Postman, "The Basic Psychology of Rumor," *Transactions of the New York Academy of Sciences*, 2d ser., 8, no. 2 (1945): 61–81; Gordon W. Allport and Leo J. Postman, *The Psychology of Rumor* (New York: Henry Holt, 1947).

[15]Nineteenth-century sociology (then still more or less a branch of history) was highly speculative, while contemporaneous historians tended to slight theory in favor of "digging out the facts" and polishing the narrative. A joke among sociologists is that "sociology is like history but without the work, while history is like sociology but without the brains." The late BYU historian Russell B. Swensen used to counsel history students (only half in jest) that "the eleventh commandment for historians is 'thou shalt not commit sociology.'"

[16]Referring to the Zealots as well as to the Sicarii, Josephus also used such pejorative terms as "brigands," "wretches who deserved punishment," "the most depraved elements," and "murderers." From such language, Rapoport and Ben-Yehuda feel justified in using the modern term "terrorists" (43).

[17]Jodi Magness, "Masada: Arms and the Man," *Biblical Archaeology Review* 18 (July/August 1992): 58–67. Compare Ehud Netzer, "The Last Days and Hours at Masada," *Biblical Archaeological Review* 17 (November/December 1991): 20–32; and Ehud Netzer, "Masada," in *New Encyclopedia of Archaeological Excavations in the Holy Land*, 4 vols. (New York: Simon and Schuster, 1993), 3:973–85.

[18]Ben-Yehuda cites Arthur Milner's play "Masada," which was first staged during 1990 in Canada. Among the drama's closing lines are these:

> Compromise with the Arabs? Live side-by-side in peace—a Jewish state, a Palestinian state? Compromise is for the weak. . . .
>
> But if the United States decides its interests are better served by Syria or Saudi Arabia, we will take care of ourselves. . . . Let the Arabs send their armies against us. If we are resolute, if we are ready to sacrifice, we shall not be defeated. We shall take strength from the land. . . .
>
> Yes, we want peace and we shall have peace—on our terms. We shall choose a never-ending war over an Israel cut up and divided. . . . If we fight with the courage and determination of the Zealots—and if we are willing to die a thousand deaths—we cannot be defeated. (220)

[19]Yehoshafat Harkabi, "Reflections on National Defence Policy," *Jerusalem Quarterly,* no. 19 (spring 1981): 108-19; Amos Oz, *In the Land of Israel* (New York: Vintage Books, 1983), 152.

[20]Benjamin Kedar, "Masada: The Myth and the Complex," *Jerusalem Quarterly,* no. 24 (summer 1982): 57-63.

[21]Baila R. Shargel, "The Evolution of the Masada Myth," *Judaism* 28, no. 3 (1979): 357-71 (esp. 369).

[22]"Fall of Herodio [*sic*]—Machaerus—Masada—Fate of Josephus—Agrippa—Bernice," *Times and Seasons* 2, no. 18 (July 15, 1841): 476-78.

[23]Neal A. Maxwell, *"For the Power Is in Them . . .": Mormon Musings* (Salt Lake City: Deseret Book, 1970), 50.

[24]James E. Talmage, *Jesus the Christ* (Salt Lake City: Deseret Book, 1988), 225.

[25]Many LDS observers have tended to see Zionist immigration to Palestine, culminating in the state of Israel's creation (1948), as fulfilling scriptural prophecy. Very early publications included: "The Zionites," *Millennial Star* 58, no. 32 (August 6, 1896): 510-11; George Q. Cannon, "The Zionist Congress," *Millennial Star* 59, no. 41 (October 14, 1897): 644-45; J. M. Tanner, "The Zionist Movement," *Improvement Era* 3 (November 1899): 1-8; "Logic of Zionism," *Millennial Star* 64, no. 37 (September 11, 1902): 582-83; and Jan M. Sjodahl, "Prophecies Being Fulfilled," *Millennial Star* 77, no. 9 (March 4, 1915): 136-38.

More recent pro-Zionist LDS pronouncements include: LeGrand Richards, *Israel! Do You Know?* (Salt Lake City: Deseret Book, 1954); Eldin Ricks, "Zionism and the Mormon Church," in *Herzl Yearbook* 5 (1963): 147-74; W. Cleon Skousen, *Fantastic Victory: Israel's Rendezvous with Destiny* (Salt Lake City: Bookcraft, 1967); Truman G. Madsen, "The Mormon Attitude toward Zionism" (series of lectures on Zionism, Haifa University, May 1981); and Michael T. Benson, "Harry S. Truman as a Modern Cyrus," *BYU Studies* 34, no. 1 (1994): 6-27.

Jerald Johansen, "Masada, Citadel of Freedom's Cry," *Ensign* 2 (May 1972): 44-50. The article informs that "Dr. Johansen, who teaches at the Ogden (Utah) Institute of Religion adjacent to the Weber State College campus, has traveled and studied in the Middle East." Other articles in that same "Holy Land issue" of the *Ensign* make comparable assertions—especially W. Cleon Skousen, "The Birth of Modern Israel" (51-57), Eldin Ricks, "Judah Must Return" (94-95), and Daniel H. Ludlow, "The Future of the Holy Land" (96-103). Yet articles presenting alternate views—for example, William E. Berrett's "For the Law Shall Go Forth from Zion" (105-8) and especially Rodney Turner's "The Quest for a Peculiar People" (6-11)—suggest that the LDS discussion of Zionism has included more diverse and more subtle positions than that of "Mormon Zionism." See also my "Jews in LDS Thought," *BYU Studies* 34, no. 4 (1994-95): 137-64, and "What Mormons Have Thought about, *inter alia,* the Jews" (forthcoming).

[26]LaMar C. Berrett and D. Kelly Ogden, *Discovering the World of the Bible* (Provo, Utah: Grandin Book, 1996), 207-10; David B. Galbraith, D. Kelly Ogden, and Andrew C. Skinner, *Jerusalem: The Eternal City* (Salt Lake City: Deseret Book, 1996).

[27]"Accuracy and reliability are of the essence of scholarship. All scholars worth their salt have wrestled long with the questions of what can and cannot, what should and should not, what must or must not be said. They acknowledge and evaluate data both for and against their ideas and theories. They eschew all

forms of plagiarism and generously recognize their indebtedness to other scholars. They guard on all sides against the covert influences of unstated assumptions, bias, and esoteric terminology. They describe shades of grey where they exist. They identify clearly their personal opinions as such. They avoid material omissions, for often what is not said can be as misleading as what is said." John W. Welch, "Into the 1990s," *BYU Studies* 31, no. 4 (1991): 25.

Illustration Credits

Illustrations on the pages noted are provided courtesy of the following institutions and individuals:

Hebrew University of Jerusalem, pp. 51, 58, 66, 103, 104, 131, 163, 173, 175e, 176, 181f, 183, 187, 200, 201, 211, 214, 235, 252, 262, 263, 311, 383

Hebrew University of Jerusalem, Renate Rosenthal and Renee Sivan, *Qedem* (Jerusalem, 1978), pp. 173a and b, 175a–c, 179, 181a–e, 185, 186

Kelsey Museum of Archaeology, University of Michigan, pp. 155, 156, 160, 161, 163 top, 165

Menil Foundation, Houston, Texas, p. 167

Royal Ontario Museum, Toronto, p. 65

LaMar C. Berrett, pp. 59, 60, 270, 278, 345, cover

Michael Lyon, pp. 22, 274, 280, 340, 341, 350, 353

Brent F. Ross, p. 89

David Slee, pp. 158, 159, 162

Tihamér Szentléleky, *Ancient Lamps* (Chicago: Argonaut, 1969; Budapest: Akadémiai Kiadó, 1969), p. 30a

Andrew Teasdale, pp. 94, 96

John W. Welch, pp. 52, 281, 354

Yigael Yadin, p. 16

Index

*References to illustrations are printed in **boldface** type.*